"Rev. McGourty's book restores the importance of rituals, such as the Order of the Dedication of the Church, as essential components of evangelization, the revitalization of parish communities, and the praxis of journeying together as a community of faith."

—John Elmer Abad, associate professor of systematic and historical theology, St. Augustine's Seminary of Toronto

"While liturgical ceremonies for the Dedication of a Church are not very frequent in our day, Fr. McGourty believes that the Order of the Dedication of a Church articulates powerfully the evangelizing mission of every parish community. I am certain that this work will help parish communities and local churches to reflect upon the vocation that the church building, through its symbolism, inspires in each of us. *Sent Out into the World* presents a badly needed liturgical theology for the contemporary Church."

—Thomas Rosica, CSB, SSL, founding CEO, Salt and Light Television

"An insightful and practical liturgist, Michael McGourty draws out the theological riches that are in the Order of the Dedication of a Church to illustrate how our understanding of who and what we are as Christians (the Church) is manifest in the building (the church) in which we gather to worship and from which we are sent out."

—Gary Franken, bishop, Diocese of St. Paul in Alberta

"Fr. McGourty's very thoughtful, well-researched, and well-written book invites the local parish community to discover its mission as part of the Mystical Body of Christ and to become a visible sign on earth of the Church in heaven. In our unprecedented era of the 'virtual parish,' this book offers a timely reminder that in order for the parish community to realize its 'authentic ecclesial and spiritual identity,' the faithful must never lose their focus upon the real presence of Christ, who journeys with us on our pilgrim way."

—A. Robert Nusca, president, St. Augustine's Seminary of Toronto

# Sent Out into the World

# Sent Out into the World

A Liturgical Theology for a Parish Community and the New Evangelization—A Reading of *The Order of the Dedication of a Church*

MICHAEL McGOURTY

WIPF & STOCK · Eugene, Oregon

SENT OUT INTO THE WORLD
A Liturgical Theology for a Parish Community and the New Evangelization—A Reading of *The Order of the Dedication of a Church*

Copyright © 2024 Michael McGourty. All rights reserved. Except for brief quotations in critical publications or reviews, no part of this book may be reproduced in any manner without prior written permission from the publisher. Write: Permissions, Wipf and Stock Publishers, 199 W. 8th Ave., Suite 3, Eugene, OR 97401.

Wipf & Stock
An Imprint of Wipf and Stock Publishers
199 W. 8th Ave., Suite 3
Eugene, OR 97401

www.wipfandstock.com

PAPERBACK ISBN: 979-8-3852-0621-6
HARDCOVER ISBN: 979-8-3852-0622-3
EBOOK ISBN: 979-8-3852-0623-0

01/23/24

Excerpts from the *Lectionary for Sundays and Solemnities*, copyright © Concacan Inc., 1992, 2009 and the *Lectionary: Ritual Masses, Masses for Various Needs and Occasions, Votive Masses, Masses for the Dead*, copyright © Concacan Inc., 2014. All rights reserved. This edition of the Lectionary follows the *Ordo Lectionum Missae, editio typica altera, Typis Polyglottis Vaticanus*, 1981.

The Scripture quotations contained herein are based on the New Revised Standard Version of the Bible, copyright © 1989 National Council of Churches of Christ in the USA. Adapted and used by permission. All rights reserved.

Adaptations were prepared by and are the sole responsibility of the Canadian Conference of Catholic Bishops. Adaptations copyright © 2009, 2014 National Council of the Churches of Christ in the USA. Used by permission. All rights reserved.

Excerpts from the English translation of *The Roman Missal* © 2010, International Commission on English in the Liturgy Corporation (ICEL); excerpts from the English translation of *The Order of the Dedication of a Church and an Altar* © 2014, ICEL. All rights reserved.

This manuscript adheres to the SBL Handbook of Style's capitalization guidelines.

Dedicated to Anne and Brian, parents who through the church of the family connected me to the church through the parishes in which we worshiped.

And to

Stella and Michael and Alma and James, their parents who did it for them a generation earlier

And

Father Cassian Folsom, O.S.B.
A priest, scholar, and Christian gentleman

# Contents

Preface | ix
Abbreviations | xi
Introduction | 1

## PART ONE | THE PARISH AND ITS DEVELOPMENT

Chapter One: The Parish: Its Development, a Definition, and References to the Parish in the Ecclesiology of Vatican II | 13
    Introduction | 13
    The History of the Parish | 14
    References to the Parish in the Ecclesiology of Vatican II (1963–1965) | 30
    The Parish in Canon Law | 47
    Summary | 54

## PART TWO | THE STUDY OF THE RITE OF THE DEDICATION OF A CHURCH

Chapter Two: Order of the Dedication of a Church: Introduction | 59
    Introduction | 59
    The Introduction of ODC | 60
    Summary | 86

Chapter Three: Order of the Dedication of a Church: The Introductory Rites | 88
    Introduction | 88
    The Introductory Rites of ODC | 88
    Summary | 113

Chapter Four: Order of the Dedication of a Church: The Liturgy of the Word | 117
Introduction | 117
The Liturgy of the Word of ODC | 118
Summary | 141

Chapter Five: Order of the Dedication of a Church: The Prayer of Dedication and the Anointings | 144
Introduction | 144
The Rites of The Prayer of Dedication and the Anointings in ODC | 145
Summary | 177

Chapter Six: Order of the Dedication of a Church: The Liturgy of the Eucharist | 183
Introduction | 183
The Rites of The Liturgy of the Eucharist in ODC | 184
Summary | 219

## PART THREE | A LITURGICAL THEOLOGY FOR A PARISH COMMUNITY AND THE NEW EVANGELIZATION

Chapter Seven: A Liturgical Theology for a Parish Community and the New Evangelization | 231
Introduction | 231
The Relevance of the Rites of ODC for the Construction of a Liturgical Theology of a Parish Community | 233
The Parish Is a Cell of the Body of Christ | 237
The Parish Is a Part of the One, Holy, Catholic, and Apostolic Church | 257
The Parish Is a Portion of the People of God, Sharing in Christ's Priestly, Prophetic, and Kingly Mission | 263
Summary | 270

## CONCLUSION

Conclusion | 281

Bibliography | 285

# Preface

*Though He was in the for of God, Jesus did not count equality with God as something to be grasped at.*

—Phil 2:6

The Incarnation, in which Jesus Christ, the Son of God, became a human being, lived among us, and redeemed us by his death and resurrection, is the foundation of the Christian faith. Christianity is a response to the reality that God became a human being and entered into time and space. Because of the incarnation, we today are saved in time and space through our encounter with Christ in a living Church.

For the Christian, time and space are where we encounter Christ today and where we are saved. We are saved in the reality of our lives.

The pandemic has changed the way in which we live in time and space.

Many people now live and relate to the world and others virtually. They watch Mass in a church far away, where they do not know anyone and are not called to do anything. When Mass is over, they change the channel without leaving their armchairs. If they are challenged to become what Christ calls them to be, they move on to another Mass broadcast from somewhere else. Many people now think of themselves as belonging to virtual communities.

*The Order of the Dedication of a Church* is celebrated for a real community that is called to worship within the church building and come into contact with the living God through the Word and sacraments that Christ left his church.

It is hoped that what lies within this book will help to rediscover why it is so important that we meet in real communities, are challenged

## PREFACE

to love by real people, and are sent out from these celebrations to live with and serve the real people we encounter in our communities. Christ really became one of us and dwelt among us. In our parish communities we are called to gather with other real people, in real celebrations where we really encounter Christ in his Word and sacrament. Jesus came to save real people and to do so he really became one of us.

Virtual parishes are not real and they do not challenge us to become real as Christ did.

It is my prayer that this book may help us to become real again and discover once again the reality of Christ who is to be encountered in the living parish communities that call us to be his people in the reality and space of our own times.

Fr. Michael McGourty
Solemnity of All Saints
November 1, 2023.

# Abbreviations

| | |
|---|---|
| *AAS* | *Acta Apostolicae Sedis.* |
| Can. | Canon (used for citing canons from Code of Canon Law). |
| CCL | Corpus Christianorum. Series Latina. Turnout, 1954—. |
| CSEL | Corpus scriptorum ecclesiasticorum Latinorum, Vienna, 1886–. |
| *PG* | *Patrologia Greca.* Edited by J. P. Migne. Paris: N.p., 1857–66. |
| *PL* | *Patrologia Latina.* Edited by J. P. Migne. Paris: N.p., 1878–90. |
| ODC | *The Order of the Dedication of a Church, The Order of the Dedication of a Church and an Alter,* English translation according to the Typical Edition (Ottawa, Ontario, Canadian Conference of Catholic Bishops 2018), 29–70. |

# Introduction

Pope Francis has written about the role of the parish in the new evangelization, in his apostolic exhortation *The Joy of the Gospel* (*Evangelii gaudium*), in the following manner:

> The parish is the presence of the Church in a given territory, an environment for hearing God's word, for growth in the Christian life, for dialogue, proclamation, charitable outreach, worship and celebration. In all its activities the parish encourages and trains its members to be evangelizers. It is a community of communities, a sanctuary where the thirsty come to drink in the midst of their journey, and a center of constant missionary outreach. We must admit, though, that the call to review and renew our parishes has not yet sufficed to bring them nearer to people, to make them environments of living communion and participation, and to make them completely mission orientated.[1]

The deeply held conviction of this book is that within *The Order of the Dedication of a Church* (henceforth *ODC*), as it was revised after the Second Vatican Council, each parish community can discover a liturgical theology for itself that will show its members how to become and live the mission which belongs to them and their community through confirmation and baptism.[2] The reason for this, as will be seen, is that this

---

1. Francis, *Joy of the Gospel*, no. 28: 16. The paragraph number is given first and the page number is given after the colon.
2. CCCB, *Order of the Dedication of a Church* (*ODC*). In the ritual, the individual paragraphs or components of the ritual are identified with an individual section or paragraph number. For the convenience of the reader, these paragraphs or section numbers will be given in the citations which follow. When quoting from the ritual, the first number which is given will be the paragraph or section number from which the text is taken. This will be followed by a colon and a number that will indicate the page number from which the text is taken.

The text of *ODC* that is cited in this study is from the 2018 English translation of the

rite is intended to create of the church building a symbol which speaks of the nature and theological identity of the living church community that meets within the building. This is a fact that is entirely new to these revised rites of dedication. As this study will show, the rites that make up ODC are intended to make of the church building a sign which calls the local Christian community to be what it is to be as a portion of the body of Christ in the territory where it resides. This study will also clearly demonstrate that this is a sign which is intended to speak most directly to a parish community and to state what it is that a parish is called to be as an evangelizing community in our world today. The intention of this book is to articulate the liturgical theology for a parish community and the new evangelization that can be discovered for every parish community within *The Order for the Dedication of a Church*.

Not insignificantly, it was on the Solemnity of Pentecost, May 29, 1977, that the Sacred Congregation for the Sacraments and Divine Worship published the reformed rites for the dedication a church and an altar. The *Decree* that promulgated these new rites, *The Order of the Dedication of a Church and Altar*, stated that the church building exists as a special kind of image of the church, which is God's temple built of living stones.[3] It goes on to speak of the altar, around which God's holy people gathers, as a sign of Christ himself, who is priest, offering, and altar of his own sacrifice.[4] Even though these rites, which had been previously found in the second book of the Roman Pontifical, had been revised and simplified in 1961, the *Decree* of the 1977 rites stated that it was necessary to revise them again and to adapt them to the norms set out in the liturgical reform that was called for by the Second Vatican Council and to contemporary conditions.[5] These new rites, as they themselves state, regard the

---

Typical Edition. The *editio typica* of this rite was first published in Latin in 1977 under the following title: *Ordo dedicationis ecclesiae et altaris*.

3. ODC, V. While the rest of the rite is divided into section and paragraph numbers, the *Decree* is not. Only the page number is given here. The *Decree* states, "[the church building] is a special image of the Church, which is God's temple built from living stones."

4. ODC, V. In this regard the *Decree* states, "Moreover, the altar, around which the holy people gather to participate in the Lord's Sacrifice and to be refreshed at the heavenly banquet, is a sign of Christ, who is the priest, the victim, and altar of his own Sacrifice."

5. ODC, V. The *Decree* states, "These rites, found in the second book of the *Roman Pontifical*, were revised and simplified in 1961. Nevertheless it seemed necessary to revise the same rites again and to adapt them to the conditions of our times in view of the purpose and the norms of the liturgical renewal that Second Vatican Ecumenical

# INTRODUCTION

visible church building as a sign of the pilgrim church on earth and an image of the church in heaven.[6] It is because the building represents the living church ("*Ecclesia*") that meets within it that the structure itself is given the name "church" ("*ecclesiae*").[7] As can be seen from the material cited here, the 1977 revised rites for the dedication of a church point to the nature of the eccleisal community that meets inside of the building. This study will also show, that as these rites were revised in keeping with the documents of the Second Vatican Council, they offer a liturgical theology for a parish that is particularly steeped in the theology and vision of a parish that is articulated in the documents of the Second Vatican Council. This study will rely on the 2018 English translation of the 1977 *Editio Typica* as published by the Canadian Conference of Bishops.

The main goal of the investigation that is undertaken in this book is to present the revised rites for the dedication of a church, ODC, in order to apply them to a parish community to demonstrate what they have to say that is unique to them in regard to the liturgical theology of a parish community. The rites for the dedication of a church that make up *ODC* are found in the second chapter of *The Order of the Dedication of a Church and an Altar*.[8] The rites of *ODC* represent the primary rites of this ritual, as it is through the celebration of them that a church and

---

Council set in motion and fostered."

6. *ODC*, no. 2:31. While the *Decree* is not divided by paragraph and section number, the rest of the ritual is. Here is given paragraph number, with page number following the colon. The *Introduction* states, "Because the church is a visible building, this house is a special sign of the pilgrim Church on earth and an image of the Church dwelling in heaven."

7. *ODC*, no. 1:31. The *Introduction* states, "Rightly, therefore, from ancient times the name "church" has also been given to the building in which the Christian community is gathered to hear the Word of God, to pray together, to take part in the sacraments, and to celebrate the Eucharist."

8. See *ODC*. This ritual is made up of eight chapters, as well as the *Decree*. The structure of the complete ritual is as follows:

*Decree* (p. V).
I. *The Order of Laying of a Foundation Stone or Commencement of Work on the Building of a Church* (pp. 3–28).
II. *The Order of the Dedication of a Church (ODC)* (pp. 29- 70).
III. *The Order of the Dedication of a Church in Which Sacred Celebrations Are Already Regularly Taking Place* (pp. 71- 98).
IV. *The Order of the Dedication of an Altar* (pp. 99–131).
V. *The Order of Blessing of a Church* (pp. 133- 153).
VI. *The Order of Blessing of an Altar* (pp. 147–153).
VII. *The Order of Blessing of a Chalice and Paten* (pp. 155–166).
Appendix: *Chants of the Antiphons and Other Texts* (pp. 169–206).

its altar are dedicated. The assumption upon which this study is based is that if the building is to be a sign that points to the nature of the living "church" that meets within it, the rites that make the building such a sign should say something concrete about the type of ecclesial community which is most common in the church's lived reality. They should offer a theology for a parish community by which its members may come to understand their identity in the church built of living stones. Those parishes which celebrate the rites of dedication for their church building can find in these rites significant content to assist them to understand what it means for them to be the pilgrim church on earth that the visible church structure is to represent. Parish communities that have already dedicated their church buildings will discover in revisiting these rites a liturgical theology that will call them back to their roots and keep them focused upon the mission which Christ calls all Christians to deepen in through the church's liturgical and sacramental life.

The investigation that is put forward here is important because it seeks to articulate what material the rites of *ODC* contain that will assist those parish communities that dedicate their churches to understand the nature of their eccleisal identity. The pastoral effectiveness of this ritual is dependent upon its ability to assist the community that celebrates it to appreciate how its theological nature is expressed in the dedicated church building. *ODC* contains many beautiful images that represent the church as a city on a mountain, a vine or a bride,[9] but what does this

---

9. See *ODC*, 62:56. The prayer for the dedication of a church puts forward a number of beautiful images of the church. A number of them are contained in this short excerpt from the prayer:

> Holy is the Church,
> the chosen vine of the Lord,
> whose branches fill the whole world,
> and whose tendrils, borne on the wood of the Cross,
> reach upward to the kingdom of heaven.
>
> Blessed is the Church,
> God's dwelling place with the human race,
> A holy temple built of living stones,
> Standing upon the foundation of the Apostles
> with Christ Jesus its chief cornerstone.
>
> Exalted is the Church,
> a City set high on a mountain for all to see,
> resplendent to every eye,
> with the unfading light of the Lamb,
> and resounding with the sweet hymn of the Saints.

mean to Christians who worship in their dedicated parish church? How does this help them to understand the vocations which belong to them as members of that living church for which the building has become a sign? This study will demonstrate that the rites of *ODC* contain material that can be used to construct a concrete liturgical theology to help define and animate that type of community in which most Christians live their faith life within the church—that of a parish community. The liturgical theology which is contained in these rites has a positive pastoral value in that it may be used as a type of catechesis to help the parish preparing to dedicate its church to understand its ecclesial identity. It also has a mystagogical content for the parish that is celebrating the anniversary of the dedication of its church. This may be used to help the community reflect upon the vocation that the church building, through its symbolism, is calling it to live within the church and local community in which the building announces the presence of the living church. In particular, this investigation is concerned with what these rites have to say specifically to a parish community. It will be shown why the contents of *ODC* are particularly orientated to calling a parish community and its members to assume their mission within the church and in the world into which the members of the community are sent to announce the good news.

A number of different methods will be utilized in this study in order to analyze and present the rites of *ODC* and articulate the theology for a parish community that is contained within this ritual. The methods that are utilized include those of the historical, descriptive, and theological analysis and synthesis.

The first part of this book, which consists of just one chapter, presents a historical overview of the development of the parish as a structure in the life of the church and follows the different forces that have shaped the definition that has been given to the parish. One of the main objectives of this chapter is to demonstrate why the parish community is an important entity that merits theological treatment. This brief survey of the history of the parish will show how it emerged as an ecclesial body as a result of the church's attempt to realize its mission to bring the good news of Christ's saving death and resurrection to all the nations of the world. This historical study is important because it points to the concerns and struggles that have helped to shape the nature of the parish in its present reality and indicates those factors that need to be kept in mind when attempting to form a theology for a parish community. Attention will be given to the manner in which the parish has been defined, and the persons and parties involved in this understanding will be highlighted. Particular emphasis will be placed upon the developments impacting upon the way in which the parish community has been described in the years following the Second Vatican Council. The documents of the council clearly annunciate the role that the parish is to have in the life of the church. These in turn greatly influenced the definition of a parish community that is to be found in the 1983 revised Code of Canon Law. These two sources will be carefully considered in this chapter. Both the conciliar and canonical definitions of a parish community are sought in this investigation in order to determine what questions must be asked of *ODC* to develop the theology of a parish that is contained in it. These questions are brought to the theological analysis of the ritual that takes place in the second part of this investigation.

On the basis of what has been said above, in Part One, Chapter One, the reader will find an examination of the historical development of the parish and a presentation of the factors that are necessary to understand the essential role that the parish has to play in the life of the church today. It discusses: 1) the history of the parish; 2) references to the parish in the ecclesiology of the Second Vatican Council; and 3) the parish in the 1983 Code of Canon Law. This chapter concludes with a summary of those factors that must be given attention in the second part of the investigation.

The second part of this book is made up of five chapters. In these chapters a thorough analysis of the rites of *ODC* is presented. The purpose of this analysis is to present the rites of *ODC* in a manner that demonstrates the importance of their contents for the construction of a liturgical theology of a parish community and its mission in the world. The success and validity of this study demands that the entire ritual be given the serious attention that it deserves. This makes for a lengthy investigation. The intention of this lengthy study is to draw out of the rites of *ODC* that data, and only that data, that is necessary to construct the theology for a parish community that can be found in the rites of *ODC*.

The five chapters that constitute this theological analysis are arranged according to the five sections that make up *ODC*. They are: 1) the *Introduction*; 2) *The Introductory Rites*; 3) *The Liturgy of the Word*; 4) *The Prayer of the Dedication and the Anointings*; and 5) *The Liturgy of the Eucharist*. Each of these sections is analyzed to discover what material can be found in them for the construction of the theology of a parish contained in this ritual. While most of the material that is necessary for

INTRODUCTION

this inquiry can be found in the ritual of dedication itself (*ODC*), the 2018 English translation of the *Editio Typica*, a number of other sources are also required. The revised lectionary in its English translation will be necessary for the study of the rites and readings associated with *The Liturgy of the Word*. The *Missale Romanum*, third revised English translation of 2011, is referred to when dealing with the study of *The Liturgy of the Eucharist* and some of the other rites. When the prayers from *The Liturgy of the Eucharist* are found in both the Roman Missal and *ODC*, citation will be given from both sources.

The theological analysis that takes place in this study will be restricted to those categories that are necessary to uncover the theology for a parish that is contained in the liturgical text itself. The categories of concern for this argument are: *rites, prayers, sacred scripture* and *persons*.[10] The selection of these four categories is justified solely by the fact that they are the ones that are necessary for the investigation that is being pursued in this study. Within the broad scope which they encompass are necessarily included a number of other categories. For example, by its very nature, the analysis of the rites that are found in the liturgical texts will at times lead to a discussion of the objects that are used in the rite, the gestures that accompany their usage, and the symbolic value that is communicated by their use. In this way the anthropological significance of many of the liturgical actions that are called for the in the rites will be examined indirectly.[11] The anthropological significance of these texts will also be dealt with indirectly through the other categories that are utilized. To give another example, this will be seen at times as the material that relates to the category of *persons* reveals what is communicated by the places taken in the church by different members of the assembly and what is communicated by the gestures executed by them. In different ways the analysis of the related categories of *prayers* and *sacred scripture* will also have a much broader horizon than the "label" given to them indicates. These categories have been selected as a result of their ability to focus on the material that is relevant to the investigation that is being presented in this study. In a like manner, other categories have been

---

10. For an outstanding treatment on the different criteria to be considered in the "reading" and study of liturgical texts, see the following excellent works by Maggiani: "Come leggere gli elementi," 130–41; "Il linguaggio liturgico," 231–63; and "Interpretare il libro liturgico," 157–92.

11. See Valenziano, *Liturgia e antropologia*. In this excellent work on liturgy and anthropology, Valenziano points out that category of "rites" by its very nature involves a discussion of the anthropological character and significance of gestures.

excluded from this study because their inclusion did not add anything of significance to the subject matter. The fundamental objective of this investigation is to present through the reading of these liturgical texts that liturgical theology for a parish community that is contained in the rites of *ODC*. That goal requires only the use of the four categories that have been presented here.

There are a few instances in this study when these four categories do not function. They cannot be applied effectively to the material that is found in the *Introduction* of *ODC*. For this reason, the *Introduction* will be read and studied simply from the perspective of its theological content and the importance of this content for the theology of a parish. The ritual being studied also contains a number of spoken instructions or admonitions that in some way explain the significance of the rites that are celebrated. These addresses or admonitions, which do not correspond to the category of *prayers*, will be dealt with under the category of *rites*. This is justified by the fact they are often intended to explain the significance of the rites with which they are associated. Notice will be given as this occurs.

As a result of what has been said above regarding Part Two, this section will have the following structure. In Chapter Two the content of the *Introduction* of *ODC* is presented and thoroughly analyzed to determine what theological content it can offer for the construction of a theology for a parish community. A summary of the results is presented at the end of the chapter. Chapter Three deals with *The Introductory Rites* of *ODC*. Chapter Four examines the rites and readings related to *The Liturgy of the Word*. The subject of Chapter Five is the rites that make up *The Prayer of Dedication and the Anointings*. Chapter Six analyzes the rites of *The Liturgy of the Eucharist*. The structure of Chapters Three through Six is the same. In them the ritual schema of *ODC* is presented first. This is then analyzed according to the categories of *rites, prayers, sacred scripture*, and *persons*. Each chapter concludes with a summary of the findings which states what the rites of *ODC* have to offer for the development of a liturgical theology of a parish community.

The third and final part of the investigation, which consists of only one chapter, will employ the method of theological synthesis in order to draw together the results of the comparative analysis and to articulate a liturgical theology for a parish community. By doing so, it will apply the findings from the second part of this investigation to the material from the discussion about the nature and development of the parish

INTRODUCTION

community that was presented in the first part of this work. The fruit of this investigation will be an articulation of the theology for a parish community that is found in the rites of *ODC*.

The articulation of this liturgical theology for a parish community with be presented in Part Three, Chapter Seven. Here the first section of this chapter will review why it is that the material found in *ODC* is particularly relevant for and significant to a parish community. The theology for a parish community that is found in the rites of *ODC* will then be presented using three models that have been developed based on the findings of the previous chapters. These three models are: 1) The Parish is a Cell of the body of Christ; 2) The Parish is a Part of the One, Holy, Catholic, and Apostolic Church; and 3) The Parish is a Portion of the People of God, Sharing in Christ's Priestly, Prophetic and Kingly Mission. This chapter will also conclude with a brief summary of this material and a look at some of the challenges that might confront a parish as it attempts to respond to the mission articulated in this liturgical theology for a parish community.

In the pages that follow, the reader will find an exciting and noteworthy liturgical theology for a parish community and its mission in the world. What makes this theology exciting and noteworthy is not that it is the creation of any specific person, rather it is one that is put forward by the church itself in one of its liturgical rites. This book is offered as a service to the rites of *ODC* through an exercise of *lex orandi, lex credendi* (the law of praying is the law of believing).[12] Within the pages of this book, the rite is read and its meaning unpacked to reveal the vision of a parish community's life that is contained within this much under-studied ritual.

What every reader will find in this rite is an invitation to encounter the same Christ who Pope Francis invites Christians to meet in their parishes in his apostolic exhortation *The Joy of the Gospel* (*Evangelii gaudium*). In the church's liturgy, *ODC* will call the Christian to meet Christ

---

12. "*Lex orandi, lex credendi*" ("the law of prayer is the law of belief") is an ancient liturgical maxim that was coined by Prosper of Aquitaine (c. 355–455) in the fifth century. It expresses the liturgical principle that one can learn what the church believes by how it prays. Based on this principle, this work is founded on the assumption that one can learn what the church believes a parish or Christian community should be by reading the liturgical rite which is intended to make a symbol of the church building in which the Christian community gathers and worships. As has been stated the sign value which the rite hopes to bestow upon the building is to be such that the building is to be a sign that points to the nature and reality of the community that meets within it.

## INTRODUCTION

who "is the the eternal Gospel," because he "is the same yesterday and today and forever (Heb. 13:8), yet his riches and beauty are inexhaustible."[13] The liturgical and sacramental catechesis which the ritual offers invites all of the faithful members of a parish community to understand that:

> In virtue of their baptism, all the members of the People of God have become missionary disciples (cf. Mt 28:19). All the baptized, whatever their position in the Church or their level of instruction in the faith, are agents of evangelization, and it would be insufficient to envisage a plan of evangelization to be carried out by professionals while the rest of the faithful would simply be passive recipients. The new evangelization calls for personal involvement on the part of each of the baptized.[14]

Through the contents of the pages that follow, it is hoped that those who come to attend the liturgical celebrations within their parish church building will be brought to understand that as they are dismissed from these same celebrations they are to be God's holy people, sent out into the world to share the good news of the salvation that is to be found in Christ Jesus the Lord.

---

13. Francis, *Joy of the Gospel*, no. 11:6.
14. Francis, *Joy of the Gospel*. no. 120:60.

# PART ONE

## The Parish and Its Development

IN THIS SECTION, CHAPTER One examines the historical development of the parish and looks at those factors that are necessary to understand the essential role that the parish has in the life of the church today. It discusses: 1) the history of the parish; 2) references to the parish in the ecclesiology of the Second Vatican Council; and 3) the parish in the 1983 Code of Canon Law. A summary articulates those factors that must be given attention in the second part of this investigation.

# Chapter One

## The Parish: Its Development, a Definition and References to the Parish in the Ecclesiology of Vatican II

### INTRODUCTION

Before beginning to develop a theology for a parish community it is necessary to articulate a definition of a parish community and to demonstrate why the parish community is an entity that merits theological treatment. In order to do this, three factors that are essential to understanding the role that the parish presently has in the life of the church will be investigated. These three factors are: 1) the history of the development of the parish; 2) references to the parish in the ecclesiology of the Second Vatican Council; and 3) the parish in the 1983 Code of Canon Law.

As will be shown, the parish structure developed as a result of the church's attempt to realize the mission that it received from Christ to bring the good news of his saving death and resurrection to all the nations of the world. As this message of salvation was carried to the different localities in which the good news was announced, slowly the local communities that made up the church developed structures by which they were organized. From this story of development the parish emerged as a community within the larger community of the church. The parish

PART ONE

develops as a local community of believers that make up a portion of the larger diocesan community.

The history of the parish also shows many of the struggles that the church encountered throughout her history in maintaining the precious gift of communion between the many different local communities of believers and the universal church. These struggles helped to determine and shape the definition that would be given to a parish community over the years. They also highlight the concerns that need to be kept in mind today in order to maintain the communion that exists between the many parish communities and the universal church.

The documents of the Second Vatican Council clearly articulate the role that the parish is to play in the life of the church. By providing the context for an understanding of the place of the parish in the church's life, the documents of the council provide the theological foundation from which the significance of the parish is to be appreciated. The parish community has a theological significance because of its place in the life and mission of the universal church.

A study of the parish in the 1983 Code of Canon Law provides the material that is necessary to supply a definition of the parish community.

The definition and the insights that are obtained through this investigation determine what questions need to be asked in the study of *ODC* in order to articulate the theology of a parish that is contained in that rite.

## THE HISTORY OF THE PARISH

### The First Communities of Believers

After Christ's death and resurrection, his disciples received the gift of the Holy Spirit and were commissioned to take his message of salvation throughout the world.[1] The apostles went out from Jerusalem and founded local Christian communities in the many different cities to which they took the good news of salvation. From the time of Pentecost onwards, the identity of those who had followed Christ during his lifetime changed drastically. The expression *ekklesia tou theou*, which was never used in the Gospels to speak of those who followed Christ during his life, became the term that was used after Pentecost to speak of those communities that continued to follow Christ and make his offer of salvation known

---

1. Acts 1:8.

to the entire world. The expression, which means "Church of God," is most likely derived from the Hebrew word *qahal* that had the meaning of "assembly, community or reunion." This expression was used twenty-three times in the Acts of the Apostles, and forty-six times in the Pauline letters, to speak about those who made up the community that witnessed to Christ's resurrection. The expression, *ekklesia tou theou*, had three different senses in the way it was used.[2] First, it was to mean the assembly of the faithful who had gathered to worship. Second, it applied to a concrete church in a specific community. Paul begins his letters to the Corinthians by addressing them to the Church of God (*ekklesia tou theou*) that is at Corinth.[3] Finally, it could be used to refer to the entire Christian community. When a local church community gathered around its bishop to celebrate the Eucharist, it made present the *ekklesia tou theou*.

These local communities that were founded by the apostles devoted themselves to the teaching of the apostles and to communal life, to the breaking of the bread and to prayers.[4] Just as each of these local communities was gathered together through the Holy Spirit, each community was also linked with the other communities by the Holy Spirit. In each community that gathered to celebrate the Eucharist around its bishop, the one body of Christ was made present in the assembly.[5] This binding together of the church by the Holy Spirit was described by the Greek word *koinonia* ("communion"). Through this *koinonia*, the one Church of God manifested itself in the celebrations of each particular Christian community. *Koinonia*, the work of the Holy Spirit, is what built all of the local Christian communities into the one Church of God.

From the very beginning of the church's life, the gift of *koinonia* did not come easily. It has always demanded obedience to the Holy Spirit. Paul must write to the many communities that he founded to ensure that their own faith remained in communion with the other Christian communities. Paul himself went up to Jerusalem to ensure that his teachings were consistent with that of the apostles.[6] In the pastoral letters that were written to Timothy, the importance of adhering to sound doctrine and the qualities that were necessary of church leaders were articulated. In the pastoral letter to Titus the important characteristics of the *presbyteroi*

---

2. Garijo-Guembe, *Communion of the Saints*, 10–11.
3. 1 Cor 1:2 and 2 Cor 1:1.
4. Acts 2:42.
5. Garijo-Guembe, *Communion of the* Saints, 11–13.
6. Gal 2:1–4.

and the *episkopoi* (terms of similar meaning at this date) were outlined for the good of the church. In these early times, the whole assembly was usually able to gather together at one liturgical celebration that was presided over by an apostle or his successor. The bishop (*episkopoi*) was seen as the one who had to maintain unity within his community and preserve unity with the other communities. Each member of the community was likewise called to be a living stone in the body of Christ, offering spiritual sacrifices acceptable to God through Jesus Christ.[7] Membership in each local church, which one gained through baptism and sharing in the body and blood of Christ, was also membership in the one living body of Christ.[8] This incorporation into Christ's body made Christ present to the believer, called the believer to be transformed into Christ's likeness, and to witness to the salvation received from Christ to others. This sacramental presence of Christ, in and through the church, is always the work of the Holy Spirit. The dignity that belonged to every member who lived this *koinonia* in the church is best spoken of in the First Letter of Peter:

> You, however, are a "chosen race, a royal priesthood, a holy nation, a people he claims for his own to proclaim the glorious works" of the One who called you from darkness into his marvelous light. Once you were no people, but now you are God's people; once there was no mercy for you, but now you have found mercy.[9]

Throughout the development of the parish system, maintaining this *koinonia* in the body of Christ, which is the church, will be a great challenge.

## The Etymology of the Word "Parish"

The word "parish," which is the English equivalent of the Latin word *paroecia*, has been used to refer to local Christian congregations since the second century.[10] The Latin word *paroecia* developed from the Greek word *paroikia*. The Greek word was used in biblical and ecclesiastical usage and had the meaning of "those living near or beside," or technically to be an alien. The verb and its derivatives "were used of immigrants who

---

7. 1 Pet 2:5.
8. 1 Cor 12:13–14.
9. 1 Pet 2:9–11.
10. Coriden, *Parish in the Catholic Tradition*, 19.

have settled somewhere and dwell there as aliens without citizenship."[11] In this secondary sense, its meaning was often related to Christians who live in the world as having no lasting city but who seek a city that is to come.[12] The earliest Christian writers used the word in this sense to speak of Christians as those who have no home here on earth but are on their pilgrimage to their heavenly home.[13]

By the second century, the Greek word *paroikia* began to be used to describe the individual Christian communities that existed in the different cities. From the second to the sixth centuries the word was used as a technical term to describe the individual Christian community, "whether that of a city or a rural bishop or one headed by a priest or deacon."[14] Only in the sixth century did the word *paroecia* begin to be used to refer exclusively to those communities in the country that were not headed by a bishop. The word *dioecesis*, which had been used interchangeably with *paroecia* to describe the local Christian community, began to be used to designate the bishop's territory. *Paroecia* and *dioecesis* developed from being words which were originally used to describe the local Christian community, to becoming by the time of the Council of Trent, words which were applied to the territories of division within the church. *Dioecesis* became the word used to describe that territory governed by a bishop and *paroecia* the word to describe that portion of the diocese that a bishop entrusted to the governance of a priest. Unless otherwise stated, these words will be used in this investigation according to the understanding given above.

### The Early Urban Christian Communities

During the first three or four centuries of the church's existence it was mainly in the cities that organized Christian communities were founded. These urban communities were referred to as *paroecia*, and this was to signify a community dwelling together in Christian charity. The term was also intended to carry the sense that this dwelling together of the Christians in the earthly city was merely a temporary situation while they awaited the Lord's coming. The term applied to a community of

---

11. Blöchlinger, *Modern Parish Community*, 21.
12. Heb 13:14.
13. Blöchlinger, *Modern Parish Community*, 25.
14. Blöchlinger, *Modern Parish Community*, 28.

individual believers and not to a geographical area that they occupied.[15] A bishop headed each individual community, and the necessary members of the major and minor orders assisted the bishop. Up until the fourth century it was common for the bishop to preside at all liturgical celebrations. The members of the clergy, both in minor and major orders, were dependent upon the bishop for the exercise of their orders. Even in Rome, where there were many titular churches at this time, the Pope exercised direct pastoral care over the churches. The Pope celebrated all baptisms, and the consecrated elements from the papal liturgy were carried by acolytes to be distributed in the differing titular churches. Clerics were also dependent upon the bishop for their financial support. Church property was administered by the bishop, and from it the bishop paid his clergy.

The titular churches were served by one or two presbyters and sometimes a deacon. Often these churches began in the private homes of members of the community. With the passage of time, the homes often became the possession of the community and were dedicated by the community for the worship of God. These titular churches had more of a personal nature than that of a territorial. The people that came to these titular churches to worship did so by personal choice. They had not been assigned to a particular church as a result of territorial boundaries that determined to which church individuals belonged. Originally these churches simply took the name of the person who owned the house. Later on they were named after martyrs or renowned Christians.[16]

These early urban Christian communities, despite the fact that they often existed at great distances from one another, were also very much aware of being connected to one another. There was a very strong sense among the different assemblies of believers of being in communion through the one baptism of Christ and sharing in his body and blood. Letters and greetings were sent with travelers from different communities, and these travelers were always received with generous hospitality.

## The Beginnings of the Parish System

The peace which the church enjoyed after the Edict of Milan (313) resulted in the spread of Christianity to many rural areas. These new and

15. Addleshaw, *Beginnings of the Parochial System*, 4–5.
16. Coriden, *Parish in the Catholic Tradition*, 21–22.

smaller communities were placed under the care of a priest or deacon, rather than creating new bishops to head these very small communities.[17] This process, which was quite new in the fourth century, became quite routine by the fifth century. Martin of Tours established six new parishes during his episcopacy (371–397), and often traveled his diocese to monitor the affairs of these parishes.[18] The life in these communities was often modeled on that of the mother diocesan cathedral, with a priest aided by deacons, sub-deacons, and the minor orders leading the assembly in worship. Although there was no unified pattern of development for these parish communities, in most regions penance, the sealing with chrism, orders, and the blessing of the oils was reserved to the bishop. There were at this point no territorial divisions by which dioceses were divided into separate parishes. The baptismal churches (*ecclesiae baptismales*) were those churches with a baptismal font, which were often staffed by a number of priests and were found in the larger villages. These churches had a mandate from the bishop to baptize the people who lived in the surrounding smaller parishes, chapels, oratories, or monasteries.[19]

At the same time that bishops began to establish parishes, so too begins the practice of private landowners building oratories on their property to care for the needs of their families and workers. Often landowners had slaves ordained by bishops from outside of the territory. The result was that many "oratory" priests had no relationship to the local church and were intended merely to serve the needs of the landowner. Much church legislation was needed at this time and in the centuries to come to ensure that these communities would be able to exist in communion with the local and universal church. The Council of Orleans in 541 required that for an oratory to be raised to the status of a parish, it was to be given to the bishop as a perpetual gift.[20] The owner was also expected to provide an endowment sufficient to ensure the upkeep of the clergy who would serve in it. It was also expected that owners would present their candidates for the priesthood to the local bishop so that they could be judged as worthy of their appointment. Slaves were to be freed before they were to be ordained. Once these "oratory" priests were part of the diocesan clergy, they were required to attend diocesan synods and give an account of their preaching and sacramental ministry.

17. Bo, *Storia della parrocchia*, 1:41.
18. Bo, *Storia della parrocchia*, 1:51.
19. Coriden, *Parish in the Catholic Tradition*, 25.
20. Bo, *Storia della parrocchia*, 1:88–89.

PART ONE

Some of the other developments that accompanied the beginning of the parish system included a new attitude regarding the appropriateness of clerics doing manual labor. The fourth century witnessed an increased sensitivity about the possibility of people being scandalized by clerics involved in certain types or work. It also became necessary for priests to devote themselves to many of the functions that had been fulfilled previously by the bishops in their churches.[21] In the face of this situation, the church became more dependent upon the offerings of the faithful to replace the manual labor of the clergy.

One of the major tasks that faced the rural parish at this time was to confront a culture that was often more comfortable with pagan practices.[22] This task of forming a Christian community in a newly converted territory involved the parish in carrying out the bishop's missionary work and task of evangelization, dealing with the local problems as they arose, and making the church visible to the faithful in the region. In the years following the break-up of the Roman Empire and the Barbarian invasions, the parishes contributed enormously to conserving and strengthening the spirit of cohesion among the many different peoples.[23] Although different regions displayed differing organizations for the parochial system, the parish was instrumental in bringing Christianity to various cultures and situations in which these people lived. Once Christianity had been established in these differing territories, bishops had to call pastors to be on guard against laxity in the faith, failure to respect the Sunday obligation, and failures in Christian values.[24]

Significant often in this period is the amount of legislation introduced to ensure that communion was maintained between the local and universal church. The Council of Toledo, held in 633, stated that all parishes were to be ready to receive the bishop for his pastoral visit and to receive the chrism.[25] The parish visit was intended to ensure that the priests were celebrating the rites of the church in the proper manner, providing proper pastoral care, and living a life in keeping with their vocation. The Council of Vaison (529) required pastors to take young lectors who were not married into their homes so that they could be instructed to sing

---

21. Bo, *Storia della parrocchia*, 1:93–110.
22. Bo, *Storia della parrocchia*, 1:493.
23. Bo, *Storia della parrocchia*, 2:34.
24. Bo, *Storia della parrocchia*, 2:48–60.
25. Bo, *Storia della parrocchia*, 2:51.

the psalms and provide for their successors.[26] By the end of the seventh century, the parish and the parish priest had become an important point of contact between those living in the rural areas and the whole church.

## The Expansion of the Parochial System under Charlemagne (768–814)

The Holy Roman Empire brought to parts of western Europe a unity that had been lost since the dissolution of the Roman Empire. The reign of the Emperor Charlemagne (768–814) was accompanied by an assertive effort for the establishment of a church and priest in every town.[27] Charlemagne's plan was distinguished from the previous efforts at expanding the parochial system in that it placed the burden of constructing the new parishes on the local feudal landowner. Before this the responsibility had fallen on the bishop. During the time of Charlemagne's rule, this plan was made successful by a delicate balance between the rights of the feudal lord and the local bishop. Under this system, which has come to be called the *eigenkirche* or proprietary church system, a church could only be built with the bishop's permission. The priest appointed to the church had to be approved by the bishop as being qualified and could only be removed by the bishop. An appropriate income had to be guaranteed to the priest. The priest had to attend the diocesan synod and welcome the bishop every year when he came on his pastoral visit to the parish. The feudal lord would invest the new priest in the new church by a ceremony that usually involved the priest placing his hand on the key in the door of the church. Once invested in a parish, the priest was expected to serve the people of that community for life. The revenues for each parish were to be generated by an arrangement that was established by Charlemagne's father, Pepin the Short (+768), for parishes and territories under his rule in 765. Pepin required that a tithe of ten percent, which had previously been voluntary, should be obligatory. Boundaries were established to ensure that the tithe was paid to the proper church by those living in the parish territory.[28]

With the break-up of the Carolingian Empire, the church was no longer able to maintain the delicate balance that existed between what

---

26. Bo, *Storia della parrocchia*, 2:45.
27. Addleshaw, *Development of the Parish System*, 3.
28. Addleshaw, *Development of the Parish System*, 4.

had come to be referred to as the right of the *gubernatio* of the bishop and the *dominium* of the feudal lord. Parishes fell into the hands of the local feudal lords and civil authorities. With this, the parishes suffered a great break in relations with the local bishop and secularization. Their religious dimension took second place to the concerns of the lay authorities that controlled them. Parish churches began to be seen by the landowner as a source of revenue and were often traded, sold, and passed on to other family members as mere property.[29] Landowners often had a serf of their choice ordained and invested with the care of the parish so that they could collect the tithes. When a bishop refused to ordain the candidate of their liking, the landowner would often find another bishop and pay him to perform the service. Those parishes that were owned by monasteries often fared better in this system. In 1059, Anselm of Braga reported that only five of the fifty parishes in his diocese were under the bishop's control.[30] Many of those who were appointed to parishes for the purpose of collecting the tithe could not even read.[31] Some priests did not even reside in their parishes, and others were only concerned to hand their office on to their children as an inheritance.

Despite the many weaknesses of the *eigenkirche* system, the parish church came to establish itself in this time period as the center of the village. The feasts, devotions and processions that centered on the parish gave the rhythm and cultural heart to a people bound by work and poverty. The many religious feasts caused landowners to release workers momentarily from their work, created a sense of community and allowed the parish to form the people in the Christian faith.[32] The years that followed were to see many efforts to free the parish system from many of the weaknesses that accompanied its development

## Efforts to Reform the Parish from Saint Gregory VII (1073-85) to the Council of Trent (1545-63)

Saint Gregory VII began a process of reform in the church that sought to see the right of appointment to ecclesiastical offices returned to the

---

29. Bo, *Storia della parrocchia*, 2:159.
30. Bo, *Storia della parrocchia*, 2:167.
31. Bo, *Storia della parrocchia*, 2:191.
32. Bo, *Storia della parrocchia*, 2:231–43.

legitimate authorities.[33] His efforts were mainly directed to the appointment of bishops and abbots. Pastoral offices had in many places become political or economic appointments aimed at benefiting the recipient's personal fortune. The reforms begun by Saint Gregory VII in this Investiture Controversy were pursued for many years to follow and received a significant boost by the victory won by the church in the signing of the Concordant of Worms in the year 1122. The agreement reached at Worms between Pope Calistus II (1119–1124) and the Emperor Henry V (1106–1125) led to a great number of councils that would attempt to correct the effects of the Investiture Controversy at different levels of the church.[34] The First Lateran Council (1123) required that all bishops be chosen freely by canonical election, and it subsequently became the practice that they would be invested with the pastoral staff by an ecclesiastical official.[35] The Second Lateran Council (1139) forbade the sale of all benefices or ecclesiastical promotions.[36]

Pope Alexander III (1159–1181) began a series of reforms that would have a great effect on parish communities. During his papacy the rights of the *eigenkirche* system were drastically transformed. The property rights for churches were transferred back to the church's authorities, and the founder of the church retained the right of patronage that entitled him to present candidates to the bishop to fill a vacancy.[37] This candidate was then required to meet the standards set by the bishop and show his ability to perform the duties that would be asked of him in his pastoral office. The pastor was to receive a benefice as a result of his

---

33. Bo, *Storia della parrocchia*, 2:168.

34. The agreement reached at Worms was also known as the *Pactum Calixtinum*. Brought about through the mediation of the German princes, it ended the Investiture Controversy. The emperor Henry V renounced investiture by ring and staff of the new bishops or abbots. He also granted canonical election and free consecration. These elections were to be free of simony and violence. The pope conceded to the emperor the privilege of having the elections of all bishops and abbots in the German Kingdom held in his presence. If the electing chapter was divided between two candidates, the emperor was to settle the dispute in favor of the *sanior pars*. Before the consecration, the elected was to receive his temporalities from the emperor, who invested him with a sceptre. The emperor enjoyed these privileges only within his own kingdom. Bo, *Storia della parrocchia*, 3:9–14.

35. *Concilium Lateranense I*, canons 1 and 3, in *Decrees of the Ecumenical Councils*, 1:190.

36. *Concilium Lateranense II*, canons 1 and 2, in *Decrees of the Ecumenical Councils*, 1:197.

37. Cruce, "History of the Parish," 17.

appointment. The benefice was the financial stipend attached to an office that was usually generated by an endowment or from the tithes collected in a particular parish. Thus the *eigenkirche* system developed into the benefice system.[38]

The benefice system resulted in a legal situation that began to equate parishes with a pastoral office that provided financial support for the clergy, as opposed to being seen as a community for the spiritual welfare of the faithful. Of the benefice system, American canon lawyer James A. Coriden wrote:

> In the church's juridical order from the twelfth century until the Code revision of 1983, a parish was looked upon as a spiritual reality (the pastoral office) with the temporal reality (the endowment or other income source) united in one institution: a benefice, that is, an office with a reliable income source for the officeholder.[39]

While the benefice system managed to restore the right of approving appointments and some control over church property to the bishops, it did bring a number of its own problems. The accumulation of benefices often saw the parish's revenues taken from the parish and less than qualified candidates being chosen as *vicarius* and paid to substitute for the absent legitimate pastor.[40] The substitutes, who were chosen to fill in for the absent pastors, were often no more qualified to serve the needs of the faithful than were the serfs who had been ordained to serve in the landowners' churches in the *eigenkirche* system. Often parishes that needed dividing, in order to serve the needs of the faithful, were not divided for fear of reducing the income of those who held the parish's benefice. The pastoral care of the faithful continued to suffer.

Not all of the efforts of reform during this period were directed to addressing the issues of appointment and property rights. Much that was done centered on improving the pastoral care that the faithful received. Even some of the reforms that concerned the rights of appointment and questions of ownership were often intended to ensure the appointment of properly educated pastors who had sufficient understanding of the faith to catechize and celebrate the liturgy in a manner that could nourish the faithful. The Second Council of Leons (1274) required that

---

38. Coriden, *Parish in the Catholic Tradition*, 28.
39. Coriden, *Parish in the Catholic Tradition*, 28.
40. Bo, *Storia della Parrocchia*, 3:167.

candidates who were nominated to fill a vacancy in a parish had to be twenty-five years old, well-educated, and had to fill the nomination within one semester or the nomination became invalid.[41] The Fourth Lateran Council (1215) required that provincial synods be held yearly to root out all abuses.[42] Significant also from the Fourth Lateran Council was the requirement that all of the faithful must go to confession and receive the Eucharist each year at Easter.[43] This requirement that parishioners must confess at Easter to their proper pastor added an increased awareness to the parish as a geographical territory. Another significant instrument of reform at this time was that of the pastoral visit of the bishop to the parish. The bishop was to ensure that the priest was serving the needs of the faithful and living according to the status of his vocation. The parishioners were to have the opportunity during these visits to denounce the pastor if he had been negligent in his duties.[44] The bishop was also to check on the religious and sacramental life of the community. A concern to address the quality of preaching that the faithful were exposed to was also expressed in some of the reforms. A local council at Lambeth in 1281 determined that every three months the parish priest was required to preach on the fourteen articles of the faith, the Ten Commandments, the two commandments of charity, the seven works of mercy, the seven mortal sins, the seven virtues and the seven sacraments.[45] Despite all of these efforts at reform, it would not be until the Council of Trent that parish life would begin to be dramatically improved by effective reform.

It was also during this time period that many of the problems in the spiritual life of parishes were confronted by a different type of reform movement. The mendicant orders, especially the Franciscans and the Dominicans, proved to be enormously popular with the faithful. This was due to both the vitality of their message and the quality of their preaching. Their presence, however, also resulted in much legislation to strengthen the relationship between the faithful and the parishes in

---

41. In regard to the need to take possession of the parish in three months, see *Concilium Lugdunense II*, canon 5, in *Decrees of the Ecumenical Councils*, 1:319; for the age and qualities of the candidates, see the same, canon 13, 1:321–22.

42. *Concilium Lateranense IV*, canon 6, in *Decrees of the Ecumenical Councils*, 1:236–37.

43. *Concilium Lateranense IV*, canon 21, 1:245.

44. Bo, *Storia della Parrocchia*, 3:95–113.

45. Bo, *Storia della Parrocchia*, 3:199.

which they lived.[46] Pastors were often jealous of the loss of revenue that they faced by parishioners attending liturgical celebrations in the mendicant churches and not their own proper parish churches. However, the popularity of these mendicant preachers spoke of the significant problems in parish life and the spiritual hunger of the faithful. The mendicant orders attempted to provide solutions to the difficulties facing the church from inside the church. Others would leave the church in an attempt to find solutions to these same problems. Many of the problems would not be solved until the Council of Trent addressed them.

## The Reforms of the Council of Trent (1545-63)

Despite the many efforts to reform the church in the years leading up to the Council of Trent, none of these efforts would have the positive effects that the Council of Trent had in the life of the church. The fathers of the council placed great emphasis on reforming the internal life of the church in order to provide greater pastoral care for the faithful. Many of the problems that had affected parish life, from the poor formation of the clergy to the abuses of the church's benefice system, were given much thought by the council fathers. Great attention was also given to a proper articulation of the Catholic faith so that the faithful could be properly nourished in the faith.

The Council of Trent asked that all bishops remember their own dignity as pastors of Christ's flock.[47] The absence of so many bishops from their dioceses, often to take government positions, had only served as an example to the many pastors who were also absent. Provincial councils were to be reintroduced and held every three years. Diocesan synods, with all of the priests active in parish ministry attending, were to be held every year. Because many people could now read, it became imperative that priests receive a more formal preparation and be able themselves to read. The twenty-third session of the council dealt with the introduction of seminary formation and the requirements of those who were to be ordained.[48] The pastoral visit was to receive much greater attention as a means of insuring that the needs of the faithful were being

---

46. Bo, *Storia della Parrocchia*, 3:178–83.
47. Bo, *Storia della parrocchia*, 4:166.
48. *Canones et Decreta Sacrosancti Oecumenici et Generalis Concilii Tridentini*, twenty-third session, Decrees of Reform, canons 1–18, 152–66.

met. A process was introduced for candidates to apply for parishes that had become vacant and for examining these candidates.[49] The twenty-first session established that bishops could divide parishes, even without the pastor's consent, to create new ones that were better able to serve the needs of the faithful.[50] The accumulation of benefices was strictly forbidden, and those who accepted the offices attached to a benefice were expected to be present to fulfill their pastoral duties. Those who were absent were obliged to pay for their replacements from their own pocket. The council required that pastors preach every Sunday, on feast days, and at least three times a week during Lent and Advent.[51] The pastor was to keep a baptismal and marriage register, and no priest could celebrate the sacraments without the authorization of the parishioner's legitimate pastor, unless there was the danger of death. The obligation of the faithful to receive the sacraments and relate to their proper parish strengthened the awareness of all in regards to legitimate parish boundaries. Two other decrees—that concerning the condemnation of those who usurp church property[52] and the requirement to pay the tithe[53]—sought to ensure the parish's freedom to serve the needs of all the faithful of the parish.

The Council of Trent sought to address the pastoral problems that had plagued the church for many years by calling bishops and pastors to a higher standard in the pastoral care that they owed to the faithful. This was to be accomplished by stricter requirements for residency within the place of pastoral responsibility, an end to the accumulation of benefices, regular pastoral visits, diocesan synods, and the introduction of seminary formation. Also of fundamental importance in this reform was the emphasis upon the relationship between the pastor and the parishioners who lived within the geographical territory of which the pastor was the shepherd. After the bishop, the parish priest was given exclusive authority, with few exceptions, over his parishioners' spiritual lives.[54] Although

49. *Canones et Decreta Sacrosancti Oecumenici et Generalis Concilii Tridentini*, twenty-fourth session, Decrees of Reform, canon 18, 193–96.

50. *Canones et Decreta Sacrosancti Oecumenici et Generalis Concilii Tridentini*, twenty-first session, Decrees of Reform, canon 4, 129–30.

51. *Canones et Decreta Sacrosancti Oecumenici et Generalis Concilii Tridentini*, twenty-fourth session, Decrees of Reform, canon 4, 181–82.

52. *Canones et Decreta Sacrosancti Oecumenici et Generalis Concilii Tridentini*, twenty-second session, Decrees of Reform, canon 11, 146–47.

53. *Canones et Decreta Sacrosancti Oecumenici et Generalis Concilii Tridentini*, twenty-fifth session, Decrees of Reform, canon 12, 229.

54. Blöchlinger, *Modern Parish Community*, 90.

the Council of Trent dealt successfully with the problems that had confronted the parish in the past, it was also limited in what it was able to offer to parish communities of the future. On this matter Alex Blöchlinger wrote:

> The Tridentine legal concept of the Church had the great disadvantage in that it was too narrowly confined to the hierarchy: it condemned the lay element, the people of the Church, too much to passivity.[55]

With this one limitation aside, the Council of Trent provided the parish with the reform it needed to become a vital force in the life of the church for centuries to come. Not until the Second Vatican Council would another church council have such a great effect on parish life.

## From the Council of Trent to the Second Vatican Council (1962–65)

The Council of Trent had an extremely powerful effect in ending many of the abuses which had plagued parish life for several centuries. Under its influence, the bishop once again became the true shepherd responsible for the spiritual life of the diocese. The parish priest came to be viewed as the bishop's delegate, fulfilling his mission within a certain territory of the diocese. The responsibility which the hierarchy had to provide pastoral care for the church was clearly articulated in the Council of Trent. For four centuries, within the framework of the Tridentine parish model, the church attempted to provide pastoral care for the different circumstances in which it existed. Some of the more significant challenges to parish life in this period included the church's missionary work, the rise of strong nation-states, the industrial revolution, and the mass immigration of national groups.[56]

The missionary effort, which followed the European arrival on the two American, the African, and the Asian continents, concentrated great attention on preaching the gospel and baptizing those exposed to the faith for the first time. The challenge of nurturing new and stable communities of faith was often neglected and still requires attention today.

---

55. Blöchlinger, *Modern Parish Community*, 92. See also Coriden, *Parish in the Catholic Tradition*, 32. Coriden expresses the same opinion.

56. Coriden, *Parish in the Catholic Tradition*, 32–35.

Some of these communities continue to exist without a stable native clergy, and sometimes even a church building is a luxury.

The emergence of strong nation-states in the eighteenth and nineteenth centuries often saw the governments of countries like France, Germany, Austria, Spain, and Italy taking on a very powerful role in the life of the church. As these governments took on the rights of appointing bishops and pastors, the independence of the church was threatened. As national churches were subjected to the agendas of government officials, the communion of the universal church was often in peril. It was also often the case that these types of governments made the local clergy into a type of civil employee of the state, rather than leaving them free to do their work as ministers of the body of Christ.

The Industrial Revolution was accompanied with a huge explosion in urban population. In many cities the size of parish populations multiplied ten and twentyfold. In Paris, sixty-three parishes had an average of 26,923 Catholics living in each of them. Essen grew from a city of 6,000 in 1846 to 240,000 in 1900. During this period there remained only two parishes in the whole city to serve all of these people.[57] At this time it was often argued that it was better to allow parishes to become large, while assigning additional associate pastors, than to create new parishes. Pastoral care in such huge parishes became next to impossible.

In North America, a new type of parish developed that would establish itself as a type of exception to the territorial parish. The national parish was established to provide large groups of immigrants from a particular language or culture with a parish to celebrate the liturgy and form community together. As we shall see, this type of parish was so effective that it received recognition in the 1917 Code of Canon Law.

When the Code of Canon Law was first promulgated in 1917, it articulated in one single legal text many of the laws which had been in effect for years prior. Of particular importance was the code's understanding of a parish as a geographical territory within the division of a diocese. Specifically related to this is can. 216, §§ 1 and 3. The first paragraph states:

> The territory of every diocese is to be divided up into distinct territorial parts; to each part a specific church and determined population are assigned with its own rector as its pastor, who is over it for the necessary care of souls.

---

57. Blöchlinger, *Modern Parish Community*, 101–5.

PART ONE

Paragraph 3 goes on to clarify:

> The parts of the diocese mentioned in § 1 are parishes; the parts of the apostolic vicariate and apostolic prelature, if a specific rector has been assigned, are called quasi-parishes.[58]

Can. 94 of the 1917 code speaks of people being assigned to a parish by reason of their place of residence. The responsibility which the pastor has to care for the souls of those who reside in the parish assigned to him is spoken of in can. 451.[59] The benefice system remains intact in the 1917 code. As a special exception, and only with an apostolic indult, national parishes, which do not have a set territory, may be established.[60]

The 1917 code thus solidifies the notion of a parish as a geographical territory, which has a benefice attached to it, and is assigned to a pastor for the pastoral care of souls. It will not be until the middle of the twentieth century that the parish would once again be viewed as a sacramental community of life.[61] This change in outlook was primarily due to the work of the liturgical movement. The beginnings of this change can be seen in such documents as Pius XII's (+1958) encyclicals *Mystici Corporis* and *Mediator Dei*.[62]

## REFERENCES TO THE PARISH IN THE ECCLESIOLOGY OF VATICAN II (1963-65)

### The Documents of the Second Vatican Council

The documents of the Second Vatican Council give a great deal of attention to the reality that it is in the assembly of the entire local church that the universal church makes its epiphany.[63] Within this view of the church's structure, one finds a realistic understanding of the relationship that exists between the local church and the universal church. The nature of the Eucharist itself is that it must be celebrated in a concrete place and time by a concrete community. The Eucharistic celebration of a local church is what makes the universal church present in its fullest possible

---

58. Peters, *1917 Pio-Benedictine Code of Canon Law*, 92–93, can. 216, §§ 1 and 3.
59. Peters, *1917 Pio-Benedictine Code of Canon Law*, 55, can. 94 and 173, can. 451.
60. Peters, *1917 Pio-Benedictine Code of Canon Law*, can. 216, § 4.
61. Blöchlinger, *Modern Parish Community*, 105.
62. Pius XII, *Mystici Corporis*,193–248; and *Mediator Dei*, 521–95.
63. Marsili, "La chiesa locale comunità di culto," 30.

manifestation to a particular place and time. It does so because the Eucharistic celebration of the entire local community around its bishop is the event that serves as an epiphany or theophany of the church.[64] In the local celebrations of the liturgy the church comes alive in the "here and now" (*"hic et nunc"*) of time and space. The Catholicity of the church depends upon the liturgy of the church being incarnated and celebrated within each local community.[65] The Eucharist, which makes the church, is also what roots each individual Christian to the church and makes it present in the here and now of their lives.[66]

Of great importance in this dialectic between the local and universal church is the adherence of the local church to the faith, rites, and the communal structure that brings unity to the universal church.[67] If the local church does not adhere to those matters of faith, morals, cult, and discipline that bring unity to the universal church, the universal church will not be present in the gatherings of the local community. The documents of the Second Vatican Council give a great deal of attention to the hierarchical structures of the church that are necessary for the communion of the local churches with the universal church.[68]

The Second Vatican Council frequently relied upon the theology of the mystical body of Christ to explain the relationship between the local church and the universal church. Within this vision, the church is presented as a structured body in which there are different roles to be played by the different members. In discussing the different divisions that are to be found within the mystical body of Christ, the council documents refer to the particular church as that local community of the faithful that is under the leadership of the bishop.[69] This is the structure that can be traced back to the apostolic church founded by Christ. After the local diocesan community gathered around the bishop, the council gives a priority of place to the parish communities that gather around their duly appointed

---

64. Marsili, "La chiesa locale comunità di culto," 47.

65. Valenziano, "Chiesa particolare e liturgia dell'uomo," 54.

66. Valenziano, "Chiesa particolare e liturgia dell'uomo," 67.

67. Valenziano, "Chiesa particolare e liturgia dell'uomo," 65.

68. Tillard, *Church of Churches*, 256–317.

69. The Second Vatican Council, *Lumen gentium*, no. 23 and 27: 376–78 and 382–84. Church documents began to be issued at the time of this council with an article number. To avoid confusing page and article numbers a colon will be used to separate the article from the page number. The page number will follow the colon. As all council documents appear in the first volume of Flannery's work, there will be no need to repeat the volume number in all citations of the council documents taken from his collection.

pastors. These are the principle communities, after the diocese, in which the church is to be encountered. This is due to the fact that the church of Christ is present in all the legitimate communities where the faithful gather around their duly appointed pastors.[70] In the following section the relevant documents of the Second Vatican Council will be investigated to understand the place that the parish is given in the ecclesiology of the council. The documents are examined in their chronological order.

## *Sacrosanctum concilium (December 4, 1963)*

The Constitution on the Sacred Liturgy contains some of the most important references to the parish to be found in all of the conciliar documents. The full significance of the passages related to the parish depends upon the general context of the ecclesiology presented in the constitution. *Sacrosanctum concilium* states that it is through the liturgy, and most especially through the Eucharist, that "the work of our redemption is accomplished."[71] Each day the liturgy builds up those who are in the church and transforms them into a holy temple of the Lord. In baptism people are implanted into the paschal mystery of Christ.[72] Christ, who is always present in the liturgy, unites the church and all its members more closely to himself in each liturgical celebration.[73] In the liturgy the priestly role of Jesus Christ is enacted and the complete and definitive public expression of the worship of the mystical body of Christ, both head and members, takes place. Through the Holy Spirit the liturgy on earth is united with the heavenly liturgy, and the church on earth awaits the day of Christ's coming when the church on earth and the heavenly church will be made one. The liturgy not only calls those who have already accepted Christ to be more fully transformed into his image; it also calls those who have not accepted Christ to accept salvation. So intimately connected to the life of Christ's mystical body is the liturgy, that the constitution declares, "Nevertheless the liturgy is the summit toward which the activity of the church is directed; it is also the fount from which all her power flows."[74] The same article of the constitution states:

70. Magrassi, "Il mistero della chiesa locale," 11.
71. The Second Vatican Council, *Sacrosanctum concilium*, no. 2:1.
72. The Second Vatican Council, *Sacrosanctum concilium*, no. 6:4.
73. The Second Vatican Council, *Sacrosanctum concilium*, no. 7:4–5.
74. The Second Vatican Council, *Sacrosanctum concilium*, no 10:6.

> From the Liturgy, therefore, and especially from the Eucharist, grace is poured forth upon us as from a fountain, and the sanctification of men in Christ and the glorification of God to which all other activities of the Church are directed, as toward their end, are achieved with maximum effectiveness.[75]

The liturgy has such a great significance in the building up of the body of Christ, and in configuring the faithful to Christ, that it is essential that the faithful approach the liturgy with the proper disposition. In the words of *Sacrosanctum concilium*, "that the faithful take part fully aware of what they are doing, actively engaged in the rite and enriched by it."[76]

The church is the mystical body of Christ continuing his work by announcing his message of salvation and making him present in every age and place. Christ's saving and transforming presence is most fully and effectively communicated through the liturgy of his church. The very nature of the liturgy, however, is that it must be celebrated in a particular place and time by a necessarily limited portion of the universal church. Despite this limited nature of all liturgical celebrations, *Sacrosanctum concilium* states that the fullest expression of the church is to be encountered in those celebrations of the entire local church that take place around the bishop. At such celebrations, the local church gathers around its high priest the bishop, with all his presbyters and ministers, to most fully manifest the church. *Sacrosanctum concilium* states:

> The bishop is to be considered as the High Priest of his flock from whom the life in Christ of his faithful is in some way derived and upon whom it in some way depends. Therefore all should hold in the greatest esteem the liturgical life of the diocese centred around the bishop, especially in his cathedral church. They must be convinced that the principal manifestation of the Church consists in the full, active participation of all God's holy people in the same liturgical celebrations, especially in the same Eucharist, in one prayer, at one altar, at which the bishop presides, surrounded by his college of priests and by his ministers.[77]

The entire Christian community should be aware of the fact that it most clearly expresses its nature as church when all its members are gathered around the bishop to actively celebrate the liturgy.

---

75. The Second Vatican Council, *Sacrosanctum concilium*, no. 10:6.
76. The Second Vatican Council, *Sacrosanctum concilium*, no. 11:6–7.
77. The Second Vatican Council, *Sacrosanctum concilium*, no. 41:14–15.

PART ONE

This being said, *Sacrosanctum concilium* duly notes that it would be impossible for the bishop to always and everywhere celebrate the liturgy in his diocese. Nor is it possible for the whole flock to always be present in one assembly. The bishop must establish smaller communities where the faithful can meet more conveniently. Parishes, which are organized locally under a parish priest who acts in the bishop's place, are the most important of these local assemblies. The importance of the church's parishes is based upon the fact that they exhibit the visible church set up throughout the nations of the world. *Sacrosanctum concilium* number 42 states in its first paragraph:

> But as it is impossible for the bishop always and everywhere to preside over the whole flock in his church, he must of necessity establish groupings of the faithful; and, among these, parishes, set up locally under a pastor who takes the place of the bishop, are the most important, for in some way they represent the visible Church constituted throughout the world.[78]

The impact that the liturgy has upon the lives of those who live in the parish ought to be such as to bind them more closely to the life of the mystical body as a whole. It should transform the members of the parish community to become more like Christ and lead them to witness to Christ's salvation to all the members of their local community that they encounter. The parish community is to strive for unity within itself as well as being aware of their unity with the universal church through the diocesan bishop. The second paragraph of *Sacrosanctum concilium* 42 reads:

> Therefore the liturgical life of the parish and its relation to the bishop must be fostered in the spirit and practice of the laity and clergy. Efforts must be made to encourage a sense of community within the parish, above all in the common celebration of the Sunday Mass.[79]

In *Sacrosanctum concilium*, the church is presented as the mystical body of Christ. This body is hierarchically structured with the members joined to their head Jesus Christ. As the body of Christ, the church continues to make Christ present to the world and to call people to salvation in every place that it is present. The liturgy, and most especially the Eucharist, when it is celebrated by the diocesan bishop surrounded

---

78. The Second Vatican Council, *Sacrosanctum concilium*, no. 42:15.
79. The Second Vatican Council, *Sacrosanctum concilium*, no. 42:15–16.

by the full assembly, manifests the church most completely. The parish community, set up locally under a parish priest who takes the place of the bishop, represents the next most significant way in which the church and its saving mission are manifested to the world. This is so because the parish communities throughout the world manifest the visible church constituted throughout the world.

## *Lumen gentium (November 21, 1964)*

The Constitution on the Church, *Lumen gentium*, characterizes the church as the body of Christ and holds a fundamentally Pauline version of this theology.[80] Paul's letters emphasize the unity between all who are inserted into the church through baptism. This unity is produced by the Holy Spirit and binds all Christians together with Christ the head to constitute his body and make him present to the entire world. *Lumen gentium* states, "For by communicating his Spirit, Christ mystically constitutes as his body those brothers [and sisters] of his who are called together from every nation."[81] In Christ's body his life is communicated to all believers, who are in a real way united to him by means of the sacraments. Because Christ's message is for all peoples, and the communion built up in the body of Christ knows no boundaries or racial barriers, the church which Christ established to carry his message to the corners of the world is called the light of the nations.[82] The universality of Christ's offer of salvation depends upon the church incarnating itself in the many local communities of believers that exist around the world. These communities of believers, which are held together by the Holy Spirit building them up in communion, are by their nature hierarchical and structured.

*Lumen gentium* offers a lengthy theological reflection on the nature of the communion that exists in the church. This communion, which is the work of the Holy Spirit, is dependent upon the church's liturgical and sacramental life. Through the church's liturgy and sacraments, the Holy Spirit conveys Christ to all believers and they are assimilated more completely into his likeness.[83] The whole people of God are called

---

80. Merendino, "Eucharistia e chiesa locale," 93.
81. The Second Vatican Council, *Lumen gentium*, no. 7:354–56.
82. The Second Vatican Council, *Lumen gentium*, no. 9:359–60: "Destined to extend to all regions of the earth, it enters into human history, though it transcends at once all times and racial boundaries."
83. The Second Vatican Council, *Lumen gentium*, no. 11:361–63.

to serve God in holiness and to share in Christ's priestly, prophetic and kingly mission. This they are to do by their full participation in the liturgy, by giving themselves to serving Christ, and by transforming the world by bringing Christ to their families and work places. In order that the people of God could be nourished and continue to grow, Christ instituted a variety of ministries which are directed towards the good of the whole body. *Lumen gentium* makes it clear that these ministries were established by Christ to be of service to all the members of the church so that they might enjoy the dignity that is theirs as Christians and come to salvation. The Constitution states:

> The holders of office, who are invested with a sacred power, are, in fact, dedicated to promoting the interests of their brethren, so that all who belong to the People of God, and are consequently endowed with true Christian dignity, may, through their free and well-ordered efforts towards a common goal, attain to salvation.[84]

The ordained ministries are those of bishops, priests, and deacons. In the bishop, assisted by the priests, there is present in the midst of believers the Lord Jesus Christ, the supreme high priest.[85] It is in the individual local church gathered around its shepherd that the church of Christ is said to be truly present.

The bishop is marked by the fullness of the sacrament of orders, and he is "the steward of the grace of the supreme priesthood."[86] He preaches the good news of salvation in his diocese and oversees the local church's sacramental and pastoral life.[87] It is also through the bishop, who is a member of the episcopal college, that the local church maintains its communion with the universal church that is in communion with Rome. As *Sacrosanctum concilium* pointed out, it is not possible for the bishop to be present in each assembly at all times. Presbyters and deacons are often required to assist the bishop in his service to God's people. *Lumen gentium* states:

---

84. The Second Vatican Council, *Lumen gentium*, no. 18:369–70.
85. The Second Vatican Council, *Lumen gentium*, no. 21:372–74.
86. The Second Vatican Council, *Lumen gentium* no. 26:381.
87. The Second Vatican Council, *Lumen gentium*, no. 26:381–82. It states: "By the ministry of the word they impart to those who believe the strength of God unto salvation (cf. Rom. 1:16), and through the sacraments, the frequent and fruitful distribution of which they regulate by their authority, they sanctify the faithful."

Whilst not having the supreme degree of the pontifical office, and notwithstanding the fact that they depend on the bishops in the exercise of their own proper power, the priests are for all that associated with them by reason of their sacerdotal dignity; and in virtue of the sacrament of Orders, after the image of Christ, the supreme and eternal priest (Heb. 5: 1–10; 7: 24; 9: 11–28), they are consecrated in order to preach the Gospel and shepherd the faithful as well as to celebrate divine worship as true priests of the New Testament.[88]

Around the bishop, the priests of one diocese constitute a presbyterium. In those congregations that are entrusted to them by the bishop, priests make the bishop present. They are to be united to the bishop's mission in trust and generosity. Priests also make the universal church present in the localities where they preside over an assembly of Christ's faithful. *Lumen gentium* states:

> Those who, under the authority of the bishop, sanctify and govern that portion of the Lord's flock assigned to them render the universal Church visible in their locality and contribute efficaciously towards building up the whole body of Christ (cf. Eph. 4:12).[89]

The deacons are not ordained for the priesthood but for ministry. Strengthened by sacramental grace, they are to be at the service of the people of God in the ministry of the liturgy, the word and charity, in communion with the bishop and his presbyterium.[90] The purpose of these ordained ministries is that they are to be at the service of the entire church so that it may be built up in all its members into the body of Christ.

Unlike *Sacrosanctum concilium*, the word "parish" ("*paroecia*") does not appear in *Lumen gentium*. The constitution on the church speaks more of the general structure of those smaller communities that exist in a diocese. What it says of these local assemblies entrusted to a priest is applicable to parishes. The structure which *Lumen gentium* puts forward for the life of the church is very important for an understanding of the theology of a parish which will be found in *ODC*. In this regard, Ignazio

---

88. The Second Vatican Council, *Lumen gentium*, no. 28:384.
89. The Second Vatican Council, *Lumen gentium*, no. 28:385–86.
90. The Second Vatican Council, *Lumen gentium* no. 29:387.

PART ONE

Calabuig, a member of the study group that prepared the 1977 rite,[91] has written:

> Si può asserire che l'Ordo dedicationis ecclesiae et altaris occupa nel quadro dei libri liturgici restaurati un posto simile a quello della costituzione Lumen gentium tra i documenti conciliari: come la Lumen gentium è un documento-sintesi dei molteplici aspetti del "mistero dalla Chiesa," così l'Ordo dedicationis è un rito-sintesi dei molteplici temi cultuali delle assemblee ecclesiali.[92]

## Christus Dominus (October 28, 1965)

*Christus Dominus*, the Decree on the Pastoral Office of Bishops in the Church, has a great deal to say about parish communities and the priests who represent the bishop in the pastoral care of the parishes. Bishops take the place of the apostles and through the gift of the Holy Spirit, which is given them in ordination, they receive the mandate and power to teach all nations, to sanctify people in the truth, and to sustain them spiritually.[93] By their consecration, bishops become members of the episcopal college. As members of the episcopal college, bishops are responsible for the entire church when they act as a body in communion with, and under the authority of, the supreme pontiff. Individually bishops have responsibility for that portion of God's flock that is entrusted to their care. A diocese is that section of the people of God entrusted to a bishop in cooperation with his priests.[94] The bishop has the fullness of holy orders and both priests and deacons are dependent upon him for the exercise of their orders.[95] Bishops are the principle dispensers of the mysteries of God, and it is their function to control, promote, and protect the entire liturgical life of the church entrusted to them. In exercising this ministry

---

91. Bugnini, *Reform of the Liturgy 1948–1975*, 792, footnote no. 1.

92. Calabuig, "'Rito' per una Chiesa che vive," 41. My translation of this passage is: It can be asserted that *Ordo dedicationis ecclesiae et altaris* [ODC] occupies in the sphere of restored liturgical books a place similar to that of the Constitution *Lumen gentium* among the documents of the [Second Vatican] Council: As *Lumen gentium* is a document that synthesizes the multiple aspects of the mystery of the church, so too *Ordo dedicationis* [ODC] is a rite that synthesizes the multiple cultic (liturgical) themes of the church assembly.

93. The Second Vatican Council, *Christus Dominus*, no. 2, 564–65.

94. The Second Vatican Council, *Christus Dominus*, no. 11:569.

95. The Second Vatican Council, *Christus Dominus*, no. 15:571–72.

the bishop is to ensure that the faithful are duly involved in the affairs of the church and is to recognize their rights and duties in playing their part in building up the mystical body of Christ.[96] The bishop is to have a special concern for all of the separated brothers and sisters. This concern is also to be shown to non-Christians. Those who on account of their way of life are not adequately cared for by the ordinary pastoral ministry of the parochial clergy are to receive special attention from the bishop.[97] The diocese must be governed by the bishop in such a way that it is clear to the faithful that the diocese is a part of Christ's universal church.

*Christus Dominus* goes on to say that the main collaborators of the bishop are the parish priests, who as pastors in their own right have been entrusted a portion of the diocese. The decree states:

> Parish priests are in a special sense collaborators with the bishop. They are given, in a specific section of the diocese, and under the authority of the bishop, the care of souls as their particular shepherd.[98]

Parish priests are to exercise their office of teaching, sanctifying and governing in such a way that the faithful of the parish community feel they are members of the diocese and the universal church. The preaching of the Word of God by the priest should lead the faithful to be grounded in faith, hope and charity. In their work of sanctification, parish priests must ensure that the Eucharistic celebration is at the heart of the Christian community. They should truly know their flock so that they may respond to their needs and be able to motivate the faithful to become more involved in their apostolate. It becomes them to bear in mind the importance of being available to celebrate the sacrament of penance. They should exercise paternal charity for the poor and sick.

In order that the bishop might be able to truly care for the building up of Christ's body in the diocese, the decree called for a reform in the manner in which priests were appointed to parishes. *Christus Dominus* stated:

> Basically, however, parochial responsibility has to do with the good of souls. It follows that, if a bishop is more easily to make provision for the parishes, all rights whatsoever of presentation,

---

96. The Second Vatican Council, *Christus Dominus*, no. 16:572–73.
97. The Second Vatican Council, *Christus Dominus*, no. 18:574–75.
98. The Second Vatican Council, *Christus Dominus*, no. 30:581.

nomination and reservation should be abrogated, without prejudice, however, to the rights of religious.[99]

The decree called for an end to all rights of presentation, nomination or reservation. The distinction between movable and immovable pastors was to be ended, and the method and procedure for the transfer and removal of a pastor was to be reexamined and simplified. These requirements would effectively bring an end to the benefice system in which a pastor was appointed for life. The parish priest was to enjoy the stability of office that was required for the good of souls. The spiritual well-being of parishioners was also to be the principle that guided the creation and the suppression of parishes. The reforms called for in parish life were all orientated towards improving the pastoral care of the faithful.

## *Apostolicum actuositatem (November 18, 1965)*

The Second Vatican Council's Decree on the Apostolate of the Laity provides a theological overview of the place that the lay faithful are to play in the life of the mystical body of Christ. The church was founded to extend Christ's offer of salvation throughout the world. Every member of the mystical body of Christ is to live his or her faith with this objective in mind. *Apostolicum actuositatem* affirms:

> The Church was founded to spread the kingdom of Christ over all the earth for the glory of God the Father, to make all men [and women] partakers in redemption and salvation, and through them to establish the right relationship of the entire world to Christ. Every activity of the Mystical Body with this in view goes by the name "apostolate;" the Church exercises it through all its members, though in various ways.[100]

All Christians are brought into the church through baptism and strengthened by the power of the Holy Spirit in confirmation. By this they are consecrated as a royal priesthood and a holy people called to offer spiritual sacrifices and bear witness to Christ for all the world to see.[101] This intimate union with Christ, enjoyed by all the members of the mystical body of Christ, is maintained by the spiritual helps common to all, but chiefly by participation in the liturgy. The mission of the laity,

---

99. The Second Vatican Council, *Christus Dominus*, no. 31:582–83.
100. The Second Vatican Council, *Apostolicam actuositatem*, no. 2, 767–68.
101. The Second Vatican Council, *Apostolicam actuositatem*, no. 3: 768–69.

which is crucial for the church's mission in the world, is to bring the good news of salvation to all persons and to permeate the whole order of temporal things with the spirit of the gospel and so perfect it.[102]

The Decree on the Apostolate of the Laity speaks of the importance of the parish for fostering and nurturing the active life of the laity within the mystical body of Christ. The decree states:

> The parish offers an outstanding example of community apostolate, for it gathers into a unity all the diversities that are found there and inserts them into the universality of the Church. The laity should develop the habit of working in the parish in close union with their priests, of bringing before the ecclesial community their own problems, world problems, and questions regarding man's [and woman's] salvation, to examine them together and solve them by general discussion. According to their abilities the laity ought to cooperate in all the apostolic and missionary enterprises of their ecclesial family. The laity will continually cultivate the "feeling for the diocese," of which the parish is a kind of cell: they will be always ready on the invitation of the bishop to make their own contribution to diocesan undertakings.[103]

The parish is the place where most of the laity will go to celebrate the liturgy and receive the sacraments. It is in the liturgy that the faithful are to be strengthened to assume their role in the body of Christ. Pastors are to work with the laity so that the parish, with the help and advice of the laity, is able to fulfill its mission completely. The faithful should be active in both the life of the parish and the diocese and have a keen awareness of the church that lies beyond these communities. Because the family is of such great importance in the life of the faithful, both the diocese and parish are to support the family as the basic unit of the church.[104] As can be seen in the above passage, the decree specifically uses the word "cell" to speak of the relationship of the parish to the diocese.[105] It also speaks of the family as the "primary and vital cell of society."[106] For most members of the body of Christ, the parish is the cell through which they are linked to the entire body of the church.

---

102. The Second Vatican Council, *Apostolicam actuositatem*, no. 5:772.
103. The Second Vatican Council, *Apostolicam actuositatem*, no. 10:777–78.
104. The Second Vatican Council, *Apostolicam actuositatem*, no. 11:778–80.
105. The Second Vatican Council, *Apostolicam actuositatem*, no. 10:777–78.
106. The Second Vatican Council, *Apostolicam actuositatem*, no. 11:779.

PART ONE

## *Ad gentes divinitus (December 7, 1965)*

The Second Vatican Council's Decree on the Missionary Activity of the Church develops its theology on the church's missionary activity based upon the same theology of the mystical body of Christ which is present throughout the Council documents. The church was founded by Christ to be the universal sacrament of salvation and must fulfill Christ's command to preach the gospel to all nations.[107] The obligation to carry out this mission of proclaiming Christ's universal message of salvation falls on the particular churches that are already established. It is an obligation to preach the gospel to all who are outside the church. Regarding missionary activity, the decree states, "By means of this activity the mystical body of Christ unceasingly gathers and directs its energies towards its own increase (Eph. 4:11–16)."[108] All baptized people share in the responsibility to come together in one flock to bear unanimous witness to Christ before all nations. Missionary activity must show a concern to bring Christ to people in those lands where the gospel has not been received and to those living amongst Christian communities who have still not received the gospel. This missionary activity must express itself in the apostolate of the laity and in the preaching and liturgy of each local community. Those who have received the gift of the faith should be admitted to the catechumenate. Here they should receive both the doctrinal content of the faith and through a lived experience of the faith come to an understanding of the gospel standards of Christian discipleship. Through the sacraments of initiation new Christians come to be grafted into Christ's body.

Addressing the role of the dioceses and parishes in the church's missionary activity, the decree states:

> Since the people of God live in communities especially in dioceses and parishes by means of which, in a certain sense, they become manifest, it belongs to such communities to bear witness to Christ before the nations. The grace of renewal cannot grow in communities unless each of them expands the range of its charity to the ends of the earth, and has the same concern for those who are far away as it has for its own members.[109]

---

107. The Second Vatican Council, *Ad gentes divinitus*, no, 1, 813.
108. The Second Vatican Council, *Ad gentes divinitus*, no. 7: 821.
109. The Second Vatican Council, *Ad gentes divinitus*, no. 37:850–51.

This missionary attitude calls members of each local community to be as concerned for those who are far away as they are for their own members. The decree suggests relations with some parish or diocese in the missions, while at the same time maintaining the need to remain open to the universal church. The bishop, who shares the task of evangelization with the entire college of bishops, must see that his diocese has a vibrant concern for evangelizing all people, both inside and outside of the diocese.[110] Priests, in their pastoral work, are also to work diligently to spread the gospel and to lead Christians to an awareness of their vocations to bring Christ to the world. The decree speaks eloquently of the theology that should motivate every pastor:

> Priests represent Christ and are the collaborators of the order of bishops in the threefold sacred duty [of teaching, governing and sanctifying] which, of its nature, pertains to the mission of the Church. They must be profoundly aware of the fact that their very life is consecrated to the service of the missions. Since by their own ministry—which consists mainly in the Eucharist, which gives the Church its perfection—they are in communion with Christ the head, and are leading others to this communion, they cannot but be aware of how much is still lacking to the fullness of the Body, and of how much must therefore be done that it might grow from day to day.[111]

It would be appropriate to say, by extension of the logic expressed in the above passage, that the Eucharist, which binds all Christians to Christ's body, calls all Christians to be aware of what is still lacking to the fullness of his church as they are sent out into the world to be Christ's witnesses after every Eucharistic celebration.

## *Presbyterorum ordinis (December 7, 1965)*

> Through the sacred ordination and mission which they receive from the bishops priests are promoted to the service of Christ the Teacher, Priest and King; they are given a share in ministry, through which the Church here on earth is being ceaselessly built up into the people of God, Christ's Body and the temple of the Spirit.[112]

---

110. The Second Vatican Council, *Ad gentes divinitus*, no. 38:851–52.
111. The Second Vatican Council, *Ad gentes divinitus*, no. 39:853.
112. The Second Vatican Council, *Presbyterorum ordinis*, no. 1, 863.

In the body of Christ all of the faithful are consecrated a royal and holy priesthood. However, the Lord also appointed some as ministers who would have the sacred power of order, to offer sacrifice and forgive sins, and to discharge their priestly function publicly for the people in the name of Christ. Christ sent out apostles who later chose bishops as their successors with the fullness of orders.[113] The bishop's office of service was delegated to priests in a subordinate capacity. Those ordained priests became members of the presbyterate and assisted the bishop in that portion of his mission that he entrusted to them. Priests are to preach the gospel, sanctify God's people through the celebration of the sacraments, and serve as agents for the building up of the community of God's faithful by their zealous pastoral activity. They are called to foster the vocation of the lay apostolate, collaborate with the laity and develop in the laity a sense of the universal church. They must also foster the missionary activity of the church in their own communities. Their fidelity to Christ is to lead all the faithful to a similar fidelity and intimacy. The decree also adds that fidelity to Christ must also mean fidelity to the church:

> Hence pastoral charity demands that priests, if they are not to run in vain, should always work with the bond of union with the bishops and their fellow priests. If they act in this manner, priests will find unity of life in the unity of the Church's own mission.[114]

The priest must exercise his pastoral office of service for building up the unity of the church.

The Decree on the Ministry and Life of Priests offers a synthesis on the presbyteral order that repeats many of the points that have already been seen in the other council documents. One of the more significant changes called for in this decree is that which effectively brought an end to the benefice system. Under the benefice system there were often great differences in the amount paid to pastors. The decree on priestly life stated that the remuneration paid to priests doing the same type of work should be the same. The council also stated that the actual office, which the sacred ministers fulfilled, should be of primary importance. For this reason it called for the benefice system to be abandoned, or at least reformed, so that the right to revenue would be regarded as being of secondary importance. The decree stated:

---

113. The Second Vatican Council, *Ad gentes divinitus*, no. 2: 864–66.
114. The Second Vatican Council, *Ad gentes divinitus*, no. 14: 890.

It is, however, to the office that sacred ministers fulfill that the greatest importance must be attached. For this reason the so-called system of benefices is to be abandoned or else reformed in such a way that the part that has to do with the benefice—that is, the right to the revenues attached to the endowment of the office—shall be regarded as secondary and the principal emphasis in law given to the ecclesiastical office itself.[115]

The end of the benefice system would result in a new definition of the parish and the office of pastor. The financial compensation attached to the pastor's office would no longer be a part of its definition.

## *Gaudium et spes (December 7, 1965)*

*Gaudium et spes* addresses the mission of the church in the modern world. In it the church professes that the redemption which Christ won through his death and resurrection is intended for all people living under every circumstance. Humanity was created in God's image and the church has a saving and eschatological purpose which obliges it to lead all people to their heavenly destiny.[116] The church must carry out its mission here on earth among men and women who are members of earthly cities. In the present circumstances of their earthly lives, the church must prepare all people for the coming of the Lord.[117] To carry out its universal mission the church may not be dependent upon any one culture, political, economic, or social system.[118] Maintaining its freedom the church must live intimately with the men and women who live in the different systems and strive to bring them to the salvation offered through her in Christ. Christians must know the circumstances and conditions faced by all their contemporaries so that they may evaluate the conditions of their society and illuminate the situation with an authentically Christian sense of values.[119] *Gaudium et spes* states:

> For theirs is a community composed of men [and women], of men [and woman] who, united in Christ and guided by the holy Spirit, press onwards towards the kingdom of the Father and

---

115. The Second Vatican Council, *Ad gentes divinitus*, no. 20:899.
116. The Second Vatican Council, *Gaudium et spes*, no. 10, 910–11.
117. The Second Vatican Council, *Gaudium et spes*, no. 40:939–40.
118. The Second Vatican Council, *Gaudium et spes*, no. 42:942–43.
119. The Second Vatican Council, *Gaudium et spes*, no. 62:966–68.

are the bearers of a message of salvation intended for all men [and women]. That is why Christians cherish a feeling of deep solidarity with the human race and its history.[120]

*Gaudium et spes* does not speak of the parish community in particular. However, from what has been seen in the other conciliar documents regarding the parish, it is easy to see that the content of *Gaudium et spes* is extremely important for all parish communities. The parish, which is the principle community through which most Christians encounter the church, must be a community that speaks Christ's universal message of salvation to the men and women of a particular locality. The message which is spoken from a particular parish must be one that is able to address the realities of the time and place in history in which the members of the community live. The parish must also speak a message that is consistent with the church's nature as a universal community of believers who are on their earthly pilgrimage and are awaiting the return of the Lord.

## The Parish of the Second Vatican Council

The documents of the Second Vatican Council contribute to a deepening of the theological appreciation of the place of the parish in the life of the church. This understanding leads to a change in the way a parish itself is defined. The parish is more clearly seen by the Council as an assembly of believers organized locally under a parish priest who acts in the bishop's place. The parish exists for the good of the souls which reside within that locality and for the sake of building up and making present the universal church. The priest who has been appointed pastor by the bishop is to serve the members of the parish community through his priestly ministry so that they may come to sanctification. All of the members of Christ's body are called to holiness and to live actively their priestly, prophetic, and kingly mission in the world. By doing this all of the members of the parish community are called to make Christ present to their locality in all of the different aspects of their lives. Each Christian is to be a minister of the New Evangelization. The church's liturgy is to be the very source and summit of the community's life. It is in the celebration of the Eucharist in particular that the community, gathered around its pastor, most fully manifests the church to its particular locality. The parish is a community

120. The Second Vatican Council, *Gaudium et spes*, no. 1: 903–4.

where the members of the local assembly are nourished and nurtured to become the church. Through the parish, the church, which is the body of Christ, becomes manifest to a particular locality.

## THE PARISH IN CANON LAW

### The 1983 Code of Canon Law

In 1983 the revised Code of Canon Law was promulgated for the Latin Rite of the Roman Catholic Church. The new code incorporated the theological and pastoral changes in the life of the church that had been called for by the bishops of the church at the Second Vatican Council. The section of the code that deals with parishes, pastors, and parochial vicars (can. 515–can. 552) "contains much that is new, as a result of the actions of the Second Vatican Council."[121] While some of the changes to the code are simply the result of a more pastoral nuance, others show a clearly changed approach due to the council's influence. Much of what the council had to say in regard to the apostolate of the laity has been introduced to provide a new thrust in what the code has to say in regard to parish life.

The 1983 Code of Canon Law defines a parish in the following way:

> A parish is a certain community of Christ's faithful stably established within a particular Church, whose pastoral care, under the authority of the diocesan Bishop, is entrusted to a parish priest as its proper pastor.[122]

The parish, which was described in the 1917 code as a territory of the diocese, is now described as a community of the Christian people. This community of the faithful exists within a particular church, which is understood as a diocese and is established on a stable basis. The importance of the code indicating "stably established" is to indicate that the parish community is understood as having a certain degree of permanence.[123] The pastoral care of this community, under the authority of the bishop, is entrusted to the parish priest as its proper pastor. The code continues by stating as a general rule the parish should be defined as territorial and embrace all of Christ's faithful within that territory. Where it is useful,

---

121. Coriden, *Parish in the Catholic Tradition*, 59.
122. *Code of Canon Law* can. 515 §1, 427–28.
123. Coriden, *Parish in the Catholic Tradition*, 60.

personal parishes may be established based on reasons of rite, language or nationality among Christ's faithful in a certain territory.[124] The pastor exercises the pastoral care of the community, under the authority of the bishop whose ministry of Christ he is called to share, in order that he may carry out the offices of teaching, sanctifying and ruling in this community. He is to carry out his office with the cooperation of the other priests and deacons assigned to the parish and with the assistance of the lay faithful who make up the parish.[125] The code also states that in order to be validly appointed a parish priest, one must already be in the sacred order of priesthood. The same canon also requires that the priest who is to be appointed be of sound doctrine, upright in character, zealous for souls and possessed of the qualities necessary to care for a parish. The above material from the Code of Canon Law was used by the Italian canonist Francesco Coccopalmerio to formulate the following definition of a parish:

> *La parrocchia è una comunità di fedeli, territoriale e locale, nella Chiesa particolare, il cui presidente è un parroco, cioè un presbitero, pastore proprio, il quale compie il suo ufficio sotto l'autorità del Vescovo diocesano e con la collaborazione di altri presbiteri, di diaconi e dei fedeli laici.*[126]

The problem of the shortage in clergy is also dealt with in the Code of Canon Law. The code states that under normal circumstances a parish priest is to have pastoral care of only one parish. However, where it is necessary, due to a shortage of clergy or other circumstances, the care of a number of parishes can be entrusted to one priest.[127] In all parishes only one priest is to be the parish priest, or the moderator responsible for the pastoral care of the parish. Where the shortage of clergy is so severe that no priest can be found to be pastor the code states:

---

124. *Code of Canon Law*, can. 518: "As a general rule, a parish is to be territorial, that is, it is to embrace all Christ's faithful of a given territory. Where it is useful, however, personal parishes are to be established, determined by reason of rite, language or nationality of Christ's faithful of a certain territory, or on some other basis."

125. *Code of Canon Law*, can. 521.

126. Coccopalmerio, *La Parrocchia: Tra Concilio Vaticano II e Codice di Diritto Canonico*, 11. My translation of this passage is: The parish is a community of believers, regional and local, in a particular church, whose president is a pastor, that is a priest, who is its proper pastor, who performs his office under the authority of the diocesan bishop and with the collaboration of the other priests, deacons and the lay faithful.

127. *Code of Canon Law*, can. 526.

> If, because of a shortage of priests, the diocesan Bishop has judged that a deacon, or some other person who is not a priest, or a community of persons, should be entrusted with a share in the exercise of the pastoral care of a parish, he is to appoint some priest who with the powers and faculties of a parish priest, will direct the pastoral care[128]

The effect of this canon is to make it clear that even when a shortage of clergy makes it impossible to appoint a priest as the pastor of the parish, a priest is to be appointed with the powers and faculties of a pastor to direct the pastoral care of the parish.[129] The norm for the pastoral care of a parish is that it is to be entrusted to a parish priest who exercises the office of pastor under the authority of the bishop. For that period of time when this norm cannot be followed, due to a shortage of clergy, the bishop may judge it necessary to entrust a deacon, or someone else who is not ordained, with a share in the exercise of the pastoral care of the parish. He is also to appoint some priest to oversee and direct the pastoral care in the parish. Should the shortage of clergy ever be remedied, a priest is to be appointed pastor. This investigation will follow the norm put forward by the Code of Canon Law and assume that a priest will be responsible for the pastoral care of a parish in the definition that it follows of a parish community.

The Code of Canon Law outlines the responsibilities of the pastor in such a way that it makes it clear that he is to fulfill his position in a manner that nourishes and leads the faithful to fulfill their own vocations within the church. Some of the more important functions of the pastor are outlined here briefly. The parish priest has the obligation to ensure that the Word of God is proclaimed so that the faithful may be properly formed to bring the Gospel message to all areas of the their lives. He is to ensure that the Eucharist is at the heart of the assembly's life and that the spiritual needs of the faithful are nourished by the devout celebration of the sacraments.[130] It is his duty to build the parish community up by his pastoral charity and by promoting the specific roles that the lay members of Christ's faithful have in the mission of the church.[131] He also has the responsibility of directing the activities of the parish to build it up in unity

---

128. *Code of Canon Law*, can. 517, §2.

129. Cusack and Sullivan, *Pastoral Care in Parishes Without a Pastor: Applications of Canon 517, §2*, ix–xiv.

130. *Code of Canon Law*, can. 528.

131. *Code of Canon Law*, can. 529.

and communion with the diocesan bishop and the universal church. The pastor needs to be always aware that he represents the diocesan bishop. It is the responsibility of the pastor to pray for the people who are entrusted to his pastoral care and to offer Mass for them.[132] The parish priest is also bound to care for the parish registers and in consultation with the members of the parish community to administer the church's goods.

The 1983 Code of Canon Law does not just speak of those rights and duties that belong to those in sacred orders. Following the teaching of the Second Vatican Council the Code articulates the responsibilities that belong to the members of Christ's body through baptism and confirmation.[133] The faithful are bound, according to their condition, to make a whole-hearted effort to lead holy lives and to promote the growth of the church and its continual sanctification.[134] Towards this end they are to participate actively in the liturgy and to make use of the sacraments as necessary means to sanctification. The faithful are bound to see that the message of Christ's salvation is proclaimed to the entire world.[135] To the lay faithful falls the special obligation of permeating and perfecting the temporal order with the Spirit of the Gospel. Married couples are bound to share their faith with their family and provide suitable Christian education for their children. Laypersons with the proper dispositions and abilities may be admitted to service in ecclesiastical offices and those liturgical ministries for which their services are required.[136] The faithful have a right to be assisted by their pastors with the church's spiritual goods, especially by the word and sacraments.[137] To the faithful also belongs the right and duty to participate in charitable works and to promote and support apostolic action.[138] In order that they might live

---

132. *Code of Canon Law*, can. 534.

133. *Code of Canon Law*, can. 204: This canon defines Christ's faithful as "those who, since they are incorporated into Christ through baptism, are constituted the people of God. For this reason they participate in their own way in the priestly, prophetic and kingly office of Christ. They are called, each according to his or her particular condition, to exercise the mission which God entrusted to the church to fulfill in the world." Can. 205 states that those in communion with the church are defined as: "Those baptized are in full communion with the Catholic Church here on earth who are joined with Christ in his visible body, through the bonds of profession, the sacraments and ecclesial governance."

134. *Code of Canon Law*, can. 210.

135. *Code of Canon Law*, can. 225.

136. *Code of Canon Law*, can. 228 and can. 230.

137. *Code of Canon Law*, can. 213.

138. *Code of Canon Law*, can. 215 and can. 216.

their baptismal call, all the members of the church also have the right to a Christian education which teaches them to strive for human maturity while living the mystery of salvation.[139] The faithful are to enjoy the liberty to make known to pastors their spiritual needs. To them belongs the right, and on occasion even the duty, to make known to their pastors their views on matters for which they have knowledge, competence and position. The code states:

> They have the right, indeed at times the duty, in keeping with their knowledge, competence and position, to manifest to the sacred Pastors their views on matters which concern the good of the Church. They have the right also to make their views known to others of Christ's faithful, but in doing so they must always respect the integrity of faith and morals, show due reverence to the Pastors and take into account both the common good and dignity of individuals.[140]

The right of the faithful to advise the pastor of the parish is illustrated by the requirement to establish parish finance councils.[141] Bishops are also to consult with the council of priests in their dioceses to determine whether pastoral councils should be established in the diocese. Should the bishop decide to require parish councils, these are to be established to provide the pastor with advice for the pastoral care of the parish.[142] Although the parish community is made up of members of Christ's faithful who generally reside in a certain locality, the parish does not exist solely to care for this group of the faithful. The balance between the rights and duties of the faithful indicate that those who are members of the church are responsible in their own degree for helping the church exercise its mission in the world. For this reason, the members of the parish community do not only receive pastoral care from the church but are to cooperate in assisting the church to carry out its mission in the parish. The parish community must be concerned for all those who live in their vicinity, whether they are fallen-away Catholics, Christians of other denominations, or non-Christians. All of the members of the parish community are bound to bring Christ's salvation to the world.

---

139. *Code of Canon Law*, can. 217.
140. *Code of Canon Law*, can. 212, §3.
141. *Code of Canon Law*, can. 537.
142. *Code of Canon Law*, can. 536.

Because the parish is a portion of the diocese, which is under the pastoral care of its true shepherd, the parish must be seen in relationship to the bishop. The bishop alone has the power to establish, suppress, or alter parishes. This he is to do in consultation with the council of priests.[143] The bishop appoints the parish priest to act on his behalf.[144] The bishop has the responsibility of choosing the candidate who is best qualified to care for the pastoral needs of each individual parish.[145] When a parish community has been entrusted by the bishop to a religious community, the bishop retains the responsibility for overseeing the pastoral care of the parish. The religious superior of the community is to be free to determine which member of the community is to be presented to the bishop in order that the bishop might appoint him pastor. When a group of religious priests has care of a parish, one of the group must be appointed pastor.[146] The bishop is the principle pastor of every parish in the diocese entrusted to his care.

The Code of Canon Law also puts forward a number of canons that relate to the parish building. No church is to be built without the express and written consent of the bishop. Before giving his consent, the bishop is to consult with the council of priests and neighboring churches. He is also to be certain that the new church will serve the good of souls and that the necessary funds are available.[147] Every parish church must have a baptismal font.[148] The blessed Eucharist is to be reserved in every parish church.[149] The code also states that "Churches, especially cathedrals and parish churches, are to be dedicated by a solemn rite."[150] It also stipulates that the dedication of a place belongs to the diocesan bishop and to those who are equivalent to him in law. The diocesan bishop may depute another bishop to do a dedication in his territory or, in exceptional cases, a priest.[151]

---

143. *Code of Canon Law*, can. 515, §2.
144. *Code of Canon Law*, can. 519.
145. *Code of Canon Law*, can. 521.
146. *Code of Canon Law*, can. 520. See also Coccopalmerio, *Parrocchia*, 291–98.
147. *Code of Canon Law*, can. 1215.
148. *Code of Canon Law*, can. 858, §1.
149. *Code of Canon Law*, can. 934, §1.
150. *Code of Canon Law*, can. 1217, §2.
151. *Code of Canon Law*, can. 1206.

## A Definition to Help Form a Theology for a Parish Community

Canonically a parish is defined in the new code as a community of Christ's faithful that is stably established within a diocesan church. Normally this portion of the faithful is established as a group because they live together in the same local territory that the diocesan bishop has designated as being within the parameter for their parish community. Such a parish is known as a territorial parish. Less frequently, personal parishes may be established by a bishop to serve the needs of Christ's faithful who are of a certain rite, language, or nationality. To a certain extent, these personal parishes are also territorial in that the members of these communities are from specific linguistic or national groups that are to be found within the confines of a certain territory. An example would be a Korean parish that is made up of all the Korean members of Christ's faithful living within a particular city, or even in an entire diocese. The members of these communities are brought together not only because of their national or linguistic origins, but also because they live in the vicinity of one another in a certain locality. Because in both types of parishes, members are constituted on the basis of some kind of territorial criteria, this study will take as its model for investigating the theology of a parish found in *ODC* the more common territorial parish.

Because members of Christ's faithful who make up the parish community are grouped together as a result of dwelling in a common locality within a diocesan church, the bishop of the diocese is their legitimate and true pastor. The diocese is divided into parishes because the entire diocesan population cannot always gather in one location for one liturgical celebration, and the bishop is unable to be present at every individual celebration. The bishop appoints a priest as pastor to serve in his place. The pastor is to act under the authority of the bishop and as the representative of the bishop in the pastoral care of the parish. The pastor is the proper pastor of the parish entrusted to him. Whether the pastor is a diocesan priest, a religious priest, or a priest who is a member of a clerical society of apostolic life, in the pastoral care of the parish he represents the bishop and shares in his teaching, sanctifying and ruling offices for the service of the community. The pastor is called to cooperate with the other priests and deacons assigned to the parish, and to work with the assistance of the lay members of Christ's faithful, so that the parish community may make the church present and carry out Christ's mission in that locality where the community exists. The parish is a part of a diocese. The diocese

PART ONE

is a part of the universal church that is entrusted to a bishop. The bishop must be in communion with the pope and the college of bishops.

This rather lengthy definition of a parish, which is based upon the canonical material presented in the preceding section, provides the criterion with which *ODC* must be read in order to construct the theology for a parish community that it contains. From this definition it can be seen that a theology of the parish must include an articulation of the role of the bishop, the pastor, the other ordained ministers, and all of the members of Christ's faithful. When speaking of the lay members of Christ's church, it will be necessary to speak also of those who exercise liturgical ministries within the parish community. The theology of the parish that will be developed must also speak of the relationships that exist between the parish and the diocesan and universal church. The investigation must also consider what the rite says about the relationship between the members of Christ's faithful who make up the parish and those who are not members of the church, as well as those who have fallen away from the church. All of these questions must be answered in the study of *ODC*.

## SUMMARY

The parish, as it is known today, does not have its origins in scripture. It is a product of history. The origins and history of the parish are intimately linked with the mission and history of the church that Christ established to bring his offer of salvation to all persons. As the church expanded into the many different communities of believers around the world, it was necessary for these communities to take on a pattern or structure of life that would allow the church to flourish in them. After the diocese, the parish has come to be the next most significant expression of the church's life in a particular locality. One can speak of a theology of the parish only if the parish is seen in the context of its place within the mission of the universal church established by Christ to spread the good news to all people.

The history of the parish community demonstrates very clearly that it has not always been easy for the parish to enjoy its proper place within the church. The parish itself can only exist as a healthy unit within Christ's body when its members, animated by the Holy Spirit, live in communion with the entire mystical body of Christ. Many councils in the church's lengthy history have fought hard to protect and maintain the relationship of communion between the church and the parish community. Often, the church's councils were required by the circumstances of the times to protect the communion of the parish with the church through exclusively juridical means. This they did to defend the parish from the differing forms of intrusion on the parish's freedom that were associated with the *eigenkirche* and benefice systems, the Investiture Controversy, and the differing interferences from the civil authorities. These efforts led to an overly juridical definition of the parish, resulting in the parish being defined at times as a territory, a benefice, or an office.

The Second Vatican Council articulated a rediscovery of the deeper theological significance of the place of the parish in the life of the church. The documents of the council recognize the parish as an assembly of Christ's faithful organized locally by the bishop and set up under the leadership of a priest who acts in the bishop's place. *Sacrosanctum concilium*, article forty-two, stated that when these parish communities meet to celebrate the liturgy, mindful of their communion with the bishop, they manifest the visible church set up throughout the nations of the world. In each individual parish community the universal church of Christ is to be made visible to the locality in which it exists.

The fact that the Second Vatican Council spoke about the value and place of the parish within the body of Christ's church does not mean that the members of the parish are fully aware of the mission of their community within the church or their personal mission within the assembly of believers. In many ways it is the role of the liturgy itself to form, nourish and call the parish, and the individual members, to be what they are called to be as members of Christ's church. This is done most perfectly through the celebration of the Eucharist. The next part of this thesis will demonstrate that the 1977 *ODC* is a liturgical rite that communicates to the parish what it is called to be within the communion of the mystical body of Christ. In articulating this for the parish community, it also does this for the individual members. Our discussion turns now to the theology for a parish contained in *ODC*.

# PART TWO

## The Study of the Rite of the Dedication of a Church

PART TWO IS MADE up of five chapters. In chapter two, the Introduction of *ODC* is studied. It is analyzed to determine what theological content is has to offer for the construction of a liturgical theology for a parish community. A summary of the results is presented at the end of the chapter. Chapter three deals with *The Introductory Rites* of *ODC*. Chapter four examines the rites and readings related to *The Liturgy of the Word*. The subject of chapter five is the rites that make up *The Prayer of Dedication and the Anointings*. In chapter six, the rites of *The Liturgy of the Eucharist* are investigated. The structure of chapters three through six is the same. The ritual schema of *ODC* is presented first. Then it is then analyzed according to the categories of *rites, prayers, sacred scripture,* and *persons*. Each of these chapters is concluded with a summary of the findings which articulate what *ODC* has to contribute to a theology for a parish community.

# Chapter Two

# Order of the Dedication of a Church: Introduction

## INTRODUCTION

One of the distinctive features that is to be found in the liturgical books that have been issued as part of the liturgical reforms that followed the Second Vatican Council are the *Praenotanda* (henceforth referred to by their English name as *Introduction*) or *Institutio generalis* (henceforth referred to by their English name as *General Instruction*) that introduce these liturgical books. The *Introductions* and *General Instructions* provide a theological and pastoral foundation for the celebration of the rites. Their content is quite different from what was found in the liturgical books issued prior to the Second Vatican Council.

In this chapter the *Introduction* of *ODC* will be studied. The significance of its theological content and pastoral guidelines will be investigated. Because this is also the first chapter in which the rites themselves are studied, it contains a brief introduction to these rites and the liturgical book in which it is found.

PART TWO

# THE INTRODUCTION OF ODC

## Introduction to ODC

The rite under study in this investigation, *ODC*, is to be found in the second chapter of *The Order of the Dedication of a Church and an Altar*.[1] The rites for dedicating a church that predate these were found in the second part of the Roman Pontifical.[2] These rites were reformed and simplified as a result of the criterion for the revision of the liturgy that was established in *Sacrosanctum concilium*. The nature of this reform was such that:

> The rites should be distinguished by a noble simplicity. They should be short, clear and free from useless repetitions. They should be within the people's powers of comprehension, and normally should not require much explanation.[3]

The rites of dedication were revised in 1961 when the *Pontifical Romanum* was promulgated with dramatic modifications to the second part. The changes to the rites of dedication that followed the Second Vatican Council were part of the restoration that effected all of the Roman liturgical books. The work of renewing the rites of dedicating a church fell to a group appointed in May of 1970 that was called "Study Group 21 bis." This group was charged with revising the rites found in the second and third books of the Roman Pontifical. The relator of this group was the French liturgist Pierre Jounel. The other members of the group were Ignazio Calabuig of Spain, André Rose of Belgium, Domenico Sartore of Italy and the Italian Latinist Rosella Barbieri.[4] Domenico Sartore was initially the secretary, however, Ignazio Calabuig later replaced him. Archbishop Annibale Bugnini (+1982), who was the secretary of the Congregation for Divine Worship at this time, credits Ignazio Calabuig with a major part of the work on this rite.[5]

---

1. *ODC*, 29–70.
2. For a brief history of the rites of dedication see: Calabuig, "Rito della dedicazione della chiesa," 373–420; and Chengalikavil, "Dedicazione della chiesa e dell'altare," 65–109. A more complete history of the rites of dedication can be found in the less accessible complete doctoral dissertation which was submitted by Luke Chengalikavil to the Pontifical Institute for Sacred Liturgy at Saint Anselmo in Rome. See Chengalikavil, *Mystery of Christ*.
3. The Second Vatican Council, *Sacrosanctum concilium*, no. 34:12.
4. Simons, *Holy People, Holy Place*, 26.
5. Bugnini, *Reform of the Liturgy (1948–1975)*, 792, Footnote # 1.

ORDER OF THE DEDICATION OF A CHURCH: INTRODUCTION

This group met with the Congregation for Divine Worship between 1970 and 1972 and made important studies of the rites of dedication. At this time the rites of the Pontifical were studied to determine which were in keeping with the criterion established by the Second Vatican Council. The most important question decided by this group was that the "proper locus for the dedication [of a church] is the celebration of the Eucharist."[6] A provisional liturgical book was published in Latin in 1973. This liturgical book was entitled *Ordo dedicationis ecclesiae et altaris deque aliis locis et rebus sacrandis*.[7]

The 1973 provisional rite contained a letter of presentation and twelve chapters. These twelve chapters, with English translation given in parentheses, were:

1. *Ordo imponendi primarium lapidem vel inchoandi opus ad domum ecclesiae aedificandam* (*The Order for Laying the Foundation Stone or For Beginning Work on the Church Building*).

2. *Ordo dedicationis ecclesiae* (*The Order for the Dedication of a Church*).

3. *Ordo dedicationis altaris* (*The Order for the Dedicating an Altar*).

4. *Ordo benedictionis ecclesiae* (*The Order for Blessing a Church*).

5. *Ordo ad altare mobile benedicendum* (*The Order for Blessing a Movable Altar*).

6. *Ordo ad inaugurandum locum celebrationibus liturgicis aliisque usibus destinatum* (*The Order for Beginning Liturgical Celebrations in a Location Destined for Other Uses*).

7. *Ordo benedictionis calicis et patenae* (*The Order for Blessing a Chalice and a Paten*).

8. *Ordo benedictionis novae crucis publicae venerationi exhibendae* (*The Order for Blessing of a New Cross to be Displayed for Public Veneration*).

9. *Ordo ad campanam benedicendam* (*The Order for Blessing a Bell*).

10. *Ordo ad coemeterium benedicendum* (*The Order for Blessing a Cemetery*).

---

6. Bugnini, *Reform of the Liturgy (1948–1975)*, 793.

7. *Ordo dedicationis ecclesiae et altaris deque aliis locis et rebus sacrandis*, bozze di stampe (1973).

11. *Publica supplicatio peragenda cum gravis iniuria domui ecclesiae est illata* (Public Rite of Prayer when Serious Harm has Been Done in a Church Building—Scandal).

12. *Ordo coronandi imaginem beatae Mariae* Virginis (*The Order for the Crowning of an Image of the Blessed Virgin Mary*).

The letter of presentation that accompanied this provisional liturgical book asked that all responses in regard to these rites should be received by November 15, 1973. A great deal of feedback was obtained as a result of the consultations that followed the publication of these provisional rites. It was observed by some respondents that occasionally churches were dedicated after they had been in use for several years. Other churches were inaugurated after a complete renovation. A rite for such occasions was requested. The study group therefore prepared a rite entitled *Ordo dedications ecclesiae in que iam de more sacra celebrantur* (*Dedication of a Church in Which Mass is Already Being Celebrated*). Others requested that there be a rite for the inauguration of a new baptistry.[8]

After the responses had been given consideration, the rites were then sent to the Congregation of the Doctrine of the Faith and the Secretariats for Christian Unity and Non-Christians. After all of the doctrinal, pastoral, and liturgical clarifications were agreed upon, confidential copies of the rites were sent to the international translation committees. The text was about to go to the pope for his approval when the responsibilities of the Congregation for Divine Worship were integrated into those of the newly created Congregation for the Sacraments and Divine Worship in the curial reform of 1975.

Not until May 29, 1977, on the solemnity of Pentecost, was the text of the Latin *Editio typica* of *Ordo dedicationis ecclesiae et altaris* officially promulgated. The new ordo, which was issued by the Congregation for the Sacraments and Divine Worship, consisted of only seven chapters. Chapter six and chapters eight through twelve of the provisional 1973 rite were not included. The new rite for the dedication of a church that was already in use was included. The structure of *Ordo dedicationis ecclesiae et altaris* is:

*Decretum* (*Decree*).

---

8. Bugnini, *Reform of the Liturgy (1948–1975)*, 794.

I. *Ordo imponendi primarium lapidem vel inchoandi opus ad ecclesiam aedificandam* (*The Order of Laying of a Foundation Stone or the Commencement of Work on the Building of a Church*).

II. *Ordo dedicationis ecclesiae* (*The Order of the Dedication of a Church*).

III. *Ordo dedicationis ecclesiae in qua iam de more sacra celebrantur* (*The Order for Dedication of a Church in Which Scared Celebrations are Already Regularly Taking Place*).

IV. *Ordo dedicationis altaris* (*The Order of the Dedication of an Altar*).

V. *Ordo benedictionis ecclesiae* (*The Order of the Blessing of a Church*).

VI. *Ordo benedictionis altaris* (*The Order of Blessing an Altar*).

VII. *Ordo benedictionis calicis et patenae.* (*The Order of Blessing a Chalice and Paten*).

Appendix: *Cantus antiphonarum et aliorum textuum* (*Chants and other Texts*).

The other rites, which were not included from the 1973 provisional rite, were later integrated into the new book of blessings or published separately. This study will be concerned with a closer examination of the official English translation of the second chapter of this liturgical book, ODC. This first English translation of this order appeared in 1978. This work has made use of the 2018 English translation according to the Typical Edition, as it appeared in the edition published by the Canadian Conference of Bishops.

## The Introduction of ODC

In the history of liturgical books, the *Introduction* (*Praenotanda*) represents a new genre.[9] Most of the new liturgical books that were revised after the Second Vatican Council contain an *Introduction* or a *General Instruction* (*Institutio generalis*). They are intended to fulfill several tasks in keeping with the objectives of the Second Vatican Council. Most contain

---

9. The word *"Praenotanda"* is used in two ways in the *Editio typica* of the revised rites. It may be used in the singular to refer to the entire chapter in which the introduction to the rite is contained. It may also be used in the plural to refer to the many different norms which are contained in the introductory chapter. In our study the word *Introduction* will be used to refer to these introductory notes as this is the word that has been used for many of the English translations of the rites.

PART TWO

a theological and a doctrinal element that aims to lead those who are celebrating the rites to a more complete comprehension of them. It is hoped that this deeper comprehension will lead the community celebrating the rites to have a clearer spiritual orientation.[10] Their theological component is commonly grounded in an articulation of the faith of the church and a formulation as to how that truth is being celebrated in the liturgical ritual. An effort is often made to explain how the mysteries of Christ are incarnated in the liturgical rite. The theological aspect may also seek to show how the new liturgical rite is related to the liturgical traditions of the past and the renewal that was called for by the Second Vatican Council.

The *Introduction(s)* also contain a pastoral and liturgical dimension that addresses issues in regard to how the rite is to be celebrated. The pastoral dimension is solidly based upon the theological dimension. It is orientated towards the full and active participation in the liturgy that the Second Vatican Council stated was one of its goals.[11] To this end the *Introduction(s)* contain norms for an authentically ecclesial celebration of the liturgy. These norms address such issues as how the people are to participate in the liturgy, how the liturgical ritual is to be celebrated, the roles of the members of the assembly, times for celebrating the rite, and the possible adaptations. The pastoral dimension of each *Introduction* is concerned to see that the members of Christ's faithful are engaged as fully as possible by the mysteries of Christ that are celebrated in the liturgy.[12] Completely engaged in the liturgy, the members of Christ's church are to be transformed more fully into the likeness of Christ.

The *Introduction* that introduces ODC follows the structure that is common to most of those that have been included in the new liturgical rites. It is made up of twenty-seven paragraphs that are divided into seven different sections. Some of the sections have been further divided. The content is as follows:

I. The Nature and Dignity of Churches (no. 1–3).

II. The Title of a Church and the Relics of the Saints to be Deposited in It (no. 4–5).

III. The Celebration of the Dedication (no. 6–17).

---

10. Donghi, "Significato dei *Praenotanda*," 8–17.
11. The Second Vatican Council, *Sacrosanctum concilium*, no. 14:7–8.
12. Pistoia, "Assemblea come soggetto della celebrazione," 91–126.

- The Minister of the Rite (no. 6).
- The Choice of Day (no. 7).
- The Mass of the Dedication (no. 8–9).
- The Office of the Dedication (no. 10).
- The Parts of the Rite (no. 10–17).

IV. Adaptation of the Rite (no. 18–19).

- Adaptations within the Competence of the Conferences of Bishops (no. 18).
- Accommodations within the Competence of the Ministers (no. 19).

V. Pastoral Preparations (no. 20).

VI. The Requisites for the Dedication of a Church (no. 21–25).

VII. The Anniversary of the Dedication (no. 26–27).

- The Anniversary of the Dedication of the Cathedral Church (no. 26).
- The Anniversary of the Dedication of a Particular Church (no. 27).[13]

The *Introduction* of ODC has not developed the theological and doctrinal aspects as heavily as have some of the other *Introduction*(s). Two different explanations for the limited doctrinal content of the *Introduction* of ODC have been offered by two people who were connected with the preparation of the rite at different stages. Ignazio Calabuig stated in his commentary of the rite that it was preferred that the rite itself should convey the rich theological content.[14] It was feared that if there was too much explanation of the doctrinal content, the rite might be restricted and less able to communicate its theological wealth. On the other hand, Archbishop Annibale Bugnini stated in his book on the reform of the liturgy that the *Introduction* had been "seriously mutilated" during its preparation by the Congregation for the Sacraments and Divine Worship.[15]

---

13. ODC, nn. 1–27: 31–38.
14. Calabuig, "'*Ordo dedicationis ecclesiae et altaris*,'" 393.
15. Bugnini, Reform of the Liturgy (1948–1975), 795.

PART TWO

The content of the *Introduction* will now be studied section by section.

## The Content of the Introduction

### *Nature and Dignity of Churches*

The *Introduction* of *ODC* begins with a theological and doctrinal explanation of the rite that, despite its brevity, is rich in content. The three articles which make-up this theological introduction are substantial enough to merit very close examination. The orientation that they give to the rite provides a valuable insight into the significance of the entire rite.

The first article of the *Introduction* of *ODC* reads:

> Through his death and resurrection, Christ became the true and perfect temple of the New Covenant and gathered together a people to be his own. Moreover, this holy people, made one by the unity of the Father, Son and Holy Spirit, is the Church, that is, the temple of God built of living stones, where the Father is worshipped in spirit and in truth.[16]

There are three essential points that must be taken from this article in order to have a proper understanding of the theology of *ODC*. These are: 1) Christ is the temple through whom God is to be encountered; 2) the church united to Christ through the Holy Spirit[17] is the temple of God

---

16. *ODC*, no. 1:31.

17. The church is bound together as one in unity with Christ by the power of the Holy Spirit. *Lumen gentium* notes that Saint Cyprian has written that as a result of the unity produced by the Holy Spirit the church can be see as: "a people brought into unity from the unity of the Father, the Son and the Holy Spirit." This unity of the church with Christ is achieved through the indwelling presence of the Holy Spirit in all the baptized.

*Lumen gentium* provides an excellent synthesis of the way in which the church is united to Christ through the Holy Spirit. It states: "When the work which the Father gave the Son to do on earth (cf. Jn. 17:4) was accomplished, the Holy Spirit was sent on the day of Pentecost in order that he might continually sanctify the Church, and that, consequently, those who believe might have access through Christ in one Spirit to the Father (cf. Eph. 2:18). He is the Spirit of life, the fountain of water springing up to eternal life (cf. Jn. 4:47; 7:38–39). To men, dead in sin, the Father gives life through him, until the day when, in Christ, he raises to life their mortal bodies (cf. Rom. 8:10–11). The Spirit dwells in the Church and in the hearts of the faithful, as in a temple (cf. Cor. 3:16; 6:19). In them he prays and bears witness to their adoptive sonship (cf. Gal. 4:6; Rom. 8:15–16 and 26). Guiding the Church in the way of all truth (cf. Jn. 16:13) and unifying her in communion and in the work of ministry, he bestows on her varied hierarchic and charismatic gifts, and in this way directs her; and he adorns her with his

where the Father is worshiped in spirit and truth; and 3) the building in which the church has gathered to carry out its worship in spirit and truth has since early times also been called "church" (*"ecclesia"*). These three points require elaboration.

## 1) Christ is the True Temple

In the Old Testament the God of heaven manifested himself to his people in specific and chosen places.[18] This can be seen in God's calling Abraham to a new land, the experience of Jacob and the rock at Bethel, and Moses and the tent of meeting.[19] These are but transitory manifestations of God's presence with his people that yield to the more permanent manifestation of God's dwelling among them that is to be found in the great temple to be built by Solomon. The permanent construction of a temple had to wait the day when the people of Israel were no longer on the move.[20] Solomon's prayer at the dedication of the temple makes it clear that while the people of Israel do not believe that the temple can contain the God who dwells in the heavens, it is the place where the Jews may come to encounter God and know that their prayers are heard.[21] In the temple at Jerusalem the Jews may offer sacrifice to God, and he will receive it, beg for relief from difficulties and obtain it, and seek refuge from the trials of this world. Even if a foreigner should approach the temple and pray, God who is in the heavens will hear the petition that the foreigner makes at, or in the direction of, the temple.[22] Should the day ever come when the people of Israel are dispersed from Jerusalem, they must merely pray facing the temple, from all the corners of the earth, and

---

fruits (cf. Eph. 4:11–12; 1 Cor. 12:4; Gal. 5:22). By the power of the Gospel he permits the Church to keep the freshness of youth. Constantly he renews her and leads her to perfect union with the Spouse. For the Spirit and the Bride say to Jesus, the Lord: 'Come!' (cf. Apoc. 22:17).

Hence the universal church is seen to be 'a people brought into unity from the unity of the Father; the Son and the Holy Spirit.'"

See The Second Vatican Council, *Lumen gentium*, no. 4:351–52.

18. Congar, *Il mistero del tempio: L'economia della Presenza di Dio dalla Genesi all'Apocalisse*, 6.

19. For Abraham see Genesis 12:1; for Jacob at Bethel see Genesis 28:16–17; and for Moses and the tent of meeting see Exodus 40:16–35.

20. Cattaneo, "Tempio pagano, ebraico, cristiano," 121.

21. 1 Kings 8:28–39.

22. 1 Kings 8:41.

PART TWO

God will hear them in his dwelling in the heavens. The temple is an essential point of encounter between the people of Israel and the God who dwells in the heavens. It is a sacred place.[23]

The New Testament proclaims a radically new point of encounter between God and humanity. Jesus Christ, the Word made flesh, is the full revelation of the Father to all humanity. Following the salvific event of his incarnation the temple of God is to be found in the body of Christ.[24] The announcement of Christ as the new point of encounter between God and humanity is richly treated in the Gospel of John. Christ tells Nathaniel that he will see angels descending and ascending on the Son of Man just as Jacob had seen them ascending and descending on the sacred rock of encounter.[25] The clear association between Christ and the temple is to be found in the story of the cleansing of the temple. In John's Gospel, Jesus declares that if the temple is destroyed he will raise it up again in three days. As the writer of the Gospel of John clarifies: "But the temple he had spoken of was his body."[26] Christ also announces the fact that worship will no longer be restricted to the temple in Jerusalem in his encounter with the Samaritan women. Jesus tells the Samaritan women that in the future those who worship God are to do so "in Spirit and in truth."[27] These same words are used in the first article of the *Introduction* of *ODC* to speak of the worship that is to be given by Christ's people. Because of Christ's death and resurrection, God's presence among his people is no longer mediated through a place, like the temple, but in the person of his Son made man. Christ eliminates the need for the temple and sacred places in order to encounter God.[28]

## 2) The Church is the temple of God

Through his death and resurrection Christ won for himself a holy people. At Pentecost this people was sealed with the gift of the Holy Spirit and made one with Christ their head as the Father, Son, and Spirit are one. The apostolic letters begin to present an idea of the temple as not tied

---

23. For a treatment of the sacred see: Eliade, *Sacred and the Profane*.
24. Marsili, "Tempio locale al tempio spirituale," 54.
25. John 1:51.
26. John 2:15–22.
27. John 4:24.
28. Giavini, "Per una teologia biblica del tempio," 568–70.

exclusively to Christ but to the church as the body of Christ, in communion with Christ its head. Yves Congar points out that in Paul's letters there are two different aspects of the notion of temple to be found. The first notion presents the idea that each Christian is a temple made for God and capable of encountering him interiorly through the Holy Spirit.[29] This is seen in the passage from 1 Cor 3:16–17. The body of the individual Christian is the temple of the Holy Spirit, and each Christian has received this gift from God. Yet Paul also speaks of a second notion of the church composed of all its members, playing their different roles, founded upon and in union with Christ its head. Ephesians 2:19–23 presents a picture of the church as the temple of the Holy Spirit in which each individual must be seen as a member of the one body founded upon Christ the cornerstone and rising upon the prophets and apostles to realize perfect communion with God. The church is the spiritual temple, which is founded on Christ, where each believer as a living stone animated by the Holy Spirit is to encounter God.[30] Through this encounter that the Christian has with God in the church, God is to be worshiped in spirit and truth.

### 3) The building where the community gathers is also called "*ecclesiae*" ("church")

For the early Christians there was no temple in the sense of a specifically sacred place where one had to go to encounter God. The only temple is Jesus Christ and the community of his church which lives in communion with him, their head, through the power of the Holy Spirit. The importance for the Christian community of encountering God within the lived *koinonia* (communion) of the church means that the experience of the assembled community will come to signify the most profound expression of the Christian community's existence. So important was this aspect of gathering for the church's existence that it began to be identified by the Greek word "*ekklesía*," which signified its status as a convoked community. What was important for this convoked assembly was not where they gathered, but that the place where they gathered accommodated the Christian assembly.[31] The community needed a place

---

29. Congar, *Mistero del tempio*, 177–185.
30. 1 Pet 2:5.
31. Grasso, "Perché le chiese," 555–56.

PART TWO

to hear the Word of God, to come together to pray, to receive the sacraments, and to celebrate the Eucharist in order to be church. Initially these gatherings simply took place in the homes of the Christians that were large enough to accommodate the community.[32] So important are these houses for the existence of the community that they took on a number of names that spoke more precisely of their function: *Domus ecclesia, domus Dei, domus orationis,* and *dominicum* ("house of the church," "house of God," "house of prayer" and "the Lord's"). Eventually by the third century the church building itself was referred to as *ecclesia*.[33] With the passage of time, the church building itself began to be mistaken for the significance of the church, *ekklesía*, and it was necessary for the church fathers and subsequent church leaders to remind the people of the authentic nature of the church. Yves Congar illustrated this phenomenon in a 1962 article entitled *"L'église, ce n'est pas les murs mais les fidèles."* In this article, Congar shows that as early as the fourth-century church leaders, such as Saints Hilary of Poitiers (+367), Ambrose of Milan (+397), and Augustine of Hippo (+430), were writing to remind Christians that it is the members of the church, in union with Christ their head through the power of the Holy Spirit, that make up the true nature of the church and not the building where the church meets.[34] In very positive terms, the first article of the *Introduction* of *ODC* repeats this fact. The church building is that place where the Christian community gathers to celebrate those events that make the community church.

The link between the liturgical celebrations which make the Christian community into the temple of God and the building in which the liturgy is celebrated by the community is so strong that the *Introduction* goes on to say in the second article:

> Because the church is a visible building, this house is a special sign of the pilgrim Church on earth and an image of the Church dwelling in heaven. Moreover, when a church is constructed as a building destined solely and permanently for gathering the People of God and for carrying out sacred functions, it is fitting that it be dedicated to the Lord with a solemn rite, in accordance with the ancient custom of the Church.[35]

32. See Acts 20:7–12 and 1 Cor 16:19.

33. Chengalikavil, *Mystery of Christ*, 35.

34. Congar, "Église, ce n'est pas," 106–7. My translation of this title is: The church, it is not the walls but the faithful.

35. *ODC*, no. 2: 31.

The church building, as a result of its quality as a visible reality, is a sign of the pilgrim church on earth and an image of the church in heaven. The content of this article is also pertinent enough to the study at hand to deserve significant treatment.

The incarnation of Jesus Christ and the church's identification with Christ's body have changed the Christian notion of the sacred.[36] In the incarnation, Jesus took on flesh and made visible to humanity the image of the invisible God. God's revelation of himself in Jesus Christ allowed humanity to apprehend the deepest spiritual realities by means of those signs that are necessary to the human condition for understanding.[37] Jesus is the Word or sacrament of God. For the Christian to speak of the sacred means to speak of those things, times, or places which have been set aside as signs of the holiness diffused in the world. These signs point to the greater spiritual reality that they represent. The church building points to the greater reality of the mystery of the church which it represents. In the words of the Italian theologian Cettina Militello: "*La chiesa-edificio, insomma, è icona spaziale della Chiesa-mistero.*"[38]

The sign value that the church building takes on is dependent upon a number of factors. The church building is where the local community gathers to celebrate the liturgical celebrations that make Christ present to them in the assembly, his ministers, the word, sacraments and the Eucharist.[39] The liturgical space itself makes memorial of Christ in the cross, ambo, altar, and liturgical art. Christ is present in the reserved sacrament of the Eucharist. The structural design of the church building ought to reflect the structured nature of the church. The church's walls and stones point to the church's nature as the living stones that are built up as the body of Christ.[40] The church building, as a structure in time and space, also speaks of the church's nature as a pilgrim community. The universal church cannot gather here in its entirety. The local community that gathers here must leave after the celebration to go back into the world. The members have not reached their final destination. They are still on their pilgrimage. The community must await the day when the liturgy of the

---

36. Grasso, "Perché le chiese," 557–58.

37. Grasso, "Perché le chiese," 559–60.

38. Miletello, "Teologia dello spazio liturgico," 438. My translation: The church building is a spacial icon of the mystery of the church.

39. The Second Vatican Council, *Sacrosanctum concilium*, no. 7: 4–5.

40. 1 Pet 2:5.

PART TWO

heavenly Jerusalem will encompass all time and space for eternity.[41] The regular celebration of the liturgy, most especially the Eucharist, contributes a great deal to constituting the church building as a sign that points to the nature of the pilgrim church on earth.

The experience that the Christian assembly has of Christ in the liturgical celebrations that take place in the church building also contributes to the building being seen as an image of the heavenly church. Here through Christ and in the Holy Spirit the assembly worships and glorifies God the Father and participates in the heavenly liturgy. The community momentarily, within the limits of time and space, takes part in the celestial liturgy to which they are ultimately called as followers of Christ. The celebration of the liturgy brings the community into communion with all the angels and saints who worship the Father in heaven. The members of the assembly are reminded as they gather as a local community in the church building that they are called to be and reflect on earth an image of the church in heaven. A number of signs are used in the dedication of a church building, such as the anointing of the church walls, to reinforce the metaphor of the church building as an image of the heavenly church. Many of these signs and symbols have their origin in the references to the heavenly liturgy that are found in the book of Revelation. The specific signs and symbols which come together in the church building to communicate this sign value will be described as the rite of dedication is studied in its specific parts.

The second article of the *Introduction* goes on to state that when a church is destined solely and permanently for assembling the people of God and carrying out liturgical functions, it is fitting that the building be dedicated to God with a solemn rite. This follows naturally from the description of the church building as a sign of the pilgrim church and image of the church in heaven. The sign value of the church building depends upon it being set apart from other uses.[42] To be an effective sign pointing to the sacred, the building cannot be used for various other purposes that contradict or confuse its sign value.

In order that the church building, which has been set aside permanently for the worship of God and the celebration of the liturgy, might attain its full sign value, it is to be dedicated to God by a solemn rite. The celebration of the rite of dedication bestows upon the church building

---

41. Rev 21:21–22.
42. Eliade, *Sacred and the Profane*, 10–15.

its full value sign. Through the complex use of symbols that make up the rite of dedication, the *domus* of the church is put forward as an image of the church.[43] The ritual schema of the rite of dedication places the living church of men and women in a symbolic relationship with the image of the church that is represented in the church building. In the rite the *domus* ("house") of the church building finds its full relation to the *ecclesia* ("church") constituted by the Holy Spirit through Christ. The entire rite of dedication serves to underline the liturgical functions and the identity attributed to the church building, and causes it to have a significance in relation to those liturgical realities.[44] Ultimately, it is the rite that establishes the church building as a sacred sign giving it the power of mediation.[45]

The fact that the rite is capable of bestowing this sign value upon the church building, making it an object of mediation, must be explained in relation to sacramental theology. Sacramentals are sacred signs that bear a resemblance to the sacraments and the effects that they signify are obtained through the intercession of the church. For this reason, the sacramentals are effective through the "Church's petition of prayer (*ex opere operantis Ecclesiae*)."[46] Sacramentals have traditionally been divided between those that are the result of constitutive blessings and invocative blessings.[47] The dedication of a church is a type of constitutive blessing

    43. Maggiani, "Teologia e sacro: Per una sintattica del sacro nella liturgia," 117. When used in the context of a church building, the word "*domus*" can mean both "house," as in "house of prayer," or building, as in "church building."
    44. Cattaneo, "Tempio pagano, ebraico, christiano," 34.
    45. Maggiani, "Teologia e sacro: Per una sintattica del sacro nella liturgia," 94.
    46. Vorgrimler, *Sacramental Theology*, 316.
    47. Sacramentals are established by blessings that have been instituted by the church and carry with them a spiritual effect that is obtained by reason of the church's intercession. The blessing itself has the effect off putting the created reality in relationship to the Mystery of Christ. In a very distinct way, blessings have the effect of producing a type of "iconization" of the relationship between the Trinitarian God and all of the created goods that have their origin in his goodness. By relating those things that have been blessed to the paschal mystery of Christ, blessings place the item or person within the *Christus totus*, giving them a significance that can be found in this relationship alone. To bless something or someone is also to unite them to God, in the context of God's offer of salvation and his alliance with humanity, and to ask that the thing or person become a manifestation of this salvation here and now.
    Blessings are distinguished as "constitutive" or "invocative." An invocative blessing upon a thing is dependent upon the church's intercession and asks that this thing might become a sign of salvation pointing toward the coming of God's reign and leading to his praise. An example of invocative blessing is the blessing of a new house. A constitutive blessing of a thing or place separates it from the rest of created reality and

that separates the church building from the rest of created reality and ecclesiastically deputes it for sacred worship. By making intercession to God, and by ecclesiastically deputing the building, the church bestows a sign value on the church building.

The third article of the *Introduction* refers to the architectural requirements that are necessary so that the church building may truly represent that to which it points as a sign. The *Introduction* states:

> A church, as its very nature requires, should be suitable for sacred celebrations, dignified, evincing a noble beauty, not merely costly display, and it should truly be a sign and symbol of heavenly realities. "Hence the general arrangement of the sacred building must be such that in some way it conveys the image of the assembled congregation and allows the appropriate ordering of all the participants, as well as facilitating each in the proper carrying out of his function.[48]

The ability of the church building to communicate as a sign pointing to the mystery of the church is dependent upon it representing something in which the image of the church can be recognized. The building must be designed for liturgical celebrations and allow the members of the assembly to participate in the liturgy according to their proper liturgical roles. The building should be planned with the distinct purpose of facilitating liturgical celebrations with the liturgical environment determined by the guidelines contained in the *General Instruction of the Roman Missal* and the rituals of the other sacraments.[49] The art and design of the building are to point the assembly towards the reality of the heavenly liturgy. There should be no need to explain the significance of the building to the community—it ought to speak for itself. The significance of the building is either sufficiently evident or it is not at all.[50] The building must resemble that for which it stands.

---

ecclesiastically deputes it for a specific purpose in the life of the church. An example of a constitutive blessing is the dedication of an altar or church. Constitutive blessings of things or places are not normally repeatable. When blessed items are destroyed or returned to profane use, the effect of the blessing is considered to be lost. This is because the sign value has been eliminated.

See Triacca, "Le benedizioni 'invocative' in genere, e su 'persone,'" and "Le benedizione 'invocative' su 'realtà cosmiche,'" 110–66.

48. *ODC*, no. 3: 31.

49. See *Roman Missal. Third Edition. The General Instruction of the Roman Missal* nn. 288, 294, 295, 296–308, 310–17.

50. Grasso, "Perché le chiese," 562.

This opening section of the *Introduction* on the nature and dignity of church buildings contains a number of very important points that need to be applied to the nature and dignity of the parish church building. In a particular locality, the universal church is manifested in the liturgical celebrations of the local church, most especially in the celebration of the Eucharist. In the first chapter of this investigation, the special significance which *Sacrosanctum concilium* attributed to the manifestation of the visible church in the liturgical celebrations of the parish community was discussed. The parish community makes the universal church present within its specific locality. To this degree, the parish church, in which the parish community celebrates the church's liturgy, must also be regarded as a sign of the pilgrim church and image of the heavenly church present within the specific parish community.[51] The building is to be a sign of the nature of the church to those who are members and to those who are not. It is also very likely that the church building may be an expression of the dialectic between the universal church and its local manifestation within a specific time, place, and culture. In the church building one should reasonably hope to find incarnated the universal realities of the faith within the specific artistic, architectural, and cultural expressions of the time and place in which the church is constructed. The guidelines recommended in the third article of this *Introduction* provide a solid foundation for achieving this balance. The parish church is to stand for all as a sign of the pilgrim church and an image of the heavenly church present in the locality in which it stands.

---

51. The fact that it is more important that a church building in which a parish community worships be given the sign value that is bestowed by the Order of Dedication as a means of speaking of its identity to the local community can be seen in the *Introduction* of *The Order of the Dedication of a Church in Which Sacred Celebrations are Already Regularly Taking Place*. The *Introduction* of this rite suggests that it is more important that a parish have this sign value than other types of church buildings. The *Introduction* states that one of the reasons that a church building that has already been standing for a long time, without having any structural changes, might be dedicated is that it has been raised to the status of a parish church. This portion of the *Introduction* states as the condition for dedicating such a building: "that there is something new or greatly changed with respect to the building (for example, the church has been completely restored) or to its juridical status (for example, the church has been raised to the rank of a parish church)." See *Order of the Dedication of Church in Which Sacred Celebrations are Already Regularly Taking Place*, in ODC, n. 1:73.

PART TWO

## *Titular of a Church and the Relics of the Saints to be Placed in It*

The second section of the *Introduction* addresses the requirement that each church to be dedicated must have a title and treats the practice of depositing relics under the altar of the church. No church may be dedicated without a title.[52] The title that is given to a church building must meet a number of very specific requirements. The church may be named after the blessed Trinity, the Lord Jesus Christ invoked according to one of the mysteries of his life, or one of his titles that is accepted in the liturgy. A church may also be named after the blessed Virgin Mary or one of her titles that is accepted in the liturgy, one of the angels, or one of the saints of the church. A church may not be named after a *beatus* without a special *indult* from the Apostolic See. A church may have only one title. It may be named after two saints only in those cases where they are listed together in the church's calendar, as for example Saints Cosmos and Damian. The naming of the church according to the above criterion contributes to the sign value of the church building. It helps to point the parish community to a reality beyond itself. This occurs as the community's identity is formed by the specific divine mystery, or the qualities of the saint, after which the church is named. In the case of a church named after a saint, the life of the saint may be held up as a model for the community. The community named after a saint should also be aware that it has a member of the heavenly liturgy capable of interceding there on its behalf. Recently, it has become a common practice for the members of a new parish to select a number of possible titles that are submitted to the bishop for final selection and approval.[53] The importance of the church's title is significant enough to the community's identity that it is not to be changed after the church has been dedicated.

The symbolic link between the church building and the heavenly Jerusalem is strengthened by the placing of the relics of a martyr or saint beneath the church altar. Symbolically this gesture has been understood as linking the sufferings of Christ with those of the martyrs who have suffered for the faith.[54] The martyrs who died for Christ have triumphed

---

52. *ODC*, no. 4: 31–32. See also *Code of Canon Law*, can. 1218: "Each church is to have its own title which cannot be changed after the church has been dedicated."

53. Simons, *Holy People, Holy Place*, 32.

54. The rite shows a preference for the relics of martyrs in the expression "placing relics of Martyrs or of other Saints under the altar . . ." See *ODC*, no. 5:32. Calabuig explains the reason for this preference as being the result of the more perfect witness of the martyrs and the closer connection of the shedding of their blood with the shedding

through Christ's sacrifice and are now in Christ's presence in the heavenly liturgy. The placing of the relics of a saint under the altar also speaks of the unity of the earthly church with the heavenly church. Just as the saint whose relics are placed under the altar was once a member of the pilgrim church, so too the members of the pilgrim church who gather around the altar hope to one day participate in the heavenly liturgy. The *Introduction* of *ODC* states that this tradition of the church is to be continued, if possible.[55] It adds a number of stipulations that are intended to assure that the relics are of sufficient size to be recognized as parts of the human body.[56] Great care should be taken to determine that the relics are authentic. When it cannot be shown that the relics are authentic, or they are too small to be recognized as parts of the human body, the *Introduction* states that it is better that relics not be used. In this way the *Introduction* recognizes that the placing of the relics beneath the altar is not essential to the rite of dedication. It has a symbolic value only if it can be done in a meaningful and significant way. The *Introduction* also calls for a return to the more traditional practice of placing the relics beneath the altar instead of upon the altar or setting them into the *mensa* (table) of the altar. Where the relics of a saint are placed beneath the altar of a parish church, they provide a powerful symbolic link between the members of the local parish community and the church in heaven.

## *Celebration of the Dedication*

The third section of the *Introduction* addresses the actual celebration of the rite of dedication. This section has been further divided into five subsections. These are: 1) The Minister of the Rite; 2) The Choice of Day; 3) The Mass of the Dedication; 4) The Office of Dedication; and 5) The Parts

---

of Christ's blood on the cross of the altar. See Calabuig, "Ordo dedications ecclesiae et altaris," 423–24.

55. This tradition was added to the Roman Liturgy in the late fourth century. Originally some Christian churches were built over the tombs of martyrs. The practice of placing relics under the altar is first witnessed to in a letter from Saint Ambrose to his sister Marcellina in the year 386. Saint Ambrose, *Epistola XXII* (22), 126–40. At this time only the celebration of the Eucharist was deemed necessary for the dedication of a church. Saint Ambrose regards the deposition of relics beneath the altar to be pastorally wise as a result of the demands of the people to follow the Roman custom in the dedication of their new basilica. The demand of the people to place relics beneath the altar of the new church is accompanied by the timely discovery of the relics of Saints Gervasius and Protasius. See Calabuig, "Rito della dedicazione della chiesa," 383.

56. *ODC*, no. 5: 32.

of the Rite. Only the first four of these sections will be examined here. The lengthy theological description that makes up "Parts of the Rite" will be incorporated into the actual descriptions of the different parts of the rite as they are examined within the context of the ritual.

Before actually turning to what the *Introduction* has to say about the celebration of the rite of dedication, it will be profitable for an understanding of this material to return briefly to the content of *Sacrosanctum concilium*, article forty-one, which was discussed in the first chapter of this book. The article speaks of the role of the bishop as the high priest of his flock. It also states that the fullest manifestation of the church takes place when the Eucharist is celebrated with the full and active participation of God's people, presided over by the bishop surrounded by his priests and ministers.[57] The first three subsections of this section are intended to insure that the celebration of the dedication of a church is accompanied by such a full manifestation of the church. The Italian liturgical theologian Mauro Paternoster has described the celebration of the dedication of a church as follows: *[L]a dedicazione è l'epifania della comunità locale che, per la prima volta, si riunisce nel nuovo luogo di culto per celebrarvi l'Eucharistia.*"[58]

The *Introduction* states that it is the responsibility of the bishop who has care of a particular church to dedicate all of the new churches that are built in his diocese. When the diocesan bishop is unable to dedicate the church himself he may appoint another bishop to do so in his place. Only in very special circumstances may a priest be appointed to dedicate a church.[59] This connection between the diocesan bishop and his role in dedicating all new communities in his diocese speaks powerfully of the link between the new community, the diocese, and the universal church. In the case of a parish it speaks of the identity of the parish within the larger community shepherded by the bishop.

The selection of the day for the celebration of the dedication of a church is to be done in such a way as to insure that as many members of the community as possible can be present.[60] The dedication is to take place at a time that would allow the nature of the church to manifest itself

---

57. The Second Vatican Council, *Sacrosanctum concilium*, no. 41:14–15.

58. Paternoster, "Analasi rituale e contenuti teologici dell," 606. My translation of this passage: The dedication is the epiphany of the local community as it meets for the first time in a new place of worship for the celebration of the Eucharist.

59. *ODC*, no. 6:32. See also *Code of Canon Law*, can. 1206.

60. *ODC*, no. 7:32.

in the most complete assembly that is possible. The selection of the day no longer involves a fast that must be announced to the people, as was the case in the previous rituals. It is most appropriate that the dedication take place on a Sunday. Where the church is to be dedicated for a parish community, the selection of a Sunday would correspond to the attention which *Sacrosanctum concilium* 42 states should be given to building the parish community through the celebration of the Sunday Mass.[61] There are a number of days on which a church may not be dedicated. This is due to the fact that the theme of dedication pervades the entire rite, and it would not be proper to disregard the mystery being commemorated on a number of the church's most solemn days.

The rite for the dedication of a church in ODC is inseparably bound up with the Eucharist. It now forms a single, continuous celebration.[62] One of the great accomplishments of this revised rite for dedication is that it reasserts the Eucharist as the principle act of dedication[63] The *Introduction* states that when a church is dedicated it must be done with the celebration of the Eucharist and the use of the texts proper to the rite for the liturgy of the Word and Eucharist.[64] It is also fitting that the bishop should concelebrate the Mass with all of the priests who take part in the celebration with him and most especially with those who are going to have care of the parish or community for which the church is being dedicated.[65] This concelebrated Eucharist, presided over by the bishop, with as many of the faithful from the community participating as possible, brings about a full manifestation of Christ's church in this first Eucharistic celebration to take place in the new church. As will be shown through the study of the parts of the rite, this manifestation of the church, which

61. The Second Vatican Council, *Sacrosanctum concilium*, no. 42: 15.

62. Simons, *Holy People, Holy Place*, 33.

63. Marsili, "Dedicazione senza consacrazione," 579.
In the early Roman Rite a church was dedicated simply through the celebration of the Eucharist. The earliest witness to this practice is Eusebius who speaks of the dedication of the new church in Tyre through the celebration of the Eucharist in 314. For Eusebius on this please see: *Historia ecclesiae*, X, 3, 3–4, ed. Bardy, 80–81. Pope Vigilius also writes to Profuturo, the bishop of Braga, in 538 to tell him that the dedication of a church is accomplished solely through the celebration of the Eucharist. See Vigilius, *Epistola ad Profuturum episcopum Bracarensem*, IV: PL 69, col. 18.

64. *ODC*, no. 8: 32.

65. *ODC*, no. 9: 33. The *Introduction* states: "It is fitting that the bishop should concelebrate the Mass with the Priests who are associated with him in carrying out the rites of dedication and with those who have been given the office of directing the parish or community for which the church has been built."

takes place within the rites of dedication, is intended to help those who are having their church dedicated appreciate the identity and nature of their community within the church.

The fourth subsection of this section deals with the celebration of the liturgy of the hours on the day of the dedication of a church. This day is to be kept as a solemnity by those in that church.[66] The office for the dedication of a church is to be celebrated from Evening Prayer I. When the rite of depositing the relics takes place, the *Introduction* recommends that a vigil take place before the relics to be placed under the altar. The vigil may consist of the office of readings taken from the common or proper most appropriate for the saint whose relics are to be placed under the altar. This vigil should follow the norms found in The Liturgy of the Hours, but may be adapted to encourage the people's participation.

The last subsection of this section deals with the different parts of the rite.[67] It is divided into: 1) The Entrance into the Church; 2) The Liturgy of the Word; 3) The Prayer of Dedication and the Anointing of the Church and the Altar; and 4) The Celebration of the Eucharist. The content of each of these will be incorporated into the discussion of the respective part of the rite.

## *Adaptation of the Rite*

In keeping with the criteria of the Second Vatican Council, the *Introduction* of *ODC* states the conditions by which the conference of bishops may adapt the rite of dedication to the character of their particular region and culture.[68] The section addressing the changes and adaptations that are possible in the celebration of a rite has become a regular feature in many of the *Introduction(s)* to be found in the rites that have been revised since the council.[69] The adaptations that are permitted are intended to allow the people celebrating the rite from many different cultures to enter more completely into the mysteries of the liturgy. The limits that are placed upon the adaptations are to ensure that the church's rites retain their essential elements. The *Introduction* of *ODC* states:

---

66. *ODC*, no. 10: 33.
67. *ODC*, no. 11-33-37.
68. The Second Vatican Council, *Sacrosanctum concilium*, nn. 38–39: 14.
69. Donghi, "Significato dei *Praenotanda*," 16.

Conferences of Bishops can adapt this Order, as circumstances suggest, to the practices of each region, but in such a way that nothing detracts from its dignity and solemnity.[70]

In making these adaptations it is never permitted to omit the celebration of the Mass with its proper preface and the dedication prayer. Those rites that have a special meaning and force in the liturgical tradition are also to be retained. These rites include the anointing of the altar and the church walls, the burning of incense on the altar, the covering of the altar, and the lighting of the altar and church. In regard to any changes that are to be made by the conference of bishops, they are to be made in consultation with the Holy See and introduced only with the consent of the Holy See.

More important to the celebration of the rite in a particular parish are those adaptations that the *Introduction* allows to the competence of the ministers who will be celebrating the rite and preparing the community for the ceremony. It belongs to the competence of the bishop and those in charge of the celebration to determine which of the three options for entering the church is to be used, what ritual gestures should be chosen to hand the church over to the bishop, and whether the relics should be deposited under the altar.[71] All of these matters will need to take into consideration the local conditions of the parish or community. A public procession to the church will not be possible in some circumstances. The manner for handing over the church should employ symbols that will be understood by the community. To the rector of the church being dedicated, and those who assist him in the pastoral care of the community, belongs the work of choosing and preparing the readings and music and other pastoral aids. The readings must be selected from those that are found in the lectionary for the dedication of a church. The readings and music are to be selected keeping in mind the goal that they should contribute "to foster the fruitful participation of the people and to promote a dignified celebration."[72] The adaptations that the local bishop and those preparing the celebration may make are to be implemented with the objective of allowing the local community to enter more fully into the liturgical celebration.

---

70. *ODC*, no. 18:35.

71. *ODC*, no. 19:36. The relics should not be deposited under the altar if they do not meet the conditions contained in article 5 of the *Introduction* regarding the size and authenticity of the relics.

72. *ODC*, no. 19:36.

PART TWO

## *Pastoral Preparation*

Because one of the main purposes of the *Introduction(s)* in the new liturgical books is to aid the Christian assembly to participate in the liturgy with a greater awareness of the mysteries which are being celebrated, the section on the pastoral preparation of the community is an important component of the *Introduction*.[73] The purpose of the instruction that is called for in ODC is that it should lead the assembly to understand the nature of the church building and the symbolic value that it is to have for the community. To bring this about, the preparation of the community should be such that its members understand the meaning of the liturgical rites to be celebrated at the dedication and the various uses and importance of the different parts of the church. It would be appropriate that the contents from the sections of the *Introduction* that deal with the "Nature and Dignity" of the church building and the "Parts of the Rite" be communicated to the assembly. As it would be difficult to convey the richness of the rite in a short period of time, its explanation should in fact play a part in the entire process of the construction of the church building. The pastoral preparation that is called for in the *Introduction* is to be such that the assembly achieves the full and active participation in the liturgy called for in *Sacrosanctum conciium*.[74] The *Introduction* states:

> Accordingly, the faithful are to be instructed about the various parts of the church and their use, the Order of Dedication, and the chief liturgical symbols employed in it, so that, fully understanding the meaning of the dedication of the church through its rites and prayers, with appropriate help, they may take a conscious, devout, and active part in the sacred action.[75]

The nature of the instruction that the community receives should be such that it communicates the power of the rite according to its spiritual, ecclesial, and missionary aspect.[76] Such instruction, which is the

---

73. Donghi, "Significato dei *Praenotanda*," 11.

74. The Second Vatican Council, *Sacrosanctum conclium*, no. 14:7–8. The Constitution on the Liturgy states: "Mother Church earnestly desires that all the faithful should be led to that full, conscious, and active participation in liturgical celebrations which is demanded by the very nature of the liturgy, and to which the Christian people, "a chosen race, a royal priesthood, a holy nation, a redeemed people (1 Pet. 2:9, 4–5) have a right and obligation by reason of their baptism."

75. *ODC*, no. 20:36.

76. *ODC*, no. 20:36. The *Introduction* states: "...are to instruct them on the spiritual, ecclesial, and missionary importance and value of the celebration."

responsibility of the rector of the church to be dedicated and those in the community experienced in the pastoral ministry, ought to lead the members of the community to see in the church building a sign which speaks to them of their spiritual and ecclesial identity as Christians and their responsibility to spread the gospel. Such a preparation may play a fundamental role in the formation of a new parish community. A powerful and explicit statement of the nature of this threefold preparation was found in the 1973 provisional edition of the rite. Although this section was dropped from the *Introduction* of the 1977 *Editio Typica*, it is worth summarizing here as it called for: 1) a spiritual preparation which called the liturgical assembly to understand itself as God's chosen people where he dwells among his people; 2) an ecclesial preparation that allowed the assembly to know itself as called to live in communion and charity with the universal church through its local bishop; and 3) a preparation that helped the liturgical assembly to understand its mission to bring the gospel it hears in the liturgy and Christ's light to all whom they encounter in their area.[77]

For the parish community preparing for the dedication of its church building, the pastoral preparation leading up to this event ought to be such that the members of the community are able to experience in the celebration of the rite, and thereafter in the church building that has been dedicated, a rich sense of their personal and corporate Christian identity from a spiritual, ecclesial and missionary point of view. The need for a thorough and solid preparation is also called for as a result of the nature of the rite. The rite of the dedication of a church is a rite that is rarely celebrated and not likely to be familiar to even well educated Christians.

## *Requisites for the Dedication of a Church*

In order that the rite of dedication may be celebrated smoothly, this section contains an article that lists the many items that are required for the celebration of the rite.[78] There are also three articles that address the following practical concerns respectively: the manner for setting up the crosses and candles for the anointing of the walls of the church, the vestments that are required for the celebration, and those objects that are

---

77. *Ordo dedicationis ecclesiae*, in *Ordo dedicationis ecclesiae et altaris deque aliis locis et rebus sacrandis*, bozze di stampa (1973) no. 22:26.

78. *ODC*, no. 21:36–37.

necessary in the event that relics are to be deposited under the altar during the rite.[79] This section also contains an article that addresses the need to record the act of dedication as an important historic event in the life of the church.[80] A record of the dedication is to be signed by the bishop who presides at the dedication, the rector of the church, and some members of the community for which the church is dedicated. A copy of the record is to be kept in the archives of the church and the diocese. When the relics of a saint are deposited beneath the altar a third copy is to be deposited in the reliquary. An inscription is also to be placed in the church to testify to the fact that the building has been dedicated. This record is to bear the date of the dedication, the name of the bishop, and the titular of the church. Because the dedication of a church is such a rare event in the life of a community, the inscription of this event that is to be found in the church should serve as a testimony to the sign value that was bestowed upon the building to many succeeding generations. This public record should be an important monument that testifies to the historic, ecclesial, and spiritual identity of every parish church that has been dedicated.

## *Anniversary of Dedication*

The final section of the *Introduction* addresses the celebration of the anniversary of the dedication of a church. The anniversary of the dedication of the diocesan cathedral is to be celebrated with the rank of a solemnity in the cathedral itself and as a feast in all of the other churches of the diocese. If the date for celebrating the anniversary is always impeded, the celebration is to be assigned to the nearest free day. The purpose for celebrating the anniversary of the dedication is stated as being: "In order that the importance and dignity of one's own Church may stand out with greater clarity."[81] So that the full nature of the local church may be expressed in the celebration of the anniversary of the cathedral church, the *Introduction* states that it is appropriate that the bishop concelebrate the Eucharist with the chapter of canons or the council of priests and the participation of as many people as possible. The celebration of the anniversary of the diocesan cathedral as a feast in the parish communities of the diocese highlights the relationship of the parish church with the

---

79. *ODC*, nn. 22–24:37.
80. *ODC*, no. 25:37–38. See also *Code of Canon Law*, ca, 1208.
81. *ODC*, no. 26:38.

mother church of the diocese. It would be appropriate for each parish community to send representatives to the celebration at the diocesan cathedral.

The anniversary of a church's dedication is to be celebrated as a solemnity within that church.[82] The celebration of the anniversary of the church's dedication provides an extremely important opportunity to bring to the community's attention the significance that was bestowed on the building at its dedication and to remind the members of the community of what this implies about their identity. The need to revisit the church's dedication on the anniversary is heightened by the fact that in many communities it may be that the people presently living in the parish were not even born when the building was dedicated. Italian liturgist Salvatore Marsili has written of the importance of the parish community celebrating the anniversary of the dedication of the parish church:

> *Non parliamo qui soltanto di ricordare il giorno anniversario della Dedicazione, ma la Dedicazione stessa, come una realtà che ha dato un valore e una dimensione particolare alla nostra chiesa. Pensiamo che la cosa dovrebbe avvenire ogni anno, nel tempo migliore per la parrocchia, anche se non corrisponde alla data storica della Dedicazione.*[83]

Marsili suggests that the anniversary of the dedication of a parish church should be celebrated with a gathering of the entire community where all of its members might reflect upon the rite of dedication assisted by the proper commentary. He also suggests that it would be appropriate for them to be re-exposed to certain aspects of the rite on the anniversary, such as the sprinkling of the walls, the lighting of the twelve candles on the church walls, or perhaps even reading from the life of the saint whose relics were placed under the altar at the dedication. The celebration of the anniversary of dedication ought to lead the parish community to comprehend more completely their identity within the church. How *ODC* articulates this identity will be explained in the following chapters that investigate the content of the rite.

82. *ODC*, no. 27:38.

83. Marsilli, "Dedicazione senza consacrazione," 601. My translation of this passage: We do not speak here only of remembering the day of dedication, but the actual fact of dedication itself as a reality that has given a value and a particular dimension to our church. We think that this event [celebration] should happen every year, at a time which is best for the parish [and at which most parishioners might attend], even if it takes place at a time that does not correspond with the actual historic date [of the dedication].

PART TWO

## SUMMARY

The nature of the material found in the *Introduction* to *ODC* is such that it contributes a great deal of positive substance to the construction of a liturgical theology of a parish community based upon the reading of the rites for the dedication of a church.

In the *Introduction* of *ODC* the church building is described as a sign of the pilgrim church on earth and an image of the church in heaven. The church itself is regarded as that holy people that Christ gathered to himself through the New Covenant he established through his death and resurrection. The church is the temple of God, made of living stones, where the Father is worshiped in spirit and truth. The *Introduction* explains that the church building has this sign value because within this building the Christian community celebrates those liturgical mysteries that through the Holy Spirit configure it to Christ and allow it to offer worship through Christ to the Father. In the celebration of the rite of dedication, a rite of the church is celebrated to ask God to bestow this sign value upon the building. This significance is given to the building by God through the church's petition of prayer, the community's offering of the building to God for his exclusive worship, and through the ritual association of the building with the liturgical mysteries for which the building is being dedicated. Through the rite of dedication, the *domus* ("house") of the church building finds its full relation to the *ecclesia* ("church") constituted of the members of the church through the Holy Spirit in Christ. This is accomplished by the fact that in the rite of dedication the *domus* of the church building is put forward through the symbols and gestures of the rite as an image of the church. This is accomplished most completely in the celebration of the Eucharist. In the rite of dedication, principally through the church's intercession, the building is endowed with the significance to mediate a sign value. The building is established through the rite of dedication as a sacramental of the church that points to the mystery of the church. The actual content and symbols that are used in the rites of dedication, and what they have to say about the image of the church that is put forward in the ritual, is the subject matter of the chapters that follow.

In the *Introduction* of *ODC* there is to be found an ecclesiology that communicates an awareness of the local ecclesial assembly for which the rites of dedication are to be celebrated. The spirit of the ecclesiology that is found in the *Introduction* of *ODC* is that of the Second Vatican

Council. This is demonstrated by the norms of the *Introduction* that address the following: the responsibility of the diocesan bishop to dedicate the churches founded in the diocese entrusted to his care, the centrality of the Eucharist in the celebration of the rites of dedication, the concern to have as many of the faithful as possible present at the Mass of dedication, and the recommendation that the Mass of dedication be celebrated by the bishop with the concelebration of those priests that are to have pastoral care of the parish. All of these liturgical norms are orientated to ensuring that the Mass of dedication will result in that epiphany of the church that is spoken of in *Sacrosanctum concilium*, article forty-one. The *Introduction* of ODC also shows an awareness of the local church's connection to the diocesan church by requiring that the anniversary of the dedication of the diocesan cathedral should be celebrated in all of the churches of the diocese. The *Introduction* of ODC offers a positive articulation of how the church is to be manifested in the local Christian assemblies that are dedicating their church buildings. The positive articulation of this reality provides an important foundation for the construction of the theology for a parish community that is found in *ODC*. The doctrinal content of ODC speaks of the theological significance of the rites of dedication for the communities for which the rite is celebrated. By doing so, it offers the local community material with which to understand the significance of the rites in relation to the community's place within the universal church.

The *Introduction* of ODC aims to communicate the spiritual and theological significance of the rite to the members of the community. This is true whether the rite is celebrated for a cathedral church, a religious community, or a parish community. To the extent that this study is concerned with the theology of a parish community contained in *ODC*, the *Introduction* develops the theological orientation from which the rite of dedication must be read and through which its significance can be appreciated. In the four remaining chapters that make-up this section, the rites of dedication will be studied to discover more clearly the theology of a parish community that is to be found in *ODC*.

# Chapter Three

# Order of the Dedication of a Church: The Introductory Rites

## INTRODUCTION

In this chapter *The Introductory Rites* of ODC will be studied in order to discover what they have to offer towards the construction of a theology of a parish community. The investigation presented in this chapter will involve an analysis of these rites according to the four categories of *rites, prayers, sacred scripture,* and *persons*.

## THE INTRODUCTORY RITES OF ODC

### The Content of The Introductory Rites of ODC

The first of the four parts into which ODC has been divided is entitled *The Introductory Rites*. This initial portion of the rite has been further broken down into three different sub-sections. These are: 1) the entrance into the church; 2) the blessing and sprinkling of water; and 3) the hymn and *collect*.

## *The Entrance into the Church*

The rite is to begin with an entry into the church that is being dedicated. According to the different circumstances of the time and place, there are three different possibilities provided for the entrance. It should be recalled that the *Introduction* stated that it was for the bishop and those in charge of the celebration to decide which of those is the most appropriate for the particular church in question.[1] The first alternative that is supplied, which involves a procession to the new church, is regarded as the most complete form of the ritual, even if it may not be the option that is most frequently used.[2]

When it has been decided that the building will be entered by a procession, the rubric states that the doors of the church to be dedicated should be closed. The people are to assemble in a neighboring church, or in some other convenient place, from which the procession may go to the new church. When the relics of a martyr or a saint are to be placed beneath the altar, they are to be prepared in the place where the people assemble.[3] The bishop, the concelebrating priests, the deacons and the ministers,[4] all dressed in appropriate vestments,[5] are to go to the place where the people are assembled.[6] The bishop then greets the people saying, "The grace and peace of God be with all of you in his holy church" or some other words that are taken from scripture. After the people have

---

1. *ODC*, no. 19:36.
2. Calabuig, "*Ordo dedicationis ecclesiae et altaris*," 398.
3. *ODC*, no. 29:39.
4. In 1972 Pope Paul VI issued the *motu proprio*, *Ministeria quaedam*, which put an end to the minor orders and established the ministries of lector and acolyte. When the word "ministers" is used in *RDC* it is referring to acolytes and lectors. In January 1973, the Congregation for the Discipline of the Sacraments issued the instruction *Immensae caritatis* to permit the use of extraordinary ministers of the Eucharist to facilitate the distribution of Communion. Extraordinary ministers of the Eucharist were to be permitted to ease the distribution of Communion in large crowds. These could also be included among the ministers referred to in the rite. In practice, in most parishes, due to the lack of persons officially installed as lectors and acolytes, the lay faithful usually generously fulfill the different roles of altar servers, acolytes, lectors and extraordinary ministers of the Eucharist and contribute greatly to the prayerful celebration of the liturgy by their committed and faithful fulfillment of these ministries. See Paul VI, *Ministeria quaedam*, 1:427–32; and Sacred Congregation for the Discipline of the Sacraments, *Immensae caritatis*, 1:225–32. Power, *Gifts that Differ*, 3–43.
5. *ODC*, no. 23: 37. For the appropriate vestments for the celebration see this number in the *Introduction*.
6. *ODC*, no. 30: 39–40.

responded to his greeting, the bishop is to address the people about the nature of the celebration. He may do so in his own words, or in the words that are provided in the rite. As the words that are suggested in the rite are the same in the first two options, they will be quoted here:

> Beloved brothers and sisters,
> we have gathered with joy
> to dedicate a new church
> by celebrating the Lord's Sacrifice.
> Let us take part in these sacred rites with loving devotion,
> listening to the Word of God with faith,
>
> so that our community,
> reborn from the one font of Baptism
> and nourished at the same table,
> may grow into a spiritual temple
> and, brought together at one altar,
> may advance in love from on high.[7]

After the bishop has addressed the people, he receives the miter and the pastoral staff and the procession to the new church begins. The only candles that are to be used in the procession are those that surround the relics. Otherwise, candles and incense are not to be used until the incensing and lighting of the church and altar. The assembly is to process according to a very clear order. The crossbearer leads the procession, followed by the ministers; next come the relics carried by the priests or deacons and accompanied by ministers or lay persons carrying candles; after these come the concelebrating priests; then the bishop and two deacons; and finally the faithful. The procession is to make its way to the new church singing Ps 121 (122) with the antiphon, "Let us go rejoicing to the house of the Lord." The rite does allow that another appropriate hymn may be sung at this time.[8]

Once the procession has reached the doors of the church it comes to a stop. At this point representatives of those who have been involved in the building of the church come forward to hand the building over to the bishop. The rubric states that these people may be "the faithful of

---

7. *ODC*, no. 30:39–40.

8. *ODC*, no. 32:40–41. It should be noted that the *Introduction* to the rite stated that it is for the rector of the church to be dedicated and those who assist him to determine what readings and songs should be used in the celebration. See *ODC*, no. 19: 36.

the parish or of the diocese, donors, architects or workers."[9] The manner in which the building is to be handed over is a matter to be decided by the bishop with those in charge of the celebration.[10] The rite suggests that this may be done by handing over either the deed, the keys, the plan of the building, or a book that describes the progress of the building's development. The handing over of the building to the bishop is regarded by the *Introduction* as one of the most significant rituals that make up *The Introductory Rites*.[11] If it is necessary, one of the representatives may briefly address the bishop and the assembly to explain what the church expresses in its art and design. The bishop then calls upon the priest to whom pastoral care of the church has been entrusted and invites him to open the door of the church, which as mentioned earlier should be closed.

After the door has been opened, the bishop invites the people to enter the church. He may either say, "Enter the gates of the Lord with thanksgiving, his courts with songs of praise" or use some similar other words. Then, following the crossbearer, the bishop and all the others enter the church. As the procession enters the church, Ps 23 (24) is sung with the antiphon, "Grow higher, ancient doors. Let him enter, the King of glory."[12] Some other suitable song may also be sung. The bishop is to go directly to the celebrant's chair without kissing the altar. The concelebrating priests, deacons and ministers go to the places assigned to them in the sanctuary. The relics are also to be placed in the sanctuary between lit torches. This is followed by the blessing of the water. Some other suitable song may also be sung. The bishop is to go directly to the celebrant's chair without kissing the altar. The concelebrating priests, deacons and ministers go to the places assigned to them in the sanctuary. The relics are also to be placed in the sanctuary between lit torches. This is followed by the blessing of the water.

The second possible way of entering the church, which is a solemn procession, is introduced by the qualification: "If the procession cannot take place or seems inopportune, the faithful assemble at the door of the church to be dedicated, where the relics of the Saints have been placed

---

9. *ODC*, no. 33:41.

10. *ODC*, no. 19:36.

11. *ODC*, no. 11:33. The *Introduction* lists this as one of the two important gestures that take place in the *Introductory Rites*. The second important ritual gesture that the *Introduction* refers to as being significant in the opening rites is the sprinkling of the people and the building with holy water.

12. *ODC*, no. 34: 42.

PART TWO

privately."[13] This rubric indicates a preference for the first option. When this cannot take place the faithful are to congregate outside of the church. The doors to the church should be closed. The bishop greets the people and addresses them in the same manner that was indicated in the first option. If it seems appropriate the people sing Ps 121 (122) with its antiphon while standing at the doors of the church. Another suitable hymn may be sung in its place. Representatives of the community are to come forward to hand the church building over to the bishop in the same manner suggested in the first option. The bishop asks the priest who will have pastoral care of the church to open the doors of the church, and then the faithful are invited to enter. The psalm that the people sing, and the manner for entering the church, is to be the same as in the first option. Once all have arrived in their places, the water is blessed for the aspersion of the people and the building.

The third option for entering the church begins with the rubric: "If the solemn entrance cannot take place, the simple entrance is used."[14] This also indicates that the simpler options are to be used only when the more complete are not possible. This third alternative, which goes by the name "The Simple Entrance," begins with the people already assembled in the church. When the celebration begins, the crossbearer leads the bishop with the concelebrating priests, the deacons and the ministers from the sacristy through the main body of the church to the sanctuary. If there are relics to be placed under the altar, these are to be brought in the entrance procession to the sanctuary from the sacristy or chapel where they had been exposed for the vigil and the veneration of the people. For a good reason, the relics may have been placed in the sanctuary between lit torches before the beginning of the celebration. The procession to the sanctuary takes place with the singing of the entrance antiphon and Ps 121 (122). For this third option a different antiphon may be used to reflect the fact that the entire assembly is not in procession. This antiphon states: "God is in his holy place, God who unites those who dwell in his house: he himself gives might and strength to his people."[15] The antiphon given in the first two options may also be used, as may another song if it is deemed appropriate. Once the procession has reached the sanctuary, the bishop, priests, deacons and ministers take their places

13. *ODC*, no. 36:43.
14. *ODC*, no. 43:46.
15. *ODC*, no. 45:46.

in the sanctuary. The bishop is to greet the people, but there is no indication that he should address them about the nature of the celebration with the words that are provided for the first two options.[16] After the bishop's greeting, the representatives from the community come forward to hand the church over to the bishop. The water for the aspersion of the people and the building is then blessed.

## *Blessing and Sprinkling of Water*

The rubric that introduces the blessing of the water and the sprinkling states:

> When the entrance rite is concluded, the Bishop blesses the water for the sprinkling of the people as a sign of repentance and as a reminder of their Baptism and for purifying the walls and the altar of the new church. The ministers bring the vessel with the water to the Bishop, who stands at the chair.[17]

The sprinkling of the people with water is to be recognized as a sign of penance and a reminder of baptism. The aspersion of the walls and the altar are intended to purify them.[18] The *Introduction* states that the people are sprinkled because they are a spiritual temple.[19] The bishop is to deliver an admonition explaining the significance of the rite. He may do this in the words that are given or in his own. The words that are supplied also emphasize that the sprinkling is a sign of repentance and a reminder of baptism. The bishop also states the hope that God's grace will help those gathered to remain faithful members of the church, open to the Spirit. The recommended text states:

> Dear brothers and sisters,
> as we solemnly dedicate this house,
> let us humbly call upon the Lord our God
> to bless this water he has created

---

16. *ODC*, no. 46:47.

17. *ODC*, no. 48:48–49.

18. The sprinkling of the church with holy water can be traced in the Roman Rite back to the time of Pope Gregory the Great. Saint Gregory wrote to the missionaries of England to tell them that it was not necessary to destroy the temples that the pagans had used. The Christians could use these if they were first purified with holy water.
See Saint Gregory the Great, *Registrum* XI, *Epistola*, 150A, 961.

19. *ODC*, no. 11:33. The *Introduction* states: "the Bishop blesses water and with it sprinkles the people, who are the spiritual temple, the walls of the church, and the altar."

PART TWO

> with which we are to be sprinkled
> as a sign of repentance and a memorial of Baptism
> and by which the new walls and altar will be purified.
> May the Lord support us with his grace,
> So that, docile to the Spirit whom we have received,
> We may remain faithful in his Church.[20]

The bishop's admonition is followed by a period of silence, during which all are to pray. The bishop then proceeds to bless the water, praying:

> O God, through whom every creature
> comes forth into the light of life,
> you accompany all people with such great love
> that not only do you nourish them with fatherly care,
> but you mercifully cleanse them from their sins
> with the dew of charity
> and constantly lead them back to Christ the Head.
>
> For in your merciful plan you established,
> that those who descend as sinners,
> into the sacred waters to die with Christ
> should rise free from guilt
> and be made his members,
> heirs with him to an eternal reward.
>
> Sanctify + therefore with your blessing
> this water you have created,
> that, sprinkled on us
> and on the walls of this church,
> it may be a sign of the cleansing waters of salvation,
> in which we have been washed in Christ
> and made a temple of your Spirit.
>
> Grant that, with all our brothers and sisters
> who will celebrate the divine mysteries in this church,
> we may come at last to the heavenly Jerusalem.
>
> Through Christ our Lord.
> R/. Amen.[21]

The bishop, with the two deacons, goes through the main body of the church, sprinkling the people and the walls with the holy water.

---

20. *ODC*, no. 48:48–49.
21. *ODC*, no. 48:48.

When he returns to the sanctuary he sprinkles the altar. While this is taking place the following antiphon is sung: "I saw water flowing from the temple, from its right-hand side, alleluia. And all to whom this water came were saved and shall say: alleluia, alleluia." In Lent the antiphon to be sung is: "When I prove my holiness among you, I will gather you from all the foreign lands; and I will pour clean water upon you and cleanse you from all your impurities, and I will give you a new spirit."[22]

Another appropriate song may also be sung. Once the sprinkling has been completed, the bishop returns to the chair and says, "May God, the Father of mercies, dwell in this house of prayer and, by the grace of the Holy Spirit, cleanse us who are the temple where he dwells."[23]

This concludes the rite of the aspersion of the building and the people.

## *Hymn and Collect*

After the sprinkling the *Gloria* is sung. When the hymn is finished the bishop invites the people to pray. All are to pray silently for a short period of time. The bishop then prays the opening prayer:

> Almighty ever-living God,
> pour out your grace upon this place
> and extend the gift of your help
> to all who call upon you,
> that the power of your word and of the Sacraments
> may strengthen here the hearts of all the faithful.
>
> Through our Lord Jesus Christ, your Son,
> who lives and reigns with you in the unity of the Holy Spirit,
> one God, forever and ever.[24]

Once the opening prayer has been prayed, the initial rites are concluded, and the celebration moves on to the liturgy of the word.

---

22. *ODC*, no. 49:49.
23. *ODC*, no. 50:50.
24. *ODC*, no. 52:50.

PART TWO

## The Analysis of the Introductory Rites

This section presents an analysis of the initial rites of *ODC* in order to determine what these rites have to contribute toward developing the theology for a parish that is contained in *ODC*. The content of the text of *The Introductory Rites* will be examined according to the four different categories of *rites*, *prayers*, *sacred scripture* and *persons*. Within the category of the *rites* will also be included the episcopal admonitions that are addressed by the bishop to the assembly at certain points in the rite. It has been decided to include these optional addresses of the bishop in the category of the *rites* because they are intended as a type of catechesis that speaks to the significance of the ritual gestures. The fact that these admonitions are optional and may not necessarily be given in the form they are found in the rite also makes it difficult to give them their own proper category.

### *Rites*

There are six ritual actions that need to be pointed out as contributing to a theology of the parish in *The Introductory Rites* of *ODC*. These are: the act of gathering to form the local assembly, the procession of the assembly to the new church, the handing over of the new church to the bishop, the opening of the doors of the church by the priest who is to have pastoral care of it, the taking of their places by the members of the assembly as the procession enters the church, and the sprinkling of the assembly and the walls and altar of the church with holy water. Each of these aspects needs to be investigated separately.

    The community that gathers to dedicate a new church is not just any assembly of people. It is a gathering of the local church in which one encounters a manifestation of the universal church.[25] As the people gather and are joined by the bishop, concelebrating priests, deacons, and ministers, the celebrating assembly becomes a theophany of the church within that particular locality. The presence of the bishop and other ordained ministers signifies that the group that gathers is not just a congregation of people living in the same area. The universal church is present in their gathering and they are one with the universal church.[26] This convocation of the people of God has the effect of producing a type of "station"

---

    25. Lathrop, *Holy People*, 61–71. See also The Second Vatican Council, *Sacrosanctum concilium*, no. 41: 14–15.

    26. de Lubac, "Particular Churches in the Universal Church," 206–9.

liturgy of the local church. As they gather, it is also clear that they are the subjects and protagonists of the celebration.[27] They will process, when this option is to be used, to the building that is the object of the celebration. The assembly that gathers also manifests the communal nature of the salvation brought by Christ. Christ has willed to save people not as isolated individuals but as members of his holy people.[28]

When the option to make a procession is exercised, it begins after the bishop has greeted and addressed the people. The ritual procession of the assembly from a church already in use speaks powerfully of the relationship of the new community to the rest of the church. The new community is generated from and receives its life from the mother church that is a part of the diocese.[29] The community that processes is a hierarchically structured community, made up of many different members, that reflects the nature of the local assembly.[30] In the procession, the community is to follow the crucified Christ to the new church that stands as a symbol of the heavenly church. The relics of one who is already a member of the heavenly church may accompany them on the way. The procession symbolizes a people on a journey to their heavenly destiny. It serves to highlight the identity of the members of the new community as members of the pilgrim church.

Once the procession has reached the doors of the church, representatives of the community are to come forward to hand the church over to the bishop. This gesture also has its proper place in the second and third options. This action speaks powerfully of the ecclesial identity of the new church that is to be dedicated. Often constructed through the efforts of the men and women who make up the community, the church is to be handed over to the bishop to become part of the diocesan patrimony.[31] This gesture recognizes the place of the bishop as the true shepherd of the diocesan community. It also recognizes the efforts of the local community that has brought the church building into existence.[32] The action symbolizes the reality that the community dedicating its church is a part of the universal church.

---

27. Paternoster, "Analisi ritual e contenuti teologici dell'," 606.
28. The Second Vatican Council, *Lumen gentium*, no. 9: 359–60.
29. Trudu, "*Haec aedes mysterium adumbrat ecclesiae*," 110–11.
30. Mazzarello, "Nuovo rito della dedicazione di una Chiesa," 685.
31. Calabuig, "*Ordo dedicationis ecclesiae et altaris*," 402.
32. Crichton, *Dedication of a Church*, 28.

PART TWO

In the first and second options, after the representatives of the community have handed the church over to the bishop, the bishop asks the priest who has pastoral care of the church to open the doors of the church. This represents the chief shepherd of the diocese asking the priest with the pastoral care of the community to open the doors so that the faithful may enter the church to celebrate the sacred mysteries. It is the priest who at the bishop's appointment will serve as shepherd of the local community and celebrate the sacraments for its members. He will not only open the door to Christ at this moment but, throughout his ministry, to this community.[33] By representing the bishop in his particular community, the priest cooperates in his absence to allow the universal church of Christ to be manifested to this local community.[34]

Once the pastor has opened the doors, the procession continues into the building in the same ordered manner in which it made its way to the church. Following the image of Christ crucified that is carried by the crossbearer, the different members of the body of Christ make their way to their prescribed places. The bishop goes directly to the celebrant's chair, while the priests, deacons, and ministers take their proper places in the sanctuary. The other members of the assembly go to their places in the body of the church. The celebrating assembly is thus constituted as a structured hierarchical community where all play their roles as members of the body of Christ.[35] Although the taking of the presidential chair by the bishop for the first liturgy to be offered in the church is not properly a ritual gesture, Ignazio Calabuig has described its importance in these words:

> *Ma la prima occupatio cathedrae, anche se non è oggetto di un particolare gesto rituale, ha un significato perspicuo: colui che, in virtù dell'ordinazione episcopale, in modo eminente e visibile, sostiene le parti dello stesso Cristo maestro, pastore e pontefice, e agisce in sua vece, occupa per primo il luogo della presidenza cultuale e*

---

33. Calabuig, "'Ordo dedicationis ecclesiae et altaris,'" 403–4.

34. See the Second Vatican Council, *Lumen gentium*, no. 28: 385–86. It states: "The priests, prudent cooperators of the episcopal college and its support and mouthpiece, called to the service of the People of God, constitute, together with their bishop, a unique sacerdotal college (*presbyterium*) dedicated it is true to a variety of distinct duties. In each local assembly of the faithful they represent in a certain sense the bishop, with whom they are associated in all trust and generosity; in part they take upon themselves his duties and solicitude and in their daily toils discharge them. Those who, under the authority of the bishop, sanctify and govern that portion of the Lord's flock assigned to them render the universal Church visible in their locality and contribute efficaciously towards building up the whole body of Christ (cf. Eph. 4:12)."

35. "General Instruction of the Roman Missal," no. 294.

*della funzione magisteriale; e quel luogo che è semplice sedes celebrantis, in questa occasione è vera* cathedra Episcopi, *come studiatamente—mi sembra—la chiama l'* Ordo *lungo tutto il rito.*[36]

The whole community is convoked by the bishop to become the celebrating assembly.

The sprinkling of the people and the walls and altar of the church, which takes place after the bishop's greeting, is a rite that speaks very powerfully about the identity of the people who make up the new church. The rubric for this rite makes it clear that the sprinkling of the people is a sign of penance and a memorial of baptism.[37] The walls and altar of the church are sprinkled in order that they may be purified. By reminding the people of their baptism, the rite of aspersion draws attention to what has made each individual a member of the local church. Each one is made a member of the community because of his or her baptism into Christ.[38] Baptism does not simply bring the individual membership in the local community or parish; it primarily incorporates the person into the one body of Christ that is made present in a certain area through the local community. To be a member of Christ's body must be regarded as a grace from God. The aspersion of the people is also to symbolize the initiation of the community as a people for God. The sprinkling of the walls and altar of the church ritually associates the building with a symbolic value that causes it to be seen as a sign of the living temple that is made up of

36. Calabuig, "L' *'Ordo dedicationis ecclesiae et altaris'*: Appunti di una lettura," 406. My translation of this passage is: But the first occupation of the *cathedra*, even if it is not the object of a particular ritual action, has a special significance: he who, in virtue of his episcopal ordination, in an eminent and visible way, in his role as Christ the teacher, shepherd and pastor, and acting on Christ's behalf, occupies for the first time the place of presidency and teaching; and that place, which is normally simply the celebrant's chair, becomes on this occasion the true *cathedra* of the bishop, as it is studiously—in my opinion—called throughout the ritual.

The commentary by Father Calabuig is based upon the Latin *editio typica* of the Rite for the Dedication of a Church. Throughout this Latin edition, the ritual explicitly refers to the presider's chair in the church that is to be dedicated as the "*cathedra.*" As Father Calabuig notes, this is clearly done to emphasize the idea of the local church making a full theophany in this celebration with its bishop presiding at the dedication of the new church building. See *Ordo dedicationis ecclesiae* in *Ordo dedicationis ecclesiae et altaris*, editio typica, no. 42: 36. The 1978 English translation has simply used the word "chair" throughout. This does not have the same significance as the use of "*cathedra*" on this occasion throughout the Latin rite.

37. *ODC*, no. 48: 48. It states: ". . .the bishop blesses the water for the sprinkling of the people as a sign of repentance and as a reminder of their Baptism and for purifying the walls and altar of the new church."

38. 1 Cor 12:13.

PART TWO

the people. The faithful are also to be reminded by the rite of sprinkling of their responsibility to continue Christ's work in the world by evangelizing those to whom they are sent in their daily lives and contributing to the growth of the church by inviting them to receive the new life which Christ always gives in the waters of baptism. As a penitential sign the rite symbolizes the new beginning that is called for as the community begins or renews its common life together. All past divisions and grudges must be put aside for the new life to which the community is called. For this reason, the sprinkling takes the place of the penitential rite. This rite also establishes a parallelism between the sacraments of initiation and the dedication of a church.[39] It also serves to remind all of the members of the community that they have been brought together through Christ's grace to experience salvation and to become the temple of God. The church building is to stand as a sign of what they are called to be.

The first part of ODC, *The Introductory Rites*, contains two optional addresses that may be given by the bishop to explain the significance of the rites that are to be celebrated. They offer a type of catechesis on the meaning of the rites. The first of these appears only in the first two alternatives for entering the church. In this first admonition the bishop points out that the church will be dedicated by the offering of the sacrifice of Christ within it.[40] The words in this address also go on to state the hope that all those who are celebrating the rite may open their hearts and minds to receive Christ's word with faith. Once they have done this, they are to speak this word in the world and make Christ present in their actions, words, and deeds. Also expressed is the hope that the communion born of the one font of baptism may be sustained at the altar of the Lord and built up to become the one temple of his Spirit.[41] These words serve as a type of catechesis on the whole purpose of the celebration. They point out that the church is dedicated by the celebration of the Eucharist and that it is through the Eucharist itself that the community is built up to become the one temple of the Spirit. The building up of the assembly also depends upon openness to Christ's word. The communion that is

---

39. Ferraro, "Mistero della chiesa," 252.

40. *ODC*, no. 30: 39–40; and no. 38: 43–44. The text states: ". . .we have gathered with joy to dedicate a new church by celebrating the Lord's Sacrifice."

41. *ODC*, no. 30: 39–40; and no. 38: 43–44. The text states: "Let us take part in these sacred rites with loving devotion, listening to the Word of God with faith, so that our community, reborn from the one font of Baptism and nourished at the same table, may grow into a spiritual temple and, brought together at one altar, may advance in the love from on high."

## THE INTRODUCTORY RITES

shared by all the members was born from the one baptismal font that has made them into members of Christ's body. The address points to the Christological nature of the community. It is founded, nourished and comes to completion in Christ alone. The bishop's words and the rites of dedication are intended to focus the community on the entire reason for its existence—the salvation found in Jesus Christ.

The second episcopal admonition that is found in this first part of the rite is directed more specifically to explaining the significance of the rite of the sprinkling of the people and the walls and altar of the church. After asking the people to pray to God to bless the water, the bishop explains to them that it is to be used as a sign of the community's repentance, a reminder of baptism, and as a symbol of the cleansing of the walls and altar of the church.[42] The bishop also expresses the hope that God's grace will help all of the members of the church to remain faithful and open to the Spirit they have received. The text of this admonition offers a catechetical explanation to the people in regard to the significance of the rite of aspersion. Like the rubric related to the sprinkling that has already been examined, the bishop's words speak of the sprinkling as a sign of penance and a reminder of baptism. The text provides an explicit reminder to the people that membership in the liturgical assembly is a gift from God received in the saving waters of baptism. It calls the faithful to share the gift of life they have received through the waters of baptism with others in their local community. The ritual expresses the truth that to continue to live as a faithful member of the church depends on the grace that comes from God.

The initial rites of *ODC* speak about both the parish community's ecclesial nature and its identity as an assembly founded upon Christ and sustained by the Holy Spirit. The gathering of the community, its procession to the new church, and the places that are taken by the members of the assembly in the church reveal that the parish community is part of the larger church and like it is constituted by a hierarchical structure. The relationship of the parish community with the larger diocesan community is also demonstrated in the handing over of the church building to the bishop and the invitation that he extends to the pastor to open the doors of the church. The rite of sprinkling is symbolic of the Christological identity of the community. Individuals are incorporated into this community through baptism into Christ's death and resurrection. By remaining open

---

42. *ODC*, no. 48:48. This portion of the admonition states: "as a sign of repentance and a memorial of Baptism and by which the new walls and altar will be purified."

PART TWO

to the grace that is received through the Holy Spirit in the celebrations that are to take place in the new church, each Christian is to be sustained as a member of the community. The ritual gestures that express these realities do so in a way that associates the church building with them and makes it a symbol of the community's identity.

## *Prayers*

There are two prayers in *The Introductory Rites* that need to be studied in order to understand what they have to contribute to the theology of a parish. These are the prayer for the blessing of the water and the collect for the Mass of dedication.

The prayer for the blessing of the holy water is a new prayer that was written for *ODC*.[43] It also appears in some of the other rites that are

---

43. Although cited in the text earlier, it is given here again for the convenience of the reader:

> O God, through whom every creature
> comes forth into the light of life,
> you accompany all people with such great love
> that not only do you nourish them with fatherly care,
> but you mercifully cleanse them from their sins
> with the dew of charity
> and constantly lead them back to Christ the Head.
>
> For in your merciful plan you established,
> that those who descend as sinners,
> into the sacred waters to die with Christ
> should rise free from guilt
> and be made his members,
> heirs with him to an eternal reward.
>
> Sanctify + therefore with your blessing
> this water you have created,
> that, sprinkled on us
> and on the walls of this church,
> it may be a sign of the cleansing waters of salvation,
> in which we have been washed in Christ
> and made a temple of your Spirit.
>
> Grant that, with all our brothers and sisters
> who will celebrate the divine mysteries in this church,
> we may come at last to the heavenly Jerusalem.
> Through Christ our Lord.
> R/. Amen

See *ODC*, no. 48: 48–49.

found in the *Rites for the Dedication of a Church and an Altar*.[44] The prayer begins by invoking the creator by the name "God" and recalls that God calls every creature to the light and surrounds "us" (humanity) with such great love that even when we stray he leads us back to Christ our head. This portion of the prayer highlights God's desire to lead sinful humanity back to him. Christ is spoken of in Pauline terms as the head.[45] The prayer continues by making an *anamnesis* of the covenant that God has established with humanity. In this covenant, all sinners who descend into the sacred waters of baptism die with Christ and rise with him as members of his body and heirs of his eternal covenant. Through baptism, humanity is created anew and shares in Christ's resurrection. There is an Easter theme to this portion of the prayer that is based upon Rom 6:1–8.[46] The notion of the church as the body of Christ is developed by the recollection that Christians become members of his body through baptism.

The prayer for the blessing of the water goes on to ask God to bless and sanctify the water. This is followed by the request that the water might become a sign of the saving waters of baptism in which the members of the church became one with Christ, the temple of the Spirit. Through baptism the Christian becomes a living member of the temple. The Christian community is the temple of the living God, not the building. The Holy Spirit is the force that animates this temple. Each individual Christian is also a temple of the Spirit through baptism.[47] The final objective that is sought in the prayer is that all those who celebrate the sacred mysteries in the church building may be brought in the end to the heavenly Jerusalem. The hope of the members of the community dedicating the church is that by celebrating the sacraments in their new church they may grow closer to Christ and finally be united with him in heaven. The building is to exist ultimately to lead the local community to its eschatological end.

The first part of *ODC*, *The Introductory Rites*, is concluded with the praying of the collect. This collect was taken from the *Gelasian Vetus* sacramentary and reworked. In the *Gelasian Vetus* it served as the *secreta* from an alternative formula for the dedication of a new basilica. The prayer that is found in the *Gelasian Vetus* reads:

---

44. Calabuig, "*Ordo dedicationis ecclesiae et altaris*," 409–12.
45. See Col 1:18 and Eph 4:15.
46. Calabuig, "*Ordo dedicationis ecclesiae et altaris*," 410.
47. 1 Cor 3:17 and 6:19.

PART TWO

> *Omnipotens sempiterne deus, effunde super hunc locum graciam tuam et omnibus te inuocantibus auxilii tui munus ostende, ut hic sacramentorum uirtus omnium fidelium corda confirmet: per dominum nostrum.*[48]

The collect that is given in the 1977 Latin *editio typica* of the Order of the Dedication of a Church has added the words *"verbi tui"* ("your words") to the petition of the prayer that requests God's strengthening for the hearts of the faithful.[49] The addition of these words serves to emphasize the fact that the Christian people are nourished both by God's Word and the sacraments. The importance of both the Word and the sacraments for the growth of the Christian life was heavily stressed at the Second Vatican Council.[50] The prayer asks that God pour out his grace on the place to be dedicated and extend the gift of his help to all who call upon him. God is asked that the proclamation of his Word and the celebration of the sacraments in the new church might strengthen the hearts of all the faithful. In this prayer the material church is presented as a place singled out by a special divine grace, where the community gathers to pray, hear the Word of God and celebrate the sacraments.[51]

---

48. Mohlberg et al., *Liber sacramentorum romanae*), no. 711:112. The page number follows the colon.

49. *Ordo dedicationis ecclesiae*, no. 52: 40. The prayer in *Ordo dedicationis ecclesiae* reads:

> *Omnipotens sempiterne Deus,*
> *effunde super hunc locum gratiam tuam,*
> *et omnibus te invocantibus auxilii tui munus impende*
> *ut hic* verbi tui *et sacramentorum virtus*
> *omnium fidelium corda confirmet.*
> *Per Dominum.*

Although previously given, for the convenience of the reader, the *collect* prays as follows:
Almighty ever-living God,
pour out your grace upon this place
and extend the gift of your help
to all who call upon you,
that the power of your word and of the Sacraments
may strengthen here the hearts of all the faithful.
Through our Lord Jesus Christ, your Son,
who lives and reigns with you in the unity of the Holy Spirit,
one God, for ever and ever.

ODC, no 52:50.

50. See The Second Vatican Council, *Sacrosanctum concilium*, no 48: 16–17; no. 51:17; and no. 56: 19.

51. Sartore, "Eucaristia nella dedicazione," 2:288.

The building is to be a place where the community will be confirmed in its faith and from which the members of the community will be sent out into the world to share their faith with others in that locality.

The prayer for the blessing of the water recalls God's desire to bestow salvation on humanity and conquer the power of sin through his Son. Christians receive salvation and become part of the body of Christ by dying and rising in the saving waters of baptism. It is for this reason that they become members of the church. The prayer for the blessing of the water asks that the building may be a place where those who celebrate the sacred mysteries may come to be united with Christ in the heavenly Jerusalem. The collect adds the plea that God's grace may be poured out upon the building and all who gather in it. It asks that God's Word and sacraments may keep the members of the community faithful. The parish church is to be that place where Christians in their local communities are redeemed from sin and grafted into Christ's body through baptism. In the parish community they are to be nourished by the Word and the sacraments to live their vocations and, fortified by the Holy Spirit, to continue their journey to the new Jerusalem.

## *Sacred Scripture*

The passages from Sacred Scripture that are found in *The Introductory Rites* are all taken from the Old Testament. A number of these passages are psalms that were sung by the people of Israel when they made their pilgrimage up to Jerusalem to enter the holy temple. The use of these psalms is intended to present an analogy in which the assembly entering the new church is to be understood as God's people making their pilgrimage to the new Jerusalem. Other passages are taken from the enthronement psalms that were used to celebrate the arrival of the ark of the covenant in the tent that had been prepared for it by David. From the psalms that are used for the entrance into the church, an image is created of Christ, who is the true temple, entering the new church to dwell with his people. There are also two passages from Ezekiel found in this section. These point to the saving and life-giving graces that are to be experienced in Christ. These graces will be made available to those who come to encounter Christ in the new church building. As rich as these passages from Scripture are, they can only be examined briefly here.

PART TWO

When the option to have a procession to the new church is chosen, this may be done with the singing of Ps 121 (122). The rite does permit that another suitable hymn may be used. The antiphon that is to accompany the psalm when it is sung, "Let us go rejoicing to the house of the Lord," is itself taken from the first verse of this psalm.[52] This is the song of rejoicing that was sung by the Jewish pilgrims as they were making their way up to Jerusalem and saw the holy city in the distance. The psalm also expresses the joy of the local Christian community as it processes to the new church building that is to stand as an image of the heavenly church.[53] The psalm also serves to create an image of the assembly as being on its pilgrimage towards its ultimate destination, the new and eternal Jerusalem.[54] Entering into the new church building, where they will partake in the Eucharistic banquet, the members of the assembly are reminded that their true home is in heaven. The psalm may also be sung in the second option outside the doors of the church, or in the third option as the ministers process from the sacristy to the sanctuary.[55]

In the first two options for entering the church, after the bishop has asked the priest with pastoral care for the church to open the doors, he invites the people to enter the church. The bishop may do this in his own words, or with the passage that is provided from Ps 122, verse 1–2: "I was glad when they said to me, 'Let us go to the house of the Lord!'"[56] This passage captures the spirit of joy that should animate the assembly as they enter into their new church. Psalm 122 (123) was sung by the Israelite pilgrims as they entered the temple in Jerusalem on solemn religious feasts.[57] The passage affirms the sign value of the church building as an image of the heavenly church, speaking of those going into the church as entering into the courts of God. The pilgrim church will only truly reach the courts of God in the heavenly Jerusalem.

Once the bishop has invited the people to enter the church, which he only does in the first and second options, they may do so while singing Ps 23 (24) with the antiphon that is taken from verse 7 of this psalm. The antiphon proclaims: "Lift up your heads, O gates! And be lifted up,

52. *ODC*, no. 32: 40–41.
53. *ODC*, no. 2: 31.
54. Crichton, *Dedication of a Church*, 28.
55. *ODC*, no. 39: 44; and no. 45: 46.
56. *ODC*, no. 34: 42; and no. 41: 45.
57. Calabuig, "'Ordo dedicationis ecclesiae et altaris,'" 404.

## THE INTRODUCTORY RITES

O ancient doors! That the King of glory may come in."[58] It is also possible that another appropriate hymn may be sung at this time. The king that enters into the church with the community is Christ. He enters the church with his bride, the Christian community. Christ is the head of the assembly and rules over it.[59] Entering into the church following after the crucified Christ, the community proclaims that they have come to enter with their king and head. Verses 1–6 of the psalm were also part of the ritual for the pilgrims arriving in Jerusalem.[60] This gives the entrance procession a sense of God's traveling with his people and being present among them. The psalm also speaks of the purity of heart that is necessary for those who wish to stand in the presence of the Lord.[61] The psalm affirms the dignity of the Christian assembly, which is the body of Christ, as it enters the church joined to Christ the head.

In those cases where the third option for entering the church is used, *ODC* offers the possibility of a second antiphon to accompany the singing of Ps 121 (122) during the entrance procession. This second antiphon reflects more clearly the reality that in this option the assembly has already gathered inside the church building. The antiphon proclaims, "God is in his holy place, God who unites those who dwell in his house: he himself gives might and strength to his people."[62] This is also the first option that appears among the two antiphons given in the Mass of the dedication of a church in *The Roman Missal*.[63] This antiphon is based upon portions of Ps 67 (68) that have been taken from verses 6, 7, and 36. God is spoken of as being both present in his holy dwelling and as being the one who has gathered his people in his house. Those who gather in the church building also hope to be joined to God in his dwelling at the end of their journeys. God will strengthen and console those who have gathered in his house so that they may reach his dwelling and be united with him. This strengthening will come through the proclamation of the Word and the celebration of the sacraments. Through these the assembly

---

58. *ODC*, no. 34: 42; and no. 41: 45.

59. Ferraro, "Aspetti di ecclesiologia nel rito," 196.

60. Calabuig, "'*Ordo dedicationis ecclesiae et altaris*,'" 405.

61. Simons, *Holy People, Holy Place*, 40.

62. *ODC*, no. 45: 46–47.

63. *Roman Missal*. Entrance Antiphon, 1221. Here the revised translation states: "God is in his holy place, God who unites those who dwell in his house; he himself gives might and strength to his people."

will encounter Christ in the new church. The rite also permits that another appropriate song may be sung.

The rite for the sprinkling of the people and the church may be accompanied by the singing of an antiphon from one of the two possible passages from the book of Ezekiel. Both of these passages contain a baptismal character that underlies the source of sacramental life which is depicted as flowing from the life of the ecclesial community which will worship in the new church building.[64] The antiphon for ordinary time is: "I saw water flowing from the temple, from its right-hand side, alleluia; and all to whom this water came were saved and shall say: alleluia, alleluia." This passage, taken from Ezek 47:1–2, 9, makes allusion to the water that flowed from the side of Jesus Christ, the true temple, on the cross.[65] The water and blood that flowed from Christ's side gave God's life and salvation. It is through the baptismal waters that Christians receive eternal life. The sprinkling is to remind the community of this. It is this they are also called to share with those to whom they are sent in their daily lives. The antiphon that is to be used in Lent conveys a similar message. Taken from Ezek 36:25–26 it proclaims: "I will pour clean water over you and wash away all your defilement. A new heart will I give you, says the Lord."[66] This passage also affirms the baptismal aspect to be associated with the sprinkling, while also alluding to the purifying nature of baptism. The Lord will wash away the defilement of his people and give them a new heart. The dedication, in a manner similar to baptism, is to bring about a new community.

The passages from scripture that are found in *The Introductory Rites* of ODC provide a rich complement to the ritual gestures they accompany. The psalms that are used in the procession speak of the pilgrimage that the Christian people make on their way to the heavenly Jerusalem. The church building is a temporal image of the celestial church to which the community is called. The Christian community makes its pilgrimage accompanied by Christ, who strengthens them on their way. The passages from Ezekiel that are found in the rites of sprinkling speak of the new life that the members of the community received in baptism. The community is called to this same life in the rite of dedication. As a community founded in the sacrament of baptism, the members are also to invite others to receive this gift of life through the same sacrament. The

---

64. Calabuig, "'*Ordo dedicationis ecclesiae et altaris*," 410.
65. John 20:34.
66. ODC, no. 49:49.

passages from scripture point to the eschatological destination to which the community is called and the sacramental life that must strengthen its members, and draw others to the community, so that they may reach this destiny.

## *Persons*

In *The Introductory Rites* for the dedication of a church all of the members of the Christian assembly are to gather for the celebration. Ideally, all of the different liturgical functions that make up the liturgical assembly should be present and active for the dedication of the new church. This section will examine the different roles that are played by the different members of the liturgical assembly.

The principle celebrant of the rite of dedication is to be the bishop. The *Introduction* states that the responsibility to dedicate a church belongs to the bishop of the diocese in which the church has been constructed. If the ordinary of the diocese himself cannot dedicate the church, it is appropriate that he should ask another bishop who assists him in the pastoral care of the diocese to dedicate the church.[67] The significance of having the diocesan bishop dedicate the churches in the diocese entrusted to him is to be found in the fact that he is the high priest of the flock that makes up the diocese.[68] The bishop is responsible for the liturgy in his diocese and is the chief dispenser of the mysteries of God.[69] The bishop's role as chief shepherd of the diocese is clearly displayed in the opening rites of ODC. The bishop is the celebrant of the rite and it is he who convokes the assembly and addresses the people in regard to the significance of the rites.[70] As head of the diocese he takes possession of the new church and asks the priest to whom he has entrusted the pastoral care of the church to open the doors.[71] The people are invited to enter the church building by the bishop. As the principle celebrant of the rite he takes the celebrant's chair and presides over the liturgical assembly. The prayers that the assembly presents are addressed to God by the bishop on

---

67. *ODC*, no. 6: 32.

68. The Second Vatican Council, *Sacrosanctum concilium*, no. 41: 14–15. See also Calabuig, "'Rito' per una chiesa che vive," 48.

69. The Second Vatican Council, *Lumen gentium*, no. 26: 381–82; and *Christus Dominus*, no. 15: 571–72.

70. *ODC*, no. 38: 43–44.

71. *ODC*, no. 40: 45.

their behalf.⁷² In the instructions that the bishop gives to the people he is exercising his role as teacher. By taking possession of the church, and inviting the priest entrusted with care for the church to open the doors, he exercises his role of governance. His role as high priest is exercised as he presides over the assembly and offers prayers on their behalf. In the initial rites of *RDC*, the bishop can be seen to be exercising his three roles as priest, prophet, and king.

A large number of priests from the diocese should be present for the dedication of a church. These are to concelebrate the Mass of dedication with the bishop. The place of these priests in the procession and in the sanctuary of the church, testifies to their role as coworkers in the bishop's mission.⁷³ Their common care and solicitude for the diocese is demonstrated by their presence at the dedication of a church for which they do not have direct pastoral care. The specific role of the priest who will have pastoral care of the new church is testified to by the bishop inviting this priest to open the doors to the new church. The parish priest will be the one who opens the door to Christ for the faithful of the parish.⁷⁴ In the absence of the bishop the pastor is the one who must build up the community in Christ through the celebration of the sacraments and preaching of the Word of God.⁷⁵

The rite for the dedication also calls for deacons to be present at the celebration. With the participation of the deacons, all three ordained orders of the church come to participate in the rite. The rite indicates that it is desirable that there should be at least two deacons present. The deacons are not concelebrants but have a role in the rite that is consistent with their functions of assisting the bishop to preach the Word of God, minister to charity and assist at the liturgy.⁷⁶ .Their role of assisting the bishop in the liturgy is demonstrated in the opening rites by the fact that two deacons are to accompany the bishop in the procession and during the sprinkling of the people and the church.⁷⁷ The reestablishment of the permanent deaconate by Pope Paul VI (+1978) also provides for the possibility that the deacons who are assisting at the liturgy may be deacons who have been assigned by the bishop to exercise their ministry in the

---

72. *ODC*, no. 52: 50.
73. The Second Vatican Council, *Presbyterorum ordinis*, no. 2: 864–66.
74. Lara, "Dedicazione della chiesa e dell'altare," 610.
75. The Second Vatican Council, *Christus Dominus*, no. 30: 581–82.
76. The Second Vatican Council, *Lumen gentium*, no. 29: 387.
77. *ODC*, no. 31: 40; and no. 49: 49.

community for which the new church was being dedicated.[78] When there are more than two deacons present, these may assist in carrying the relics or follow the concelebrating priests in the procession.

The dedication of a church is also to be complemented by the presence of those who exercise a liturgical ministry.[79] Following the *motu proprio, Ministeria quaedam,* the ministries of acolyte and lector are to be exercised by the lay faithful.[80] This means that those who fulfill the ministries of lector and acolyte at the celebration will likely be members of the community that is dedicating its new church. Prior to *Ministeria quaedam,* these roles were fulfilled by those in minor orders. This required that the bishop be accompanied by a number of seminarians that would fulfill these roles. Many of these seminarians were probably strangers to the community that was having its church dedicated. *Ministeria quaedam* also indicates that members of the lay faithful may also be appointed temporarily to assist at the liturgy by carrying the missal, the cross or the candles.[81] The need for such assistance at the rite of dedication is called for in the *Ceremonial of Bishops.*[82] A number of cantors are required to sing the different psalms and hymns that are found in these rites. It would be very appropriate that those who exercise these liturgical functions be members of the community dedicating its church.

---

78. Paul VI, *Ad pascendum*, 1:433–40. *Ad pascendum* does not require that the permanent diaconate must be restored in every diocese. It permits the diocesan bishop to determine whether the permanent diaconate may assist the local church that has been entrusted to his care. It is up to the episcopal conference of the region to determine the formation required for those being ordained to the permanent diaconate. This formation must also meet the requirements established by the Holy See and receive its approval.

79. *ODC*, no. 37: 43.

80. Paul VI, *Ministeria quaedam*. Rarely, if ever, does one find a parish where those who exercise the ministries of acolyte and lector are actually men who have been properly instituted by the diocesan bishop. Despite this fact, it is as a result of *Ministeria quaedam* that the minor orders were abolished. Prior to this, these ministers were to be exercised by persons who were in minor orders who were preparing for holy orders. After the promulgation of this *motu proprio,* these roles began more commonly to be fulfilled by generous and capable members of the lay faithful.

81. Paul VI, *Ministeria quaedam*, 427–28.

82. *Ceremonial of Bishops*, no. 882: 239–40. The *Ceremonial* states: "The cross bearer leads the procession, without the usual candle bearers on either side; the ministers follow; then the deacons or presbyters with the relics of the saints, ministers or faithful accompanying them on either side with lighted torches; then the concelebrating presbyters; then the bishop, followed by two deacons; then the ministers who assist with the book and miter; and lastly the faithful."

PART TWO

    As has been made clear in the analysis of the rites and prayers that make up *The Introductory Rites*, the subject and protagonist of these rites is the celebrating assembly. This assembly, which consists of members who fulfill different functions, is made up for the most part of members of the lay faithful. These rites are intended to call and strengthen the members of the celebrating assembly to be what they have been called to be through their baptisms. The liturgical ministries that are exercised in these rites are intended to serve this end and to assist the faithful to intercede to God for the graces they need from him. The rites demonstrate this fact as the pastor opens the door so that the faithful may enter the church. The people are sprinkled by the bishop so that they may be reminded of their dignity as members of the body of Christ redeemed by his death and resurrection. The prayer for the blessing of water speaks of this dignity as it recalls the fact that in baptism the members of the community became one in Christ, who is the temple of the Spirit. Their gratitude for the saving graces that they have received by being incorporated into Christ's body through baptism is to be shown by the manner in which the lay faithful invite others to share this new life in Christ through the sacraments of initiation. The same prayer also requests that all those who celebrate the sacred mysteries in the new church may go on to share in the communion of the heavenly Jerusalem. The collect of the Mass prays that God's Word may be proclaimed and his sacraments celebrated in the new church so that the hearts of the faithful may be confirmed. The prayers that are found in this section also seek to obtain from God the gift of the Holy Spirit, upon whom the faithful are dependent to live the vocations they have received. The rites that make up this opening section are also intended to bestow a sign value upon the church building that will call the faithful to live their baptismal vocations. In the end, the rites and prayers that make up *The Introductory Rites*, and the building that is the object of the celebration, are intended to achieve the objective of bringing God's temple, which is the church, the grace from the Holy Spirit upon which it is dependent to reach its goal—the new and eternal Jerusalem.

    The celebration of the rites that are contained in *The Introductory Rites* ought to lead the members of the parish community that is dedicating its church to understand the place that belongs to them and their community within the mystical body of Christ. They should be led to see that through their baptism they have become members of the one body of the church.[83] This recognition, and the graces of the Holy Spirit that the rite asks from God for them, is to strengthen the members of the community so that they may go out into the world to announce the message of Christ's salvation in their daily lives.[84] In short, through the sacramental celebrations that take place in the dedicated church building, the lay faithful are to be nourished through Word and sacrament in order that they may take Christ to their neighbors as ministers of the New Evangelization. The rites contribute to establishing the church building as a sign that calls the members of the parish to the dignity that belongs to them as living stones in God's temple.

## SUMMARY

The *Introduction* of *ODC* refers to the holy people won by Christ through his death and resurrection as the temple of God built of living stones, where the Father is worshiped in spirit and in truth.[85] The church building is regarded as a visible sign of the pilgrim church on earth that reflects the church dwelling in heaven.[86] The study of *The Introductory Rites* of *ODC* that has taken place in this chapter has illustrated that this holy people, who are the living stones of the temple of God, are the subject and protagonist of these rites. The ritual gestures and prayers that are found here are intended to make of the dedicated church building a sign that speaks to the members of the Christian community about their worth as members of the body of Christ and the place of their community within the universal church.

These rites point to the dignity that belongs to the individual members of the local community through the baptismal imagery that is employed in them. The people are sprinkled with holy water so that they may be reminded of their baptismal calling and as a sign of penance for the times that they have failed to live up to it. The prayer for the blessing of the holy water is to remind them that it was through baptism that they

---

83. Ginami, "Nel Rito Dedicazione," 459.

84. The Second Vatican Council, *Apostolicam actuositatem*, no. 5: 772.

85. *ODC*, no. 1: 31. *ODC* states: "Moreover, this holy people, made one by the unity of the Father, Son, and Holy Spirit, is the Church, that is, the temple of God built of living stones, where the Father is worshiped in spirit and in truth.

86. *ODC*, no. 2: 31. *ODC* states: "Because the church is a visible building, this house is a special sign of the pilgrim Church on earth and an image of the Church dwelling in heaven."

PART TWO

were freed from sin and became members of Christ's body, which is the temple of God's spirit. As the church and altar are sprinkled, the faithful are reminded that they make up one living community gathered around Christ. The rites remind the members of the parish community that it is not mere geography that binds them together, but their communion in the one body of Christ.

The 1983 Code of Canon Law states that as a rule adults are to be baptized in their proper parish church and that children are to be baptized in the proper parish of their parents.[87] Yet, this is not to be taken to mean that they are to be baptized into the parish community. The parish is but that local community of contact through which the individual is incorporated into the universal church of Christ. The initial rites of *ODC* also indicate how the members of the local community are to live out their vocations in relationship to the universal church.

In the initial rites of *ODC* the diocesan bishop is to preside as the high priest of the local church. Through him the local community is linked to the universal church.[88] That the individual community is not to exist as an independent entity is demonstrated by the handing over of the church building to the bishop. The communion that is to be maintained between the bishop and the community will be secured through the priest that the bishop entrusts to care for the community. The priest, who is given care of a community or parish, represents the bishop in his absence and makes the universal church present in the liturgical assemblies of the community.[89] The fact that the bishop calls upon the priest to open the doors of the church for the faithful in the initial rites of *ODC* is an indication of the role of service that the priest is to have in assisting the faithful in their Christian vocations. As the community prepares to dedicate its church, the bishop says:

> Beloved brothers and sisters,
> we have gathered with joy
> to dedicate a new church
> by celebrating the Lord's Sacrifice.
> Let us take part in these sacred rites with loving devotion,

---

87. *Code of Canon Law*, can. 857, § 2. The canon states: "As a rule and unless a just reason suggests otherwise, an adult is to be baptized in his or her proper parish church and an infant in the proper parish church of the parents."

88. The Second Vatican Council, *Lumen gentium*, nn. 23–24: 376–78.

89. See The Second Vatican Council, *Lumen gentium*, no. 28: 384–87; and *Christus Dominus*, no. 30: 581–82.

listening to the Word of God with faith,

so that our community,
reborn from the one font of Baptism
and nourished at the same table,
may grow into a spiritual temple
and, brought together at one altar,
may advance in love from on high[90]

The responsibility for announcing the Word, celebrating the Eucharist and the sacraments, and building the community up in love is the service that the parish priest is called to render to the community. To the baptized members of the community belongs the responsibility of announcing Christ's word and bringing his presence to their homes and workplaces as they play their roles in the church's mission of evangelization.

The heavy emphasis on the baptismal imagery in the *Introductory Rites* is not only intended to remind the faithful of their own baptisms but also to help them record that they are called to be a baptismal community. To each Christian belongs the responsibility of bringing Christ to others. As the building is sprinkled to be a sign, the community is called to remember that each member has the responsibility of inviting others to celebrate the Rites of Christian Initiation and so become part of the body of Christ. Through their baptisms, the faithful are to participate in the evangelization of those to whom they are sent through the course of their daily lives. They also have an important role of welcoming and preparing others who come to their community. The Rites of Sprinkling remind the community that dedicates its church that an essential part of its mission within the local community is to be an evangelizing community which invites others to share in the life Christ gives to all through baptism. The dedicated church building is to stand as a sign that should invite all in the area to consider receiving Christ's gift of life, which is given through baptism.

*The Introductory Rites* of ODC also indicate that Christians are to nourish their vocations within the community by coming to the dedicated church with the entire community to hear the word of God, be fed with Christ's body and blood, celebrate the other sacraments, and grow in Christian fellowship. These rites also orientate the members of the Christian community to the eschatological destination to which they

---

90. *ODC*, no. 30: 39–40; and no. 38:43–44.

are called. Through an openness to the Holy Spirit, they are to live in communion with the church on earth so that they may be brought to full communion with God and the heavenly church at the end of time. This reality will also be emphasized in the sprinkling rites of the funerals of the members of the community which are celebrated in the church building as the departed are entrusted to the church in heaven. The church building on earth, in which Christians receive a foretaste of their heavenly destiny, is an image of the church in heaven. In *The Introductory Rites* of ODC, the sprinkling of the church takes place to purify the church building so that it may worthily represent this image.

All of the rites that have been studied in this section have been concerned to dedicate the church building so that it may be a place where Christians may come to encounter God and be nourished in their faith. The rites of *ODC* are unique in the content that they offer for catechizing the members of the local community about the dignity that belongs to them as members of Christ's body and the place that their local community has within the universal church. *The Introductory Rites* of ODC have a great deal to offer for the construction of a theology of a parish.

# Chapter Four

## Order of the Dedication of a Church: The Liturgy of the Word

### INTRODUCTION

The second section of *ODC* is entitled *The Liturgy of the Word*. In this chapter the rites and readings associated with the liturgy of the word in the reformed 1977 rites will be examined. This investigation will consist of two sections. In the first, the rites and readings of *ODC* are studied. The second section of this chapter provides a summary of these findings and articulates the implications that they have for the construction of that theology of a parish community that is contained in *ODC*.

In order to carry out the inquiry that is proposed in this chapter, it is necessary to turn to other sources. While the rites of *ODC* have been integrated into the celebration of the Mass, not all of the material required to celebrate the dedication of a church is to be found in the text of the ritual itself. The readings that are used in *The Liturgy of the Word* are to be found in the second and third volumes of the revised lectionary. For this reason, it will be necessary to draw upon the lectionary in the first section of this chapter in order to consider the readings that are found in the Common for the Dedication of a Church.

In the second section of this chapter, the rites are analyzed according to the categories of *rites, prayer, sacred scripture* and *persons*.

PART TWO

# THE LITURGY OF THE WORD OF ODC

## The Content of The Liturgy of the Word in ODC

The second part of *ODC*, entitled *The Liturgy of the Word*, begins immediately after the bishop has prayed the collect of the Mass. Once he has done this, he and the members of the assembly are to be seated.[1] The two readers and the psalmist are to come forward and approach the bishop. One of the readers is to carry the lectionary and present it to the bishop. He is to stand and show the lectionary to the people. While he is showing the lectionary to the people, the bishop is to proclaim: "May the word of God resound always in this building, to open for you the mystery of Christ and bring about your salvation within the church."[2] After he has done this, the bishop gives the lectionary to the first reader. The two readers and the psalmist go to the ambo. As they go, the first reader is to proceed "carrying *The Lectionary* for all to see."

When they arrive at the ambo, the first reader is to proclaim the mandatory first reading from the Book of Nehemiah (Neh 81–4a, 5–6, 8–10).[3] This reading from the Old Testament is to be read at all Masses for the dedication of a church, even those that occur in the Easter season. After this, the psalmist is to sing Ps 18 (19):8–9, 10, 15 with the response: "Your words, Lord, are spirit and life." The second reading and the Gospel are to be chosen from the texts indicated in the lectionary. Outside of the Easter season, the lectionary offers four possibilities for the second reading. These are: 1 Cor 3:9b-11, 16–17; Eph 2:19–22; Heb 12:18–19, 22–24; or 1 Pet 2:4–9.[4] During the Easter season it is also possible to take the second reading from Rev 21:1–5a or Rev 21:9b-14, which are also found among the first readings for the Mass on the anniversary of the dedication of a church in the Easter season.[5] The Gospel is to be chosen from

---

1. *Ceremonial of Bishops*, no. 895: 206.
2. *ODC*, no. 53: 51.
3. *ODC*, no. 54: 51.
4. See *Common for the Dedication of a Church*, in *Lectionary of the Roman Missal*, 320–28.
5. See *Common for the Dedication of a Church*, in *Lectionary for the Roman Missal*, 1882. The rubric indicating the possible use of these readings during the Easter Season is found on this page in the *Common for the Dedication of a Church* which lists all of the possible readings. This rubric states: "When three readings are desired, the first reading is chosen from the Old Testament, except in the Easter Season when the first reading is traditionally chosen from the Acts of the Apostles or the Book of Revelation." However, as it is required at the dedication of a church that the first reading always be

among the five texts that are given in the lectionary. These passages are: Matt 16:13–19; Luke 19:1–10; John 2:13–22; John 4:5–10, 19–24; and John 10:22–30. It is the responsibility of the rector of the church that is being dedicated, with the assistance of those who support him in the pastoral work, to decide what readings should be used for the celebration.[6] The Gospel should be read by the deacon, or in the absence of a deacon, by one of the concelebrating priests.[7] Neither candles nor incense are to be used during this first proclamation of the Gospel in the church.[8] All of the members of the assembly are to stand for the proclamation of the Gospel.

Once the Gospel has been proclaimed, the bishop is to give the homily.[9] The *Introduction* indicates that in the homily the bishop should explain the meaning of the readings and the significance of the dedication of the church.[10] When the homily is finished all are to stand for the profession of faith. This concludes *The Liturgy of the Word*. In the Mass for the dedication of a church, the prayers of the faithful are omitted. Their place is taken by the singing of the Litany of the Saints.[11] The third part of the rite, *The Prayer of Dedication and the Anointings*, begins with the singing of the Litany of the Saints.

---

from the Book of Nehemiah, chapter 8—even in the Easter Season—these readings should be considered as possibilities for the second reading during the Easter Season. The selection of readings which occurs in this volume of the lectionary is intended for the celebration of the anniversary of a church's dedication.

6. *ODC*, no. 19: 36. The *Introduction* states: "It is, however, for the rector of the church to be dedicated, helped by those who assist him in the pastoral work, to decide and prepare everything concerning the readings, the singing, and other pastoral aids to foster the fruitful participation of the people and to promote a dignified celebration."

7. See *Ceremonial of Bishops*, no. 22: 23; and no. 140: 54.

8. *ODC*, no. 54: 51 The rubric states: "Neither lights nor incense are carried at the gospel."

9. *ODC*, no. 55: 51.

10. *ODC*, no. 13: 33. The *Introduction* states: "After the readings, the Bishop gives the Homily, in which he explains the biblical readings as well as the meaning of the dedication of a church."

11. *ODC*, no. 56: 51. The rubric states: ". . .and the Creed is sung or said. The Universal Prayer (Prayer of the Faithful or Bidding Prayers), however, is omitted since in its place the litany of the Saints is sung."

PART TWO

## The Analysis of The Liturgy of the Word.

Volumes have been written on the significance and effect of God's word in the liturgy. The analysis presented in this section is restricted to the content of the rites found in *The Liturgy of the Word* in ODC. This material is investigated in order to determine what it can contribute to an understanding of the theology of a parish that is found in ODC. According to the approach that is being used in this study, *The Liturgy of the Word* will be analyzed by the categories of *rites, prayers, sacred scripture,* and *persons*.

By its nature, the material found in *The Liturgy of the Word* has a much greater scriptural content than the other sections of ODC. This is reflected in the investigation that follows. The category of *sacred scripture* is the most significant in this chapter. There are no prayers found in this portion of the rite, meaning that there is no material to be dealt with within the category of *prayers*. The words that the bishop speaks when holding up the lectionary will be investigated in the category of *rites*, as they are intended to explain the significance of this gesture.

### *Rites*

The proclamation and reception of God's word is important in every liturgical celebration, but it is particularly relevant in the dedication of a new church.[12] This is because the Christian community is born of the word, is nourished by it, and grows and develops by means of it.[13] In his word, God communicates himself to his people, reveals his plan of salvation to them, and calls them to respond to him.[14] *Lumen gentium* speaks of the power of the Gospel to constantly call the church to that vitality for which Christ established it.[15] When the scriptures are proclaimed in the liturgy, Christ himself is present to his people speaking to them.[16] When they hear the word of God and reflect upon it, the faithful receive the grace to act upon it in faith, hope and charity and are built up to live the Christian life. It is the Holy Spirit acting in the church that gives the word

---

12. Calabuig, "'*Ordo dedicationis ecclesiae et altaris*,'" 413.
13. Paternoster, "Analisi ritual e contenuti teologici dell'," 607.
14. The Second Vatican Council, *Dei verbum*, no. 6, 752.
15. The Second Vatican Council, *Lumen gentium*, no. 4: 351–52.
16. The Second Vatican Counciul, *Sacrosanctum concilium*, no. 7: 4–5.

its efficacious effect.[17] Through the proclaimed word, the Christian community receives the covenant from God, is renewed in it, and is called to respond to it today.[18] The word of God constitutes the church to be what it is supposed to be and calls it to grow in the likeness of Christ.[19] The liturgy of the word also has a dialogue nature to it. It calls the community to relate to God, to respond to him and entrust its needs to him.

ODC shows an awareness of the importance of the liturgy of the word that is based upon the theology of the word that was developed in the documents of the Second Vatican Council.[20] According to this understanding, "the proclamation of the word in the liturgy is a *kairos*,"[21] a privileged and graced moment when God's saving presence is manifested to his people. This awareness is evidenced by the new and significant rites that are related to the liturgy of the word in ODC. These rites attempt to emphasize the importance of the word that is proclaimed in the assembly, to highlight the place from which the word is proclaimed, and to explain the end that the proclamation of the word seeks to achieve.[22]

The rites that accompany the first reading of God's word in the new church unfold as a sort of dedication of the new ambo.[23] The lectionary is presented to the bishop by members of the community and is held up by him to proclaim the primacy of Christ and his word. As the bishop holds up the book, the gesture proclaims that one of the greatest responsibilities of the community is to announce the word of God. The elevation of the book for all to see is also to indicate that those who hold a teaching office in the church, as well as the other members of the church, are servants of the living word of God.[24] It is the duty of the entire church to make God's

---

17. Mancini, "Spirito Santo costruttore del tempio," 145.

18. *General Instruction of the Lectionary*, in *Lectionary of the Roman Missal. Sundays and Solemnities*, no. 48: xviii–xix. The page number appears after the colon.

19. *General Instruction of the Lectionary*, in *Lectionary of the Roman Missal. Sundays and Solemnities*, no. 45: xviii.

20. Crichton, *Dedication of a Church*, 31.

21. Crichton, *Dedication of a Church*, 31. This is particularly evident in *Sacrosanctum concilium*, no. 7: 4–5. The Constitution states: "He (Christ) is present in his word since it is he himself who speaks when the holy scriptures are read in the Church."

22. Simons, *Holy People, Holy Place*, 41–42.

23. Lara, "Dedicazione della Chiesa e dell'altare," 610.

24. Calabuig, "'Ordo dedicationis ecclesiae et altaris,'" 414. This is in keeping with the teaching of *Dei verbum*, which states: "Yet this Magisterium is not superior to the Word of God, but its servant. It teaches only what has been handed on to it. At the divine command and with the help of the Holy Spirit, it listens to this devotedly, guards it with dedication and expounds it faithfully. All that it proposes for belief as being divinely

word known to all. The fact that the lectionary is first presented to the bishop and is then handed by him to the first reader indicates the role of the bishop in assuring the authenticity of the word that is proclaimed. The word is to be passed on by the successors of the apostles who hand it on to the entire church.[25] From the word that is preached by the bishops, all Christians are to be nourished to carry Christ to the entire world.

The words which the bishop is to say as he holds the lectionary up for the people to see provide a powerful description of the role that the word of God is to have in the community that is dedicating its church. By saying, "May the word of God resound always in the building," the bishop speaks of one of the principle reasons that the church is dedicated and why the community is to gather in that building. It is to be a place where God's word resounds. Because the building is to stand as an image of the living church, it is to signify that the word of God must resound forth in the life and works of the living church.[26] As the body of Christ is to be animated by God's word, so too this word must always ring out in the building that represents Christ's body. The bishop also expresses the purpose that the word is to serve in the community's life as he continues by saying: "to open for you the mystery of Christ and bring about your salvation within the Church." Through it, the mystery of Christ is opened up for the faithful, and they are to come to salvation in and through the church. This expresses the reality that the faithful are fed on Christ's word, that they come to know Jesus through his word, and that it is the responsibility of the church to transmit Christ's saving message to all people. As Christians come to know and experience Christ's salvation in the Eucharist, so too, through his word they encounter him and are transformed by him. It is for this reason that the church has always spoken of the table of the word and the table of the Eucharist. Christ is to be venerated in both of these forms of his presence.[27] The ability of Christ's word to feed and nourish the members of the church is also emphasized in the prayer of dedication.[28] The bishop's proclamation serves to point

---

revealed is drawn from the single deposit of faith." See *Dei verbum*, no. 10: 755–56.

25. The Second Vatican Council, *Dei verbum*, nn. 7–10: 753–56.

26. Falsini, "Dalla Chiesa-comunità alla chiesa-luogo," 57.

27. The Second Vatican Council, *Dei verbum*, no. 21: 762.

28. *ODC*, no. 62: 57. This portion of the prayer of dedication states: "Here may your faithful, gathered around the table of the altar, celebrate the memorial of the Paschal Mystery and be refreshed by the banquet of Christ's Word and his Body." This portion of the prayer of dedication is also based upon *Dei verbum*, no. 21: 762.

out the role that is to be played by God's revealed word in building the local community up into the body of Christ.

After the bishop has expressed the significance of the word that is contained in the lectionary, he hands it to the first reader, and there is a procession to the ambo as the readers and psalmist make their way to it. There is no mention in ODC of a separate Gospel procession that is intended to distinguish the primacy of Christ's presence in the Gospels over the other books of scripture. There are to be no candles or incense used when the Gospel is proclaimed.[29] The subdued nature of the rites that accompany the Gospel have been criticized for failing to show the appropriate signs of reverence toward it and for not distinguishing it from the other readings.[30] The absence of the use of incense and candles during the first proclamation of the Gospel in the church is not consistent with the importance that is attributed to Christ's word in the bishop's proclamation.

The first reading of God's word that takes place from the ambo is regarded by ODC as marking its inauguration.[31] The importance that is attributed to the word of God in the revised liturgy is expressed through the attention that is given to the ambo. No longer is the word to be read merely from the epistle or Gospel side of the Eucharistic altar.[32] The ambo is to stand as a sign in the new church of the importance of announcing God's word. It is to remind the members of the community of their responsibility to proclaim Christ's resurrection in the events of their lives.[33] In order that this sign value may be properly attributed to the ambo, all of the announcements that are made from it should be of a scriptural nature.[34] Its dignity suggests that only a minister of the word should approach it. It is also appropriate that the ambo should be located in a place where the ordained ministers and readers who proclaim God's word from it can be easily seen and heard. The fact that the rites connected to this first proclamation of the word are not to be celebrated in the rite for *The Order of the Dedication of a Church in Which Sacred Celebrations are Already Regularly Taking Place*, indicates that the first proclamation

---

29. ODC, no. 54: 51.

30. Chengalikavil, "Dedicazione della chiesa e dell'altare," 81.

31. See Calabuig, "'Ordo dedicationis ecclesiae et altaris,'" 413; Ferraro, "Mistero della Chiesa nella liturgia," 258; and Simons, Holy People, Holy Place, 41.

32. Simons, Holy People, Holy Place, 34.

33. Donghi, "Liturgia come itinerario educativo," 446.

34. *General Instruction of the Roman Missal* (Third Edition), no. 309.

of the word of God in the church is regarded as the inauguration of the ambo.[35] The rites that are associated with the first reading from scripture in *ODC* are intended to make of the ambo a symbol of the vocation that belongs to each Christian to proclaim Christ's salvation in his or her life.

The structure of the liturgy of the word that is common to every Mass takes on greater significance in the celebration for the dedication of a church. This is particularly true when the dedication of the church marks the beginning of the community's life together as a parish or as an ecclesial entity. As the word is read for the first time, it enters into the community directly, creates it, and sustains it in faith.[36] Through the word, the church receives the Holy Spirit,[37] and believers are enlivened to live their baptismal and chrismal faith.[38] The psalm and its response are an important expression of the assembly's reception of the word and their response to it in faith.[39] Because God is active and present in his word, he touches the hearts of those who hear it and calls them to praise him in song. This they do as they recite the responsorial to the psalm. In the *alleluia* that they are to sing prior to hearing the Gospel, the assembly expresses its joy and confidence that they will hear Christ speaking to them in it.[40]

Through the homily the word is actualized in the midst of a particular people living in a specific time and place.[41] The bishop must explain to the faithful what the scriptures and rites are to mean for them.[42] Within the context of the Mass of dedication, the homily should speak to the people about how the mystery of the church that is expressed in these rites ought to manifest itself in their lives. The homily should call those who are attending the dedication to incarnate in their local community the pilgrim church on earth, of which the building is to stand as a sign.

---

35. See the *Introduction* of *The Order of the Dedication of a Church in Which Sacred Celebrations are Already Taking Place Regularly*, no. 2 d: 74.

36. Mazzarello, "Nuovo rito della dedicazione di una chiesa," 680.

37. Mancini, "Spirito Sancto construttore del tempio," 141.

38. Donghi, "Liturgia come intinerario educativo," 446.

39. Deiss, "*Célébration de la Parole*," 64.

40. Deiss, "*Célébration de la Parole*, 171–74."

41. Chénu, "Homélie, action liturgique de la communauté eucharistique," 27.

42. *ODC*, no. 55: 51. The rubric states: "After the gospel, the Bishop sits and, having received according to custom the mitre and pastoral staff, gives the Homily, in which he explains the biblical readings and the meaning of the rite."

When the homily is concluded, the entire assembly is to stand and recite the creed. By so doing, it expresses the faith that has been communicated to it by the word that was proclaimed in its midst.[43] By this faith, they are united by the Holy Spirit to the entire church. The word leads the assembly to profess its faith and by this faith they are bound to the One, Holy, Catholic, and Apostolic Church that they confess. The voice of Christ, which speaks to the assembly when the scripture is read in their midst, builds the local Christian community up to take its place within the mystical body, the church.

The rites of *The Liturgy of the Word*, which are new to *ODC*, emphasize the importance of God's revealed word in the life of the Christian community. They call the community to recognize that in and through God's word they encounter the mysteries of Christ and are brought to salvation in his church. The Christian community is not founded upon a human doctrine or ideology. Its origins are Divine and it is called to respond to the Divine intervention by which it was established. Only through the grace of the Holy Spirit can the members of the church come to the eschatological destiny to which they are called. Through the word of God, the church, which is the body of Christ, is created, strengthened and sustained, so that it may manifest itself in the liturgical assembly where the scriptures are proclaimed.

## *Prayers*

The principle contents of *The Liturgy of the Word* are the scripture readings that are proclaimed during the celebration of the dedication of a church. While there are a few ritual gestures, accompanied by the bishop's explanatory words, in this portion of *ODC*, there are no prayers. Thus, there is no material to be analyzed in this section. This study moves on to investigate the scripture passages that are found in *The Liturgy of the Word*.

## *Sacred Scripture*

In the Latin *editio typica* of the lectionary, the readings that are to be proclaimed in *The Liturgy of the Word* are to be found in the third volume of the lectionary, entitled *Pro missis de sanctis, ritualibus, ad diversa,*

---

43. *General Instruction of the Lectionary*, no. 29: XVI.

*votivis et defunctorum*. Within the section called *Commune dedicationis ecclesiae*, there are three sections named: 1) *In die dedicationis ecclesiae*; 2) *In dedicatione altaris*; and 3) *In anniversario dedicationis ecclesiae*. The mandatory first reading for the dedication of a church is to be found in *In die dedicationis ecclesiae*. The second reading and the Gospel are to be chosen from among those contained in *In anniversario dedicationis ecclesiae*.[44] In the revised English translation of the Canadian Lectionary, all of the readings that are required on the day of the celebration of a church's dedication can be found together in the revised common for the dedication of a church in the *Lectionary: Ritual Masses, Masses for Various Needs and Occasions, Votive Masses, Masses for the Dead*. Those readings which are used for celebrating the anniversary of the dedication are to be found in another volume of the lectionary entitled, *Lectionary Weekday B: Proper of Seasons—Ordinary Time (Weeks 6–34) Years I and II. Proper of Saints (May 12—December 4)*.[45] As mentioned, ODC indicates that the mandatory first reading and accompanying responsorial psalm are to be Neh 8:1–10 followed by Ps 18 (19):8–9, 10, 15.[46] The rich variety of readings from which the second reading and Gospel may be selected represent the fuller selection from scripture that was called for by the Second Vatican Council.[47] The pastor or rector of the church to be dedicated is to determine which of the readings would best serve the needs of the community. This he is to do with those who assist him in the pastoral care of the church.[48] Clearly, those who gather for the celebration will only hear one of the possible second readings and Gospel texts. It is

---

44. See *Lectionarium*, vol. III: *Pro missis de sanctis, ritualibus, ad diversa, votivis et defunctorum*, 252–54.

45. See footnotes 4 and 5 from this chapter for citations for these lectionary volumes.

46. ODC, no. 54: 51. The rubric states: "The first reading is always taken from the Book of Nehemiah 8:2–4a, 5–6, 8–10, followed by the singing of Psalm 19B, 7, 8 9, 14 (*Lectionary Ritual Masses, Masses for Various Needs and Occasions, Votive Masses, Masses for the Dead, no. 816*) with the response."

47. The Second Vatican Council, *Sacrosanctum concilium*, no. 51: 17. It states: "The treasures of the Bible are to be opened up more lavishly so that a richer fare may be provided for the faithful at the table of God's word. In this way a more representative part of the sacred scriptures will be read to the people in the course of a prescribed number of years."

48. ODC, no. 19: 36. The *Introduction* states: "It is, however, for the rector of the church that is to be dedicated, helped by those who assist him in the pastoral work, to decide and prepare everything concerning the readings, the singing, and other pastoral aids to foster the fruitful participation of the people and to promote a dignified celebration."

important, however, to look at all of the possible readings to understand the complete theological idea that they are intended to communicate. They contain a rich theology of the nature and dignity of the ecclesial community. Their proclamation is intended to prepare the gathered assembly to understand the significance of the ritual action that takes place in the dedication of the church building.

The first reading at the dedication of a new church must always be from Neh 8:1–4a, 5–6, 8–10. This is to be the case even in the Easter season when it is the custom to not read from the Old Testament. The choice of this reading is new to the Roman rite and does not have a precedent in the tradition.[49] It highlights a concern to focus upon the role that is played by God's word in creating the community that lives in a covenant relationship with him. The passage recounts how Ezra first read the Law of Moses from an elevated platform so that all could hear it after they had returned from their exile from Jerusalem in 445 B.C. It recalls how the people recognized God in the reading of his word and how it moved their hearts toward him. By its reading, the people were constituted as God's people and called to transform their lives. Many commentators are in agreement that Judaism was born with the event that is described in Neh 8:1–10.[50] The reading of the law in Nehemiah had the effect of making people aware of their sins and focusing them upon their reliance on God.[51] At the dedication of a new church, Neh 8:1–10 emphasizes the irreplaceable role of God's word in constituting the Christian community. The assembly has been founded as a result of God's incarnated word and it is nurtured and sustained by it. The local community is to exist as a faith community living in response to God's covenant with humanity.

*ODC* indicates that the responsorial psalm for the dedication of a church is to be based upon excerpts taken from Ps 18 (19):8–9, 10, 15.[52] The response to the psalm, which is to be said by the entire community is: "Your words, Lord, are spirit and life." The extracts from Ps 18 (19) and the responsorial provide an excellent complement to the reading from Nehemiah. God's laws and precepts are praised in the psalm for their perfection, trustworthiness and wisdom. They provide guidance and strength to all who follow them. Those who are faithful to God's word experience him as their rock and redeemer. The responsorial psalm is a

---

49. Calabuig, "'*Ordo dedicationis ecclesiae et altaris,*'" 415–16.
50. Crichton, *Dedication of a Church: A Commentary*, 32.
51. Fensham, *Books of Ezra and Nehemiah*, 219–20.
52. *ODC*, no. 54: 51.

PART TWO

reminder to those who are celebrating the dedication of their church that their lives must always be based upon God's teachings if their Christian community is to come to the destiny for which God called it into being.

The lectionary indicates that the second reading is to be chosen from among the four options that are provided. These are: 1) 1 Cor 3:9b-11, 16–17; 2) Eph 2:19–22; 3) Heb 12:18–19, 22–24; and 4) 1 Pet 2:4–9. During the Easter season, the second reading may be chosen from an additional two possibilities that are found among the options for the Easter season. These are: Rev 21:1–5a and Rev 21:9b-14. Each of these readings provide significant material to complement the image of the mystery of the church that is communicated in *ODC*. For this reason, each reading must be given brief attention here.

The text from 1 Cor 3:9b-11, 16–17 communicates that message which is at the heart of the rites of *ODC*. It states that those who make-up the Christian assembly are God's building. Each member is a part of the one temple of God that is animated by the Holy Spirit.[53] The building has this dignity because it is constructed upon Jesus Christ. The assembly, and those who make it up, are holy because they are God's temple. As the *Introduction* states, the church building is to be dedicated so that it may stand as a sign which points to the dignity which belongs to the living church that is God's temple.[54]

Ephesians 2:19–22 presents the same theme of God's people forming a temple that is built up by the Holy Spirit. However, it also points to the universal quality of the membership in this body. It is not restricted only to the Jews. By his death and resurrection Christ has established a universal covenant to save all. There are no longer any aliens. All who belong to the church form one communion with the saints in God's household.[55] This one structure rises upon the foundation of the apostles and prophets. The church is bound together by Jesus Christ, the cornerstone, to be the dwelling place for God in the spirit. The reading addresses the universal dimension of the church's nature. No single community may have an isolated existence. All are part of the household of God, sharing in communion with the saints.

Hebrews 12:18–19, 22–24 draws attention to the radical nature of the new covenant that has been established in Christ's blood. The old covenant with the Jewish people came from Mount Sinai, a mountain

---

53. Grosheide, *Commentary on the First Epistle to the Corinthians*, 84–90.
54. *ODC*, nn. 1–2: 31.
55. Bruce, *Epistles to the Colossians, to Philemon, and to the Ephesians*, 302–7.

## THE LITURGY OF THE WORD

that could not be touched, and was based upon words that were difficult to hear. In the new covenant, based upon the blood of Christ, all are called to live in intimacy with God and to enjoy a status similar to that of a first-born child. Through a spiritual union, Christians share in the heavenly liturgy that is attended by a myriad of angels. Having drawn near to this great celebration, those who have been sprinkled with the blood of the mediator of the new covenant are pilgrims on their way to the heavenly liturgy.[56] The reading points to the eschatological destiny of the members of the local assembly, while also articulating the dignity that belongs to Christians, who have been bought by Christ's blood. It also emphasizes the communion between the church on earth and that in heaven.

The dignity that belongs to the members of the church is also articulated in 1 Pet 2:4–9. Here they are described as living stones that are built as an edifice of the spirit into a royal priesthood that offers spiritual sacrifices that are acceptable to God through Jesus Christ. The building has value and is acceptable to God because it is built upon Jesus Christ, the precious cornerstone. All those who put faith in Christ will be saved and find themselves building upon a firm foundation. Those who reject Christ reject God and his offer of salvation. All who have accepted Christ and become members of his royal priesthood are called to proclaim in their lives the marvelous works of him who called them out of darkness into his light.[57] Membership in his body is to have the effect of transforming each member more and more into the likeness of Christ. Those Christians having their church dedicated are called to understand the dignity that belongs to them as members of Christ's chosen people. As living stones in the one temple, they are called to offer spiritual sacrifices with their lives and witness to his truth in the world. The local community is a part of the one people redeemed by Christ and must proclaim his saving works. It exists so that it might be built up into the one edifice of living stones founded upon Christ. In *ODC*, the dedicated church building is to stand as a sign that points to the church's identity as a structure of living stones built on Christ.

The lectionary provides two additional choices for the second reading in the Easter season. The first of these is from Rev 21:1–5a. This passage presents John's vision of the new heaven and earth coming down to

---

56. Bruce, *Epistle to the Hebrews*, 369–79.
57. Davids, *First Epistle of Peter*, 85–93.

transform the old order. The vision reveals the glorious reality of God dwelling with his people and the new covenant in which the new heaven and earth by far surpass the beauty of the old.[58] A voice proclaims that in this city God will dwell intimately with his people and that there will be no more pain and suffering. The church is presented as a bride prepared to meet her groom. The city represents the eternal felicity of those who follow the Lamb. Revelation 21:1–5a serves to remind the members of the community that is having its church dedicated of their eschatological destiny and of the intimacy they are called to enjoy with God as a result of the new covenant. The communion which Christians are called to enjoy with God is to be found by living within his bride, the church. This is to be experienced by the faithful when they participate in the church's sacramental and liturgical life within their local faith communities. For this reason, the dedicated church building is to stand as an image of the heavenly church.[59]

The church is also presented as the bride of the Lamb in Rev 21:9b–14. The new Jerusalem, which comes down from heaven, is described as a great city with four walls constructed of precious gems. The walls have twelve gates named for the twelve tribes of Israel and twelve courses of stones for its foundation on which are written the names of the twelve apostles of the Lamb. The city that is viewed by John, in the spirit from the top of the mountain, is the eternal city to come at the end of time. Its radiance reflects the purity it enjoys as a result of its communion with the Lamb who has redeemed it.[60] The twelve gates facing in all directions reflect the universality of the church's mission. This mission is based upon the preaching of the apostles and builds upon the old covenant which God had with the twelve tribes of Israel. Like the first reading from Revelation, this one points to the church's eschatological destiny. Salvation for all persons is to be found in the church that Christ has ransomed with his blood. The church itself can only fulfill its mission by basing its efforts on the teaching of the apostles. The traditional twelve anointings of the walls of the church are intended to assimilate the building to the image of the heavenly church. The door of Christ's universal offer of salvation is to be entered by those residing in a certain area through the local Christian

---

58. Mounce, *Book of Revelation*, 368–73.

59. *ODC*, no. 2: 31. The *Introduction* states: "Because the church is a visible building, this house is a special sign of the pilgrim Church on earth and an image of the Church dwelling in heaven."

60. Mounce, *Book of Revelation*, 375–85.

community. Here they will have that experience with Christ that will carry them to the heavenly church.

The Gospel for the Mass of dedication is to be chosen from one of the five that are provided for in the lectionary. These are: 1) Matt 16:13–19; 2) Luke 19:1–10; 3) John 2:13–22; 4) John 4:5–10, 19–24 and 5) John 10:22–30. Due to the importance of their contents, these will also be examined here.

In the Gospel from Matt 16:13–19, Jesus asks his disciples who they say that he is. Peter answers that he is the Messiah, the Son of the living God. Jesus tells Peter that it is the heavenly Father that has revealed this truth to him. He then tells Peter that he is "Rock" and upon this rock he will build his church. Whatever Peter declares bound on earth will also be bound in heaven; whatever he declares loosed on earth will be loosed in heaven. This Gospel articulates the basic truth that Jesus builds his church on the apostles' profession of faith in his divinity.[61] The ability to accept Jesus as divine and profess him as such is a gift of faith that can be granted only by the Father. The church is called to have an entirely Christological identity. It is to be built upon the profession of Christ's divine and human nature and the preaching of the apostles and their successors. The bishops are to succeed the apostles in teaching the sound doctrine of the faith. The teaching of this faith by the bishops establishes each local church in communion with the universal. It is the profession of this apostolic faith that is to unite the church around the world. The individual ecclesial community that is celebrating the dedication of its building must share the faith that is preached by the successors of the apostles. It must not profess some different theology or ideology. That this is a theme to be emphasized in the Gospel is demonstrated by the verse from Matt 16:18 that accompanies the *alleluia*: "You are Peter, and on this rock I will build my Church; the gates of Hades will not prevail against it."

Luke 19:1–10 is the Gospel that was required at the dedication of a church in the *Missale Romanum* of 1570 and 1962. It recounts the story of Zacchaeus the tax collector and his desire to see Jesus. The line of central importance for the dedication of a church in this Gospel is "Today salvation has come to this house." The house represents the church building that is a sign of the living church.[62] The church is brought into

---

61. Mounce, *Matthew*, 159–63.
62. Ferraro, "Aspetti di ecclesiologia nel rito," 200–201.

relationship with Christ's salvation by the fact of his becoming flesh and founding it. Today (*hodie*), salvation comes to humanity and is encountered in Christ's living church. The effects of Christ's saving presence are seen instantly in the changes that take place in Zacchaeus. By his contact with Christ he is immediately changed and saved.[63] He is transformed and begins to share in the spirit of Christ's loving generosity. The story represents a call for all to accept Jesus' salvation today, to repent and become like him. Christ's salvation is to be encountered in his church. As the church building is a sign that represents the living church, all are called to encounter Christ in the liturgical life of the local church which is celebrated in the building. By doing so, they may encounter Christ's salvation in the "*hodie*" ("today") of the here and now of their lives. The intimacy that is to be enjoyed by all who seek Christ in his house is described in the verse for the *alleluia* from Matt 7:8: "In my house, says the Lord, everyone who asks receives, everyone who searches finds, and for everyone who knocks the door will be opened."

There are three possible readings from the Gospel of John. The first of these is from John 2:13–22. This tells the story of Jesus cleansing the temple in Jerusalem as he visits it at Passover. When the Jews ask Jesus for a sign to show that he is authorized to do this, he tells them that if they destroy the temple, he will raise it up in three days. An important line in this Gospel states, "But Jesus was speaking of the temple of his body." Under the old covenant, the Jews were required to encounter God at the temple in Jerusalem. However, as the *Introduction* to ODC indicates, referring to this passage from scripture:

> Through his Death and Resurrection, Christ became the true and perfect temple of the New Covenant and gathered a people to be his own. Moreover, this holy people, made one by the unity of the Father, Son, and Holy Spirit, is the Church, that is, the temple of God built of living stones, where the Father is worshipped in Spirit and in truth.[64]

In the new covenant, God is to be encountered in Christ and his church, which is his body. Living in intimate communion with the Trinitarian God, the church prolongs Christ's presence throughout time and space.[65] The church, joined to Christ its head, is the temple of God. The church

---

63. Geldenhuys, *Commentary on the Gospel of Luke*, 469–72.
64. *ODC*, no. 1: 31.
65. Ferraro, "Aspetti di ecclesiologia nel rito," 208.

## THE LITURGY OF THE WORD

building is dedicated so that it may be a sign of the church's presence in a particular locality. It is to serve to remind all who see it that they are to encounter God in his living and true temple—Christ and his church.

The fact that Christ's body is to replace the temple of the old covenant and to be the place where God is encountered is also enunciated in the verse to accompany the *alleluia*. Taken from God's promise to Solomon after the construction of the first temple, the text from 2 Chr 7:16 states, "I have chosen and consecrated this house, says the Lord, that my name may be there forever."

The second possible Gospel passage from John, that of John 4:5-10, 19-24, contains the amazing story of Jesus and the Samaritan women. There was great hatred between the Jews and Samaritans. Much of this had to do with their disagreement over where God was to be worshiped. The Samaritans were convinced that Joshuah had brought the Ark of the Covenant to Mount Gerizim when the Jews entered the Holy Land. They therefore believed that it was on this mountain, and not Mount Zion as the Jews claimed, that God was to be encountered. As he speaks with the Samaritan women in this passage, Jesus is alluding to the New Covenant that will be established by his death and resurrection. By the sending of the Holy Spirit after his ascension into heaven, people will no longer have to encounter God in one specific place. Nor will this encounter be restricted to any particular gender or people—all will be welcome as members of this new people that make up Christ's body. All those who open their hearts humbly to Christ in faith will encounter him in "spirit and in truth." This means that all who come in faith to the church that is being dedicated will encounter God in spirit and in truth through their faith. Here too, the saving water of baptism is being pre-figured in Christ's offer of a water that will permanently satisfy all thirst. The parish church is that place where most people will encounter the saving waters of baptism and where it is hoped their thirst for God will be satisfied. The samaritan women also gives that first example of the type of witness Christians are called to give after they encounter Christ in the saving waters of baptism. They are to be sent forth from their local church to call others to the good news of salvation. The Gospel acclamation from 2 Chr 7:16 that precedes this passage emphasizes that God will be encountered in Christ's body, the church, as it states: "I have chosen and consecrated this house, so that my name may be there forever."

The third Gospel passage from John (John 10:22-30) deals with another visit by Jesus to the temple in Jerusalem. This option appears only in the Latin *editio typica* of the rite and not in the English language lectionary. In the English lectionary it appears as a possible Gospel for the celebration of the anniversary of the dedication, which is where the Gospels are chosen from in the Latin *editio typica* of the lectionary. This involves Jesus' trip to celebrate the Feast of the Dedication, which celebrated the re-dedication of the temple in 165 B.C. This time, Jesus announces, to those who ask him if he is the Messiah, that all who live in communion with him will receive eternal salvation. Redemption does not come from visiting the old temple but from living in communion with Christ. This salvation is to be encountered in Christ because he and the Father are one. They live in intimate communion.[66] All who follow Christ shall be made members of this communion and shall have eternal life. No longer is the temple God's dwelling place among men. This dwelling place is now to be found in his Son and those who accept him. This is expressed in the *alleluia* verse from Rev 21:3: "Look, God's dwelling place is now among the people, and he will dwell with them." The Gospel articulates the reality that in the new covenant God and eternal salvation are to be encountered in Christ. In the context of the dedication of a church, it is to indicate that the church building is to be a sign that points to the living church in which that saving communion with God is to be experienced by the men and women of today, within their own particular locality.

The passages from scripture that may be proclaimed in *The Liturgy of the Word* in this rite contain a rich catechesis regarding the mystery of the church. They call to mind the fact that the church was established and is sustained by God's word. In the new covenant, this word is contained and revealed in the person of Jesus Christ. The church rises and stands upon the foundation of Jesus Christ, who is the word revealed for the salvation of all. It is because the church is so intimately related to Jesus Christ that it is holy and its members are able to obtain salvation. As the readings state, the church is the temple of God the Father animated by the Holy Spirit. Although composed of many members, these are bound together in the one church by the Holy Spirit to offer worship to the Father through Christ the Lord. Within the church, men and women of every nation live in communion with the Trinitarian God. Through it, God's offer of salvation is brought to all. This offer of salvation is made universal through the teaching of the apostles and their successors. The

---

66. Michaels, *John*, 185–89.

church has an apostolic mission to bring the word of God to all nations and cultures so that the offer of salvation that is revealed in Jesus Christ may be extended to all peoples. Those who accept and embrace this offer are to be made members of Christ's living body through baptism. They are to live in communion with him in the church until they arrive at the end of their earthly pilgrimages at their eschatological destiny. This destiny, as revealed in the eschatological readings contained in this section, is the new and eternal Jerusalem. The texts from Scripture discussed in this section provide material for a deep catechesis into the mystery of the One, Holy, Catholic, and Apostolic Church.

This catechesis is essential in the rites of ODC because through the rites of dedication the church building is to be made into a sign which represents the mystery of the church. The readings, therefore, present a picture of what the community having its church dedicated ought to be as a portion of the body of Christ. The readings proclaim what the church ought to call the community to be within its locality. In the homily that follows these readings, it is appropriate that the parish—or other ecclesial community—that is celebrating these rites should be led to understand what it means for it to manifest the church in its specific place and time.

## *Persons*

*Sacrosanctum concilium* stated that it was through the liturgy that the faithful are able to manifest in their lives the mystery of Christ and the genuine and true nature of the church.[67] In the rites of ODC there is to be found a powerful articulation of the nature of the church. In *The Liturgy of the Word*, the church is presented as the community that is founded upon, sustained and nourished by God's word. The task of authentically transmitting God's word and seeing to its spread throughout the world has been entrusted to the church. The responsibility for seeing that this mission is executed faithfully belongs to the bishops in their role as successors of the apostles.[68] The first duty of the bishop is to preach the

---

67. The Second Vatican Council, *Sacrosanctum concilium*, no. 2: 1–2. The Constitution states: "For it is the liturgy through which, especially in the divine sacrifice of the Eucharist, 'the work of our redemption is accomplished,' and it is through the liturgy, especially, that the faithful are enabled to express in their lives and manifest to others the mystery of Christ and the real nature of the true Church."

68. The Second Vatican Council, *Dei verbum*, nn. 7–10: 753–56. See also *Ad gentes divinitus*, no. 1: 813.

Gospel.[69] It is by the preaching of the word that the people of God are formed into one.[70]

The important role that belongs to the bishop, as a successor of the apostles, in the authentic transmission of the Gospel is evident in both the rites and readings of the *Liturgy of the Word*. Before the word is proclaimed in the church for the first time, it is first presented to the bishop who presides at the "*cathedra*" ("chair").[71] When the bishop receives the lectionary, he holds it up for all to see and declares: "May the word of God resound always in this building, to open for you the mystery of Christ and to bring about your salvation within the Church."[72] He then hands it to the reader who will proclaim the first reading. By this gesture, the bishop announces to the community the authentic purpose of God's word and passes it on to a member of the assembly so that it may be transmitted to all. Given that no church is to be built, or parish established, without the permission of the local bishop,[73] the gesture of passing on the word of God provides a powerful sign of the bishop's role in the community. As is indicated by Neh 8:1–10, the people are formed by this word that is passed on by the bishop. The fact that it is the bishop who has the responsibility for the authentic transmission and interpretation of God's word in the local church is also demonstrated by his giving the first homily in the new church. In this he is to articulate the significance of the word and the rites of *ODC* for the local church. Through his ministry of teaching, sanctifying and governing, the local church is bound to the universal. The office that the bishop exercises in this capacity is one of service for the building up of the body of Christ. This role will be continued in the new community by those priests whom the bishop appoints to exercise his office in his absence.[74]

69. The Second Vatican Council, *Lumen gentium*, no. 25: 379–81.

70. The Second Vatican Council, *Presbyterorum ordinis*, no. 4: 868. The decree states: "The People of God is formed into one in the first place by the Word of the living God, which is quite rightly sought from the mouth of priests."

71. As has already been mentioned, in the Latin *editio typica* the presider's chair is referred to throughout the rite of dedication at which the bishop presides as the "*cathedra*." This is the case in all churches that are dedicated by the bishop, not just a cathedral. In the English translation the word is translated simply as "chair." This diminishes the sense given by the word "*cathedra*" in the Latin *editio typica*. For more on this point see: Calabuig, "'Ordo dedicationis ecclesiae et altaris,'" 406.

72. *ODC*, no. 53: 51.

73. See *Code of Canon Law*, can. 1215 for the role of the diocesan bishop in the construction of new churches and can. 515 for his role in establishing new parishes.

74. The Second Vatican Council, *Lumen gentium*, no. 28: 384–87.

## THE LITURGY OF THE WORD

The importance of the bishops as successors of the apostles for the building up of the church is also spoken of in the readings contained in *The Liturgy of the Word*. The church that Jesus founded is to be built upon the apostolic confession of the faith that was first professed by Peter (Matt 16:13–19). Ephesians 2:19–22 describes the church as the building that rises up on the foundation of the apostles. This theme is also presented in Rev 21:9b-14, where the church is depicted as the city of God, with gates open to the four corners of the world, built upon the foundation of the apostles. Through the diocesan bishop's mission to preach the Gospel and teach the faith, the local church is bound to the universal and built up into the body of Christ. This occurs as the Holy Spirit makes Christ present in the faithful preaching of his word. The church receives Christ himself when it receives his living word. By receiving him in his word, the local church is assimilated into his likeness. As a result of the word that is transmitted to the assembly by the bishop, its members are led to profess their faith in Christ and his church.[75] They are also to become more like Christ.

Under normal circumstances, the rites of *The Liturgy of the Word* do not attribute any special liturgical activities to the members of the presbyterate who are present at the celebration. They should listen to God's word and respond to it with the other members of the assembly. In the absence of a deacon, a priest should read the Gospel. As the liturgy of the dedication of a church serves as a type of stational liturgy, it can be noted that in future Masses to be celebrated in the church, a priest will fulfill essentially the same role as the bishop who presides at this Mass—making him present in his absence.[76] By preaching the word of God, the parish priest collaborates with the bishop so that the faithful may be built up in faith, hope and charity, may grow in Christ, and the Christian community may witness to the charity that the Lord commanded.[77]

By liturgical tradition the responsibility for the biblical readings in the celebration of the Mass is assigned to ministers: to readers and the deacon.[78] These ministries are to be exercised as a service to the community. It belongs to the deacon, when there is one present at Mass, to

---

75. *ODC*, no. 56: 51. The rubric states: "...and the Creed is sung or said. The Universal Prayer (Prayer of the Faithful or Bidding Prayers), however, is omitted, since in its place the Litany of the Saints is sung."

76. The Second Vatican Council, *Lumen gentium*, no. 28: 384–87.

77. The Second Vatican Council, *Christus Dominus*, no. 30: 581–82.

78. *General Instruction of the Lectionary*, no. 49: xix.

read the Gospel and present the general intercessions.[79] He may, with the permission of the celebrant, also give the homily. However, within the context of the rites of *ODC*, the homily is to be given by the bishop.[80] The first and second readings are usually assigned to a member of the lay faithful. As a result of Paul VI's *motu proprio, Ministeria quaedam*, the readings are no longer reserved to those in minor orders.[81] As has already been stated, the document did away with the minor orders. The 1983 Code of Canon Law states that any baptized and confirmed member of the faithful may be called upon to cooperate with bishops and priests by exercising the ministry of the word.[82] These readers may be deputed by the rector or pastor of the church in which they are to exercise their ministry.[83] Because the exercise of the ministry of the word is to serve the building up of the body of Christ, it is important that all who read at Mass be truly qualified to fulfill their duties—both in the spiritual and technical sense.[84] Only those who are capable of proclaiming the word in such a way that it will lead those who hear it to love scripture should exercise this ministry. This is a ministry to be exercised for the benefit of the assembled community—not a personal honor to reward certain members of the faithful.

The proclamation that the bishop makes at the beginning of *The Liturgy of the Word* indicates that the word of God is announced in the church building so that it may unfold for the faithful the mystery of Christ and achieve their salvation in the church.[85] The faithful who make up the assembly are the subjects of the proclamation of the liturgy of the word in *ODC*. As is the case in every liturgy of the word, but in a way that is more obvious in the rites of dedication, the members of the assembly are formed into the people of God by the proclamation of his word.[86] Through the word, men and women are drawn to the faith, they are led

---

79. *General Instruction of the Roman Missal*, no. 94.

80. *ODC*, no. 55: 51. It should also be noted that the Code of Canon Law states that only a bishop, priest or deacon may give the homily at Mass. See *Code of Canon Law*, can. 767 §1.

81. Paul VI, *Ministeria quaedam*, 427–32.

82. *Code of Canon Law*, can. 759.

83. *General Instruction of the Roman Missal*, no. 99.

84. *General Instruction of the Lectionary*, no. 55: xix–xx.

85. *ODC*, no. 53:51. The bishop is to say: "May the word of God resound always in this building, to open for you the mystery of Christ and to bring about your salvation in the Church."

86. The Second Vatican Council, *Presbyterorum ordinis*, no. 4: 868–70. See also Calabuig, "'*Ordo dedicationis ecclesiae et altaris*,'" 413.

## THE LITURGY OF THE WORD

to baptism and are prepared to receive Christ's body and blood. They are brought to maturity through the word and prepared by it for salvation.[87] In the liturgy of the word, the congregation still receives today the covenant through the faith that comes from hearing.[88] In the context of the liturgy, the assembly responds ritually to the covenant that God offers by praising him in the responsorial psalm and by professing their faith in common. When the word is heard, the faithful receive the Holy Spirit and are drawn to the mystery of Christ. By being placed in relationship to Christ, they are transformed and receive the grace and charity that are necessary to manifest him to the world. Through the word, the faithful are also placed in relationship with the Trinitarian God and are made aware of their eschatological destiny. In the word is contained God's offer of salvation for all who act upon it with faith and charity.

The readings that may be used in *ODC* are of particular importance to the faithful who are celebrating the dedication of their church because they speak to them of the dignity that belongs to them as members of the church. These scripture texts articulate the nature of the intimate relationship that exists between the members of the church and Jesus Christ the Son, the Holy Spirit, and God the Father. The assembly is the temple of God where the Holy Spirit dwells (1 Cor 3:9–16). Each member is a living stone in God's temple, called to offer spiritual sacrifice to the Father through Christ (1 Pet 2:4–9). No individual has done anything to merit this gift. As in the case of Christ's coming to Zacchaeus (Luke 19:1–10), salvation has come to each and everyone who receives the word as a result of God's unlimited generosity. The only way to respond to such a gift is by responding in kind with love and charity. This good news must be shared with others, so that they too may come to the salvation announced by Christ. The word is to be carried to the four corners of the world by the faithful, so that the city of God may be open to all peoples. In the new covenant which he establishes, Christ wishes to bring all people to dwell in intimate communion with the Father in the new and eternal Jerusalem. All who hear the word are called to receive the Holy Spirit that they may be strengthened to come to this salvation. The faithful are to be the subjects of the liturgy of the word so that they might know God's salvation.

---

87. The Second Vatican Council, *Lumen gentium*, no. 17: 368–69.
88. See *General Instruction of the Lectionary*, no. 45: xviii.

PART TWO

The people who hear the word proclaimed are also to be aware of the responsibilities that belong to those who make up the church. The readings speak of the mystery of the church in which people are to be saved. As was the case with Zacchaeus, the word must produce a faith that gives yield to charity. The people of God are a holy people and a royal priesthood who are called to bear witness to the marvelous works of God (1 Pet 2:4–9). They posses a prophetic calling to spread the word to the entire world through their temporal and secular endeavors.[89] They are to offer their lives as a spiritual sacrifice to God by bearing witness to Christ and by sharing in his priesthood.[90] The call to sanctity is addressed to all who hear the word, that they too may come at the end of their journeys to share in the kingdom of God with all the saints. Ultimately, the word that is addressed to all has an eschatological end.

The readings that are proclaimed in the rites of *ODC* have great significance for the community that is dedicating its church. They proclaim the divine origins of the community and the dignity that belongs to the members of the assembly as a result of God's loving intervention in the world. They situate the faithful and their community within the body of Christ's living church. The assembly is to be led to see itself as a living portion of the one temple of God that is animated by the Holy Spirit and offers true worship to the Father through Jesus Christ. The readings call the parish community that is dedicating its church building to actualize the word within its own particular context and situation. How this is to be done is to be the subject of the homily. The parish should bring to realization the word that is proclaimed within it, by bringing it to bear on the problems and challenges of the daily lives of its members.[91] From the parish, the word of God is to be announced in that corner of the world in which its members live.[92] Through the parish community, the mystery of the church, which is the subject of the readings found in *ODC*, is to be manifested in a particular locality.

---

89. The Second Vatican Council, *Lumen gentium*, nn. 34–35: 391–93.
90. The Second Vatican Council, *Lumen gentium*, no. 10: 360–61.
91. The Second Vatican Council, *Apostolicam actuositatem*, no. 10: 777–78.
92. The Second Vatican Council, *Ad gentes divinitus*, no. 37: 850–51.

THE LITURGY OF THE WORD

## SUMMARY

As has become apparent throughout this chapter, the subject matter of the rites and readings found in *The Liturgy of the Word* of ODC is the ecclesial community that meets within the church building. This community is the temple of God, built of living stones, where the Father is to be worshiped in spirit and truth.[93] It was founded by Jesus Christ as a result of the New Covenant that he established by his death and resurrection. Animated by the Holy Spirit, it is the body of Christ present in the world today, announcing the good news of salvation to all. In and through this community, men and women hear the word of God announced in their midst and are brought to the eschatological destiny that the Father has prepared for those who accept his Son—the Word made flesh. The church building is to stand as a sign of the mystery of the church in which God's salvation is to be found and as a symbol of the eternal Jerusalem to which all are called. The rites and readings of *The Liturgy of the Word* speak to the nature of the mystery of the church that is expressed in the church building. In doing so, they articulate the theology by which the community having its building dedicated ought to define itself. For the parish community that is dedicating its church, they annunciate how it is to cooperate with the Holy Spirit so that the body of Christ may be manifested within its particular location.

*The Liturgy of the Word* communicates the role that God's word must play within each and every community in the church. As the universal church itself was founded upon the Word Incarnate revealed by the Father, so too each individual Christian community, parish or otherwise, must be founded upon and nurtured by God's word. The parish community must be constituted by this word and strive to actualize it. Through the word it has access to the Holy Spirit and is bound to the body of Christ. The parish must serve this word alone and cannot give itself to the service of political agendas or human ideologies. It cannot develop and grow around the popularity of some local figure. As the bishop's words indicate when he presents the lectionary, it is through Christ's word that the mystery of Christ is revealed and those who make up the church are to come to salvation.[94] The reading from Nehemiah is intended to emphasize that it is through God's word that those who gather in the building are made a part of the New Covenant people established by

---

93. *ODC*, no. 1: 31.
94. *ODC*, no. 53: 51.

Christ. It is also through this word that the community is nurtured and new members are drawn to it. The parish community must be rooted in the word of God if it is to manifest the body of Christ within its locality.

*ODC* also makes it clear that the transmission of the word of God is an ecclesial endeavor. The word must be received in and through the church. As the readings indicate, Christ established the church upon the testimony of the apostles. Strengthened by the Holy Spirit, these men carried it to the four corners of the earth that it might ring out among all nations. It is through the bishops of the church, the successors of the apostles, that the authentic transmission of this word is to be assured.[95] This is demonstrated by the fact that the word is presented by the bishop to the community as it meets for the first time in the church, it is handed on by him to those who will proclaim it, and it is he who interprets it in the homily that follows. He is to ensure that the community remains in communion with the church by guaranteeing that the word is always authentically proclaimed and preached there. In the subsequent celebrations of the Mass, the bishop fulfills his mission through the cooperation of those ordained ministers who will act on his behalf.[96] The priests and deacons who serve in the parish community are to act in service to the word, so that it may be carried to all and the body of Christ may be built up in love.

*The Liturgy of the Word* also emphasizes that the transmission of the word is not a responsibility that belongs to only the ordained members of the church. Each and every member is dependent upon the word for his or her life within the body of Christ. By it they are led to embrace the baptism by which they are incorporated into the church. Through it they are nourished and their hearts are open so that they may receive the Holy Spirit and be nourished with Christ's body and blood. Active participation in the liturgy is to be the means by which they are to have the mystery of Christ revealed to them and through which they are to achieve salvation within the church. The faithful are here built up into the body of Christ, and strengthened in their own lives to carry Christ's light to all the nations of the world.[97] That this dignity and responsibility

---

95. See The Second Vatican Council, *Dei verbum*, nn. 7–10: 753–56.

96. *Code of Canon Law*, can. 756 and can. 757.

97. The Second Vatican Council, *Sacrosanctum concilium*, no. 2: 1–2. The Constitution states: "The liturgy daily builds up those who are in the Church, making of them a holy temple of the Lord, a dwelling-place for God in the Spirit, to the mature measure of the fullness of Christ. At the same time it marvellously increases their power to preach Christ and thus show forth the Church, a sign lifted among the nations, to those who are outside, a sign under which the scattered children of God may be gathered

## THE LITURGY OF THE WORD

belongs to the laity is communicated by the bishop's act of entrusting the lectionary to lay members of the assembly so that it may be proclaimed by them. The readings also articulate this fact by reminding all Christians that they are living stones in God's temple who are called to offer sacrifices to the Father and proclaim his good works in their lives (1 Pet 2:4–9). The recitation of the creed that is made by all of the faithful testifies to the fact that it is through the word that they receive the Holy Spirit and are built up to profess the church's faith. It is their prophetic vocation to preach and witness to this word in every area of their lives.[98] When the members of the parish community do this, the parish is able to be that organ of the body of Christ by which God's word is carried to all the nations. In this regard, the Vatican Council's Decree on the Missionary Activity of the Church has stated: "Since the people of God live in communities especially in dioceses and parishes by means of which, in a certain sense, they become manifest, it belongs to such communities to bear witness to Christ before the nations."[99]

The rites and readings of *The Liturgy of the Word* serve to call the parish community to recognize its identity. From it, the word of God is to ring out to the world so that the mysteries of Christ may be revealed and all people may be brought to salvation in the church. The parish community must manifest within its particular locality the living body of Christ from which the word of God is announced. Within it is to be experienced the temple of God built of living stones, where the Father is worshiped in spirit and truth.[100] As a result of this encounter, men and women are to be brought to the heavenly liturgy, where they will praise the Father for all eternity.

---

together until there is one fold and one shepherd."
  98. The Second Vatican Council, *Lumen gentium*, nn. 34–35: 391–93.
  99. The Second Vatican Council, *Ad gentes divinitus*, no. 37: 850–51.
  100. *ODC*, no. 1: 31.

# Chapter Five

## Order of the Dedication of a Church: The Prayer of Dedication and the Anointings

### INTRODUCTION

In the rites of *ODC*, the church building is dedicated through the celebration of the Eucharist.[1] Despite this fact, the rites in the third section of this ritual, entitled *The Prayer of Dedication and the Anointings*, contain the richest theological exposition regarding the significance of the dedication of a church that can be found in the ritual. In this chapter, these explanatory rites are investigated in order to determine what they have to offer towards the construction of a theology of the parish.

As has been the case in previous chapters, the first aspect of this inquiry is a study of the rites from *ODC*. To begin with, a complete description of the ritual schema of *The Prayer of Dedication and the Anointings* is presented. This is followed by an analysis of these rites according to the categories of *rites*, *prayers*, *sacred scripture*, and *persons*. This chapter concludes with a summary of the results of this investigation.

---

1. *ODC*, no. 8: 32–33; and no. 17: 35.

# THE RITES OF THE PRAYER OF DEDICATION AND THE ANOINTINGS IN ODC

## The Content of the Rites of The Prayer of Dedication and the Anointings in ODC

The third part of *ODC* is entitled *The Prayer of Dedication and the Anointings*. The rites that are found here have been divided into six subsections. These are: 1) *The Litany of the Saints*; 2) *The Depositing of the Relics*; 3) *The Prayer of Dedication*; 4) *The Anointing of the Altar and the Walls of the Church*; 5) *The Incensation of the Altar and the Church*; and 6) *The Lighting of the Altar and the Church*.

### *The Prayer of Supplication*

The rites that are found in the third section of *ODC* begin after the assembly has recited the creed. They commence with the singing of the litany of the saints, which takes the place of the general intercessions. The bishop addresses the people, who remain standing after the creed, in these or similar words:

> Dearly beloved, let us pray to God the almighty Father, who makes the hearts of the faithful into spiritual temples for himself, and may the supplications of the Saints, our brothers and sisters, be joined with our voices.[2]

After the bishop has invited the people to pray, the deacon asks them to kneel. On Sundays and during the Easter season he does not do this, as the people remain standing on these days. The cantors then begin the litany, adding at the proper places the names of such saints as the titular of the church, the patron of the place, and the saints whose relics are to be deposited beneath the altar. The version of the litany that is to be sung is given in chapter eight of the ritual.[3] It contains minor changes that are to facilitate its use during the celebration of the dedication of a church. The intercession "Consecrate this church for your worship" has been added for these occasions.[4] In the previous rites of 1595 and 1962, a petition

---

2. *ODC*, no. 57: 52.
3. *Litany of the Saints*, *ODC*, 59:52–54.
4. *Litany of the Saints*, *ODC*, 59: 54.

PART TWO

similar to this was repeated three times and expanded upon each time.[5] When the litany has been concluded, the bishop stands and prays with hands extended:

> Mercifully accept our petitions,
> We pray, O Lord,
> through the intercession of the Blessed Virgin Mary
> and all the Saints,
> so that this building to be dedicated to your name
> may be a house of salvation and grace
> where the Christian people, gathering as one,
> will worship you in spirit and in truth
> and be built up in charity.
>
> Grant this through Christ our Lord.[6]

When the dedication does not take place on a Sunday or during the Easter season, the deacon invites the people who have been kneeling to stand. The relics are then to be deposited beneath the altar. If there are no relics of the saints, the bishop says the prayer of dedication after the litany.

## *The Depositing of the Relics*

It will be recalled from the discussion of the *Introduction* that the placing of the relics beneath the altar are not required in the rites of ODC. This traditional element of the Roman rite of dedication is to be preserved only if the conditions set forth in the *Introduction* can be observed.[7] In

---

5. *Pontificale Romanum*, editio princeps (1595–1596), no. 530: 317; and *Pontificale Romanum. Reimpressio editionis iuxta typicam anno 1962 publici iuris factae, partibus praecedentis editionis ab illa omissis, introductione et tabulis aucta*, study edition with notes prepared by Anthony Ward and Cuthbert Johnson (Rome: C.V.L. Edizioni Liturgiche, 1999) no. 445: 133. In both of these references the page number appears after the colon and the paragraph number is before the colon.

6. ODC, no. 60: 54.

7. The *Introduction* states:
"a) Relics for deposition should be of such a size that they can be recognized as parts of human bodies. Hence, enclosing excessively small relics of one or several Saints is to be avoided.
b) The greatest care must be taken to determine whether relics intended for deposition are authentic. It is better for an altar to be dedicated without relics than to have relics of doubtful authenticity deposited under it.
c) A reliquary must not be placed on the altar or on the table of the altar but under the table of the altar, in a manner suitable to the design of the altar."
See ODC, no. 5: 32.

those cases where the relics of the martyrs or saints are to be placed under the altar, the bishop approaches the altar after the litany. A deacon or a priest brings the relics from the location in the sanctuary where they had been placed after the entrance procession and gives them to the bishop. He rests them in the aperture beneath the altar that has been prepared for them. While this takes place, Ps 14 (15) is sung with one of the two antiphons that are supplied. The first antiphon says, "Beneath the altar of God you have been placed, O Saints of God: intercede for us before the Lord Jesus Christ." The second possible antiphon is: "The bodies of the Saints are buried in peace, and their names will live for all eternity (E. T. Alleluia)."[8] Another appropriate song may be sung to accompany the depositing of the relics. A stonemason seals the relics into the enclosure and the bishop returns to the chair (or as is it referred to in the Latin *edition typica*, the *"cathedra."*).

## *The Prayer of Dedication*

After the relics have been deposited under the altar—or after the litany of the saints in those cases where there are no relics to place under the altar—the bishop says the prayer of dedication. This prayer is a new composition for the rite of dedication. Although the celebration of the Eucharist is the most essential and only necessary aspect of the rite of dedication, in accordance with the tradition of the church in both the East and West, the prayer of dedication remains an important element in the rite of ODC.[9] The bishop offers it, as he stands without the miter, either at the chair (*"cathedra"*) or near the altar. The whole prayer is quoted here:

> O God, sanctifier and ruler of your Church,
> it is right for us to celebrate your name
> in joyful proclamation;
> for today your faithful people desire
> to dedicate to you,
> solemnly and for all time,
> this house of prayer,
> where they worship you devoutly,
> are instructed by the word,
> and are nourished by the Sacraments.

---

8. *ODC*, no. 61: 55.
9. *ODC*, no. 15: 34.

PART TWO

This house brings to light the mystery of the Church,
which Christ made holy by the shedding of his blood,
so that he might present her to himself
as a glorious Bride,
a Virgin resplendent with the integrity of faith,
a Mother made fruitful by the power of the Spirit.

Holy is the Church
the chosen vine of the Lord,
whose branches fill the whole world,
and whose tendrils, borne on the wood of the Cross,
reach upward to the Kingdom of Heaven.

Blessed is the Church,
God's dwelling-place with the human race,
a holy temple built of living stones,
standing upon the foundation of the Apostles
with Christ Jesus its chief cornerstone.

Exalted is the Church
a City set high on a mountain for all to see,
resplendent to every eye
with the unfading light of the Lamb,
and resounding with the sweet hymn of the Saints.

Therefore, O Lord, we beseech you:
graciously pour forth from heaven your sanctifying power
upon this church and upon this altar,
to make this for ever a holy place
with a table always prepared for the Sacrifice of Christ.

.Here may the flood of divine grace
overwhelm human offences,
so that your children, Father,
being dead to sin,
may be reborn to heavenly life.

Here may your faithful,
gathered around the table of the altar,
celebrate the memorial of the Paschal Mystery
and be refreshed by the banquet
of Christ's Word and his Body.

Here may the joyful offering of praise resound,
with human voices joined to the song of the Angels,
and unceasing prayer rise up to you
for the salvation of the world.

Here may the poor find mercy,
The oppressed attain true freedom,
And all people be clothed with the dignity of your children,
Until they come exultant
to the Jerusalem which is above.

Through our Lord Jesus Christ, your Son,
who lives and reigns with you and the Holy Spirit,
one God, for ever and ever.[10]

## *The Anointing of the Altar and the Walls of the Church*

The anointing of the altar and the walls of the church follow the prayer of dedication. This ritual gesture, along with the incensing of the altar and church and the lighting of the same, are explanatory rites composed in the same manner. For each, the bishop offers a formula aloud and follows this by carrying out the liturgical action, which is accompanied by the singing of a biblical hymn or a psalm.[11] The rites of anointing have been associated with the dedication of a church.[12]

When it is time for the anointing, the bishop may remove the chasuble and put on a linen gremial. He approaches the altar with the deacons and other ministers, one of whom is to carry the chrism. From the altar, the bishop is to say:

---

10. *ODC*, no. 62: 56–57.

11. Calabuig, "L' '*Ordo dedicationis ecclesiae et altaris*': Appunti di una lettura," 430.

12. The rites for the anointing of the altar in the dedication of a church are witnessed to in the Western Church in the early sixth century. The Council of Adge decreed in 506 that altars must be consecrated not only by anointing them with chrism, but also with a sacerdotal blessing. Canon 14 of this Council stated: "*Altaria uero placuit non solum unctione chrismatis sed etiam sacerdotali benedictione sacrari*" (Not only with the anointing with chrism, but also with priestly blessing). See *Concilium Agathense*, canon 14: 200.

In 517, the Council of Epoana stipulated that only those altars that were made of stone could be anointed. Canon 26 of this Council stated: "*Altaria nisi lapedea crismatis unctione non sacrentur*" (Altars that are not made of stone should not be made sacred with anointing of the oil of chrism). See *Concilium Epaonense*, canon, 30.

See also Braun, *Der Christliche Altar in seiner geschichtlichen Entwicklung*, 670–74.

> May the Lord by his power
> sanctify this altar and this house,
> which by our ministry we anoint,
> so that as visible signs
> they may express the mystery of Christ and the Church.[13]

After this he is to pour the sacred chrism on the middle of the altar and on each of the four corners of the altar. It is recommended that he anoint the whole altar with this.[14] When the altar has been anointed, the walls of the church are to be anointed. *ODC* provides a number of options for the anointing of the walls. This may be done in either twelve or four places. The first option, which is in keeping with the tradition, calls for the walls to be anointed on the twelve crosses that have been distributed around the church.[15] The second possibility found in *ODC*, which might be more suitable to a small church, is that the walls are anointed in only four places.

*ODC* also provides for the alternative that the walls may be anointed by some of the priests who are assisting the bishop at the celebration. In this case, after the altar has been anointed, the bishop hands vessels of chrism to the priests who will be assisting him and they then go to anoint the walls. The rite suggests that he may have the assistance of two or four priests for this purpose.[16] It would be very appropriate that some of those who assist in this be from among the priests who will have pastoral care for the parish or the community. It is up to the discretion of the bishop to determine whether he wishes to be assisted by members of the presbyterate for the anointing of the walls. He may decide to anoint the walls in twelve or four places on his own. While these ritual gestures take place,

---

13. *ODC*, no. 64: 58.

14. In the two rites of dedication immediately prior to the 1977 ritual, that of the *Pontifcal Romanum* of 1595 and that of 1961, the bishop was to anoint the altar in the form of five crosses, one in the centre and one on each of the four corners. In *ODC* it is recommended that the entire altar be anointed. This represents a return to an earlier practice that was found in the Romano-Germanic Pontifical of the tenth century. The rubric for the anointing of the altar found in *Ordo ad benedicendam ecclesiam* stated: "*Et unguat manu sua totum illud altare de oleo sancto semper incensum in circuitu ipsius altaris alio sacerdote ferente*" (He is to anoint with his own hand the whole altar with holy oil while another priest is always circling and incensing the altar). See *Ordo ad benedicendam ecclesiam*, in *Le Pontifcal romano-germanique du dixième siècle*, vol. 1, ord. XL, no. 53: 144. The page number follows the colon.

15. The practice of anointing the twelve crosses on the walls of the Church goes back to the end of the eighth century in *Ordo XLI*, no. 1, page 339; and no. 26: 345.

16. *ODC*, no. 64: 380.

Ps 83 (84) is sung with one of the two possible antiphons that are provided. The first is: "Behold God's dwelling with the human race. He will live with them and they will be his people, and God himself with them will be their God (E. T. Alleluia)." The second antiphon that is given is: "Holy is the temple of the Lord, God's own structure, God's own building."[17] Another appropriate hymn may be sung in place of the psalm. Once the altar and walls of the church have been anointed, the bishop returns to the chair ("*cathedra*" as the *editio typica* states), sits and washes his hands. He then takes off the gremial and puts the chasuble back on. The priests who assisted with the anointing also wash their hands.

## *The Incensation of the Altar and the Church*

After the rite of anointing, a brazier is to be placed on the altar for the burning of incense and aromatic gums. The possibility also exists that instead of a brazier, a heap of incense mixed with tapers and small candles may be placed upon the altar. The bishop either places incense in the brazier or lights the heap of incense with a small candle that is handed to him by another minister. He then says:

> Let our prayer rise, O Lord,
> like incense in your sight;
> and as this house is filled with a pleasing fragrance,
> so let your Church be fragrant with the aroma of Christ.[18]

Having completed this, he puts incense into several censers and proceeds to incense the altar. Once he has incensed the altar, the bishop returns to the chair ("*cathedra*" in the Latin *editio typica*), is incensed by another minister, and is then seated. A number of other ministers then walk through the church incensing the people and the walls of the church. While the altar and the church are being incensed, Ps 138 (137) is sung with one of the two antiphons that are supplied. The first antiphon that is given states, "An angel stood by the altar of the Temple, holding in his hand a golden censer." The second antiphon is "In the presence of the Lord arose clouds of incense from the hand of the Angel."[19] Another appropriate hymn may be sung.

---

17. *ODC*, no. 64: 58–59.
18. *ODC*, no. 66: 60.
19. *ODC*, no. 68: 60–61.

PART TWO

## *The Lighting of the Altar and the Church*

When the incensing of the church has been completed, a few ministers approach the altar and wipe the table (*"mensa"*) with cloths. If it is necessary, they should cover the altar with an impermeable cloth. Having done this, they cover the altar with an altar cloth and, if it seems opportune, they may decorate it with flowers. They then arrange the candles for the celebration of the Mass and, if there is need, the cross. A deacon approaches the bishop, who stands, and hands a small lighted candle to him. The bishop declares to the assembly: "Let the light of Christ shine brightly in the Church, that all nations may attain the fullness of truth."[20] The bishop is then seated and the deacon goes to the altar and lights the candles for the celebration of the Eucharist. The "festive" illumination of the entire church is then to take place as all the candles in the church are lit, including those that mark the spots where the walls were anointed. Even the rubric expresses the joy that is associated with the illumination of the church.[21] While the candles are being lit, the Canticle of Tobias is sung with the antiphon, "Your light has come, Jerusalem: the glory of the Lord has risen upon you, and the nations will walk in your light, alleluia." During Lent the antiphon is "Jerusalem, city of God, you will shine with splendid light; and all the ends of the earth will pay you homage." The rubrics also permit that another hymn may be sung, stipulating that it would be appropriate for it to be one that honors Christ as the light of the world.[22] This concludes the third part of the rite. It is followed by the celebration of the Eucharist.

## The Analysis of The Prayer of Dedication and the Anointings

This section is concerned to present an analysis of the content found in *The Prayer of Dedication and the Anointings* in order to determine what these rites have to contribute to the development of the theology of a parish contained in ODC. These rites are studied here according to the categories of *rites, prayers, sacred scripture,* and *persons*. The admonitions that the bishop addresses to the people will be investigated in this chapter in relation to the prayer or rite that they are intended to introduce. The

---

20. *ODC*, no. 70: 61.

21. *ODC*, no. 71: 61. The rubric states: "Then the festive lighting takes place: all the candles, including those at the places where the anointings were made, and the church's other lamps are lit as a sign of rejoicing."

22. *ODC*, no. 71: 61.

words of invitation spoken by the bishop prior to the litany of the saints will be discussed in relationship to the litany under the category of *prayers*.

## Rites

There are four sets of ritual gestures in *The Prayer of Dedication and the Anointings* that need to be investigated. These activities are the depositing of the relics, the anointing of the altar and walls of the church, the incensation of the altar and church, and the lighting of the altar and church. These four aspects will be analyzed separately.

The Second Vatican Council spoke of the importance of the tradition of venerating the relics of the saints.[23] In *ODC*, the practice of placing these beneath the altar has become conditional on the possibility of obtaining relics that are large enough to be recognized as parts of the human body.[24] Despite this difficult requirement, it is still hoped that the relics of a martyr or a saint may be placed under the altar. When this does occur, the new rite insists that they are to be deposited in a space underneath the altar to present more clearly the idea of burial under it.[25] This is to illustrate to the faithful, who are members of the mystical body of Christ, the relationship between the sacrifices of Christ the head and those of the members.[26] Saint Ambrose emphasized this point when he wrote:

> *Succedant victimae triumphales in locum, ubi Christus hostia est. Sed, ille super altare, qui pro omnibus passus est. Isti sub altari, qui illius redempti sunt passione.*[27]

The saints and the martyrs serve as teachers to be imitated by those who hope to follow Christ. The placing of their relics beneath the altar calls the members of the community to offer their lives in a similar manner.

---

23. The Second Vatican Council, *Sacrosanctum concilium*, no. 111: 31. The Council stated, "The saints have been traditionally honoured in the Church, and their authentic relics and images held in veneration. For the feasts of the saints proclaim the wonderful works of Christ in his servants and offer to the faithful fitting examples of their imitation."

24. *ODC*, no. 5: 32.

25. Évenou, "Le nouveau rituel de la dédicace," 97.

26. Rev 6:9. See also *ODC*, no. 14: 34; and Ferraro, "Il mistero della chiesa nella liturgia della dedicazione," 254.

27. Saint Ambrose, *Epistola XXII* (22), 133–35. My translation of this passage is: "Let the triumphant victims be brought to the place where Christ is the victim. Although he upon the altar, who has suffered for all; they are beneath the altar, who have been redeemed by his blood."

PART TWO

The presence of the relics of the martyrs and saints under the altar also helps to demonstrate to the local community the communion that exists between the heavenly liturgy and that which is celebrated in the particular church. At the earthly liturgy the local community partakes in the heavenly liturgy.[28] The members of the community on earth hope to one day join the saint whose remains lie beneath the altar at the liturgy in the eternal Jerusalem. The community does not have a merely earthly existence; it is called to the eschatological destiny that belongs to the universal church of Christ. The communion that exists between the two dimensions of the one church is further emphasized by the fact that the deposition of the relics follows the litany of the saints in ODC. The rite points to the reality of the one church found in heaven and earth.

The prayer of dedication is followed by three sets of liturgical rites that are intended to explain the content of this prayer.[29] The first of these consists in the anointing of the altar and the walls of the church. The altar is to be anointed first, so that it may become a symbol of Christ, the Anointed One.[30] It is to represent Christ, who is the priest, altar and sacrifice, because he gives his body, offering the sacrifice of his life for the salvation of the world. This is in keeping with the Old Testament practice of anointing altars.[31] These all prefigured the one true altar that is Jesus Christ. This ritual gesture points to the centrality of the altar in the life of the church.[32] The entire community gathers around it and receives from it the saving food that Christ offers his people. It stands as a sign that Christ alone is the foundation of the community that gathers around him to celebrate the Eucharist. The altar is that cornerstone, Jesus Christ, around which the entire building of the church is constructed.[33] The Christian people are also to see in the altar a sign of the sacrificial nature of the mystery of Christ that calls them to offer their lives in sacrifice to

---

28. The Second Vatican Council, *Sacrosanctum concilium*, no. 8: 5.

29. *ODC*, no. 16: 34. See also Paternoster, 607.

30. *ODC*, no. 16 a: 34. For an excellent summary on the significance of the altar, see *Dedication of an Altar*, in *Dedication of a Church and an Altar*, nn. 1–11: 101–4.

31. See Genesis 28:18; Exodus 30:27–28; and 40:10; and Numbers 7:11.

32. Dongi, "La liturgia come intinerio educativo: La dedicazione della Chiesa e dell' altare," 445–51.

33. The Second Vatican Council, *Lumen gentium*, no. 6: 353–54. See also Matt 21:42; Acts 4:11; and 1 Pet 2:7.

the Father. The bishop alone is to anoint the altar, "for, in the celebration, he is the representative of the *Christos*."[34]

After the bishop has anointed the altar, he may either anoint the walls himself or invite a number of presbyters to do this. Should he decide to entrust this task to other priests, this gesture speaks powerfully of the role that presbyters have as collaborators with the bishop.[35] Inviting the priests, who have pastoral care for the community, or the parish, to assist in this would provide an excellent form of catechesis for the assembly in regard to the relationship of cooperation that exists between the bishop and the clergy appointed to serve them. The church may be anointed in twelve or four places. The traditional twelve anointings are intended to make the building into a symbol of the church that Christ founded upon the twelve apostles.[36] Faithful to their teaching, the church is to be built up around Christ in love, through the power of the Holy Spirit, to become the one temple of God. The stones that make up the walls of the church are to be symbols of the living church made up of Christians.[37] This community rises up around, and receives its life from, the altar. This points to the reality that Christ is to be at the center and heart of every Christian community. The church walls may also be anointed in four places. This is to represent the church that is gathered from the four corners of the world.[38] The identification of the building with the living church remains the same in this case.

The anointing of the walls is also intended to call all of the faithful to the mission that belongs to them as Christians who were sealed with the Holy Spirit in confirmation.[39] As Christ the altar is anointed, so too they are anointed and called to witness to his love. In the same way that the building is a visible sign, testifying to Christ and his church, Christians, both as individuals and as a community, must witness to Christ in the world. Because they are members of the living Christ, incorporated into him through baptism, confirmation and the Eucharist, Christ's

---

34. Crichton, *Dedication of a Church: A Commentary*, 65.

35. See The Second Vatican Council, *Presbyterorum ordinis*, no. 2: 864–66; and *Christus Dominus*, no. 28: 580.

36. See Rev 21:14; 1 Cor 3:11; and *Lumen gentium*, no. 6: 353–54.

37. Ginami, "Nel Rito della Dedicazione i cristiani si riconoscono Chiesa," 459. See also 1 Pet 2:5.

38. Rev 21:13.

39. Ferraro, "Aspetti di ecclesiologia nel rito di dedicazione della chiesa e dell'altare," 191.

disciples have an obligation to collaborate in the expansion of his kingdom throughout the world.[40] It is the vocation of every believer to carry Christ's saving message into every area of his or her life.[41] In speaking of the responsibility that the laity have in this regard, *Apostolicam actuositatem* describes the parish as that unit in the church that provides an outstanding means for unifying and coordinating the efforts of the faithful in carrying out this mission.[42] For this reason, the parish church should also be seen as a sign of the unity that should animate the living stones of the local church as the members of the parish live their faith in the world. Founded upon Christ, and bound together by the Holy Spirit,[43] the parishioners are to live in communion with one another, their pastor, the bishop and the universal church.

The catechetical impact that the anointing of the altar and the walls of the church is to have in pointing out the symbolic value of the building, is announced to the faithful gathered for the celebration through the words the bishop addresses to them prior to the anointing. He says:

> May the Lord by his power
> sanctify this altar and this house,
> which by our ministry we anoint,
> so that as visible signs
> they may express the mystery of Christ and the Church.[44]

The second set of explanatory rites that follow the prayer of dedication are those for the incensing of the altar and the church. The *Introduction* states that incense is to be offered on the altar of the new church to signify that on it the sacrifice of Christ is perpetuated *in mystery* and rises up to God as a sweet offering.[45] As God received the offering of Noah as it burned on the altar, even more so, the Father with great joy receives

---

40. The Second Vatican Council, *Lumen gentium*, no 11: 361–63; and *Ad gentes*, no. 36: 850.

41. The Second Vatican Council, *Apostolicam actuositatem*, no. 2: 767–68.

42. The Second Vatican Council, *Apostolicam actuositatem,*, no. 10: 777–78.

43. The Second Vatican Council, *Lumen gentium*, no. 13: 364–65. The Constitution states: "This character of universality which adorns the People of God is a gift from the Lord himself whereby the Catholic Church ceaselessly and efficaciously seeks for the return of all humanity and all its goods under Christ the Head in the unity of his Spirit."

44. *ODC*, no. 64: 58.

45. *ODC*, no. 16 b: 34. The *Introduction* states: "Incense is burned on the altar to signify that Sacrifice of Christ, which is there perpetuated in mystery, ascends to God as an odour of sweetness; this is also a sign that the pleasing and acceptable prayers of the faithful rise up to the throne of God."

the true and perfect sacrifice of Christ.[46] The Christian altar is both the altar of sacrifice and the table of the paschal supper.[47] This incensing is intended to draw the attention of the faithful to the altar's sacrificial nature. The gesture also highlights the reality that when Christians join their own prayers to the sacrifice offered here, these rise up to God and are received by him.[48] All of Christ's disciples are called to offer the hopes and fears of their lives as a spiritual offering to the Father. In the Eucharistic sacrifice, the prayers of each and every Christian are presented to the Father through the mediation of his only Son. The altar is also to remind the members of the assembly that they are called, like Christ, to live their lives as a spiritual offering to the Father.

That the faithful are to be a spiritual altar, called to offer their lives in praise to the Father, is reflected by the fact that they are to be incensed before the building. They are the true and living temple of God.[49] As the temple of the Old Testament announced and made known God's presence among his people, in the New Testament God's people are to do this by offering their lives in service to him. This is attested to by the prayer that the bishop offers prior to incensing the altar.[50] The church is incensed after the people because as a result of its being dedicated for Christian worship, it is to become a house of prayer.[51] The incensing of the people before the building provides another example of the way in which *ODC* has taken the church building as the object of its ritual action, and the church community as its subject.[52]

---

46. Gen 8:20.

47. See *Ordo dedicationis altaris*, no. 3: 406. See also Michiels, "Rituel de la dédicace," 138–45; and Sirboni, "Dedicazione dell'alatre," 39–48.

48. Based upon Rev 8:3–4, this image of the prayers of the faithful rising up to God is at the heart of the Eucharistic spirituality that calls every Christian to offer his or her life in thanksgiving to God in the Eucharistic sacrifice. This reality is recognized in the celebration of the Eucharist with the words: "Pray, brethren (brothers and sisters), that my sacrifice and yours be acceptable to God the Father almighty."

49. 1 Cor 3:16–17. See also The Second Vatican Council, *Lumen gentium*, no. 6: 353–54.

50. *ODC*, no. 66: 60. The prayer states: "Let our prayer rise, O Lord, like incense in your sight; and as this house is filled with a pleasing fragrance, so let your Church be fragrant with the aroma of Christ."

51. *ODC*, no. 16 b: 34. The *Instruction* states: "Moreover the incensation of the main body of the church indicates that the dedication makes it a house of prayer; but the People of God are incensed first, for they are the living temple in which each faithful member is a spiritual altar."

52. Bargellini, "Ecclesiologia e tempio," 8.

PART TWO

The third set of explanatory rites following the prayer of dedication is entitled *Lighting of the Altar and Church*. These begin with the covering of the altar, its preparation with the candles and cross, and possibly even its decoration with flowers. The dressing of the altar is to clearly signify the second aspect of the altar's nature. It is the Lord's table where all of God's people are to joyously meet to be refreshed with the body and blood of Christ sacrificed.[53] From here, and through the gift that Christ offers of himself in the Eucharist, the Christian community is bound together in love and built up into the body of Christ.[54] The Eucharistic sacrifice offered on the altar is to be the heart of the parish community's life and that which binds it to the universal church.

After the altar has been covered, the bishop is to stand and proclaim, "Let the light of Christ shine brightly in the Church, that all nations may attain the fullness of truth."[55] This is very similar to the Easter proclamation that announces Christ as the light of the world.[56] In order to indicate that it is Christ alone who illuminates the entire church, the deacon receives a candle from the bishop and lights all of the candles on the altar. Only after the altar has been made a symbol of the radiant light of Christ are the other candles in the church to be lit. The church, which receives its light from Christ, is to transmit this light to the rest of the world.[57] The symbolism contained in the illumination of the altar and the church presents a synthesis of the first article of *Lumen gentium*.[58] It reminds the members of the community that is having its church dedicated that Christ is to be the light of truth by which they guide their lives and that they too must carry his light to all the corners of the world.[59] For the

---

53. *ODC*, no. 16 c: 34–35. The *Introduction* states: "The covering of the altar indicates that the Christian altar is the altar of the Eucharistic Sacrifice and the table of the Lord; the Priests and the faithful stand around it and, in one and the same action but with a difference of office, celebrate the Memorial of the Death and Resurrection of Christ and eat the Lord's Supper. For this reason, the altar is prepared as a table of the sacrificial banquet and adorned as a feast."

54. The Second Vatican Council, *Lumen gentium*, no. 3: 351; and no. 7: 354–56.

55. *ODC*, no. 70: 61.

56. Luke 2:31; and John 8:12.

57. *ODC*, no. 16 d: 35 The *Introduction* states: "The lighting of the altar, which is followed by the lighting of the church, reminds us that Christ is "a light for the revelation to the Gentiles," whose brightness shines out in the Church and through her upon the whole human family."

58. The Second Vatican Council, *Lumen gentium*, no. 1: 350.

59. The call which belongs to all of Christ's faithful to carry his message of salvation to all persons is addressed in a number of the documents of Vatican II. A few examples

parish the rite provides a reminder that from it the radiance of Christ's Gospel must shine out to the entire local community and beyond.

The rite for the dedication of a church is intended to make the building a sign of the mystery of the church. The explanatory rites that make up *The Prayer of Dedication and the Anointings* associate the church building with the mystery of the church. At the heart of the church, in both its local manifestations and universal reality, is Jesus Christ. He is the foundation of the church and from him alone the church receives its life. The liturgical gestures that make up this section communicate this reality by placing the altar at the center of the building and associating it with Christ and his life giving sacrifice. The ritual also calls the Christian faithful who gather around the altar to understand that the church building is to stand as an image of the church made up of living stones. Constructed on the apostles, with Christ as the cornerstone, the church is to imitate the Savior and communicate his message of salvation to all. The church must also be united around Christ, through the ministry of the apostolic successors, in the same way that the building stands as one edifice around the altar. Anointed by the Holy Spirit, the members of the one body of Christ are called to make him present in the world. These rites call the parish to recognize its origin in Christ and challenge its members to make him present within their local community.

## *Prayers*

There are four prayers in *The Prayer of Dedication and the Anointings*. These are: the litany of the saints; the prayer which the bishop offers after the litany of the saints; the prayer for the dedication of the church; and the prayer that is said before incense is offered on the altar. Of these, the prayer for the dedication of the church is the most important and it will receive the greatest attention in the analysis that follows.

In *ODC* the litany of the saints is to take the place of the general intercessions.[60] In many ways the litany follows the same structure as the prayers of the faithful in that they are introduced by the celebrant, consist of petitions and response by the people, and are concluded with a final prayer asking God to accept them. The text of the optional admonition

---

of this may be found at: The Second Vatican Council, *Lumen gentium*, no. 13: 364–365; *Ad gentes*, no. 19: 835–36; and *Apostolicam actuositatem*, no. 5: 842–43.

60. *ODC*, no. 56: 51.

and the concluding prayer for the litany are both new to this ritual.[61] The singing of the litany emphasizes the union of the earthly liturgy to be celebrated in the new church with that of the heavenly liturgy celebrated by the saints before God's throne.[62] It also points to the role of intercession taken by the saints on behalf of their brothers and sisters who are on their earthly pilgrimage.[63] The optional words that are supplied for the bishop to introduce the petitions ask the saints to support the assembly's prayers to the Father. The admonition also alludes to the call to sanctity that belongs to all Christians by speaking of the hearts of God's people as spiritual temples.[64]

The singing of the litany should include the name of the patron of the church, the patron saint of the place, and the saints whose relics are to be deposited under the altar. The rubrics add the stipulation that other petitions suitable to the nature of the celebration or the circumstances of the people may be added to the litany.[65] These two considerations recognize the concerns of the local community and allow the members of it to seek the intercession of the saints who are important to them. There is also a petition specific to the dedication of a church included in the litany. This states, "Consecrate this church for your worship."[66] This includes the only use of the word "consecrate" found in the rite. A number of other petitions ask for God's protection and blessing for the universal church. The unity between the heavenly and earthly church, which the litany reflects, is further emphasized when the litany of the saints is followed by the depositing of the relics beneath the altar.

When the litany is concluded, the bishop offers a prayer asking that the intercession of the blessed Virgin Mary, and of all the saints, may

---

61. Calabuig, "L' 'Ordo dedicationis ecclesiae et altaris': Appunti di una lettura," 418.

62. The Second Vatican Council, *Sacrosanctum concilium*, no. 8: 5; and *Lumen gentium*, no. 50: 410–12.

63. The Second Vatican Council, *Sacrosanctum concilium*, no. 104: 29.

64. ODC, no. 57: 52. The admonition states, "Dearly beloved, let us pray to God the almighty Father, who makes the hearts of the faithful into spiritual temples for himself, and may the supplication of the Saints, our brothers and sisters, be joined with our voices."

65. ODC, no. 59: 52. The rubric states, "In the Litany there are added, at the proper place, invocations of the Titular of the church, the Patron Saint of the place, and the Saints whose relics are to be deposited, if this is to take place. There may be added other petitions that take into account the particular nature of the rite and the circumstances of the faithful (cf. App., no. 10)."

66. ODC, *Litany of the Saints*, 59: 52–53.

make the assembly's petitions acceptable to God.⁶⁷ The requests of the local community are strengthened with the aide of the heavenly church. This oration goes on to ask that the building being dedicated to God's name may become a "house of salvation and grace." Here Christians are to gather as one to worship in spirit and truth⁶⁸ and to be built up in charity. As the church in heaven is a community united in charity to worship the Father in spirit and truth, so too the local community wishes to be such in the building which they dedicate to God.

The prayer for the dedication of a church is a new composition that was written for *ODC*. Strangely, the prayer seems to have been included only in the last stages of preparation, since it cannot be found in the rites for the dedication of a church published in the 1973 provisional *ordo*.⁶⁹ The prayer of dedication represents the solemn proclamation of the intentions of the people to dedicate the new church for the worship of God.⁷⁰ The ecclesial community declares its decision to do this through the person of the bishop, who in turn asks God to pour his graces upon the building. The prayer of dedication speaks of the link between the building and the sacramental life of the community.⁷¹ It also offers a beautiful meditation on the mystery of the church—a mystery that is to be reflected in the church building.

The prayer of dedication can be divided into five sections. These consist of the introduction (lines 1–10); a first part (lines 11–231) that speaks of the relationship between the church building and the mystery of the church; a second part (lines 32–36) that represents the epiclesis; a third part (lines 37–55) which speaks of the saving presence of God which is to be experienced in the church building; and a conclusion (lines 56–58).⁷² The prayer of dedication is of such significance in the rite that each of these sections will be examined separately.

---

67. *ODC*, no. 60: 54. The prayer states, "Mercifully accept our petitions, We pray, O Lord, through the intercession of the Blessed Virgin Mary and all the Saints, so that this building to be dedicated to your name may be a house of salvation and grace where the Christian people, gathering as one, will worship you in spirit and in truth and be built up in charity. Grant this through Christ our Lord."

68. John 4:23.

69. See *Ordo dedicationis ecclesiae*, in *Ordo dedicationis ecclesiae et altaris deque aliis locis et rebus sacrandis* (1973) 68–69.

70. Calabuig, "L' 'Ordo dedicationis ecclesiae et altaris': Appunti di una lettura," 426.

71. Ferraro, "Aspetti di ecclesiologia nel rito di dedicazione della chiesa e dell'altare," 205–8.

72. Paternoster, "Analasi ritual e contenuti teologici dell' 'Ordo dedicationis

PART TWO

The prayer begins by invoking God the Father, who is referred to as both the source of holiness and true purpose of his church.[73] It goes on to state the purpose of the celebration that is taking place. God's people have gathered so that they may dedicate the church in perpetuity to him. It is to be a house of prayer[74] where God can be given true worship. Here God's word is to be heard, the sacraments to be celebrated and solemn rites to be fulfilled.[75] The church building is to be dedicated to God so that it may be a place where his people encounter him in prayer, in his word and through the sacraments.

The first of the three sections (lines 11–31), which make up the body of the prayer, begins by stating, "Here is reflected the mystery of the Church."[76] The four paragraphs that make up this section contain a reflection on the mystery of the church and the manner in which this is expressed by the church building. In the next paragraph, a number of biblical images are attributed to the church, which Christ has made holy by his blood.[77] She is spoken of as a virgin splendid in the wholeness of faith, a bride made radiant with glory,[78] and a blessed mother. Many of these titles are intended to point to the image of Mary, who is an icon of the church.[79] The following paragraph speaks of the church as a vine whose branches envelop the world, bringing the salvation won by Christ on the cross, and reaching up to heaven.[80] This image of the vine draws upon

---

ecclesiae et altaris,'" 608–9. Paternoster divides the prayer and numbers the lines based on the Latin version given in the *editio typica*. The division and line numbering that is given here is based upon the English translation, as it appears in *The Rites* and as it has been given here in this chapter.

73. *ODC*, no. 62: 56. The introduction states: "O God, sanctifier and ruler of your Church, it is right for us to celebrate your name in joyful proclamation; for today your faithful people desire to dedicate to you, solemnly and for all time, this house of prayer, where they worship you devoutly, are instructed by the word, and are nourished by the Sacraments."

74. Mark 11:17; Matt 21:13; and Luke 19:45.

75. *ODC*, no. 62: 56–57.

76. *ODC*, no. 62: 56–57.

77. *ODC*, no. 62: 56. This paragraph reads: "This house brings to light the mystery of the Church, which Christ made holy by the shedding of his blood, so that he might present her to himself as a glorious Bride,
a Virgin resplendent with the integrity of faith, a Mother made fruitful by the power of the Spirit."

78. Eph 5:25.

79. Calabuig, "L' *Ordo dedicationis ecclesiae et altaris*': Appunti di una lettura," 426. See also The Second Vatican Council, *Lumen gentium*, nn. 52–69: 413–23.

80. *ODC*, no. 62: 56. This paragraph reads: "Holy is the Church the chosen vine of

John 15:1 and alludes to the eschatological fulfillment in heaven that is to be enjoyed by those who receive the salvation offered by Christ through the church. The church is then spoken of as a dwelling place of God on earth.[81] It is that temple which is built of living stones, founded upon the apostles with Jesus as its cornerstone.[82] The content of this paragraph is manifested in the rites of dedication through the anointing of the altar and the church. The final paragraph of this section speaks of the church as a city built upon a mountain.[83] Reference is made here to the eternal Jerusalem to which all Christians are called. Illuminated by the glory of the Lamb,[84] the church is to shine out to all the world, while echoing the prayers of all the saints. The church is here portrayed according to the ecclesiology of *Lumen gentium*, article one.[85] The imagery contained in this paragraph is developed through the ritual lighting of the altar and then the entire church. This section provides a powerful articulation of the way in which the mystery of the church is to be encountered in the building that is being dedicated.

The second section of the body of the prayer (lines 32–36) represents the epiclesis.[86] God is asked to send his Spirit from the church in heaven to make the church building on earth a holy place.[87] The Lord is also asked to send his Spirit so that the altar may also become holy and Christ's sacrifice may be offered upon it for all time.[88] Not only does this section of the prayer contain the epicletic aspect, it contains the most

---

the Lord, whose branches fill the whole world, and whose tendrils, borne on the wood of the Cross, reach upward to the Kingdom of Heaven."

81. *ODC*, no. 62: 52. This paragraph reads: "Blessed is the Church, God's dwelling-place with the human race, a holy temple built of living stones, standing upon the foundation of the Apostles with Christ Jesus its chief cornerstone."

82. The image of the Church that is presented here draws heavily upon The Second Vatican Council, *Lumen gentium*, no. 6: 353–54. See also 1 Pet 2:4–5.

83. *ODC*, no. 62: 56–57. This paragraph reads: "Exalted is the Church a City set high on a mountain for all to see, resplendent to every eye with the unfading light of the Lamb, and resounding with the sweet hymn of the Saints."
The image of the Church as a city set on a hill draws upon Matt 5:14–16.

84. John 8:12.

85. See The Second Vatican Council, *Lumen gentium*, no. 1: 350.

86. Paternoster, "Analasi ritual e contenuti teologici dell," 608.

87. Ferraro, "Mistero della chiesa nella liturgia," 259–60.

88. *ODC*, no. 62: 57. This paragraph states: "Therefore, O Lord, we beseech you: graciously pour forth from heaven your sanctifying power upon this church and upon this altar, to make this for ever a holy place with a table always prepared for the Sacrifice of Christ."

compact indication of the prayer's Trinitarian dimension. It is addressed to the Father, who is asked that the Holy Spirit may sanctify the church, so that Christ may be made present in the sacrifice that is to take place on the altar.[89]

The third section (lines 37–52) contains four paragraphs that articulate the effect of the Holy Spirit's work in the church by describing how Christ is to be sacramentally encountered in the new church building.[90] By doing this, it also explains how the images of the mystery of the church that were developed in the first section of the prayer are to be encountered in the church building. Each of these four paragraphs begins with the word "here," indicating that the experience of God that is being spoken about is to occur "here," in the building that is being dedicated. The first of these asks that the waters of baptism might overwhelm the shame of sin, so that people might die to sin and live again through grace as God's children reborn in the church's baptismal font.[91] The church is presented as a mother who generates her children in the womb of the font and through the grace of the Holy Spirit grafts them into Christ's body. In the second paragraph, it is asked that in the building that is being dedicated, the faithful might gather around the altar to celebrate the memorial of the Paschal Lamb and be fed at the table of Christ's word and body.[92] This petition requests that the edifice might become that place where the faithful are nourished to be built up into the body of Christ. In the third of this set, it is asked that prayer, which is the church's banquet, might resound through heaven and earth, and rise up to God as a prayer for the salvation of the world.[93] The church building is thus associated with the temple of God where he is to be worshiped in truth and spirit. In the final subsection, it is requested that the poor may find justice and the victims of oppression might find

---

89. Ferraro, "Il mistero della chiesa nella liturgia della dedicazione," 260.

90. Ferraro, "Aspetti di ecclesiologia nel rito di dedicazione della chiesa e dell'altare," 205.

91. *ODC*, no 62: 57. This paragraph states: "Here may the flood of divine grace overwhelm human offences, so that your children, Father, being dead to sin, may be reborn to heavenly life.."

92. *ODC*, no. 62: 57. This paragraph states: "Here may your faithful, gathered around the table of the altar, celebrate the memorial of the Paschal Mystery and be refreshed by the banquet of Christ's Word and his Body."

93. *ODC*, no. 62: 57. This paragraph states: "Here may the joyful offering of praise resound, with human voices joined to the song of the Angels, and unceasing prayer rise up to you for the salvation of the world."

true freedom within the church.[94] In this way the light of Christ is to shine out of the church and to bring authentic freedom and liberation to those who are bound by the darkness of sin. In the particular building that is being dedicated to God, the Holy Spirit is asked to make Christ present so that "here" all may experience the salvation conveyed through his mystical body, the church.

The conclusion of the prayer (lines 53–55) points to the eschatological reality to which the experience of Christ in the church is to bring all humanity. It asks that from the church all people ("the whole world") may come to be clothed with the dignity of God's children so that they may go with gladness to God's city of peace—which is the new and eternal Jerusalem.[95] The church building is to be that place where men and women encounter Christ's saving presence in the present and are led to their eschatological destiny. It is not just the place where the individual or the community are to find salvation, but all of humanity. It must be that place where Christians are nourished and built into Christ's body and from where Christ's love is announced to the whole world.

What is said in the prayer of dedication about the church building has particular importance for the parish church. From here is reflected the mystery of the church to a particular community. Here the people of a certain locality experience the church as a mother when they come to be reborn in the baptismal font and are made members of the universal church. Here those who live in the vicinity come to be nourished by Christ's word and sacraments. Receiving his body and blood, they are built up here into the one body of Christ. Here, they are united to the temple of God and live out their vocations as living stones in this structure. From here they join their voices to the entire church, and with those of the angels, in their praise of God. The faithful are to be sent out from here into the world to bring the light of Christ to all their brothers and sisters. In doing this they are to make known the generosity of the liberty and mercy found in Christ. From the parish church the mystery of the church is to manifest itself to the local community. From here, the risen Christ, who is always present to his church by the power of the Holy Spirit, is to be brought to all people so that they may be transformed by his grace and come one day to the new and eternal Jerusalem.

---

94. *ODC*, no. 62: 57. This section of the prayer states: Here may the poor find mercy, The oppressed attain true freedom."

95. *ODC*, no. 62: 57. The conclusion states: "and all people be clothed with the dignity of your children, until they come exultant to the Jerusalem which is above."

PART TWO

The final prayer that is to be found in *The Prayer of Dedication and the Anointings* is the formula pronounced by the bishop before the incense is burned upon the altar.[96] The first half of this prayer is based upon Ps 140 (141), verse 2, and it draws attention to the purpose of the liturgical rite that it accompanies.[97] God is asked to accept the prayers of his people like incense that rises up to him. The second petition of the prayer (found in the last three lines) asks that as the building is filled with the fragrance of incense, the living church of men and women may also fill the world with the fragrance of Christ.[98] It is hoped that the liturgical symbols that the Christians experience in the rite will demonstrate to them what they are called to be in the world. As the incense permeates and transforms the atmosphere inside the church building with its sweet aroma, so the faithful are to permeate and transform the environment in which they live with the message of the Gospel.

The prayers that are found in *The Prayer of Dedication and the Anointings* present the image of the church that the faithful are to encounter in the church building and articulate how it is to be a sign that calls them to become living members of the church that the edifice represents. These prayers speak to the members of the parish community about the manner in which their parish church is to be a sign calling them to manifest the living church of Christ in their area.

## Sacred Scripture

There are four ritual gestures in the *The Prayer of Dedication and the Anointings* that are accompanied by the singing of a psalm or an Old Testament canticle. These hymns are also accompanied by antiphons that have been inspired by scripture. Two of the three psalms that are sung in this section of the rite, Ps 14 (15) and 137 (138), are new to the dedication of a church, as is the Canticle of Tobit. These texts from scripture have been selected to complement the significance given to the rites that they are associated with in *ODC*.

---

96. *ODC*, no. 66: 60. The prayer states: "Let our prayer rise, O Lord, like incense in your sight; and as this house is filled with a pleasing fragrance, so let your Church be fragrant with the aroma of Christ."
97. Calabuig, "'*Ordo dedicationis ecclesiae et altaris*,'" 438.
98. 2 Cor 2:14–15.

The depositing of the relics under the altar of the church is to be accompanied by the singing of Ps 14 (15).[99] This psalm begins by asking, "O Lord, who may abide in your tent? Who may dwell on your holy mountain?" It then goes on to recount the qualities of the righteous man who will be worthy to dwell in God's house. This serves to point to the qualities by which the martyr or saint whose remains are being placed under the altar came to stand in God's presence in the heavenly liturgy. By doing this, a reminder is provided to all those attending the dedication, and to those who will visit the church in the future, that they too are called to sanctity by living a holy life. The selection of Ps 14 (15) for the depositing of relics was also directed by the meaning of the deposition itself.[100] The mortal remains of the martyr or saint are deposited under the eucharistic altar, a place of holiness and peace. The psalm promises this reward to those who live a holy life. Because the church building is to reflect the church dwelling in heaven,[101] it represents the final destiny where all the saints are to find the peace that Christ offers to those who follow him faithfully. By placing the remains of the martyr or saint under the altar, all of the Christian faithful are given a sign of the eternal communion with Christ that awaits those who persevere in following him.

The first of the two antiphons to be sung with the psalm draws its inspiration from the vision of the martyrs under the altar of God in Rev 6:9. It goes on to mention the power of intercession that the saints have because of their proximity to Christ. The second antiphon refers to the peace that is to be enjoyed by those who die in Christ.

The first explanatory rite to follow the prayer of dedication is the anointing of the altar and the walls of the church. The *Introduction* states that the anointing of the walls is to signify that the church is an image of the holy city Jerusalem.[102] As the anointing takes places, Ps 83 (84) is to be sung. This psalm speaks of the psalmists yearning to stand one day in God's dwelling place. In doing so, it expresses the longing of the pilgrim people to come at the end of their journeys into God's house.[103]

---

99. *ODC*, no. 61: 55.

100. Calabuig, "'Ordo dedicationis ecclesiae et altaris,'" 425.

101. *ODC*, no. 2: 31.

102. *ODC*, no. 16 a: 34. The *Introduction* states: "Moreover, the anointing of the church signifies that it is given over entirely and perpetually to Christian worship. Twelve anointings are made in accordance with liturgical tradition, or, as circumstances suggest, four, signifying that the church is an im age of the holy city of Jerusalem."

103. Calabuig, "'Ordo dedicationis ecclesiae et altaris,'" 435.

PART TWO

The people who gather in the building come to be nourished by Christ and strengthened so that they may reach their final destiny. In the church building they are to find a sign of hope, pointing them to their much-desired homeland. Psalm 83 (84) calls attention to the transitional nature of the building and articulates the desire of the community for the heavenly church to which the visible structure points.

There are two antiphons that may be sung with Ps 83 (84). The first of these states, "Behold God's dwelling with the human race, He will live with them and they will be his people, and God himself with them will be their God (E. T. Alleluia)."[104] This antiphon is based upon Rev 21:3, where the old heaven and earth pass away and the new Jerusalem comes down from heaven. In the building, Christians are to experience communion with God, through the sacraments, in his word, and through the community that will strengthen them to come one day into his presence in the new Jerusalem.[105] The second antiphon states, "Holy is the temple of the Lord, God's own structure, God's own building." Ignazio Calabuig has written in his commentary on the rite that this antiphon was inspired by a Pauline theme that is present in 1 Cor 3:9.[106] The church, for which the building stands as a symbol, grows and comes to fulfillment only because the Lord is its builder.

The incensing of the altar is intended to signify that the prayers of the people rise up from there to the throne of God, while the walls are incensed to show that the church is a house of prayer.[107] Psalm 137 (138), which is used in *ODC* to accompany this gesture, voices the psalmist's certitude that God hears the words from his mouth.[108] The text also speaks of the psalmist's conviction that he will stand in the presence of the angels and worship in God's holy temple. This aspect of the psalm alludes to the fact that the community in the church building is united with the heavenly liturgy,[109] and that this is the destiny to which the earthly community is called. The psalm goes on to articulate that God hears the prayers of both the great and the lowly when they call out to him. The psalmist gives thanks to God for having delivered him and prays that all of the kings of the world might acknowledge God's greatness. The psalm

104. *ODC*, no. 64: 58–59.
105. The Second Vatican Council, *Sacrosanctum concilium*, no. 7: 4–5.
106. Calabuig, "'*Ordo dedicationis ecclesiae et altaris*,'" 436.
107. *ODC*, no. 16 b: 34.
108. *ODC*, no. 68: 60–61.
109. The Second Vatican Council, *Sacrosanctum concilium*, no. 8: 5.

## THE PRAYER OF DEDICATION AND THE ANOINTINGS

calls the community gathered in the church that is being dedicated to a confidence that God will hear the prayers that it addresses to him from there and that he will give them the strength to go forth to bring his salvation to the world.

The antiphons that accompany this psalm are both from Rev 8:3–5, where an angel stands at the altar of incense before the throne of God with a gold censer. From this censer rise up clouds of incense that carry the prayers of God's people to him. Both of the antiphons reaffirm the intention of the ritual gesture that they accompany by asserting that God hears the prayers of his people. These prayers are to rise up to him from the community that gathers in the building, because its members make up the true temple in which each Christian is a spiritual altar.[110]

The Canticle of Tobit (Tobit 13:10; 13–14ab; 14c-15; 17) is to accompany the lighting of the altar and the church.[111] This canticle is taken from excerpts of the prayer offered to God by Tobit in thanksgiving for the fact that God had heard his plea for help and delivered him from the suffering and hardships that he had encountered. The passages that make up the canticle exhort God's chosen people to praise him for his works; declare that the light of God's splendor will be seen shinning out from his holy city; and prophecy of the final gathering that will take place in the new Jerusalem when the people of all lands are united there at the end of time to praise God. Thus, the canticle calls the members of the community dedicating its church to praise God for his many gifts; to remember their missionary duty to announce Christ's good news to the

---

110. *ODC*, no. 16 b: 34.
111. *ODC*, no. 71: 62. The canticle reads:

> "Bless the Lord, all you his chosen ones,
> Proclaim a day of gladness and give him glory.
> R/.
> Jerusalem, city of God,
> you will shine with the splendid light
> and all the ends of the earth will pay you homage.
> Nations will come from afar,
> and, bearing gifts, will adore you, Lord
> R/.
> Your land will be called holy,
> and your name shall be invoked as great.
> You shall rejoice in your children,
> for all shall be blessed
> and gathered before the Lord."
> R/.

PART TWO

whole world[112] and to be aware of the eschatological destiny to which all persons are called. The canticle provides a beautiful complement to the ritual gestures of the lighting of the altar and church—an action that communicates the church's saving mission.[113] The church is to be regarded as a light on a hill radiating the good news of salvation to all people. The canticle also points to the building's sign value as an image of the pilgrim church and reflection of the church in heaven. The illuminated building is to represent this. Through it the local Christian assembly is to be reminded of its responsibility to bring Christ's message to all people.

The two antiphons that are to accompany this canticle share many of its themes. The first antiphon is taken from Isa 60:1–3 and states, "Your light has come, Jerusalem: the glory of the Lord has arisen upon you, and the nations will walk in your light, alleluia." Here, again, the future glory of the heavenly Jerusalem is proclaimed. The holy city is spoken of as that place to which all nations will be led by the light that shines out of it. This light is the radiance of the glory of the Lord. The antiphon and canticle emphasize the building's identity as a sign that points to the community's eschatological destiny. The second antiphon, which is to be sung in Lent, proclaims, "Jerusalem, city of God, you will shine with splendid light, and all the ends of the earth will pay you homage. Nations will come from afar and, bearing gifts, will adore you, Lord." Taken directly from the prayer of Tobit (Tobit 13:11–13), this antiphon also echoes themes that are found in the canticle. It too refers to the church's mission to bring Christ's light to all people. The canticle and antiphon also exude a confidence that God's plan for salvation will in the end overcome all of the barriers that confront the church. These passages speak to the local community of the need for it to bring Christ's message to the whole world.[114] They also emphasize the transitory nature of the building as an image of the heavenly Jerusalem, that will eventually give way to the new and eternal city where God will be praised forever.

For the local community that is dedicating its church, these scripture passages provide an excellent complement to the rites contained in

112. The Second Vatican Council, *Ad gentes divinitus*, no. 16: 831–33.

113. The Second Vatican Council, *Lumen gentium*, no. 1: 350.

114. The Second Vatican Council, *Presbyterorum ordinis*, no. 6: 872–74. The decree states: "A local community ought not merely to promote the care of the faithful within itself, but should be imbued with the missionary spirit and smooth the path to Christ for all men [and women]. But it must regard as its special charge those under instruction and the newly converted who are gradually educated in knowing and living the Christian life."

*The Prayer of Dedication and the Anointings.* These texts point to the holy city to which the members of the community are called. In the new Jerusalem, the local assembly will be united completely and perfectly with all of the redeemed. For this reason, they must be concerned not only with the members of their own community, but also with bringing the light of Christ's message to all persons. In the parish building, the members of the church who live in a particular area experience that communion with Christ and the heavenly liturgy to which all are called for eternity at the end of their pilgrim journeys. The building is to be a sign pointing them towards their eschatological goal. It must also call them to the awareness that in the new Jerusalem they will worship God united with the entire church. The visible structure should be a sign that enhances the local community's awareness of its relationship with the church in heaven and the entire pilgrim church on earth.

## *Persons*

In *The Prayer of Dedication and the Anointings*, the bishop proclaims, "May the Lord by his power sanctify this altar and this house, which by our ministry we anoint, so that as visible signs they may express the mystery of Christ and the Church."[115] Because the rite of dedication makes the building into a visible sign of the mystery of the church, both the rite and the building have a great deal to say about the nature of the church and the roles that are played by the different people who make it up.

The Second Vatican Council described the bishop as the principle dispenser of the mysteries of God and stated that it was his function to direct, promote, and protect the entire liturgical life of the church entrusted to his care.[116] It also stated that it is the bishop who is to preside over the flock of God and make Christ present among the faithful.[117] In the rites of *The Prayer of Dedication and the Anointings*, the bishop can be clearly seen as fulfilling these roles. It is he, in his role of dispensing the sacred

---

115. ODC, no. 64: 58.

116. The Second Vatican Council, *Christus Dominus*, no. 15: 571–72. The decree states, "It is therefore bishops who are the principal dispensers of the mysteries of God, and it is their function to control, promote and protect the entire liturgical life of the Church entrusted to them."

117. The Second Vatican Council, *Lumen gentium*, no. 21: 372–72. The Constitution states, "In the person of the bishops, then, to whom the priests render assistance, the Lord Jesus Christ, supreme high priest, is present in the midst of the faithful."

PART TWO

mysteries of God, who dedicates the building to God on behalf of the community and sets it aside as a place for the celebration of the liturgy in the prayer of dedication. In this same oration, the bishop calls down the Holy Spirit and asks that the church may be a place where Christ is experienced in his word and sacrament, so that the local community may be built up into the body of Christ. By anointing the altar, the bishop transforms it into a symbol of Christ and establishes it as the foundation stone around which the entire Christian community gathers. The bishop also exercises his function of preaching in this section of the ritual as he proclaims Christ to be the light that shines forth from the church to all the nations.[118] The rites make it clear that the community that is having its church dedicated is to be one based on listening to God's word, praise and supplication, celebrating the sacraments, and living out the teaching of Christ by bringing his light to the world and reaching out to the needy and the oppressed. Within this community, the bishop who dedicates the church to God so that it may be a place where Christ's body may be built up by his word and sacraments exercises his mission of sanctifying, teaching, and governing.[119]

The rite of dedication also communicates an important lesson about the role of the bishop as a successor of the apostles in building up the communion of the church. The building, which is a symbol of the one church, is to be built upon the foundation of the apostles with Christ as the cornerstone.[120] The unity of the building, which represents the church, is based upon Christ and is held together by the apostles that he sent out into the world. The twelve crosses that are placed in different locations in the one structure are to represent the apostles through whom the church is bound together by the Holy Spirit. In and through the local bishop, the community that is involved in the dedication of its church is joined in communion with the rest of the universal church. The Second Vatican Council's Decree on the pastoral office of the bishop, *Christus Dominus*, has spoken of the bishop's role as follows:

---

118. The Second Vatican Council, *Lumen gentium*, no. 25: 379-81. *Lumen gentium* states: "Among the more important duties of bishops that of preaching has pride of place." The proclamation which the bishop makes states, "Let the light of Christ shine brightly in the Church, that all nations may attain the fullness of truth." See *ODC*, no. 70: 61.

119. The Second Vatican Council, *Lumen gentium*, no. 21: 372-74. The constitution states, "Now, episcopal consecration confers, together with office of sanctifying, the duty also of teaching and ruling, which, however, of their very nature can be exercised only in hierarchical communion with the head and members of the college."

120. The Second Vatican Council, *Lumen gentium*, no. 6: 353-54.

deacons are not asked to anoint the walls of the church demonstrates the difference that exists between the presbyteral order and the deaconate. This difference is expressed in the following words of *Lumen gentium*: "At a lower level of the hierarchy are to be found deacons, who receive the imposition of hands 'not unto the priesthood, but unto the ministry.'"[132] Within the local community, the deacon is to play an important role in the instruction of all people so that they may come to the light of Christ.

The many complicated liturgical actions that are found in *The Prayer of Dedication and the Anointings* require the assistance of a number of lay ministers in order that they might be properly carried out. These lay ministers are required to assist in the liturgy for the anointing of the altar,[133] the incensing of the bishop, people and walls of the church,[134] and for the wiping and preparing of the altar for its illumination.[135] As with the other sections of *ODC*, these rites also require the participation of a number of cantors so that they may be accompanied by the music that is to complement them. The presence of a stone mason may also be required for depositing the relics of the martyr or saint under the altar. These ministries are to be exercised in keeping with the criteria that were set out by Pope Paul VI in *Ministeria quaedam*—they are to be of service to the proper ordering of worship and to God's people.[136]

Mauro Paternoster has written that the importance of the rites found in *The Order of the Dedication of a Church and an Altar* is to be attributed to the fact that they display a rediscovery of the mentality of the early Christian community in regard to the relationship between the church as temple and the church as the People of God.[137] In *ODC*, the rites of dedication are celebrated for the sanctification of the Christian assembly. The dedicated church building is to point to the nature and identity of the living church of God that is made up of the baptized disciples of Christ. Although the building is actually dedicated through the celebration of the Eucharist, the explanatory rites that are found in *The Prayer of Dedication and the Anointings* articulate the manner in which

---

132. The Second Vatican Council, *Lumen gentium*, no. 29: 387.

133. *ODC*, no. 63: 58.

134. *ODC*, no. 67: 60.

135. *ODC*, no. 69: 61.

136. Paul VI, *Ministeria quaedam*, 433–34.

137. Paternoster, "Analasi ritual e contenuti teologici dell' 'Ordo dedicationis ecclesiae et altaris,'" 605–6. In this regard see the previously cited excellent article by Congar, "Église, ce n'est pas."

PART TWO

the Christian assembly is to discover the nature of its identity in the sign value that the rites bestow upon the building. The local community that is dedicating its church edifice must be understood as the subject and protagonist of these rites, while the visible structure is their object.[138] The building is to constitute a sign that reminds the community of what it is and calls it to become what it is to be through the grace of God's Holy Spirit.

The catechesis that is communicated by these rites calls the local assembly to recognize its communion with the heavenly church, as well as the call to sanctity that is addressed to each one of its members in the litany of the saints and the depositing of the relics beneath the church's altar. The prayer of dedication reminds the faithful that they are to be the living stones of the one church founded by Christ and built upon the apostles. The same prayer also challenges the assembly to realize that its origins are to be found in the baptism received from Christ; that its life is radically dependent upon the Holy Spirit; that its continued growth and sustenance must be based upon the nourishment found in Christ's word, sacraments and his body and blood; and that its ultimate destiny lies in praising God the Father in heaven for all eternity. Both the prayers and rites of this section testify to the responsibility that belongs to all those who have received the gift of faith. They are to open their hearts to the power of the Holy Spirit so that they may witness to the good news of salvation with their own lives. In the rites of anointing, the assembly is called to place Christ, the anointed one, at the center of its life and to recall that each individual member has also been anointed by the Holy Spirit and is called to offer his or her life in loving service to the Father. The rites of incensing and lighting of the church point to the fundamental responsibility that belongs to the laity to take the good news of salvation into the world to which they are sent as ministers of the Gospel after the liturgical celebrations which take place within the church building have concluded. The laity are to fill the world with the fragrance of Christ and the light of his Gospel. The ritual content of *The Prayer of Dedication and the Anointings* also makes the building into a sign that reveals the universal church's nature as a unified entity built upon the apostles and their teaching. In and through their local bishop and legitimate pastors, the local assembly is to be a living part of the body of Christ. Through these ritual actions, the building is transformed into a sign that provides

---

138. Bargellini, "Ecclesiologia e tempio," 38.

a constant mystagogical testimony to the Trinitarian dimension of the community's identity within the mystical body of Christ.

The rites and prayers contained in *The Prayer of Dedication and the Anointings* provide the local church with the opportunity to take stock of what it is—the temple of the living God—and call the members of this assembly to renew their openness to the Holy Spirit so that they may be built up as the one church of God manifesting itself in a particular area.[139]

## SUMMARY

Once again, it can be observed that in *ODC* the community that is dedicating its church edifice can be seen as the subject and protagonist of the ritual activities. The visible structure is the object of the rites of *ODC* and it becomes, as a result of these rites, a sign that is to call the community to become what it is to be as a portion of the church, which is the body of Christ. This is something that is completely new in the history of the rites for the dedication of a church building. Prior to these rites of *ODC*, the subject of the ritual for the dedication of a church was always the building which was being dedicated to God.[140] The older rituals for dedication do not say anything explicit about the nature of the living church which is to meet within the building. They strove only to set the building aside to God through rites that are similar to those celebrated when Christians are confirmed. The subject of the previous rites was the building and the purpose of the rites was to make the building into a sacred place where God might be encountered. The new rites contained in *The Prayer of Dedication and the Anointings* display a novelty that was best described by Ignazio Calabuig when he wrote:

> . . .ognuna di esse è orientata non a "santificare" le pareti e l'altare del nuovo edificio cultuale, ma a ravvivare la conscienza che il cristiano è il vero tempio di Dio e a recordare i sacramenti attraverso i quali egli è divenuto dimora santa del Padre, del Figlio e dello Spirito.[141]

---

139. Lara, "Dedicazione della chiesa e dell'altare," 599.

140. McGourty, *Theology for a Parish Community*.

141. Calabuig, "Rito della dedicazione della chiesa," 413. My translation of this passage is: Each of these [rites from *ODC*] is orientated not to sanctifying the walls and altars of the church building, but to reviving in the consciousness of each Christian that he or she is the true temple of God and to help him or her remember the sacraments through which he or she became a holy dwelling place of God the Father, of the Son

Because the rites of *The Prayer of Dedication and the Anointings* seek to make the building into a sign of the mystery of the church, they provide a rich theological content which describes how the church manifests itself within a particular community. This material lays the foundation for the theology of a parish that is contained in *ODC*.

The content of *The Prayer of Dedication and the Anointings* builds upon that of the *Introductory Rites*. It will be recalled from the discussion in chapter three that the *Introductory Rites* of *ODC* was fundamentally concerned to articulate the dignity that belonged to each Christian as a baptized member of the church. Baptism is the sacrament by which one enters the church and becomes a member of Christ's body. In *The Prayer of Dedication and the Anointings*, the ritual gestures are concerned to articulate what it means for the living church to be the anointed body of Christ present in the world. The rites call the church and its members to manifest Christ to the world and point them towards the sacramental realities that are to strengthen them to accomplish their mission. They indicate that Jesus Christ is to be the source and foundation of the church's life and that only by being assimilated to him, through his word and sacraments, can individual Christians and the church accomplish his saving mission in the world. By living their vocations within the body of Christ, each individual member is brought into communion with Christ and receives the graces that will be necessary to bring him or her to eternal communion with God. As is clearly indicated in *The Prayer of Dedication and the Anointings*, the church is built up in unity and strength by the Holy Spirit to accomplish its task in the world. The individual ritual gestures and prayers of this section of *ODC* articulate the different ways in which the mystery of the church is to be manifested in a particular community.

Through the rites of the deposition of the relics, when these occur, and the Litany of the Saints, the local parish community is reminded of its communion with the heavenly church. It is not a separate and independent entity. It is united to the entire celestial choir. By placing the relics of a saint beneath the altar of Christ's sacrifice, the baptized are also reminded of their vocations to live their lives in sacrifice to Christ. The ultimate destiny of the pilgrim church on earth is the church in heaven. While here on earth, the members of the body of Christ are united to

---

and of the Holy Spirit.

## THE PRAYER OF DEDICATION AND THE ANOINTINGS

those in heaven most perfectly in the celebration of the liturgy.[142] Within their local parish community, Christians are to celebrate their faith until the day that the whole church is brought from the four corners of the earth to the new and eternal Jerusalem.

In the prayer of dedication is to be found a twofold reminder of the ways in which the church is to be built up in the local community and of the obligations that belong to its members. The work of building up the church and making it present in a particular community belongs essentially to Christ. He does this as he is made present through the power of the Holy Spirit. New Christians are generated by Christ in baptism. The members of Christ's body are nourished by his word in the liturgy, fed with his body and blood at his altar, and fortified by the celebration of the diverse sacraments. As a result of the graces that the members of the assembly receive in the celebration of the liturgy, which takes place in the dedicated church building, they are to become more like Christ and through his church are to make him present in the world.[143] Strengthened by the liturgy, the faithful are to bring Christ to all the areas of their lives.[144] As the many different members come together, the parish serves as a unifying force, bringing together the different talents of the people in a particular area and focusing them upon their individual missions within the universality of the church.[145] In the parish community, those who make up Christ's body in a specific area are to be transformed into Christ's likeness and strengthened to make him present to their brothers and sisters. They are to witness to Christ's charity and love and announce the good news in their locality. From their midst the praise of the local church is to rise up to God. The prayer of dedication asks that the church building may become a sign calling the members of the community to realize their ecclesial identity and to manifest it where they live.

The prayer of dedication is followed by three sets of explanatory rites; the first of which is the anointing of the altar. The bishop is to announce to the assembly that by this gesture the altar and church are to become signs of the mystery of Christ and his church.[146] The altar be-

---

142. The Second Vatican Council, *Lumen gentium*, no. 50: 410–12.

143. See The Second Vatican Council, *Sacrosanctum concilium*, no. 2: 1–2; and no. 59: 20.

144. See The Second Vatican Council, *Apostolicam actuositatem*, no. 3: 768–69; and no. 13: 781–82.

145. The Second Vatican Council, *Apostolicam actuositatem*, no. 10: 777–78.

146. *ODC*, no. 64: 58–60. The bishop states: "May the Lord by his power sanctify

comes a symbol of Christ who is to be the center of the community and Christian life. It is he alone who gathers the community together and he is to be the principle reason for its existence. As the altar makes present the mystery of Christ as priest, prophet, and king, it calls all of the faithful to model their lives on his. They too are to offer themselves in sacrifice to the Father. The centrality of the altar in the church also calls the members of the community who gather around it to nourish their faith on Christ's body and blood. Focusing its attention on the altar whenever it assembles, the community is reminded that it is Christ who brings it together, not mere geographical proximity.

The anointing of the walls of the church is to remind all of the faithful of the dignity that belongs to them as the members of Christ's body. Just as Christ was anointed, so too they have been anointed by the Holy Spirit in the sacraments of initiation. The Holy Spirit binds the whole church into one entity and makes all of the members into one body. Through the power of the Holy Spirit, all of the faithful are called to make Christ present in the world. The building is to become a sign of the one church that encompasses all of those who have been incorporated into Christ. When the walls are anointed in the twelve places, this gesture has a great value in communicating the apostolic nature of the one church. Each Christian community, whether a parish or not, is joined to the One, Holy, Catholic, and Apostolic Church of Christ through its union with the local bishop.[147] The nature of the link between the bishop, who is a successor of the apostles, and the local community can be demonstrated in those cases when the bishop sends the priests to anoint the walls of the church. As the stones that make up the walls are to represent the living members, the priests who are sent to anoint the walls may be regarded as those who will be sent by the bishop to minister to God's people. The ministry of priests in the communities that they serve is to be one of service to the faithful so that the body of Christ may be built up in unity.[148] Through the priest, the bishop is made present in the liturgy and the one church is manifested.[149] The gesture of anointing the walls calls the

---

this altar and this house, which by our ministry we anoint, so that as visible signs they may express the mystery of Christ and the Church."

147. The Second Vatican Council, *Christus Dominus*, no. 11: 569.

148. The Second Vatican Council, *Presbyterorum ordinis*, no. 1: 863. See also Wood, *Sacramental Orders*, 117–42; Wood, "Priestly Identity: Sacrament of the Ecclesial Community," 109–27.

149. See The Second Vatican Council, *Presbyterorum ordinis*, no. 3: 866–68; and no. 5: 870–72.

## THE PRAYER OF DEDICATION AND THE ANOINTINGS

faithful to embrace the vocations that have been given them through the anointing which they received in the sacraments of initiation. Through them Christ must be made present in the world. The parish community is to be a cell of the one body of Christ manifesting the salvation he offers within a specific locality.[150]

The ecclesial obligations that belong to the faithful are more clearly expressed in the explanatory rites that follow those of anointing. The incensing of the altar and people serves to remind the faithful of Christ's sacrifice and that they too must offer their own lives as a fragrant offering to God. The primacy that is consistently given to the altar in these rites is intended to draw the community's attention constantly to Christ. The faithful are to follow his example and are to be strengthened to do this by feeding on his body and blood. The fruits of Christ's sacrifice are to transform the members of his body into his likeness. The incense that rises up to God is to remind Christians that they are called to be a people of prayer, which always gives praise to the Father. The missionary aspect of the church's vocation is spoken of in the prayer that accompanies this gesture. It asks that as the building is filled with the fragrance of incense, so too may the church fill the world with the fragrance of Christ.[151] For the members of the parish community that is dedicating its church, the incensing implies a call to be transformed by the sacrifice of Christ so that they might permeate their environment with his sweet and saving message. The building is incensed because it is to be a visible sign of the church in the world.

In a similar way, the vesting and lighting of the altar, followed by the illumination of the church, communicates in a powerful manner the mission that belongs to the members of the body of Christ. The altar is to be dressed because it is the table at which the faithful are to be nourished with the body and blood of Christ. Only by coming together around it to encounter Christ can the local community hope to make him present in their lives. As the altar is lit, it emphasizes that Christ is the light of the church. The living church, which is illumined by Christ, has the responsibility of bringing him to the entire world. It belongs to the laity, the church's living stones, to bring the Gospel to all areas of their lives.[152]

---

150. The Second Vatican Council, *Apostolicam actuositatem*, no. 10: 777–78.

151. *ODC*, no. 66: 60. The prayer states: "Let our prayer rise, O Lord, like incense in your sight; and as this house is filled with a pleasing fragrance, so let your Church be fragrant with the aroma of Christ."

152. The Second Vatican Council, *Lumen gentium*, nn. 34–35: 391–93.

By doing so, they are to carry Christ's offer of salvation to all nations. This is expressed by the bishop as he proclaims, "Let the Light of Christ shine brightly in the Church that all nations may attain the fullness of truth."[153] In *ODC* the church building is illumined because it is to be a sign reminding the local community that it is to make the body of Christ present in the world.

For the parish community which gathers to celebrate the dedication of its church building, there is to be found in the rites of *The Prayer of Dedication and the Anointings* a profound theological exposition of what it means for its members to be part of the mystical body of Christ. They are to be bound to the church by the anointing with the Holy Spirit that they have received. Through the ministry of the ordained, the faithful are to be nourished by Christ's word, his sacraments and his body and blood. Transformed by the experience of Christ that they encounter in his living temple, the members of the parish community are to bring Christ's message of salvation and charity to the different corners of the earth in which they live and work. The parish is to be a cell of Christ's body that makes him present in a particular area. The rites of *The Prayer of Dedication and the Anointings* also communicate the reality that a concrete experience of Jesus Christ is conveyed by the Holy Spirit in the liturgy. Until the day when the entire church is gathered together as one in the new and eternal Jerusalem to offer praise to the Father for all time, the parish liturgy is to be that place where those who belong to this specific community worship the Father in spirit and truth. The rites remind all of the transitory nature of the church on earth and point them to their true home in heaven. The celebration of these ritual gestures is to make of the parish church a sign of what it means for this community to make Christ's body present in its specific local. This sign must call the members of the parish to manifest Christ's charity and salvation in their midst. The yearly celebration of the anniversary of the dedication should call this same community to renew its awareness of what it means for it to be the living temple of God—as should all celebrations of the Eucharist. These rites point out that in each and every legitimate parish community ought to be encountered the living body of Christ.

---

153. *ODC*, no. 70: 61.

# Chapter Six

## Order of the Dedication of a Church: The Liturgy of the Eucharist

### INTRODUCTION

The fourth and final section of *ODC* is called *The Liturgy of the Eucharist*. In this chapter the rites associated with the Eucharistic liturgy in the ritual for the dedication of a church will be examined. This inquiry will consist of three sections. In the first, the prayers and rites that are specific to the celebration of the Mass within the context of the ritual for a church's dedication will be presented. In this section, the overall general structure of the Eucharistic liturgy, as it is celebrated in the Mass within the Roman Missal that was revised after the Second Vatican Council, will be assumed. Only those aspects that are distinct to *The Liturgy of the Eucharist* in *ODC* will be discussed. In the second section these rites will be analyzed, as they have been throughout this study, according to the categories of *rites*, *prayers*, *sacred scripture*, and *persons*. The third and final section of this chapter provides a summary of these findings and articulates the implications that they have for the construction of that theology of a parish that is contained in *ODC*.

The study that is proposed in this chapter requires an additional source. While most of the prayers that are required for the celebration of the Eucharist can be found in the ritual of *ODC*, there are others, such as the Eucharistic Prayers, that are found only is the Roman Missal. The fact of the matter is that in the actual celebration of the dedication of a church, most of the prayers related to the Eucharist would in fact be taken from the Roman Missal. As has already been mentioned in this study, one of the main reasons for the 2018 revised English translation of this ritual, is to include the revised translation of the prayers that are now found in the third edition of the Roman Missal. For that reason, the texts that are presented and studied in this section cited from the revised third edition of the English Roman Missal of 2011 and the revised 2018 English translation of the Typical Edition of *The Order of the Dedication of a Church and Altar*. These prayers are to be found in the Roman Missal in the *Ritual Mass for the Dedication of a Church*.[1]

## THE RITES OF THE LITURGY OF THE EUCHARIST IN ODC

### The Contents of The Liturgy of the Eucharist in ODC

The fourth part of *ODC*, *The Liturgy of the Eucharist*, begins immediately after the church has been illuminated. Referring to this part of the rite, the *Introduction* states: "When the altar has been prepared, the Bishop celebrates the Eucharist, which is the principal part of the whole rite and also the most ancient. For the celebration of the Eucharist is in the closest harmony with the Rite of the Dedication of a Church."[2]

As the fourth section begins, the deacons and the ministers prepare the altar for the celebration of the Eucharist in the usual way. When the altar has been prepared, some of the faithful bring the bread, wine and water for the celebration of the Eucharist. The bishop receives these gifts at the chair ("*cathedra*"), where he is seated. It is significant to note here again that the Latin *editio typica* of *Ordo dedicationis ecclesiae* consistently and deliberately uses the word "*cathedra*" for the chair in which the bishop is seated.[3] This word will be emphasized in this section, as it contributes to the understanding of the Eucharist as it is celebrated in this context as a celebration of a "station Mass" of the local church. While the gifts are being brought forward, it is appropriate that the antiphon supplied in the ritual should be sung. The antiphon is "Lord God, in the simplicity of my heart I have gladly

---

1. *Ritual Mass for the Dedication of a Church*, 1214–20.
2. *ODC*, no. 17: 35.
3. *Ordo dedicationis ecclesiae*, no. 72: 52.

offered everything; and I have looked with surpassing joy upon your people present here. God of Israel, Lord God, keep this resolve in their hearts (E. T. Alleluia)."[4] When everything has been prepared, the bishop approaches the altar. Once he arrives at the altar, he puts aside his miter and then kisses it.[5] This is the first time in the ceremony that the altar is reverenced in this way. At the beginning of the celebration the altar was not reverenced in the customary manner. Bypassing it, the bishop went directly to the chair ("*cathedra*").[6] At this point, after the bishop has reverenced the altar, the rubric indicates that the Mass is to continue as usual, with the exception of the fact that the gifts and the altar are not to be incensed at this point.[7] The altar itself was incensed in the third section of the rite, *The Prayer of Dedication and the Anointings*, with the people and the church. The *Introduction* points out that the Mass is to be celebrated by the bishop with all of the priests who take part in the rite concelebrating. It also indicates that among the concelebrants should be those priests who are assigned to care for the parish or community for which the church has been built.[8] The Mass is then celebrated according to the manner that is set out in the *General Instruction of the Roman Missal*. As an in-depth analysis of the entire liturgy of the Eucharist would be beyond the scope of this chapter, only those aspects of the celebration that are specific to ODC will be highlighted in this study.

The *Introduction* of ODC indicates that the rite of dedication may only be celebrated on those dates when it is possible to use the texts that are provided as part of the rite.[9] It also states that the dedication of the

---

4. *ODC*, no. 72: 63.

5. *ODC*, no. 73: 63.

6. *ODC*, no 35: 43. The rubric states, "The bishop, without kissing the altar, goes to the chair ("*ad cathedram*"); the concelebrants, Deacons, and ministers go to the places assigned to them in the sanctuary."

7. *ODC*, no. 73: 63. The rubric states, "When all is ready, the Bishop goes to the altar and, with his mitre put aside, kisses the altar. The Mass continues in the usual way; however, neither the offerings nor the altar are incensed."

8. *ODC*, no. 9: 33. The *Introduction* states, "It is fitting that the Bishop should concelebrate the Mass with the Priests who are associated with him in carrying out the rites of dedication and with those who have been given the office of directing the parish or community for which the church has been built."

9. *ODC*, no. 8: 32. The *Introduction* states, "The celebration of the Mass is inseparably linked to the Rite of the Dedication of a Church; so when a church is dedicated, the texts of the liturgy of the day are omitted, since proper texts are used both for the Liturgy of the Word and the Liturgy of the Eucharist."

## PART TWO

church is closely connected to the celebration of the Eucharist by the fact that the Mass for the dedication has its own preface that is an inherent part of the rite.[10]

The prayer over the gifts that is offered by the bishop at the Mass of dedication is:

> May the gifts of your joyful Church
> be acceptable to you, O Lord,
> so that your people, gathering in this holy house,
> may come through these mysteries to everlasting salvation.
> Through Christ our Lord.[11]

ODC indicates that the preface for the dedication of a church is to be prayed either with the First or Third Eucharistic Prayer.[12] The preface which is found in the current English translation of the Roman Missal is as follows:

> V/. The Lord be with you.
> R/. And with your spirit.
> V/. Lift up your hearts.
> R/. We lift them up to the Lord.
> V/. Let us give thanks to the Lord our God.
> R/. It is right and just.
>
> It is truly right and just, our duty and salvation,
> always and everywhere to give your thanks,
> Father most holy.
>
> For you have made the whole world a temple of your glory,
> that your name might everywhere be extolled,
> yet you allow us to consecrate to you
> apt places for the divine mysteries.
>
> And so, we dedicate joyfully to your majesty
> this house of prayer, built by human labour.

---

10. *ODC*, no. 17: 35. The *Introduction* states: "Finally, the bond whereby the dedication of a church is closely linked with the celebration of a church is closely linked with the celebration of the Eucharist is likewise evident from the fact that the Mass of the Dedication of a Church is provided with its own Preface, which is an integral part of the rite."

11. *Prayer over the Offerings*, Ritual Mass for the Dedication of a Church, 1214 and *ODC*, no. 74: 63.

12. *ODC*, no. 75: 64. The rubric states: "Eucharistic Prayer I or III is said, with this preface, which is an integral part of the Rite of the Dedication of a Church."

> Here is foreshadowed the mystery of the true Temple,
> here is prefigured the heavenly Jerusalem.
>
> For you made the Body of your Son, born of the tender Virgin,
> the Temple consecrated to you,
> in which the fullness of the Godhead might dwell.
>
> You also established the Church as a holy city,
> built upon the foundation of the Apostles,
> with Christ Jesus himself the chief cornerstone:
> a city to be built of chosen stones,
> given life by the Spirit and bonded by charity,
> where for endless ages you will be all in all
> and the light of Christ will shine undimmed for ever.
>
> Through him, O Lord, with all the Angels and Saints,
> we give you thanks, as in exultation we acclaim:
>
> Holy, Holy, Holy Lord God of hosts. . .[13]

When the First Eucharistic Prayer is used, there is a special *Hanc igitur* ("Therefore, Lord, we pray") formula that is provided for it. This is:

> Therefore, Lord, we pray:
> graciously accept this oblation of our service,
> and of these your servants,
> who in a spirit of faith
> have offered you this church (in honour of N.)
> and built it with tireless labour.
> (Through Christ our Lord. Amen)[14]

Likewise, when the Third Eucharistic Prayer is said, a special intercession is inserted into it. After the words, "the entire people you have gained for your own," the following is said:

> Listen graciously to the prayers of this family,
> who dedicate this church to you:
> may it be for your family a house of salvation
> and a place for the celebration of your heavenly Sacraments.
> Here may the Gospel of peace resound

---

13. *Preface: The Mystery of God's Temple*, Ritual Mass for the Dedication of a Church, 1215 and *ODC*, no. 75: 64.

14. Ritual Mass for the Dedication of a Church, *Hanc igitur* ("Therefore, Lord, we pray"), 1219 and *ODC*, no 76: 65.

> and the sacred mysteries be celebrated,
> so that your faithful,
> formed by the word of life and by divine grace
> on their pilgrim way through the earthly city,
> may merit to reach the eternal Jerusalem.
> There, in your compassion, O merciful Father,
> gather to yourself all your children
> scattered throughout the world.
> To our departed brothers and sisters
> and to all...[15]

Otherwise, the Eucharistic Prayer is offered as at any other Mass.

When it is time for communion, while the bishop is receiving the body and blood of Christ, the communion song begins. Psalm 127 (128) is sung with one of two possible antiphons. The first antiphon is: "My house shall be a house of prayer, says the Lord: in that house, everyone who asks receives, and the one who seeks finds, and to the one who knocks, the door will be opened (E. T. Alleluia)." The other antiphon is: "Like shoots of the olive, may the children of the Church be gathered around the table of the Lord (E. T. Alleluia)."[16] Another song may be sung. Communion is distributed to the faithful in the manner that is customary in that particular church.

After communion has been distributed *ODC* may be concluded in two different ways. The first of these involves the inauguration of the blessed sacrament chapel. When this option is utilized, after communion the pyx containing the blessed sacrament is left on the altar. The bishop goes to the chair ("*cathedra*") and all pray in silence for a short period of time. All stand, the bishop says "Let us pray" and after a brief silence he offers the prayer after communion:

> Through these holy gifts we have received,
> O Lord, we pray,
> instill in our minds an increase of your truth,
> so that we may constantly adore you in your holy temple
> and glory in your sight with all the Saints.
> Through Christ our Lord.[17]

All are to respond "Amen."

15. Ritual Mass for the Dedication of a Church, *Intercession for Third Eucharistic Prayer*, 1219 and *ODC*, no. 77: 65

16. Ritual Mass for the Dedication of a Church, *Communion Antiphon*, 1220 and *ODC*, no. 78: 66.

17. Ritual Mass for the Dedication of a Church, *Prayer After Communion*, 1220 and *ODC* no. 79: 67.

When the prayer has been completed, the bishop returns to the altar, genuflects and incenses the blessed sacrament. He then puts on the humeral veil, takes the pyx and covers it with the veil. A procession is formed. It is lead by the crossbearer, lighted torches and incense. The blessed sacrament is carried through the main body of the church to the chapel of reservation. As the procession proceeds to its destination, Ps 147:12–20 is sung with the antiphon "O Jerusalem, glorify the Lord."[18] Another appropriate song may be sung instead of the psalm. When the procession arrives at the chapel of reservation, the bishop places the pyx on the alter or in the tabernacle, the door of which is to be left open. He then puts incense in the thurible, kneels and incenses the blessed sacrament. After all have prayed in silence for a period of time, the deacon puts the pyx into the tabernacle or closes the door. A minister then lights a lamp, which is to burn perpetually before the blessed sacrament.[19] If the chapel where the blessed sacrament has been reserved can be well seen by all of the faithful, the bishop gives the blessing that concludes Mass from there. If the chapel cannot be clearly viewed by all, the procession returns to the sanctuary by the shorter route and the bishop gives the blessing either from the altar or the chair ("*cathedra*").[20] The deacon is then to dismiss the people in the usual way.

If there is no inauguration of the blessed sacrament chapel, the celebration concludes in the manner of a conventional Mass. When the communion of the faithful has been concluded, the bishop offers the prayer after communion. This prayer is the same as that given above in the event that there is an inauguration of the Blessed Sacrament chapel. After all have responded to the prayer, the bishop puts on his miter and gives the blessing to the people. This blessing is the same that is given at the conclusion when the blessed sacrament chapel is inaugurated. The bishop says, "The Lord be with you." The people respond. The deacon, if it is appropriate, tells the people to bow their heads for the blessing. The bishop then extends his hands over the people and blesses them, saying the three separate invocations of the blessing. These are:

> May God, the Lord of heaven and earth,
> who has gathered you today for the dedication of this church,
> make you abound in heavenly blessings.
>
> May God, who has willed that all his scattered children

18. *ODC*, no 80: 67.
19. *ODC*, no. 81: 68.
20. *ODC*, no. 82: 68.

PART TWO

    be gathered in his Son,
    grant that you become his temple
    and the dwelling place of the Holy Spirit.

    May you be made thoroughly clean,
    so that God may dwell within you
    and you may posses with all the Saints
    the inheritance of eternal happiness.[21]

To each of these three invocations, all are to respond, "*Amen.*" The bishop then receives the crozier and says, "And may the blessing of almighty God, the Father, + and the Son, + and the Holy + Spirit, come down on you and remain with you for ever." The deacon then dismisses the people in the regular way. This marks the conclusion of the rite for the dedication of a church.

## The Analysis of The Liturgy of the Eucharist

Most of the liturgical actions that take place in *The Liturgy of the Eucharist* are the same as those that occur in every celebration of the Eucharist. The study which follows is restricted to those rites and texts that are specific to the celebration of the Mass at the rite for the dedication of a church. They are examined under the categories of *rites, prayers, sacred scripture* and *persons*. The purpose of this inquiry is to determine what *The Liturgy of the Eucharist* can contribute to the construction of the theology for a parish that is contained in *ODC*.

### *Rites*

There are four ritual actions that need to be looked at in order to appreciate what *The Liturgy of the Eucharist* contributes to the theology of a parish in *ODC*. These are the presentation of the gifts to the bishop, the act of reverence that the bishop makes to the altar when he kisses it before the Eucharist is celebrated, the First Eucharistic celebration within the church, and the inauguration of the blessed sacrament chapel. Each of these aspects must be examined separately.

---

21. Solemn Blessing at the End of Mass, Ritual Mass for the Dedication of a Church, 1220 and ODC, no. 84: 69–70.

## THE LITURGY OF THE EUCHARIST

Before the Eucharist is celebrated, members of the community that is having its church dedicated are to bring forward the bread, wine, and water for the celebration of the Eucharist. This they present to the bishop who is seated at the chair ("*cathedra*"). Although this gesture is a part of every Eucharistic liturgy, it has a special significance at the first Mass that is celebrated within the church that is being dedicated. Here, it parallels the presentation of the building to the bishop by the members of the community at the doors of the church.[22] The offertory is an expression of thanks from a people who have received so much from God.[23] What is offered is itself something that has been made from the gifts which God has given in his creation. The community merely offers back to God what it has received from him. More important than the simple gifts that are offered by the community is what will become of them. From the bread and wine that are offered, God will give to the Christian community the body and blood of his Son. By partaking in this food, Christians will receive the graces that they need to live in communion with God in this world and in the next. The exchange that takes place in these elements points to God's outstanding generosity and the community's radical dependence upon him. Without his intervention, the bread and wine would be incapable of sustaining the assembly. By the power of the Holy Spirit, they become the body and blood of Christ, capable of sustaining the entire community and bringing them to eternal life.

When the altar has been prepared for the celebration of the Eucharist, the bishop is to approach it and reverence it with a kiss. This very simple gesture, which normally takes place at the beginning of Mass, has great significance at this point within the context of the dedication of a church. It is an expression that acknowledges the effects of the rites that were celebrated in the third part of *ODC*, *The Prayer of Dedication and the Anointings*.[24] In the prayer for dedication the bishop declared the community's intention to dedicate the church to God. The anointing of the altar made it a symbol of Christ and the anointing of the walls of the church symbolized that the building was perpetually given over to God.[25]

---

22. *ODC*, no. 33: 41.

23. Simons, *Holy People, Holy Place*, 54.

24. Calabuig, "'Ordo dedicationis ecclesiae et altaris,'" 447.

25. *ODC*, no. 16 a: 34. The *Introduction* states, "The anointing of the altar and the walls of the church:
- By the anointing with Chrism the altar is made a symbol of Christ who, before all others, is and is called "The Anointed One"; for the Father anointed him with the Holy Spirit and constituted him High Priest, who on the altar of his Body would

These rites have effected the status of the building. In a manner that is somewhat analogous to the way that the rites of the catechumenate effect the catechumens relationship to the church,[26] the rites of *The Prayer of Dedication and the Anointings* have changed the symbolic identity of the altar and building for the ecclesial community. The anointing of the building has set it aside in order that it may perpetually assume the sign value that it will receive when the Eucharist is celebrated within it. The bishop kisses the altar so that he may acknowledge before the community that it has become a symbol of Christ. It is a worthy place for the Eucharist to be celebrated and is to be the focal point of the assembly's gatherings. The importance of the rites of *The Prayer of Dedication and the Anointings* in preparing the building for the sign value that will be perpetually attributed to it through the celebration of the Eucharist is testified to by the existence of the rite found in the third chapter of *The Order of the Dedication of a Church and an Altar*. In *The Order of the Dedication of a Church in Which Sacred Celebrations are Already Regularly Taking Place* the rites of anointing are celebrated in a church that has already had the Eucharist celebrated within it so that it might be dedicated permanently to God.[27] These rites should be understood in somewhat the same way as those that are celebrated for a person who has been baptized in an emergency outside of the regular form in *Rite for Bringing a Baptized Child to the Church within Mass*.[28] They provide

---

offer the sacrifice of his life for the salvation of all:
- Moreover, the anointing of the church signifies that it is given over entirely and perpetually to Christian worship. Twelve anointings are made in accordance with liturgical tradition, or, as circumstance suggest, four, signifying that the church is an image of the holy city of Jerusalem."

26. See *Rite of Christian Initiation of Adults*, no. 48, page 18. This appears as number 18 in the *Praenotanda* of the *editio typica* of the rite. In regard to the change in the status of the catechumens in the church after the rites of the catechumenate have been celebrated the ritual states, "From this time on the Church embraces the catechumens as its own with a mother's love and concern. Joined to the Church, the catechumens are now part of the household of Christ, since the Church nourishes them with the word of God and sustains them by means of liturgical celebrations. The catechumens should be eager, then, to take part in celebrations of the word of God and to receive blessings and other sacramentals. When two catechumens marry or when a catechumen marries an unbaptized person, the appropriate rite is to be used. One who dies during the catechumenate receives a Christian burial."

See also The Second Vatican Council, *Ad gentes divinitus*, no. 14: 828–29.

27. See *Order of the Dedication of a Church in Which Sacred Celebrations are Already Regularly Taking Place*, in *Order of the Dedication of a Church and an Altar*, 71–98.

28. See *Order for Bringing a Baptized Child to the Church*, 187–201.

the catechetical and ecclesial dimensions of the rites that are necessary for the full effects of the celebration to be profoundly apprehended and actualized by the community.

The question of what effects must be attributed specifically to the different ritual gestures and actions that make up *ODC* is a difficult question to deal with. It lies well beyond the scope of this investigation. However, it is worth noting here, that in regard to these questions, Ignazio Calabuig has written:

> *PR 1977 non ha dato una risposta piena a questi e ad altri interogativi. La liturgia è espressione del* mysterium, *che non sempre consente risposte di razionalità cartesiana. Tuttavia PR 1977 ha fornito eccellenti soluzioni ad alcuni problemi ed è riuscito ad armonizzare elementi di diversa origine.*[29]

At the beginning of the rites of *ODC*, the bishop announced to the gathered faithful that the church building was to be dedicated by offering within it the sacrifice of Christ.[30] The *Introduction* of the rite indicates that the most important and only necessary action for the dedication of a church is the celebration of the Eucharist.[31] To this extent, *ODC* must be praised for returning the Eucharist to the heart of the rite of dedication.[32] It is viewed as the one essential act for the dedication, as it had been in the early Roman rite.[33] In keeping with an opinion that was expressed by the fathers of the church,[34] in the reformed rites of *ODC*, the church and

---

29. See Calabuig, "Rito della dedicazione della chiesa," 409–10. My translation of this passage is: PR 1977 (*ODC*) did not give a full response to these and other questions. The liturgy is an expression of (sacred) mysteries that does not always yield to responses according to Cartesian logic. Overall, however, PR 1977 (*ODC*) has provided an excellent solution to some of the challenges of this rite and has succeeded in harmonizing many of the diverse traditions in its (the rite's) history.

30. *ODC*, no. 30: 40. The bishop proclaims: "Beloved brothers and sisters, we have gathered with joy to dedicate a new church by celebrating the Lord's Sacrifice."

31. *ODC*, no. 15: 34. The *Introduction* states, "The celebration of the Eucharist is the most important rite, and the only necessary one, for the dedication of a church."

32. Paternoster, "Analisi rituale e contenuti teologici dell," 610.

33. As has been previously pointed out, the earliest references to the dedication of a church in the Roman Rite emphasize only the celebration of the Eucharist. This is the case for the dedication of the Cathedral in Tyre spoken of by Eusebius in the year 314. See Eusebius, *Historia ecclesiae*, X, 3, 3–4. Some two hundred years latter, in 538, Pope Vigilius wrote to Profuturo, the bishop of Braga, to tell him that the dedication of a church is accomplished solely through the celebration of the Eucharist. See Pope Vigilius, *Epistola ad Profuturum episcopum Bracarensem*, IV, col. 18.

34. *ODC*, no. 17: 35. In this regard the *Introduction* quotes the words of John

PART TWO

altar become holy when they receive the body of Christ in the Eucharistic sacrifice. The entire structure of *ODC* is arranged to situate the Eucharist as the climax of the whole celebration. All of the other ritual gestures have been placed within the framework of the Eucharistic liturgy. They serve as the foundation to this. The rites of *The Prayer of Dedication and the Anointings* blend with the other aspects of preparation for the Eucharist that take place after the homily and before the offering of the sacrifice.[35] They must be seen as preparing the building and the altar for the crowning event of the entire celebration.

In order to understand why the celebration of the Eucharist has such a pivotal place in the rites of dedication, it is essential to recall what sign value the church asks God to bestow upon the building as a result of this ritual. The church is to be a special sign of the pilgrim church on earth and an image of the church in heaven.[36] It is to represent the church (*Ecclesia*) of living stones which gathers within it to hear the word of God, to pray together, to receive the sacraments, and to celebrate the Eucharist. The living church that meets inside the building is the true and perfect temple of God that Christ has formed out of the holy people he won for the Father by his death and resurrection. Joined to Christ, her head, the church is the body of Christ where the Father is worshiped in spirit and truth.[37] The church building is to stand as a sign that points to the mystery of the church, which is the true temple of God.

The church building takes on this sign value when, after it has been set aside permanently as a place of worship for the Christian community, the bishop celebrates the Eucharist in it with the local community gathered around him. At such a celebration, *Sacrosanctum concilium* states, the principal manifestation of the church takes place.[38] The Eucharistic

---

Chrysostom. The words from him that it cites are "This altar should be an object of awe: by nature it is stone, but it is made holy when it receives the body of Christ." The *Introduction* gives as the source for this passage the following citation: John Chrysostom, *Homilia XX*, col. 540.

35. Calabuig, "'*Ordo dedicationis ecclesiae et altaris*," 445.
36. *ODC*, no. 2: 31.
37. *ODC*, no. 1: 31. See also John 2:21.
38. The Second Vatican Council, *Sacrosanctum concilium*, no. 41: 14–15. The constitution states, "Therefore all should hold in the greatest esteem the liturgical life of the diocese centered around the bishop, especially in his cathedral church. They must be convinced that the principal manifestation of the Church consists in the full, active participation of all God's holy people in the same liturgical celebrations, especially in the same Eucharist, in one prayer, at one altar, at which the bishop presides, surrounded by his college of priests and by his ministers."

celebration that is called for in *ODC* is a station liturgy of the local church. Here, the bishop celebrates Mass with the different ministers of the local church and the full participation of the faithful. As the bishop offers the sacrifice which Christ offered on the altar of the cross to the Father, his body and blood become present on the altar and a full and complete manifestation of his mystical body takes place in the ecclesial community that gathers. The epiphany of the church that occurs at this moment becomes identified with the building that has been permanently set aside to house the assembly that offers this worship to the Father. By this action, the building is elevated from having a mere function to being an ecclesial sign of mystical realities—the mysteries of Christ and the church.[39]

The place that is given to the celebration of the Eucharist in *ODC* provides a powerful demonstration of the importance of the Eucharist for the life of the church. The Eucharistic celebration produces the most intensive manifestation of the church.[40] Through it, the individual members of the community are bound together in charity and love and transformed into the body of Christ. Christ and his church are made present in the here and now of a specific time and place when the Eucharist is celebrated. In such celebrations, the universal church becomes present and manifests itself in the particular local community.[41] By participating in the Eucharist each individual Christian is more fully identified with the body of Christ and the community to which they belong is built up to become the spiritual temple of God.[42] The Holy Spirit is conveyed to the faithful in this life-giving sacrament. The gift that Christ gives of himself in his body and blood calls Christians to realize their identities as members of a royal priesthood who have been inserted into the paschal mystery. Strengthened by this gift, they too are to go into the world and make Christ present by offering their lives in loving service to the Father. The paschal mystery is to be the reality upon which the church and its members are radically dependent for their life and salvation. Without the Eucharist the church cannot exist.

The Eucharist also has the effect of communicating the eschatological destiny that belongs to the entire church. Through it, the local assembly participates in the heavenly liturgy and is given a foretaste of the eternal banquet to which its members are called. This spiritual food

39. Calabuig, "Aegno teologico della chiesa e dell," 92.
40. Garijo-Guembe, *Communion of the Saints*, 98.
41. Valenziano, "Chiesa particolare e liturgia dell'uomo," 65–68.
42. Savatore Marsili, "Chiesa locale comunità di culto," 42–43.

strengthens Christians so that they might reach this end. By it the building is also made an image of the heavenly church.

For the parish community that is having its church dedicated the vital place that is given to celebration of the Eucharist in *ODC* provides an essential lesson. By its celebration the parish community is transformed into a living cell of the body of Christ. In fact, as *Sacrosanctum concilium*, article 42, makes clear, the parish itself is established so that the Eucharist may be celebrated for those who are unable to gather with the local bishop for the liturgy.[43] In these communities, separated from their bishop for reasons of time, space, or practical convenience, the One, Holy, Catholic, and Apostolic Church is made present whenever their legitimate pastors celebrate the Eucharist.[44] By sharing in the body and blood of Christ, the members of the parish are transformed into that which they receive. The Holy Spirit is communicated through this precious gift and the assembly is fortified in communion with the entire church. It is by the power of the Holy Spirit, received in the Eucharist, that the many different men and women who make up the parish community are bound together in one body by charity and are able to manifest the church in their locality. Without it, they remain a scattered and diverse group of people. The Eucharist must be at the heart of the life of the parish community; it must be the very source and summit of its existence.

That the parish's Eucharistic celebration is to provide the most vivid manifestation of the church in a particular area, after that of the diocese, is testified to in many church documents. *Sacrosanctum concilium* refers

---

43. The Second Vatican Council, *Sacrosanctum concilium*, no. 42: 15. The constitution states, "But as it is impossible for the bishop always and everywhere to preside over the whole flock in his church, he must of necessity establish groupings of the faithful; and, among these, parishes, set up locally under a pastor who takes the place of the bishop, are the most important for in some way they represent the visible Church constituted throughout the world.

"Therefore, the liturgical life of the parish and its relation to the bishop must be fostered in the spirit and practice of the laity and the clergy. Efforts must also be made to encourage a sense of community within the parish, above all in the common celebration of the Sunday Mass."

44. The Second Vatican Council, *Lumen gentium*, no. 26: 381–82. *Lumen gentium* states, "This Church of Christ is really present in all legitimately organized local groups of the faithful, which, in so far as they are united to their pastors, are also quite appropriately called Churches of the New Testament . . . In these communities, though they may often be small and poor, or existing in the diaspora, Christ is present through whose power and influence the One, Holy, Catholic, and Apostolic Church is constituted. For 'the sharing in the body and blood of Christ has no other effect than to accomplish our transformation into that which we receive.'"

## THE LITURGY OF THE EUCHARIST

to the parish as the most important of the local communities to be established by the bishop. It has this importance because though the diverse parishes set up in different localities, the visible church is constituted throughout the world. Within the parish community itself, this unity is to be fostered by the common celebration of the liturgy, above all the Sunday Mass.[45] In the encyclical *Dies Domini*, Pope John Paul II spoke of the importance of the parish Mass on Sunday for making visible the unity of the church in a particular area. He suggested that all other small group Masses ought to give way to the parish celebrations on Sunday.[46] When the members of the local assembly come together at the Sunday Mass it is the setting for the celebration of the "*sacramentum unitatis*" which profoundly marks the church as a people gathered by and in the unity of the Father, the Son, and the Holy Spirit.[47] The Mass for the dedication is to make the parish assembly aware of the fact that it is the community that must make the church present within its local environment.

From what has been said about the power of the Eucharist, celebrated by a validly appointed pastor, to bring about a manifestation of the church, it is important to note a reality that is also acknowledged in the *Introduction* of *ODC*. It is not absolutely necessary that the diocesan bishop be the one to celebrate the rites of dedication. He may appoint an auxiliary bishop, another bishop, or in extreme cases a priest, to replace him at the celebration.[48] The power of the Eucharist itself is such that

45. The Second Vatican Council, *Sacrosanctum concilium*, no. 42: 15.

46. John Paul II, *Dies Domini*, no. 36: AAS 90 (1988) 735–36. An English translation of the pertinent section of this paragraph states, "This is why on Sunday, the day of gathering, small group Masses are not to be encouraged: it is not only a question of ensuring that parish assemblies are not without the necessary ministry of priests, but also of ensuring that the life and unity of the Church community are fully safeguarded and promoted. Authorization of possible and clearly restricted exceptions of this general guideline will depend upon the wise discernment of pastors of the particular Churches, in view of the special needs in the area of formation and pastoral care, and keeping in mind the good of the individuals or groups—especially the benefits which such exceptions may bring to the entire Christian community."

See also *General Instruction of the Roman Missal*, no. 113. It states, "Great importance should also be given to Mass celebrated with any community, but especially with the parish community, inasmuch as it represents the universal Church at a given time and place, and chiefly in the common Sunday celebration."

47. John Paul II, *Dies Domini*, no. 36: 735–36.

48. *ODC*, no. 6: 32. The *Introduction* states, "If, however, he cannot himself preside at the rite, he is to entrust the office to another Bishop, especially to one who is his associate and assistant in the pastoral care of the faithful for whom the new church has been built; or, in altogether special circumstances, to a Priest, to whom he is to give a special mandate."

whenever it is celebrated the Holy Spirit makes Christ and his church present. The *Introduction* recommends that the local bishop celebrate the rites with the participation of the people and ministers who make up the local church so that the reality of the mystery that is celebrated may be expressed as fully as possible. It is the celebration of the Eucharist that makes the building a sign that points to the mystery of the living church that gathers within it.

After the faithful have received communion, *ODC* is to be concluded with a ritual gesture that is new to the dedication of a church. The inauguration of the blessed sacrament chapel unfolds much like the procession with the Eucharist that follows the Mass of the Lord's Supper on Holy Thursday. As the Eucharist is taken from the altar to the tabernacle a powerful statement is communicated about the relationship between the altar and the tabernacle. The sacrament reserved in the church is the fruit of the sacrifice offered on the altar. The time of prayer and the incensing of the blessed sacrament that proceeds the reservation reflects the vocation to adore the Almighty that belongs to all Christians.[49] The lighting of the candle that is to burn perpetually over the tabernacle illustrates the reality that Christ dwells within his church always. He is to be encountered there at all times. Without him the church would cease to exist. In the building that stands as a sign that represents the mystery of the church, the reserved sacrament testifies to the reality that Christ alone is the *alpha* and the *omega* of the church's life and existence. The presence of the Eucharist in the church points to the fact that until the time comes when Christians stand before Christ in the New Jerusalem, the church is that place where he is to be encountered. As the faithful are dismissed from the rites of dedication, they are to carry Christ, whom they received in the Eucharist, to the whole world. After they have dispersed, the parish building is to remain as a visible sign that announces the presence of the living church in that locality. Within every parish church is to burn a light that announces that Christ dwells with his church and that it is within the body of this church—the body of Christ—that salvation is to be found.[50] The church building, through the rites of dedication, is made a sign that points to the living church.

---

49. Calabuig, "'*Ordo dedicationis ecclesiae et altaris*,'" 35.

50. The Code of Canon Law requires the Eucharist to be reserved in all cathedral and parish churches. The code states, "The Most Holy Eucharist: 1° Must be reserved in the cathedral church or its equivalent, in every parish church, and in a church or oratory connected to the house of a religious institute or society of apostolic life." See

## THE LITURGY OF THE EUCHARIST

### *Prayers*

The fourth section of *ODC*, *The Liturgy of the Eucharist*, is rich in prayer formularies. This investigation will focus upon those orations that are specific to the rites of dedication. There are six euchological texts that pertain to this inquiry. These are: 1) the prayer over the gifts; 2) the preface for the dedication of a church; 3) the *Hanc igitur* text that is to accompany the First Eucharistic Prayer when it is used; 4) the text of intercession to be used with the Third Eucharist Prayer if it is said; 5) the prayer after communion; and 6) the special final blessing to be used at the conclusion of the dedication of a church. As either the First or Third Eucharistic Prayer is to be used at the dedication Mass, those aspects of their content that contribute to an understanding of the theology of the parish that is contained in *ODC* will be briefly commented upon. Although most of the Mass prayers that are required for *The Liturgy of the Eucharist* can be found in the present translation of *ODC*, as has been mentioned, this study draws upon the recent translation of the prayers as found in the third revised English transition of the Roman Missal. It will be from this source that the soon expected revised translation of the rites of dedication will take the prayers for *The Liturgy of the the Eucharist*.

The prayer over the gifts is a new composition. It has been inspired by the antiphon that is to accompany the presentation of the gifts, which it follows.[51] This antiphon is taken from David's prayer of thanksgiving as he presents to God the material with which his son Solomon will build the temple (1 Chr 29:17).[52] Expressing the same joy as was voiced by David, the *Prayer over the Offerings* asks that the Lord may accept the gifts of a rejoicing church ("joyful church"). It continues by requesting that these might be received so that God's people ("your people"), who have gathered in this sacred place, may obtain everlasting salvation through the mysteries that are offered there.[53] While the prayer does refer to the

---

*Code of Canon Law*, can. 934, §1.

The code also states that the presence of the Eucharist is to be marked by a lamp that burns constantly before the tabernacle. In this regard the code states, "A special lamp which indicates and honours the presence of Christ is to shine continuously before a tabernacle in which the Most Holy Eucharist is reserved." See *Code of Canon Law*, can. 940.

51. Sartore, "Eucaristia nella dedicazione," 288–89.

52. *ODC*, no. 72: 63. The antiphon states, "Lord God, in the simplicity of my heart I have gladly offered everything; and I have looked with surpassing joy upon your people, present here. God of Israel, Lord God, keep this resolve in their hearts (E. T. Alleluia)."

53. *Prayer over the Offerings*, Ritual Mass for the Dedication of a Church, 1214 and

building as "this holy house," it is God's people who are its subject. It seeks eternal salvation for the members of God's "joyful church" who have come to the church to participate in the sacred mysteries. The church is that place where the faithful are to come to receive the food of eternal life. God's people ask that their simple gifts may be received by him in order that they may receive a gift of immeasurably greater value—"everlasting salvation."

The *Introduction* of ODC states that the close bond between the dedication of a church and the celebration of the Eucharist is demonstrated by the fact that the Mass of dedication has its own preface.[54] The nature of this bond is further emphasized by the fact that the preface, which forms an essential part of the Eucharistic Prayer, contains a rich synthesis of the themes expressed throughout the rite of ODC.[55] It is also a new composition that contains a rich selection of biblical, patristic, and liturgical themes.[56] The body of the preface provides a summary of the two principle themes that are found in the rites of dedication. In the first half, the building is spoken of as a sign that foreshadows the mystery of the true temple.[57] The church is an image of the church on earth and in heaven. In the second half, there is a beautiful exposition on the nature of the true temple of God, which is the body of Christ and the church that is founded upon him.[58] As the preface points out, humanity is to find

---

ODC, no 74: 63. The prayers states, "May the gifts of your joyful Church, be acceptable to you, O Lord, so that your people, gathering in this holy house, may come through these mysteries to everlasting salvation. Through Christ our Lord."

54. ODC, no. 17: 35. The *Introduction* states, "Finally, the bond whereby the dedication of a church is closely linked with the celebration of the Eucharist is likewise evident from the fact that the Mass of Dedication of the Church is provided with its own Preface, which is an integral part of the rite."

55. Cfr., Paternoster, "Analisi ritual e contenuti teologici dell," 613.

56. See Ward and Johnson, *Prefaces of the Roman Missal*, 364–369.

57. *Preface: The Mystery of God's Temple*, Ritual Mass for the Dedication of a Church, 1215 and ODC, no 75: 64. The first half of the body of the preface states, "For you have made the whole world a temple of your glory, that your name might everywhere be extolled, yet you allow us to consecrate to you apt places for divine mysteries.

And so, we dedicate joyfully to your majesty this house of prayer, built by human labour.

Here is foreshadowed the mystery of the true Temple, here is prefigured the heavenly Jerusalem."

58. *Preface: The Mystery of God's Temple*, Ritual Mass for the Dedication of a Church, 1215 and ODC, no 75: 64. The second half of the preface goes on to say: "For you made the Body of your Son, born of the tender Virgin, the Temple consecrated to you, in which the fullness of the Godhead might dwell."

eternal salvation through membership in the true temple of God. The content of the preface is significant enough to merit additional attention.

The preface follows the structure that is common to all. After the introductory dialogue and the "It is truly right and just" ("*Vere dignum*") paragraph, follows the content that is specific to this particular preface. The first paragraph of this deals with the symbolic value that is assigned to the church building as a result of its dedication. It proclaims that the whole world is God's temple, which has been created to proclaim the glory of his name. In other words, God himself has no need of the temples built by man. Yet as the preface continues, God allows man to dedicate to his service places where they may worship him (2 Macc 14: 35). The dedicated church fulfills a need that men have to designate as a sacred space those places where they worship God.[59] The preface, which is proclaimed by the bishop on behalf of all, announces that the community dedicates the building to God with hearts that are filled with joy. The structure, which has been constructed with the work of human hands, is to become a "house of prayer." It is significant that the building that is to be transformed by God into a sacred sign is referred to in words similar to the gifts that are presented for the Eucharist—"built by human labour."[60] Repeating a theme that occurs throughout the rites of *ODC*, the preface articulates that symbolic value that is to be attributed to the building as a result of its dedication in the two lines of the third paragraph: "Here is foreshadowed the mystery of the true Temple, here is prefigured the image of the heavenly Jerusalem."

While the first half of the body of the preface speaks of the sign value to be attributed to the building as a result of its dedication, the second articulates the theological identity and nature of the true temple of God. The second paragraph of the core of the preface states that the true temple of God is the body of his Son (John 2:21), which is the dwelling place of the fullness of the divinity (Col 2:9). The body of Christ, which has been consecrated to God's glory, is that which was born of the Virgin Mary. Unspoken of in this part of the prayer, but implicit in the account,

---

You also established the Church as a holy city, built upon the foundation of the Apostles, with Christ Jesus himself the chief cornerstone: a city to be built of chosen stones, given life by the Spirit and bonded by charity, where for endless ages you will be all in all and the light of Christ will shine undimmed forever."

59. See Eliade, *Sacred and the Profane*, 10–17.

60. The bread and wine that are to be transformed into Christ's body and blood in the Eucharist are referred to as "work of human hands" when they are presented to the Lord.

is the role of the Holy Spirit, through whom Jesus took on flesh, was born of the Virgin (Luke 1:26–38) and was consecrated. God's temple becomes incarnate and manifests itself among men by the work of the Holy Spirit.

The church itself has been established as a holy city founded upon the apostles with Jesus Christ as its cornerstone. This is the subject of the third paragraph. God, it says, continues to build up the church—his living temple—with chosen stones that are enlivened by the Holy Spirit (1 Pet 2:5) and cemented together in love. The role of the Holy Spirit in the continued growth and cohesion of the church is mentioned here explicitly. This reference to the chosen stones that are enlivened by the Spirit and cemented together in love also points to the symbolic value that was associated with the anointing of the stones in the walls of the church in the third part of *ODC*.[61] In this holy city, which is the church, the preface states that God will be all in all for endless ages and that Christ will be its light forever. This image alludes to the first paragraph of *Lumen gentium* and to the ritual gestures linked to the illumination of the altar and church.[62] The standard conclusion to the preface rightly implies that the faithful, through the relationship that they have with Christ in the church, will come to praise God for all eternity with the angels and the saints.

The preface presents an integrated overview of the theology of the church, and its relationship with the Triune God, that is expressed in *ODC*. The church is founded upon Jesus Christ, the Son of God, whom the Father sent into the world. The incarnation of the Son and the extension of his body, the church, throughout time and space have been accomplished through the power of the Holy Spirit. This same Spirit continues to call men and women to God so that the church may constantly be built up. Those who respond to this call are incorporated into the church and sustained in it through the enlivening work of the Holy Spirit, which makes Christ present to them in a particularly effective manner in the church's liturgy and sacraments. Through Christ the members of the church offer praise and worship to the Father. The faithful, through their life in the church, praise God during their pilgrimage on earth in communion with all of the angels and saints. Their eschatological calling is to offer this same praise to the Father for all eternity in the kingdom that he has prepared for them. The preface ought to remind the members of the

---

61. Crichton, *Dedication of a Church*, 50.
62. The Second Vatican Council, *Lumen gentium*, no. 1: 350.

parish that is having its church dedicated that they are a portion of God's holy people. They have been made one by the saving death of Jesus, as the Father, Son, and Holy Spirit are one. In their communion with God they are to form that temple of God built of living stones, where the Father is worshiped in spirit and truth.[63]

The preface must be prayed with either the First or Third Eucharistic Prayer, it being necessary to use one of the two at the Mass of dedication.[64] When the First Eucharistic Prayer is said, *ODC* provides a special embolism that is to be used after the words, "Therefore, Lord we pray" ("*Hanc igitur*"). This asks that God may accept the gifts presented by his family and mentions in a special way those who have given and built the church with their physical and spiritual offerings.[65] It draws attention to the fact that the building has been constructed for the spiritual welfare of a specific group of people. By their offering, they hope to enjoy the blessings of God's peace in this life and to be numbered among his chosen in the next. The members of the parish community offer the building to God with the hope that the mysteries celebrated within it will bring them to salvation.

The embolism that is to be used with the Third Eucharistic Prayer is to be inserted after the words, "the entire people you have gained for your own."[66] It asks that the prayers of those who are asking to have the church dedicated to God may be heard by him. The request is made that the church may become a "house of salvation and a place for the celebration of your heavenly Sacraments," where the gospel of peace may resound and the sacred mysteries may be celebrated. It is hoped that this

---

63. *ODC*, no. 1: 31.

64. *ODC*, no. 75: 64. The rubric states, "Eucharistic Prayer I or III is said with this Preface (cf. App., no 22), which is an integral part of the Rite of the Dedication of a Church."

65. *Hanc igitur* ("Therefore, Lord, we pray"), Ritual Mass for the Dedication of a Church, 1219 and *ODC*, no. 76:65. The *Hanc igitur* states, "Therefore, Lord, we pray: graciously accept this oblation of our service, and those of these your servants, who in a spirit of faith have offered to you this church (in honour of N.) and built it with tireless labour."

66. Ritual Mass for the Dedication of a Church, *Intercession for Third Eucharistic Prayer*, 1219 and *ODC* no. 77:65. The intercession for the Third Eucharistic Prayer states, "Listen graciously to the prayers of this family, who dedicate this church to you: may it be for your family a house of salvation and a place for the celebration of your heavenly Sacraments. Here may the Gospel of peace resound and the sacred mysteries be celebrated, so that your faithful, formed by the word of life and by divine grace on their pilgrim way through the earthly city, may merit to reach the eternal Jerusalem. There, in your compassion, O merciful Father, gather to yourself all your children scattered throughout the world. To our departed brothers and sisters and to all . . ."

will happen so that God's faithful may be led by the word of life and by divine grace through their pilgrim journeys to arrive safely at the eternal Jerusalem. In that city, all of God's scattered people are to be one day joined together in peace. The embolism complements the theme of the pilgrim people of God that is expressed in the Third Eucharistic Prayer.[67] It presents the church building as the house of salvation and hall of heavenly sacraments where those who are having their church dedicated are to hear God's word and be nourished by his sacraments. By these sacred realities, the faithful are to receive the strength and graces that they will need to reach their appointed destinies. Through the sacraments that are celebrated in the parish church, the members of the parish community are to be brought with all of God's people scattered throughout the world to the one celestial home he has prepared for them.

At the heart of every Eucharistic Prayer is the life-giving covenant that Jesus offers to all humanity. It is this covenant that gathers and binds each Eucharistic community into the one body of Christ. It must also be the force that gives definition to every parish community. Despite the rich doctrinal content of the Eucharistic Prayers for the theology of the church, a complete examination of the First and Third Eucharistic Prayers would be beyond the parameters of this inquiry.[68] Here, it will suffice to briefly point out some aspects of the prayers that help to establish the place of the parish community within the church.

Common to both the First and Third Eucharistic Prayers is a petition that asks that the sacrifice that is offered in the Mass may strengthen the entire communion of the church. The nature of this request is such that it situates the community that gathers to celebrate the Eucharist in communion with the local bishop, who is in turn in communion with the bishop of Rome. In regard to the importance of this aspect of the Eucharistic Prayers, Pope John Paul II has written:

> Each community, gathering all its members for the "breaking of the bread," becomes the place where the mystery of the Church is concretely made present. In celebrating the Eucharist, the community opens itself to communion with the universal Church, imploring the Father to "remember the Church throughout the world" and make her grow in the unity of all the faithful with

---

67. The Third Eucharistic Prayer states, "Be pleased to confirm in faith and charity your pilgrim Church on earth..."

68. For a treatment of the Eucharistic Prayers see Mazza, *Eucharistic Prayers of the Roman Rite*.

the Pope and with the Pastors of the particular Churches, until love is brought to perfection.[69]

The Eucharistic Prayers also articulate the relationship of the members of the pilgrim church on earth with the heavenly church to which they are destined. This aspect of the church's identity is recalled every time the Eucharist is offered. It is a dimension that it would be suitable to highlight within the context of the rites of dedication.

The Third Eucharistic Prayer offers a particularly vivid articulation of the nature of the communion that has been produced as a result of the covenant established by Christ's death and resurrection. This covenant has resulted in people from every age and time gathering, by the power of the Holy Spirit, to offer sacrifice to the Father through Jesus Christ.[70] As they gather to be nourished by the fruit of this sacrifice, the members of the particular community who eat Christ's body and blood are filled with the Holy Spirit and are built up into the one body of Christ.[71] The many different people from around the globe who celebrate the Eucharist do so because they all share the hope that they will one day be united in the kingdom that God has prepared for all.[72] The Eucharistic prayers serve to remind every Christian community that it is a portion of the people of God that has been formed by the New Covenant.

The prayer after communion has been taken from the tenth century Sacramentary of Fulda.[73] It asks that as a result of the holy gifts received,

---

69. John Paul II, *Dies Domini*, no. 36: 734. This is an English translation of the original Latin text.

70. The Third Eucharistic Prayer states, "You are indeed Holy, O Lord, and all you have created rightly gives you praise, for through your Son our Lord Jesus Christ, by the power and working of the Holy Spirit, you give life to all things and make them holy, and you never cease to gather a people to yourself, so that from the rising of the sun to its setting a pure sacrifice may be offered to your name."

71. The Third Eucharistic Prayer states, "Look, we pray, upon the oblation of your Church, and, recognizing the sacrificial Victim by whose death you willed to reconcile us to yourself, grant that we, who are nourished by the Body and Blood of your Son and filled with his Holy Spirit, may become one body, one spirit in Christ."

72. The Third Eucharistic Prayer states, "To our departed brothers and sisters and to all who were pleasing to you at their passing from this life, give kind admittance to your kingdom. There we hope to enjoy for ever the fullness of your glory through Christ our Lord through whom you bestow on the world all that is good."

73. See Richter and Schönfelder, *Sacramentarium Fuldense*, no. 2145. This prayer appears in section 383 of the Sarcamentary, entitled "*Missa in anniversario dedicationis aecclesiae.*" Here it also served as a post-communion (*ad complendum*). The words which appear in bold print are those which still appear in the Latin version of the *editio typica* of the rite of dedication. The prayer in the Sacramentary of Fulda stated,

PART TWO

God's truth may be increased in the minds of the faithful.[74] It goes on to request that the faithful may always adore God in his holy temple and extol him in his presence with all of the saints. The Italian liturgist Domenico Sartore notes that this prayer is based upon John 4:23 ("worship the Father in spirit and truth"), pointing to the pure adoration that is to be given to the Father in spirit and truth.[75] Within the context of all that has gone before it in the rites of ODC, it is to be assumed that the "holy temple" in this prayer, from which this adoration is to be directed to the Father, is the church—the body of Christ.[76] This oration petitions that as a result of the Eucharist that they have received, the faithful may grow in God's truth, may worship him in his church, and may come to glorify him in heaven. The Eucharist is to build the faithful up and bind them more fully in communion with God and his church so that they may enjoy full communion with him for all eternity.

The final blessing at the end of ODC contains a rich summary of the celebration. It provides an excellent conclusion to the rite before the faithful are sent to live their faith in the world. The first petition of the blessing reminds the assembly that it was as a result of an intervention of the God who made heaven and earth that its members were brought together to dedicate their church. It asks that God may fill them with his heavenly blessings.[77] The second proclaims that God wishes all of his children scattered throughout the world to be one. It requests that the assembly gathered may be made into his temple, the dwelling place of his Holy Spirit.[78] .The final petition asks that God might free the members

---

"**Multiplica domine queasumus per haec sancta quae sumpsimus veritatem tuam in** *animabus* **nostris ut te in templo sancto iugiter adoremus et in conspectu tuo cum** *sanctis angelis* **gloriemur.**"

74. *Prayer After Communion*, Ritual Mass for the Dedication of a Church, 1220 and ODC, no. 79:67. The prayer states, "Through these holy gifts we have received, O Lord, we pray, instill in our minds an increase of your truth, so that we may constantly adore you in your holy temple and glory in your sight with all the Saints. Through Christ our Lord."

75. Sartore, "Eucaristia nella dedicazione," 292.

76. See ODC, no. 1: 31. The *Introduction* states, "Through his Death and Resurrection, Christ became the true and perfect temple of the New Covenant and gathered a people to be his own." As this investigation has shown, this is the dominant understanding of the word "temple" that runs through ODC.

77. *Solemn Blessing at the End of Mass*, Ritual Mass for the Dedication of a Church, 1220 and ODC, no. 84: 69–70. The first petition states, "May God, the Lord of heaven and earth, who has gathered you today for the dedication of this church, make you abound in heavenly blessings."

78. *Solemn Blessing at the End of Mass*, Ritual Mass for the Dedication of a Church,

of the assembly from sin, that he may dwell in them, and bless them with peace. It expresses the hope that they may live with him forever in the company of all the saints.[79] The blessing articulates one of the central themes running through *ODC*: God has moved his people to dedicate the church so that they may be built up into his living temple and come to stand in his presence for eternity in the New Jerusalem.

The prayers that are found in *The Liturgy of the Eucharist* call the assembly that is having its church dedicated to recognize the reality that their community receives its life, purpose and identity through the New Covenant that Jesus established with the church in his life, death, and resurrection. Every time that they celebrate the Eucharist, the members of the parish community become what Christ has called them to be. By it, the Holy Spirit transforms them into a living cell in Christ's body. The prayers found in this section provide a powerful reminder to the parish of its essential identity. As this study has shown, the Eucharistic prayers of the church provide a reminder of this reality every time Mass is celebrated. These prayers call all those who are to receive Christ in the Eucharist to recognize that their community is a portion of Christ's body, the church. For the parish community they indicate that it is a cell of Christ's body called to manifest him in the locality in which it exists. Those who receive Christ in the Eucharist must make him present in the world so that men and women from every corner of the globe may come one day to stand in his kingdom for all eternity. The parish church is to be dedicated so that in it the parishioners may receive Christ and make him known in the area where the building stands. The building is to be a visible sign that announces to all who see it that God's living temple, the church, is alive and well in their midst.

## *Sacred Scripture*

There may be as many as three different processions that take place in *The Liturgy of the Eucharist*. Two of these, that at the presentation of the gifts

---

1220 and *ODC*, no. 84: 69–70. The second petition states, "May God, who has willed that all his scattered children be gathered in his Son, grant that you become his temple and the dwelling place of the Holy Spirit."

79. *Solemn Blessing at the End of Mass*, Ritual Mass for the Dedication of a Church, 1220 and *ODC*, no. 84: 69–70. The third petition states, "May you be made thoroughly clean, so that God may dwell within you and you may possess with all the Saints the inheritance of eternal happiness."

and that of the faithful at Holy Communion, are a standard part of the celebration of Mass with a community. The third, which takes place with the blessed sacrament after Mass as it is taken to the reservation chapel, is an optional procession that may be omitted from the rites of ODC. Each of these processions may be accompanied by a psalm or scriptural hymn that is particular to them. It is also possible that they may be carried out with another appropriate song. The *Introduction* states that it is the responsibility of the rector of the church being dedicated and those who assist him in the pastoral work to determine what songs are sung.[80] The passages from scripture that are provided in *ODC* to accompany these ritual actions will be examined here.

The first procession takes place as the gifts are brought forward by members of the assembly and presented to the bishop. In regard to the music that is to complement this, the Instruction to the Roman Missal states, "The procession bringing the gifts is accompanied by the Offertory Chant, which continues at least until the gifts have been placed on the altar."[81] The antiphon to be sung as the gifts are presented is based upon a passage from 1 Chr 29:17–18. It says, "Lord God, in the simplicity of my heart I have gladly offered everything; and I have looked with surpassing joy upon your people, present here. God of Israel, Lord God, keep this resolve in their hearts (E. T. Alleluia)."[82] This is the same *antiphona ad offertorium* that was found in the *Missale Romanum* of 1570 and 1962.[83] The passage is taken from David's prayer of thanksgiving in which he presents to the Lord the many gifts that will be used by his son Solomon to build the new temple for God. Immediately prior to this line, David acknowledges to the Lord that all the gifts that are presented belong to him in the first place (1 Chr 29:16). This is also the case with the gifts that the assembly presents for the celebration of the Eucharist; they return to God what he has created and given to his people out of love. This verse from David's prayer is to emphasize the relationship between the gifts that are presented for the celebration of the Eucharist and those that were

---

80. *ODC*, no. 19: 36. The *Introduction* states, "It is, however, for the rector of the church that is to be dedicated, helped by those who assist him in pastoral work, to decide and prepare everything concerning the readings, the singing, and other pastoral aids to foster the fruitful participation of the people and to promote a dignified celebration."

81. *General Instruction of the Roman Missal*, no. 74.

82. *ODC*, no. 72: 63.

83. *Missale Romanum* (1570) no. 3793: 608; and *Missale Romanum* (1962) no. 4469: *Commune sanctorum*, 40.

given for the construction of the church. Both the building and the bread and wine have been given so that the Eucharist may be celebrated. When the bread and wine are consecrated, both they and the building will be transformed in this first Mass that takes place inside the new church. The bread and wine will become Christ's body and blood. The building will become a sign of the mystery of the church that is manifested inside of it at this celebration of the Eucharist. The antiphon expresses the thanksgiving of the people who joyfully present their gifts to God in the elements with which the Eucharist is celebrated and in the gifts and talents that built the church.[84] These are presented with joy because the donors know that in return for their simple offerings they will receive blessings of unlimited proportions from God's generosity.

The second procession takes place as the faithful come forward to receive Christ's body and blood. At this time the communion antiphon, or another song, is to be sung as an outward sign of the communicants union in spirit, which is expressed by means of the unity of their voices, to show their joy of heart, and to make the procession a more complete community act.[85] *The Liturgy of the Eucharist* indicates that Ps 127 (128) may be sung at this time, with one of the two antiphons that are provided. The first antiphon that is given is that which also appeared in the *Missale Romanum* of 1570 and 1962 as the communion antiphon.[86] It states, "My house shall be a house of prayer, says the Lord: in that house, everyone who asks receives, and the one who seeks finds, and to the one who knocks, the door will be opened (E. T. Alleluia)." The first half of the antiphon is derived from Matt 21:13 and the second is taken from Luke 11:10. The text from Matthew is based upon Christ's admonition to the moneychangers when he cleansed the temple. The dedicated building is to be a holy place, a house of prayer where people may call upon the Father. The second half, from Luke 11:10, is taken from Christ's discourse on prayer in which he assures his listeners that the Father will grant the prayers of all who call upon him. The antiphon refers to both the church

---

84. Crichton, *Dedication of a Church*, 48.

85. *General Instruction of the Roman Missal*, no 84. The *General Instruction* states, "While the Priest is receiving the Sacrament, the Communion Chant is begun, its purpose being to express the spiritual union of the communicants by means of the unity of their voices, to show gladness of heart, and to bring out more clearly the 'communitarian' character of the procession to receive the Eucharist."

86. *Missale Romanum* (1570) no. 3795: 608–9; and *Missale Romanum* (1962) no. 4473: *Commune sanctorum*, 40.

as building and the church as community.[87] The church assembly is told that it must be a people of prayer and it is assured that God will always hear the prayers of his people. Because the building is that place where the people assemble, it is a place where they may be confident of God's presence among the members of his church. The greatest sign and assurance of this presence is the Eucharist that the people are approaching to receive as this antiphon is sung.

The second antiphon that may be used at this time is taken from Ps 127 (128), verse 3. Although it has been adapted significantly, it states, "Like shoots of the olive, may the children of the Church be gathered around the table of the Lord (E. T. Alleluia)."[88] Ignazio Calabuig explained that this verse from the psalm was given an ecclesiological interpretation as the children of the just, which are spoken of in the psalm, were taken to be the "children of the Church." The family table, at which the just were to enjoy the fruits of their righteous behavior, was changed to the Eucharistic "table of the Lord," referred to in 1 Cor 10:21, at which the faithful are fed on Christ's body and blood.[89] Gathered around the Eucharistic table of the Lord, the children of the church are to be like abundant olive branches, radiating the nourishment and the life they have received through Christ's body and blood.

The blessings to be received by those who walk in God's ways are proclaimed by Ps 127 (128) as it is sung with these antiphons. It states that the man who is faithful to God will have a fruitful wife and enjoy many children at his table. He will live a long life and see his children's children. Most important of all in this context, he will see the prosperity of Jerusalem and enjoy the peace of Israel. For the Christian the psalm proclaims the eschatological hope of the New Covenant and points to the promise that Christ made to those who eat his body and drink his blood (John 6:51). The psalm voices the confidence of those who follow Christ's command, to partake in his body and blood, that they will indeed receive the blessings and eternal life he has pledged to the faithful children of the New Covenant he formed by his life-giving sacrifice.

The inauguration of the blessed sacrament chapel is an optional aspect of *The Liturgy of the Eucharist*. Its execution will depend upon the discretion of those who prepare and celebrate the rites and on the

---

87. Sartore, "Eucharistia nella dedicazione," 287.

88. *Communion Antiphon*, Ritual Mass for the Dedication of a Church, *Roman Missal*. Canadian (Third) Edition, 1220 and *ODC*, no. 78: 66.

89. Calabuig, "Rito della dedicazione della chiesa," 416–17.

architectural design of the building. When it does take place, the procession with the blessed sacrament to the chapel of reservation is to be accompanied by the singing of Ps 147:12–20, with the antiphon "O Jerusalem, glorify the Lord."[90] The antiphon is taken from the first verse of that portion of the psalm that is to be sung (Ps 147:12). The psalm is a communal hymn of praise and was offered by the people of Jerusalem in thanksgiving after their return from exile to the holy city. It praises God for strengthening Jerusalem and speaks of the peace and abundance that the exiles find under God's protection after their return. It also proclaims the generosity of the God whose word created the world and rules nature, for he has revealed this same word to the people of Jerusalem. He has given his ordinances to the people of Israel and made himself known to them in a way that he has not done for any other nation. As the body of Christ is carried in procession to the blessed sacrament chapel, this psalm speaks of the intimacy of God's revelation of himself through the person of his Son, the word made flesh. Through the sacrament of his body, God's Son dwells with his people in a manner that is far more intimate than he has with any other people in the past. The experience of Christ's presence in the Eucharist will only be surpassed by the direct and immediate contact that the faithful will have with him in the New Jerusalem. The Eucharistic presence in the church makes the building a symbol of the celestial city. It points the assembly to their eschatological destiny. As they proclaim the antiphon "O Jerusalem, glorify the Lord," the faithful are reminded that they are a pilgrim people who are called to stand in the presence of Christ at the end of their journeys.

The scriptural passages that are found in *The Liturgy of the Eucharist* complement the ritual movements with which they are associated. They identify the church building as a sacred space where God is to be encountered by his people in prayer and sacrament ("house of prayer"). They point to the intimacy that God wishes his people to have with him. The living church presents this building to God in the hopes that it may be a place where they may experience communion with him. The communion and blessings that are experienced in the assembled church that gathers in this temporal structure foreshadow those that the faithful are to know in the New Jerusalem. The building is to stand as an image of this holy city.

---

90. *ODC*, no. 80: 67.

PART TWO

## *Persons*

In order to understand the significance of the Eucharistic celebration that takes place in *ODC*, and the importance of the roles that are played by the different members of the assembly, it is essential to view this Mass, which is the principal part of the rite of dedication, within the context of *Sacrosanctum concilium* 41. This states:

> The bishop is to be considered as the High Priest of his flock from whom the life in Christ of his faithful is in some way derived and upon whom it in some way depends.
> Therefore all should hold in greatest esteem the liturgical life of the diocese centered around the bishop, especially in his cathedral church. They must be convinced that the principal manifestation of the Church consists in the full, active participation of all God's holy people in the same liturgical celebrations, especially in the same Eucharist, in one prayer, at one altar, at which the bishop presides, surrounded by his college of priests and lay ministers.[91]

*ODC* calls for a station Mass of the local church at which the entire hierarchically structured community gathers around its high priest, the bishop.[92] Ideally, the rite is to be celebrated by the local bishop.[93] When he cannot be present, it is up to him to delegate another to take his place. The members of the church's different orders and ministries are also to participate in the rites of dedication.[94] The *Introduction* indicates that the ceremony should take place on a day when as many of the faithful as possible can be present.[95] The purpose of this full assembly of the local church within the edifice being dedicated is to achieve that full manifestation of the church that is spoken of in *Sacrosanctum concilium* 41. This is to have the result of effectively making the visible structure a sign that represents the living church that gathers within it. The rites of *ODC* that have preceded *The Liturgy of the Eucharist* prepared the structure to take on this sign value. The celebration of the Eucharist actualizes within the building the reality to which it is to point. In the encounter that takes

---

91. The Second Vatican Council, *Sacrosanctum concilium*, no. 42: 111.

92. Calabuig, "'Rito' per una Chiesa che vive," 43.

93. *ODC*, no. 6: 32.

94. *ODC*, no. 31: 40. The description of the procession to the church lists the places to be taken by the members of the different orders and ministries, as well as by the faithful who are to be present.

95. *ODC*, no. 7: 32.

place between the living church and the building that has been set aside to represent it, God bestows a sign value upon the church structure.

All of the different functions that are played by the various ministers and persons who participate in *The Liturgy of the Eucharist* must be seen in relationship to *Sacrosanctum concilium* 41. The one church that meets within the building is a single body made up of different members.[96] These members are hierarchically structured, each having a different role and service to fulfill within the one body of the living church.

In *The Liturgy of the Eucharist*, as has been the case throughout *ODC*, the bishop is to be seen as the high priest of the community that has gathered. Within the liturgical assembly, it is clearly he who plays the principle role in making Christ present as priest, prophet, and king. Even though the rites of dedication will be rarely celebrated within a cathedral church, the seat that is taken by the bishop is consistently referred to as the *"cathedra"* in the Latin *editio typica* of the rite. The liturgy is to unfold as a type of station liturgy of the local church over which he clearly presides.[97] As was the case when the building itself was offered, so too the gifts are given to him, and it is he who presents them to the Father on behalf of the community. He also offers the presidential prayers to the Father on behalf of the assembly, repeats in the preface the intention to give the building to God, calls on the Holy Spirit to sanctify the bread and wine, and offers the sacrifice of Christ to the Father.[98] The place reserved to the bishop in *ODC* communicates that he is the foundation of the local church's life. He is its principle teacher, pastor, and high priest. All other ministries in the church are to be exercised in co-operation with his mission to build the church up into Christ's body.[99] As the community begins its new life in the church building, the central role that is played by the bishop in this inaugural celebration testifies appropriately to his place in the life of the local church.

Evident in every celebration of the Eucharist, but perhaps more vividly in the rites of *ODC*, is the important ministry that the bishop fulfills in binding the local church to the universal. This aspect of the bishop's ministry is mentioned whenever the Eucharistic Prayer is offered, as it refers to the sacrifice that is made in union with the Pope and local bishop. In this Eucharist, his link with the individual communities

---

96. Ferraro, "Aspetti di ecclesiologia nel rito," 203.
97. Lara, "Dedicazione della chiesa e dell'altare," 611.
98. *General Instruction of the Roman Missal*, no. 92.
99. The Second Vatican Council, *Christus Dominus*, nn. 15–16: 571–73.

within the diocese is also demonstrated by the fact that the priests who assist him are to concelebrate the Mass. ODC specifically recommends that the priests who are to be responsible for the pastoral care of the parish or community having its church dedicated be among the concelebrants.[100] In this way, the rites bear witness to the assembly that their community is bound to the universal church through its communion with the local bishop.[101] This union depends equally upon the bishop's communion with the Pope.[102] Through the ministry of the bishop, each particular church in which the Eucharist is celebrated and the gospel is proclaimed is built into a living church in which the One, Holy, Catholic, and Apostolic Church of Christ is present and active.[103] The health of the assembly that is having its church dedicated, and the particular church to which it belongs, depends upon it being conscious of this fact.[104] As it is through their own particular bishop that Christians experience their relationship to the universal church in a real and concrete manner,[105] it is extremely important that he celebrate the rites of ODC.

The *Introduction* of ODC states, "It is fitting that the Bishop should concelebrate the Mass with the Priests who are associated with him in carrying out the rites of dedication and with those who have been given the office of directing the parish or the community for which the church has been built."[106] This makes it clear that the understanding of the rite is that the bishop will entrust the pastoral care of the community or parish to another priest who is to fulfill this work on his behalf. While the role that is given to the bishop in ODC shows him to be the high priest of his diocese, the place taken by the concelebrating priests around the altar with the bishop in *The Liturgy of the Eucharist* indicates their communion with him and points to the service they are to render in the diocese as his coworkers.[107] Once the ceremony for the dedication has concluded, the bishop will depart and it will be the responsibility of the priest appointed to care for the community to build it up into a healthy portion of

---

100. *ODC*, no. 9: 33.
101. The Second Vatican Council, *Lumen gentium*, no. 23: 376–78.
102. The Second Vatican Council, *Lumen gentium*, no. 22: 374–76.
103. The Second Vatican Council, *Christus Dominus*, no. 11: 569.
104. The Second Vatican Council, *Christus Dominus*, no. 22: 576.
105. Valenziano, "Chiesa particolare liturgia dell'uomo," 70.
106. *ODC*, no. 9: 33.
107. Chengalikavil, "Dedicazione della chiesa e dell'altare," 93.

## THE LITURGY OF THE EUCHARIST

the body of Christ.[108] Priests are ordained to share in the bishop's mission of making Christ the high priest, prophet, and king present.[109] In order to do this, they are to fulfill their task in communion with the local bishop.[110] Like the bishop, they are to build the church up by preaching the gospel and celebrating the Eucharist and other sacraments. They are to give the greatest attention to the Eucharist and ensuring that the Sunday Mass is at the core of the Christian assembly's life, as no Christian community can grow if it does not have the Eucharist at its heart.[111] When priests celebrate the Eucharist in communion with their bishop, the one church of Christ becomes manifest in these communities.[112] As the principle division into which a bishop divides the diocese is the parish,[113] parish priests are to be his principle collaborators in the diocese.[114] In the parishes that they serve, the church of Christ is made manifest throughout the world.[115]

The role of the deacons in *The Liturgy of the Eucharist* is similar to that which they are to have at any celebration of the Mass where they exercise their ministry. Mentioned specifically in *ODC* is the fact that the deacons are to prepare the altar and that one of them is to give the final dismissal.[116] The assistance that the deacon of the Mass gives to the bishop at the altar witnesses to the connection of his ministry to the Eucharist.[117] This will be continued in the life of the community, if the

---

108. The Second Vatican Council, *Lumen gentium*, no. 26: 381–82; and no. 28: 384–87.

109. The Second Vatican Council, *Presbyterorum ordinis*, no. 1: 863.

110. The Second Vatican Council, *Presbyterorum ordinis*, no. 7: 875–78.

111. Cfr. The Second Vatican Council, *Christus Dominus*, no. 30: 581–82; and *Presbyterorum ordinis*, nn. 5–6: 870–75.

112. The Second Vatican Council, *Lumen gentium*, no. 28: 384–87.

113. The Second Vatican Council, *Sacrosanctum concilium*, no. 42: 15. In this regard, the Constitution states, "But as it is impossible for the bishop always and everywhere to preside over the whole flock in his church, he must of necessity establish groupings of the faithful; and, among these, parishes, set up locally under a pastor who takes the place of the bishop, are the most important, for in some way they represent the visible Church constituted throughout the world."

114. The Second Vatican Council, *Christus Dominus*, no. 30: 581. The decree states, "Parish priests are in a special sense collaborators with the bishop. They are given, in a specific section of the diocese, and under the authority of the bishop, the care of souls as their particular shepherd."

115. The Second Vatican Council, *Sacrosanctum concilium*, no. 42: 15.

116. *ODC*, no. 72: 63; and 85: 70.

117. *General Instruction of the Roman Missal*, nn. 178–83.

deacon is permanently assigned to it,[118] as he exercises these same functions at Mass and brings the Eucharist to the sick and shut-in.[119] The distinct nature of the deacon's service at the altar also distinguishes his ministry from that of the priests who are concelebrants with the bishop. The connection of the deacons' ministry with the Eucharist is also illustrated as they assist in the distribution of communion to the faithful. The presence of the deacons at the Mass is also important for the full manifestation of the church that is to be expressed at this celebration. Together with the bishop and priests, they make present all three of the church's orders.

*The Liturgy of the Eucharist* indicates that the Mass should be celebrated as usual.[120] For this reason, the assistance that is required from lay ministers in these rites does not differ greatly from that which they provide at other celebrations of this nature. Those who assist at the altar are always to do so to assist to build up the body of Christ through the liturgical celebrations.[121] Acolytes or members of the faithful who have been trained to serve will be required to serve at the altar. They will also be required to assist the procession with the blessed sacrament to the chapel of reservation should this take place. Cantors will be required to assist with the music that accompanies the different processions. The 1973 Instruction, *Immensae caritatis*, from the Sacred Congregation for the Discipline of the Sacraments, stated that specially appointed extraordinary ministers could in certain circumstances distribute communion to the faithful.[122] The main reasons for the use of such ministers is to be the absence of the ordinary ministers of communion (bishop, priest or deacon), or crowds so large that the ceremony would be excessively prolonged because of an insufficient number of ordained ministers to distribute Holy Communion. Because *ODC* requires the presence of the bishop, deacons and many priests, it is unlikely that extraordinary ministers would be required to distribute communion at the Mass for the dedication of a church. *Immensae caritatis* states that the criteria to

---

118. The reestablishment of the permanent deaconate in many places will likely mean that one of the deacons will continue to serve the community that is having its church dedicated. See Paul VI, *Ad Pascendum*; see also *Lumen gentium*, no. 29: 387.

119. The Second Vatican Council, *Lumen gentium*, no. 29: 387.

120. *ODC*, no. 73: 63.

121. Paul VI, *Ministeria quaedam*, 427–28.

122. The Sacred Congregation for the Discipline of the Sacraments, *Immensae caritatis*, 225–26.

determine such a question are to be established by the diocesan bishop. The fundamental principle to be followed in the exercise of all lay ministries is that they be of service to the proper ordering of worship and to God's people.[123]

In the Third Eucharistic Prayer there is a petition that states:

> Look, we pray, upon the oblation of your Church
> and, recognizing the sacrificial Victim by whose death
> you willed to reconcile us to yourself,
> grant that we, who are nourished
> by the Body and Blood of your Son
> and filled with his Holy Spirit,
> may become one body, one spirit in Christ.[124]

This describes the effect that the celebration of the Eucharist is to have in the lives of all the faithful.[125] The explanatory rites, which precede the Mass in *ODC*, are intended to raise the consciousness of Christians of being the true temple of God and to recall the sacraments by which they become the holy dwelling place of the Father, Son, and Holy Spirit.[126] By their participation in the Eucharist, Christians receive Christ's body and blood and are transformed by the Holy Spirit into his living temple, where the Father is to be adored in spirit and truth.[127] As they gather to celebrate the New Covenant that Jesus formed with his life-giving sacrifice, the many individuals who make up the assembly are bound together by love and charity. This bond of communion, which is the fruit of the Holy Spirit, not only binds the members of the local community to one another but also to the entire church. The memorial of this covenant also raises within Christians the awareness of being a royal, priestly, and prophetic people that have been inserted into the Paschal Mystery of Christ and are called to live their lives defined by this reality.[128] By joining their prayers to those that are offered to the Father by the celebrant, the faithful transform their spiritual sacrifices into a living sacrifice that is holy and acceptable to God.[129] In this way, the laity are strengthened to fulfill their

---

123. Paul VI, *Ministeria quaedam*, 427–28.
124. The Third Eucharistic Prayer.
125. Mancini, "Spirito Santo construttore del tempio," 122.
126. Calabuig, "Rito della dedicazione della chiesa," 148.
127. Bargellini, "Ecclesiologia e tempio," 12–14.
128. Donghi, "Liturgia come intinerario educativo," 454.
129. Kloppenburg, *Ecclesiology of Vatican II*, 283.

PART TWO

mission of bringing Christ to every corner of the world.[130] The Eucharist is the source and summit of each Christian's life. By it they are sanctified by Christ and are assimilated into his body. It is also the high point in Christian worship because in adoring God through Christ his Son, the faithful offer praise to God the Father. All of this is accomplished every time the Eucharist is offered. The place that is given to the celebration of the Eucharist in the rites of *ODC* is a reminder to the faithful and to their community of the importance that the Mass is to have in the Christian life.

The church may certainly exist without buildings. However, when the church sets a building aside through the rites of dedication, it becomes a sign that reflects the mystery of the church and an image of the church in heaven.[131] This sign points to the corporate nature of the church. God does not wish to save Christians as isolated individuals but as members of his holy people sanctified through their common life.[132] This salvation comes only through Christ and the experience of him that is transmitted by his church. The visible structure is to point to the salvation that each individual is to obtain through membership in God's Holy People.

For the parish assembly having its church dedicated, *ODC* presents a rich catechesis as to what their community is to be. The rites indicate that it is to be that portion of Christ's body present within that particular territory. Through it, the many diverse men and women who live within its vicinity are gathered into the universality of the church.[133] At the foundation of its existence must be the sacramental and liturgical life by which its members are assimilated into Christ and enabled to offer praise to the Father. Fortified by these same sacraments, the different members of the parish community must offer their lives as an oblation to the Father. They are called to bring Christ and his gospel to all whom they encounter and to transform their environments. It belongs to the many different parishes around the globe, within their respective dioceses, to bear Christ to all the nations of the world.[134] In order to fulfill this mission, each parish must be open to the entire church. This means an awareness of its connection with the diocesan and universal church. In each parish, the men and women of a particular area are to be able to encounter the one

130. The Second Vatican Council, *Apostolicam actuositatem*, no. 2: 767–68.
131. *ODC*, no. 2: 31.
132. The Second Vatican Council, *Lumen gentium*, no. 9: 359–60.
133. The Second Vatcian Council, *Apostolicam actuositatem*, no. 10: 777–78.
134. The Second Vatican Council, *Ad gentes divinitus*, no. 37: 850–51.

church of Christ. By being incorporated into the church, through their parish community, they are to become members of Christ's body and to offer true worship and praise to the Father. Here they are to receive the eternal salvation that Christ offers to all nations through his life, death and resurrection.

*Sacrosanctum concilium* 42 states that the bishop is to establish parishes under the leadership of pastors. These communities, it adds, are the most important way by which the visible church of Christ is constituted in the world.[135] The rites of *ODC* present a theological catechesis that explains to the community that is celebrating the dedication of its church how it is to manifest the church in its locality. For the parish community, the ritual provides a summons to its members to become the living church in their area. By the celebration of these rites, the church building becomes a sign calling the parishioners to embrace their ecclesial vocations. In responding to this invitation they will come to their eschatological destiny. The building is to testify to the presence of Christ's body in that locality and to witness to the salvation that is to be attained through the living church that meets there.

## SUMMARY

As this is the last chapter in which the rites of *ODC* are discussed directly, before summarizing the findings of this section for the construction of a theology for a parish community, it is worth saying a few words about the importance of the place given to the celebration of the Eucharist in these rites and its significance for the dedication of a church. At the beginning of the rites of *ODC* the bishop announces to all who have gathered, "Beloved brothers and sisters, we have gathered with joy to dedicate a new church by celebrating the Lord's Sacrifice."[136] In the *Introduction*, the celebration of the Eucharist is spoken of as the most important and one necessary act for the dedication of a church.[137] It is described as be-

---

135. The Second Vatican Council, *Sacrosanctum concilium*, no. 42: 15. The constitution states, "But as it is impossible for the bishop always and everywhere to preside over the whole flock in his church, he must of necessity establish groupings of the faithful; and among these, parishes, set up locally under a pastor who takes the place of the bishop, and the most important, for in some way they represent the visible Church constituted throughout the world."

136. *ODC*, no. 30: 40.

137. *ODC*, no. 15: 34. The *Introduction* states, "The celebration of the Eucharist is the most important rite, and the only necessary one, for the dedication of a church."

PART TWO

ing inseparably bound up with the rite for the dedication of a church.[138] The bond between the rites of dedication and the Eucharist is said to be evident by the fact that the Mass for the dedication of a church has its own preface.[139] As Mauro Paternoster has observed, *ODC* returns the Eucharist to a central position in the rites.[140] In the previous rites (those of 1595–96 and 1961–62), he stated, it had been a mere complement to the rites of dedication.

Yet, despite the greater significance that *ODC* gives to the celebration of the Eucharist in the dedication of a church, the 1977 ritual does not communicate the idea that the celebration of the Eucharist alone consecrates the church to God. It is through the celebration of the Mass within the context of the rites of dedication that a church is dedicated. Through the anointing with chrism the altar becomes a symbol of Christ, the anointed one. The anointing of the walls of the church signifies that it has been given over entirely and perpetually for Christian worship.[141] When the conferences of bishops wish to make adaptations to *ODC*, they are to retain those rites that have a special meaning and force in liturgical tradition (such as anointing, incensing, the covering of the altar, and the lighting of the altar and church).[142] The fact that even after Mass has been celebrated in a church, in order for it to be dedicated, the rites of *The Order of the Dedication of a Church in Which Sacred Celebrations are Already Regularly Taking Place* are to be celebrated within it, which

---

138. *ODC*, no. 8: 32. The *Introduction* states, "The celebration of the Mass is inseparably linked to the Rite of the Dedication of a Church."

139. *ODC*, no. 17: 35. The *Introduction* states, "... the bond whereby the dedication of a church is closely linked with the celebration of the Eucharist is likewise evident from the fact that the Mass of Dedication of a Church is provided with its own Preface, which is an integral part of the rite."

140. Paternoster, "Analisi ritual e contenuti reologici dell," 609–10.

141. *ODC*, no 16 a: 34. The *Introduction* states, "The anointing of the altar and the walls of the church:

—By the anointing with Chrism the altar is made a symbol of Christ who, before all others, is and is called "The Anointed One"; for the Father anointed him with the Holy Spirit and constituted him High Priest, who on the altar of his Body would offer the sacrifice of his life for the salvation of all.

—Moreover, the anointing of the church signifies that it is given over entirely and perpetually to Christian worship. Twelve anointings are made in accordance with liturgical tradition, or, as circumstances suggest, four, signifying that the church is an image of the holy city of Jerusalem."

142. *ODC*, no 18 b: 35. The *Introduction* states, "rites which have a special meaning and power from liturgical tradition (cf. above no. 16) must be retained, unless weighty reasons stand in the way, but the formulas may be suitably adapted, if necessary."

indicates that the act of dedication is dependent upon the celebration of the Mass within the context of the rites and prayers of dedication. The building must be handed over to God and the altar transformed into a symbol of Christ before the celebration of the Eucharist may permanently set the sign value of the living church, which is manifested during the Mass, upon the building. For this reason, the rites must be seen as a whole. The ritual of *ODC* is significant in that it has returned the celebration of the Eucharist to a significant and necessary component of this whole. The other rites associated with the dedication are now to be found within the context of the celebration of the Mass—it has become the *fulcrum* point of the entire event.[143]

As far as attempting to explain the extent to which each aspect of the ritual contributes to the dedication of a church, the ritual does not answer these questions. It is assumed that if a church is to be dedicated, and Mass has not been previously celebrated within it, the rites of *ODC*, or a ritual adapted by the appropriate Episcopal Conference and approved by the Holy See, will be celebrated in order to dedicate the church. If Mass has already been celebrated within the church, the rites of *The Order of the Dedication of a Church in which Sacred Celebrations are Already Regularly Taking Place* are to be used. The approved rites of the church, celebrated in their entirety, are to have the effect for which the church intended them. These rites are supplied by the church to obtain the desired grace from God, not to respond to the demands of Cartesian analysis.[144]

The rites of *ODC* are able to obtain the effects for which they were intended because they were created to make the building into a sacramental sign. Sacramentals are sacred signs that bear a resemblance to the sacraments and the effects that they signify are obtained through the intercession of the church. The seven sacraments are effective as a result of the "saving work of Christ made present in them (*ex opere operato*)."[145] The sacramentals, on the other hand, because they were established by the church, are effective through the "Church's prayer of petition (*Ex opere operantis Ecclesiae*)."[146] The blessings, by which the sacramentals are established, place the created reality with which they are concerned in a more profound relationship with the mystery of Christ. In a very distinct

---

143. Paternoster, "Analisi ritual e contenuti reologici dell," 609.

144. Calabuig, "Rito della dedicazione della chiesa," 409.

145. Vorgrimler, *Sacramental Theology*, 316.

146. Vorgrimler, *Sacramental Theology*, 316. See also The Second Vatican Council, *Sacrosanctum concilium*, no. 60: 20.

way, these blessings have the effect of producing a type of "iconization" of the relationship between the Trinitarian God and all of the created goods that have an origin in his goodness.[147] Because the sacramentals depend upon the church's prayer of petition, it lies within the competency of the Holy See to determine how they are to be carried out and the manner in which they are to be established.[148] It is due to this authority over the sacramentals that the church may return the Eucharist in the rites of *ODC* to the central position it enjoyed in the early Roman liturgy.

It is also as a result of the authority that the church enjoys over the sacramentals that it may determine the nature of the sign value that is given in the rites of dedication to the church building. In the rites of *ODC*, the dedicated church is to stand as a sign that points to the pilgrim church on earth and to be an image of the church in heaven.[149] The *Introduction* states, in agreement with the scriptures and the fathers of the church, that the true temple of God is Jesus Christ and the living church that he has formed into his mystical body through the power of the Holy Spirit.[150] The building is to point to the identity of that living church that meets inside of it to hear God's word, to pray together, to receive the sacraments, and to celebrate the Eucharist. This church is the body of Christ where God is to be encountered. In order that this building may take on this sign value, *ODC* has established that a "station Mass" of the local church ought to be celebrated within the church as a part of the rites of dedication. While the celebration of the Eucharist that takes place in *ODC*, and all of the rites associated with it, may be celebrated in cases of necessity by a delegated priest, the most explicit manifestation of the church's identity is made visible if the rites are celebrated by the diocesan bishop with the full participation of the differing members of the local church. As has been seen, such a liturgy is intended to bring about that epiphany of the local church that is spoken of in *Sacrosanctum concilium* 41.

The manifestation of the living church that *ODC* strives to bring about in the church building is that of the local church that will itself meet and gather within the church to praise and worship God. It is this

---

147. Triacca, "Benedizioni 'invocative' in genere," 120.

148. *Code of Canon Law*, can. 1167. The canon states, "§1. The Apostolic See alone can establish new sacramentals, authentically interpret those already received, or abolish or change any of them.

§2. In confecting or administering sacramentals, the rites and formulas approved by the authority of the Church are to be observed carefully."

149. *ODC*, no. 2: 31.

150. See *ODC*, no. 1: 31; John 2:21; and Congar, "Glise," 105–14.

grouping of the faithful within the church, which is a portion of the body of Christ, that will make Christ and his salvation present in a particular area. In order that this manifestation of the church may be truly recognized as an expression of the local church, these rites stipulate that the celebrant should be the diocesan bishop. The Eucharist should be concelebrated with the other priests of the diocese, and especially with those to whom the bishop will entrust the pastoral care of the parish or community for which the church was built. In this way, the connection of the particular community with that of the diocese is more evident. The members of this community are also to participate actively in the liturgy. It is appropriate that some of the faithful who are in attendance should present the gifts to be offered in the Eucharist to the bishop at the chair ("*cathedra*"). This demonstrates to those in attendance the link between the sacrifice offered on the altar and the sacrifice they are called to make to God with their lives. The community that gathers to celebrate the dedication of its church is to recognize that it is a part of the living church for which the building is to stand as a sign. The rites of *ODC* articulate the identity of the local assembly as a cell within Christ's body and call it to assume the responsibilities and dignity that this entails.

Having summarized the importance of the celebration of the Eucharist for the dedication of a church, this investigation can now move onto summarizing the contribution that the *Liturgy of the Eucharist* has to make towards the theology of a parish community which is contained in it. Prior to the celebration of the Eucharist in *ODC*, the altar had been anointed to signify that it was a symbol of Christ and the walls to show that the building has been set aside for the worship of God. In a very real way, however, it is the celebration of the Eucharist that provides the epiphany of the church that unites the significance of the altar, which stands for Christ, to the walls of the church, which stand for the living stones of which Christ's church is constructed. The celebration of the Eucharist creates a type of fusion by which the different symbols that were created in the rites of *The Prayer of Dedication and the Anointings* are dynamically linked to become a sign that represents the living church that gathers within it.

For the community that gathers to celebrate the dedication of its church, the Eucharist has a similar effect. It is what Pope John Paul II has called the "*sacramentum unitatis*."[151] The many diverse members of

---

151. John Paul II, *Dies Domini*, no. 36: 735–36.

PART TWO

the church who come together to celebrate the dedication of the church are likely to be mostly composed of Christians who have already been baptized and anointed in the sacraments of initiation. However, it is the celebration of the Eucharist that unites all the faithful and allows their gathering to be transformed into a true and authentic manifestation of the church, which is the body of Christ.[152] By the power of the Eucharist, the men and women gathered to celebrate the dedication of the church are gathered into the one church of Christ, are united with him and one another, and make visible his one body, extending the incarnation throughout time and space. The Eucharist makes the church, transforming all who gather to celebrate into Christ's body.[153] When it is celebrated for the first time by the community that has gathered for the dedication of its building, it marks the inauguration of the local church. Gathering for the first time as a group within their place of worship, the Eucharist transforms these Christians into Christ's mystical body. They, united with Christ and his church, make him present in their locality.

Within the rites of ODC are to be found a rich catechesis regarding the nature of the *koinonia* that is to be produced by the *sacramentum unitatis* in all those Christian communities in which it is celebrated. In his exhortation at the beginning of the ceremony, the bishop asked God that the community that was born in the church's baptismal font may grow into a spiritual temple as the members gather around the one altar in love.[154] The Eucharist, because it conveys the Holy Spirit, is the source of all charity and binds the many members of the church together as one. The Preface itself indicates this as it states, "... a city to be built of chosen stones, given life by the Spirit and bonded by charity, where for endless ages you will be all in all and the light of Christ will shine undimmed for ever."[155] That the Holy Spirit is transmitted to those who receive the

---

152. See The Second Vatican Council, *Lumen gentium*, no. 3: 351; and no. 26: 381–82; and *Sacrosanctum concilium*, no. 41: 14–15. In particular, *Lumen gentium*, no. 3 states, "Likewise, in the sacrament of the eucharistic bread, the unity of believers, who form one body in Christ (cf. 1 Cor. 10:17), is both expressed and brought about."

153. Marsili, "Chiesa locale comunità di culto," 42.

154. ODC, no. 30: 40. The exhortation states, "Let us take part in these sacred rites with loving devotion, listening to the Word of God with faith, so that our community, reborn from the one font of Baptism and nourished at the same table, may grow into a spiritual temple and, brought together at one altar, may advance in the love from on high."

155. *Preface: The Mystery of God's Temple*, Ritual Mass for the Dedication of a Church, 1215 and ODC, no 75: 64.

## THE LITURGY OF THE EUCHARIST

Eucharist, as has been seen, is also eloquently articulated in the Third Eucharistic Prayer, as it asks: "grant that we, who are nourished by the body and Blood of your Son and filled with his Holy Spirit, may become one body, one spirit in Christ."[156] As these rites of dedication indicate, Christ is to be the reason for the local church's existence and the Holy Spirit is to be the wellspring of its life, binding all of its members to Christ in love and charity.[157]

Building upon this fundamental reality of the church's nature, *RDC* also contains an ecclesiological dimension that articulates the manner in which each particular community achieves *koinonia* with the rest of the church as it gathers for Mass. The church that Jesus established in order to extend the mystery of his incarnation throughout time and space is apostolic.[158] It is founded upon the witness of the apostles and through their successors, the bishops, the church has extended Christ's body throughout the world.[159] In the person of the bishop, to whom the priests are to render assistance, Christ the high priest is present in the midst of the faithful. When he offers Christ's sacrifice to the Father, Christ himself is present and his mystical body is made manifest in the assembly. Each local church, which is presided over by a bishop, is linked to the universal church through his ministry.[160] This understanding of the role of the bishop, which is articulated in *Lumen gentium*, is at the heart of the ecclesiology that is found in *ODC*. It is for this reason that the community's first Mass in the new building, and the rites that dedicate the church, are to be celebrated by the local bishop.[161] The ecclesial health of the community that is having its church dedicated depends upon it recognizing its proper relationship to the local bishop and its place within the larger diocesan community. The particular must always be aware of its relationship to the universal.

The relationship that the community that is having its church dedicated has with the local bishop is evident in the relationship that

---

156. The Third Eucharistic Prayer.

157. Ferraro, "Aspetti di ecclesiologia nel rito," 210.

158. *Preface: The Mystery of God's Temple*, Ritual Mass for the Dedication of a Church. *The Roman Missal*. Canadian (Third) Edition, 1215 and ODC, no. 75: 64. The Preface in this regard states, "You also established the Church as a holy city, built upon the foundation of the Apostles, with Christ Jesus himself the chief cornerstone."

159. The Second Vatican Council, *Lumen gentium*, no. 21: 372–74.

160. The Second Vatican Council, *Lumen gentium*, no. 23: 376–78.

161. *ODC*, no. 6: 32.

their pastor has with him. The pastor is to collaborate with the bishop so that he might make him present in those places in the diocese where he cannot be. The service that a pastor renders to the community is to exercise the bishop's ministry of teaching, sanctifying, and governing in his place.[162] ODC implies that the bishop will hand responsibility for the pastoral care of the community over to another priest, stating that the one who will assume this task ought to concelebrate the Mass of dedication with him.[163] Parishes are to be established so that priests may aid the bishop in the pastoral care of the faithful in the many different places where he cannot regularly be in the diocese.[164] When a priest who is in communion with the bishop celebrates the Mass in these communities, the universal church is made visible.[165] In order that the celebration of the Eucharist, the *sacramentum unitatis*, may have its greatest impact on the Christian community, pastors and the faithful are to give the greatest attention to the Sunday celebration in the parish.[166] ODC shows this respect for Sunday, when it suggests that the church should be dedicated on this day so that as many of the faithful as possible can be present.[167]

By their participation in the parish Eucharist, the diverse members of Christ's body are gathered into the universality of the church.[168] Here they receive the Holy Spirit and are assimilated more fully into Christ. The table of the Lord's supper is where all Christians are to be fed with the fruit of his sacrifice and have their hearts renewed in charity and love. At this table (*"mensa"*), Christ's paschal mystery is made real and his disciples are strengthened to live in the grace of the New Covenant that Christ has established with his church. The worship that is offered to the Father at the Eucharist is that of the true temple that Christ established by his death and resurrection. The Father is worshiped here in spirit and truth. The sacrifice of the Eucharist must also remind all of the faithful that as members of Christ's body they belong to a holy and

---

162. The Second Vatican Council, *Christus Dominus*, no. 30: 581–82.

163. *ODC*, no. 9: 33.

164. The Second Vatican Council, *Sacrosanctum concilium*, no. 42: 15.

165. The Second Vatican Council, *Lumen gentium*, no. 28: 384–87. *Lumen gentium* states, "Those who, under the authority of the bishop, sanctify and govern that portion of the Lord's flock assigned to them render the universal Church visible in their locality and contribute efficaciously towards building up the whole body of Christ (cf. Eph. 4:12).

166. The Second Vatican Council, *Sacrosanctum concilium*, no. 42: 15; and John Paul II, *Dies Domini*, no. 35: 734.

167. *ODC*, no. 7: 32.

168. The Second Vatican Council, *Apostolicam actuositatem*, no 10: 777–78.

kingly priesthood. They are to offer spiritual sacrifices to God through Jesus Christ and proclaim the virtues of him who has called them from darkness into his admirable light.[169] As living stones of the true temple, every single member is to reverence Jesus in his heart and by the spirit of prophecy give witness to him.[170] The Eucharist is the food that nourishes all of the faithful in order that they may bring Christ and his salvation to all the corners of the world.[171] It extends the incarnation throughout time and space.

The Eucharist also produces that *koinonia* by which the pilgrim church is joined to the heavenly church. Through it, the church on earth praises God with all of the angles and saints. Christians receive a foretaste of the heavenly banquet when they partake of Christ's body and blood. It reveals to all people the eschatological destiny to which they are called. Not only does the *sacramentum unitatis* unite all those diverse people who worship God on earth in the body of Christ; it unites the many people of different times and places and foreshadows the day when all of the faithful are brought together in the New Jerusalem and all division is ended. Here all will be one, as the Father, Son, and Holy Spirit are one and the Father will be worshiped in spirit and truth for all eternity.

For the parish community that is celebrating the dedication of its church, the rites of *ODC* communicate a fundamental truth: it must first and foremost be a Eucharistic community. In the same way that it is through the celebration of the Eucharist that the living church becomes manifest within the building, it is the Eucharist that transforms the assembled community into that portion of the church that makes Christ's body present in a certain area. The parish becomes the body of Christ within its locality, offering God's salvation to the men and women who live there, through the graces that are received in the Eucharist. As they partake in Christ's body and blood, the members of the parish become living stones within God's temple who proclaim God's salvation within their midst. As they share this saving message, they draw those who they encounter to the salvation that is found in Christ and his mystical body is extended to all nations. The parish is bound to the universal church through the celebration of the Eucharist. In this same event, the One, Holy, Catholic, and Apostolic church is incarnated and comes to life in a particular community. As a result of the celebration of the Eucharist in

---

169. 1 Pet 2:5 and 9.
170. The Second Vatican Council, *Presbyterorum ordinis*, no. 2: 864–66.
171. The Second Vatican Council, *Apostolicam actuositatem*, no. 2: 767–68.

the different parishes of the world, the affirmation which *Sacrosanctum concilium* 42 makes about them becomes a reality: through them the visible church is constituted throughout the world.

Through the rites of *ODC* the parish church becomes a sign that announces within its locality the presence of that community which celebrates Christ's paschal banquet. In this building, men and women are to encounter the salvation that is to be received by all of the members of that New Covenant community that eats and drinks Christ's body and blood. The building proclaims the salvation that belongs to the members of Christ's body. It points to the destiny that belongs to those who are called to praise the Father in spirit and truth for all eternity through him who is the one true temple of God—Jesus Christ. The reservation of the blessed sacrament in this building, which is to represent the living church, witnesses to the truth that it is in the church that Christ is to be encountered. Within the parish church, which has the altar that symbolizes Christ at its center, the body of Christ is to be built up within that territory in which the structure stands. From this building, Christ's salvation is to be brought to all who encounter that portion of the church that meets within it. The building itself points to the salvation that is to be encountered within that community that is fed and formed within it by eating Christ's body and blood.

# PART THREE

A Liturgical Theology for a Parish Community and the New Evangelization

IN THIS FINAL SECTION of this study, Chapter Seven presents the results of this study by synthesizing the theology for a parish community that is found in *ODC*.

# Chapter Seven

## A Liturgical Theology for a Parish Community and the New Evangelization

**INTRODUCTION**

This chapter presents the liturgical theology for a parish community that is found in the rites of *ODC*. In doing so, it offers a synthesis of the first two parts of this investigation. It will show why the rites of *ODC* of dedication have something of particular value to offer to a parish to help it define and live out its mission within the church. It gives a formulation of this theology using three "images" or "themes."

In order to accomplish this, it is necessary to return to the first chapter of this investigation and to state why the rites of *ODC* have a particular relevance for the construction of a theology for a parish community. This is the topic considered in the first section of this chapter. The purpose of this phase of the presentation is not to suggest that the content of this ritual does not have significance for other types of ecclesial communities. It is to demonstrate that this ritual has material that may be applied directly to the lived reality of the parish. The liturgical, sacramental, and ecclesial life that is described in these rites is such that it corresponds completely with the nature of the parish as it is described in the documents of the Second Vatican Council and the Code of Canon

PART THREE

Law. They have an import for the parish which addresses precisely its concrete situation within the church.

The actual articulation of the liturgical theology for a parish that is contained in the rites of ODC will be achieved through the use of three separate theological "themes." The treatment of these will take place in three different sections of this chapter. Each of these correspond to one of the three elements that the *Introduction* of ODC states must be given consideration when preparing the assembly for the celebration of this ritual. This preparation is to be based upon the spiritual, ecclesial, and missiological dimensions of the rite.[1] The three themes that are put forward in this chapter as a summary of the findings that were developed in the second part—Chapters Two through Six—of this study are: 1) the parish is a cell of the body of Christ; 2) the parish is a part of the One, Holy, Catholic, and Apostolic Church; and 3) the parish is portion of the People of God, sharing in Christ's priestly, prophetic, and kingly mission. These deal, respectively, with the parish's theological identity from the spiritual, ecclesiological, and missiological perspectives. Combined they provide a complete picture of the liturgical theology for a parish that is contained in ODC. They are in some ways distinct, while in other ways they are quite similar. They are developed here independently, so that each one may stand on its own. The result is that material which is necessary for the construction of one is presented in a different light in order to build another. Each theme complements the others and at times they stand upon the same foundation. Some duplication in the material is necessary for the integrity of each one of them.

The final section of this chapter presents a summary of these findings and a few brief observations in regard to some of the factors that might impact upon the ability of the parish community to come to a full appreciation of the material that the rites of ODC are intended to communicate.

---

1. ODC, no. 20: The *Introduction* states, "In order that the faithful may fruitfully take part in the Rite of Dedication, the rector of the church to be dedicated and others experienced in the pastoral ministry are to instruct them on the spiritual, ecclesial, and missionary importance and value of the celebration."

## THE RELEVANCE OF THE RITES OF ODC FOR THE CONSTRUCTION OF A LITURGICAL THEOLOGY OF A PARISH COMMUNITY

The first part of this inquiry investigated the nature of a parish community and the history of its development. Here, it was shown that the parish is a product of the church's lived history in the world. This particular entity in the church's structure emerged with time as the followers of Jesus Christ brought the message of salvation to the many different nations and peoples of the world. As this saving message was carried to the diverse communities that make up the one body of Christ, the parish developed as a cell within this body where the men and women of a particular place would hear God's word proclaimed and be built up into his body through the celebration of the Eucharist and other sacraments.[2] It is due to the importance of the parish community in the context of its place within the mission of the universal church established by Christ that it can be spoken of as having a theological significance. In fact, every parish is founded upon a theological reality, because it is a Eucharistic community.

The documents of the Second Vatican Council address the theological nature of a parish precisely from this perspective of its identity as a Eucharistic community. As was noted, *Sacrosanctum concilium* stated that because the diocesan bishop could not be present always and everywhere to celebrate the Eucharist in the local church entrusted to his care, he must establish smaller groupings of the faithful. Among these, parishes, set up locally under a pastor who takes the place of the bishop, are the most important, for in some way they represent the visible church constituted throughout the world.[3] The parish is to be built up in communion with the whole church principally through the celebration of the Sunday Eucharist.[4] The extensive investigation of the documents of the Second Vatican Council, which took place in the first section of this

---

2. The Second Vatican Council, *Apostolicam actuositatem*, no. 11: 778–80.

3. The Second Vatican Council, *Sacrosanctum concilium*, no. 42: 15.

4. See *ODC*, no. 7: 32. The importance of the Sunday celebration of the Eucharist in building up the parish community is spoken of in *Sacrosanctum concilium*, no. 42: 15. It is also the theme of the previously cited encyclical of John Paul II, *Dies Domini*. The importance of Sunday for building up the community is also alluded to in the *Introduction*, as cited here, when it states a preference for Sunday as the day for the dedication, as it would allow the greatest number of the faithful to be present for the rite. It says, "A day should be chosen for the dedication of the new church so that as many of the faithful as possible can gather, especially a Sunday."

work, articulated the manner in which the communion between Christ's universal church and the local churches throughout the world is maintained. Each local church is bound to the universal by the work of the Holy Spirit through the ministry of the bishop in the church entrusted to his care. The bishop makes Christ the high priest present in the diocese that he serves.[5] The priests who assist him in the diocese are his principle collaborators and make him present in his absence when they celebrate the liturgy.[6] Celebrating the liturgy in communion with the bishop, and sanctifying and governing that portion of God's flock assigned to them, priests render the universal church visible in their locality and contribute toward the building up of the entire body of Christ.[7] In those communities, where a duly appointed priest celebrates the Eucharist in communion with the bishop, the church of Christ is said to be made manifest.

The principal importance that the parish community has in bringing about the manifestation of the church throughout the world is not only spoken of in *Sacrosanctum concilium*. Again, as was shown in Part One of this inquiry, the documents of the Second Vatican Council refer to the parish as a cell of the church by which the good news of salvation is brought to the nations and the many diverse peoples of the world are gathered into it.[8] The parish, as both its history and the documents indicate, must be an instrument for building up the church in communion—it must be an agent of *koinonia*.

The importance and identity that was given to the parish in the documents of the Second Vatican Council helped to define and focus the definition given to it in the 1983 Code of Canon Law. Here, the parish was defined as a certain community of Christ's faithful stably established within a particular church, whose pastoral care, under the authority of the diocesan bishop, is entrusted to a parish priest as its proper pastor.[9] The code also articulated the role that the diocesan bishop is to have in establishing parishes, appointing pastors to them, and in the oversight of their day-to-day existence. It states the obligations that pastors have in providing for the spiritual life of the parishioners, and emphasizes the place that the parish is to have in the faith life of the members of

---

5. The Second Vatican Council, *Lumen gentium*, no. 21: 372–74.
6. The Second Vatican Council, *Christus Dominus*, nn. 30–31: 581–83.
7. The Second Vatican Council, *Lumen gentium*, no. 28: 384–87.
8. The Second Vatican Council, *Apostolicam actuositatem*, no. 10: 777–78; and *Ad gentes divinitus*, no. 37: 850–51.
9. *Code of Canon Law*, can. 515, §1.

Christ's body. The canons stipulate that under normal circumstances, their proper parish is to be that place where Catholics are baptized, married, strengthened in their faith life by the Eucharist and the sacraments and entrusted to God's mercy in the funeral liturgy.[10] The functions that the code attributes to the parish priest indicate that he is normally to be the one who celebrates the sacraments by which Christ accompanies the individual on his or her journey.[11] The parish, according to the Code of Canon Law, must also have a baptismal font[12] and a tabernacle for the reservation of the blessed sacrament.[13] It is also recommended that both the parish and the cathedral church be solemnly dedicated.[14]

What the council documents and the Code of Canon Law state about the parish community are very important to the discussion at hand because they show that the parish community corresponds most fully to the type of community that is the subject of the rites of *ODC*. The Christian community that is the subject of these rites of dedication, which were studied in Part Two of this book, is to be that in which the assembly encounters Christ in the sacraments, hears his word proclaimed, and is built up into his body through the celebration of the Eucharist. As this study has revealed through the analysis of the rites and prayers of *ODC*, the dedicated church is to be that place where the faithful are grafted into Christ's body in the baptismal font. Here, the faithful are to hear God's word proclaimed, be transformed into Christ's likeness by the sacraments, celebrate the Eucharist, and be strengthened to bring the good news of his salvation to the poor and suffering.[15] Here, the rites assume that the blessed sacrament will be reserved, so that the faithful may always be able to come to the building to know Christ's unconditional love, which is always present in the reserved sacrament. In the church that is being dedicated to God, the Holy Spirit is asked to make Christ present so that from "here" all may experience the salvation that is to be obtained through his mystical body, the church. The type of community that is the subject of the rites of *ODC* corresponds most completely to

---

10. *Code of Canon Law*. For baptism see can. 857, §2; for marriage see can. 1118, §1; for funerals see can. 1117, §1; and can. 530.
11. *Code of Canon Law*, can. 530.
12. *Code of Canon Law*, can. 858, §1.
13. *Code of Canon Law*, can. 934, §1.
14. *Code of Canon Law*, can. 1217, §2.
15. *ODC*, no. 62: 56–57.

that which is described in article 42 of *Sacrosanctum concilium* as making the church manifest throughout the world—that is a parish community.

For a parish community, the relevance of the rites of *ODC* is also to be found in the ecclesial relationships that are expressed in these rites of dedication. In *ODC*, the diocesan bishop initiates the life of the community and entrusts it to the care of the priest who is to provide for its pastoral well-being on his behalf. The building is also placed in the care of the diocesan bishop at the beginning of the ceremony.[16] The assembly that will gather in the church that is dedicated is referred to in the prayers as a community that will come to the dedicated building for the events of its sacramental life. While many different types of churches may be dedicated, unless they belong to a parish community, there would be little need for a baptismal font or likelihood that the local Catholic community would gather in them to celebrate the day-to-day events of its faith life. In fact, the only type of community that is mentioned in the rites of *ODC* apart from the diocese is that of the parish. So relevant is the content of these rites to the identity of a parish community that *The Order of the Dedication of a Church in Which Sacred Celebrations Are Already Regularly Taking Place* states that a church that has existed for a long time may be dedicated, without any changes having been made to the structure, if the community that assembles within it is given the status of a parish.[17] This reflects the reality that the rites of dedication have something to say about the nature of the parish community. The contents of the rites of *ODC* speak directly to the theological identity of a parish community.

This is not to say that the rites of *ODC* do not speak to the identity of other types of Christian communities. These rites speak to the theological identity that is at the heart of every type of Christian community. However, since, as has been stated in *Sacrosanctum concilium*, the parish community is the most important type of community into which a bishop can divide a diocese, it follows that the parish structure would most fully correspond to that which is found in the theology of a Christian community found in *ODC*. These rites have been based upon the vision of such a community that was articulated in the documents of the Second Vatican Council. In this regard, the rites of *ODC* can be said to offer a theology for a parish community that conveys what this type of a community must

---

16. *ODC*, no. 33: 41.

17. *Order of the Dedication of a Church in Which Sacred Celebrations Are Already Regularly Taking Place*, no. 1: 73.

be if it is to be faithful and authentic to its mission in the church. This theology informs the members of the local parish about the relationship that their community is to have with the universal church, about those aspects of the faith that must be at the core of their parish's existence, and about the call that belongs to them as members of the body of Christ. For the parish that is preparing to dedicate its new building, these rites of dedication should help to define the community and assist its members to understand the place that they have within the church. The rites make of the church building a sign of the mystery of Christ and his church present in a particular area. The building is to both announce the presence of the church in that corner of the world and to call the members of the body of Christ to manifest his saving presence to those whom they encounter. Properly understood, these rites make the building a sacramental sign of what the church should be; they call the members of the parish community to actualize this reality in their daily lives.

This chapter will now present a synthesis of the liturgical theology of a parish that is contained in the rites of *ODC*. Here, three broad conclusions from the rite will be articulated. Each of these aspects of a parish's identity is intimately connected to the other and none of them may be ignored. In order for the parish community to authentically manifest the church in its area, it must adhere to the implications expressed in each of these conclusions.

## THE PARISH IS A CELL OF THE BODY OF CHRIST

The rites of *ODC* articulate a theology for a parish community that reveals the theological significance of the parish to be based upon the fact that it is a cell of the mystical body of Christ. As they do this, they point to the absolutely gratuitous and essential roles that are played by each of the three persons of the Holy Trinity in establishing and bringing about the parish community and maintaining it in relationship with the holy people that Jesus Christ has won for himself through his death and resurrection. They reveal the parish to be a portion of that holy people, unified through the unity of the Father, Son and Holy Spirit, that is the temple of God built of living stones, where the Father is worshiped in spirit and truth.[18] The rites of *ODC* further show that it is through the church's sacramental

---

18. *ODC*, no. 1: 31. The *Introduction* states, "Moreover, this holy people, made one by the unity of the Father, Son, and Holy Spirit, is the Church, that is, the temple of God built of living stones, where the Father is worshipped in Spirit and in truth."

PART THREE

life that God continues his saving activity within the parish community and transforms its members into a living portion of the body of Christ. In order to fully appreciate what the rites of *ODC* have to say about the identity of a parish community as a cell of the body of Christ, it is necessary to review their theological contents in regard to the following: 1) the role of each of the three persons of the Trinity in the life of the parish; 2) the importance of Christ's word and sacraments for its life and existence; and 3) the effects of these in configuring its members into a portion of the hierarchically structured body of Christ, which is the church.

## God the Father is the Origin of the Life of the Parish

The 1977 rites of *ODC* proclaim that God the Father is the source of all life and goodness.[19] The parish itself, as a cell in the body of Christ, owes its entire existence to the Father's utterly gracious and mysterious design for the salvation of all people. As the prayer for the blessing of water in the initial rites states, it is by God's infinite mercy that sinful humans are called back to the loving Father. Despite our constantly turning away from him, the Father sent Jesus Christ to form a covenant of salvation with mankind. Through the waters of baptism, all sinners who receive this life-giving sacrament are made members of Christ's body and heirs of his eternal covenant.[20] All of those who have been made members of

---

19. The Preface for the Eucharistic Prayer provides the greatest evidence for this. It states,

> "For you have made the whole world a temple of your glory,
> that your name might everywhere be extolled,
> yet you allow us to consecrate to you
> apt places for the divine mysteries.
> And so, we dedicate joyfully to your majesty
> this house of prayer, built by human labour."

See *Preface: The Mystery of God's Temple*, Ritual Mass for the Dedication of a Church, 1215 and *ODC*, no. 75: 64.

20. The prayer for the blessing of the water states,

> O God, through whom every creature
> comes forth into the light of life,
> you accompany all people with such great love
> that not only do you nourish them with fatherly care,
> but you mercifully cleanse them of their sins
> with the dew of charity
> and constantly lead them back to Christ the Head.

the church through the waters of baptism have been made beneficiaries of the Father's unbounded generosity. The ability of each individual to accept this good news and open his or her heart to salvation has itself been a result of the Father sending his word into the world in the person of his Son.

As it is in the parish community that Christians normally are to receive God the Father's offer of salvation through the sacrament of baptism,[21] it is also from here that they are joined to the body of Christ and are to offer a sacrifice of praise to the Father. The nature of the sacrifice and worship that is owed to the Father is announced in these rites by the centrality of the altar, the placement of the relics of a martyr or saint beneath the altar, the explanatory rites that follow the anointing of the altar, and most especially by the sacrifice of the Mass, which is at the heart of the ritual. All of these call the community and its members to realize that they must join their lives to Christ's sacrifice and give themselves to fulfilling the will of the all-loving Father. This reality is witnessed to by the rite for the incensing of the people, whose lives are to be offered to

> For in your merciful plan you established,
> that those who descend as sinners,
> into the sacred waters to die with Christ
> should rise free from guilt
> and be made his members,
> heirs with him to an eternal reward.
>
> Sanctify + therefore with your blessing
> this water you have created,
> that, sprinkled on us
> and on the walls of this church,
> it may be a sign of the cleansing waters of salvation,
> in which we have been washed in Christ
> and made a temple of your Spirit.
>
> Grant that, with all our brothers and sisters
> who will celebrate the divine mysteries in this church,
> we may come at last to the heavenly Jerusalem.
>
> Through Christ our Lord.
> R/. Amen.

See *ODC*, no. 48: 48–49.

21. It will be recalled that the Code of Canon Law has stated that the parish community is usually to be the place of baptism. See *Code of Canon Law*, can. 857, §2. In this regard see also the prayer for dedication, *ODC*, no. 62: 57. It states, "Here may the flood of divine grace overwhelm human offences, so that your children, Father, being dead to sin, may be reborn to heavenly life."

God as a sweet offering.[22] By the place given to the Eucharist in *ODC*, the ritual witnesses to the fact that the entire Christian life must be lived in thanksgiving to the Father for the salvation that he extends to all through his Son's death and resurrection.

The 1977 rites of *ODC* also call the parish community to realize that the Father is the eschatological end to which all its efforts are to be directed. The earthly liturgy, which is celebrated in the newly dedicated building, foreshadows the celestial liturgy to which all Christians are called. Those who are drawn to the local community, restricted by time and space, come in the hopes of attaining eternal communion with the Father. He is the origin of the community's life and existence.

## Christ the Son is the Source and Foundation of the Parish Community's Existence

The rites of *ODC* show that the parish's existence is dependent upon the Lord Jesus Christ and is sustained and nourished by him. It is he who draws new members to the community, gathers the many into his one body and gives it life and purpose. Through him the faithful have access to the Father. This reality runs throughout the entire ritual program of the 1977 *ordo* of dedication. *ODC* calls the parish to keep its life focused upon Christ and to understand that it is only through faithfulness to him that it may be what it is called to be in the church.

The centrality of Christ's role in the identity of the parish, and every other Christian community for that matter, is proclaimed in the opening paragraph of the *Introduction*. Declaring that, "Through his Death and Resurrection, Christ became the true and perfect temple of the New Covenant and gathered a people to be his own,"[23] the *Introduction* articulates the reality that Christ's paschal mystery is at the heart of the church's existence. It is through this alone that it came into being and is sustained and nourished. It is this reality that makes the liturgy the source and summit of the church's life[24] and causes it to be identified in

---

22. *ODC*, no. 16 b: 34. The *Introduction* states, "Moreover, the incensation of the main body of the church indicates that the dedication makes it a house of prayer, but the People of God are incensed first, for they are the living temple in which each faithful member is a spiritual altar."

23. *ODC*, no. 1: 31.

24. The Second Vatican Council, *Sacrosanctum concilium*, no. 10: 6. The constitution states, "Nevertheless the liturgy is the summit toward which the activity of the

the ritual program of the rites of dedication as the means through which Christ continues to build up his church. Through the liturgy, the diverse members of the parish are built into the one temple of God, where the Father is worshiped in Spirit and truth.[25] The extent to which the rites of *RDC* are orientated to calling the parish community to recognize its foundation in the New Covenant offered in Jesus Christ can be seen by a brief examination of its four parts.

In the *Introductory Rites*, the members of the parish community that gathers to dedicate its church are reminded that their community was born in the baptismal font.[26] In this font each parishioner passed through the sacred waters to die with Christ and rise restored as members of his body and as heirs of his covenant.[27] The sprinkling with holy water is to remind all that it was Christ's death and resurrection that has gathered them together and formed them into his people. It is Jesus Christ, and not mere geographical proximity, that brings them together. Their relationship is based upon their fellowship with Christ, and this is to call them beyond the concerns of their own immediate needs. In order that the parish may properly become that portion of Christ's body that it is called to be in the world, the bishop asks in the opening exhortation that all of the members of the community might open their hearts and minds to receive his word with faith and be sustained at the table of the Lord so that they may become the one temple of his Spirit. They must die to their old life of sin and live according to that new life to which Christ has called them.[28]

The rites of *The Liturgy of the Word* make it clear that Christ's word plays an essential role in the formation and continued life of the parish community. God's word is to unfold the mystery of Christ and achieve the

---

Church is directed; it is also the fount from which all her power flows."

25. *ODC*, no 1: 31. The *Introduction* states, "Moreover, this holy people, made one by the unity of the Father, Son and Holy Spirit, is the Church, that is, the temple of God built of living stones, where the Father is worshipped in Spirit and in truth."

26. *ODC*, no. 30: 40. The bishop is to begin by saying, "Beloved brothers and sisters, we have gathered with joy to dedicate a new church by celebrating the Lord's Sacrifice. Let us take part in these sacred rites with loving devotion, listening to the Word of God with faith, so that our community, reborn from the **one font of Baptism** and nourished at the same table, may grow into a spiritual temple, and, brought together at one altar, may advance in love from on high." The bold print has been added for emphasis.

27. *ODC*, no. 48: 48. The text for the blessing of the water that is cited here is given in full in footnote number 20 of this chapter.

28. The Second Vatican Council, *Lumen gentium*, no. 7: 4–5.

PART THREE

salvation of the members of the community.[29] As the mandatory reading from Nehemiah serves to point out, it is God's word—Jesus Christ in the New Covenant—that calls the community into existence.[30] It is the Word made flesh that attracts new members to the community, sustains those members who are on their pilgrim journey, and leads all Christians to their heavenly destiny. As the response to the psalm makes clear as it states, "Your words, Lord, are spirit and life," it is to be Christ's word that defines the spirit and life of the parish. This word is not to be subjected to the cult of personality or the political agenda of a particular group. It announces the truth about humanity, communicates the salvation to be found in Christ, and builds up the community to take its proper place in the body of Christ. The Word of God shows the members of the community that they form a part of the larger household of God which rises on the apostles and has Christ as its foundation stone.[31] Within this household, the pilgrim members of the body of Christ are to encounter the salvation that is offered to them in Jesus Christ "today."[32] They are also to be formed in Christ's word in order that they may bring the salvation that he offers through it to those whom they encounter in the day-to-day realities of their lives. The parish is to be that place from which the Word of God is announced in its particular locality so that all who encounter it there may come to salvation at the end of time.

In the third section of *ODC*, *The Prayer of Dedication and the Anointings*, the ritual gestures articulate what it means for the parish to be a portion of the anointed body of Christ present in the world. The community which receives its life from Christ, and is nourished by him, must be one that responds in faith to the tremendous gift of salvation that it has received from its redeemer. Thus, the relics of a martyr or a saint may be placed under the altar to signify that the sacrifice of the members has its source in the sacrifice of the head.[33] The rites of anointing, incens-

---

29. *ODC*, no. 53: 376. The bishop is to hold up the lectionary and say, "May the word of God resound always in this building to open for you the mystery of Christ and to bring about your salvation in the Church."

30. The Second Vatican Council, *Presbyterorum ordinis*, no. 4: 868–70. The Decree on the ministry and life of priests also speaks of the importance of the Word of God in forming the People of God.

31. Eph 2:19–22. This text is one of the selections that might be used in the Liturgy of the Word at the dedication Mass.

32. Luke 19:1–10. This is one of the Gospels that might be proclaimed at the dedication Mass.

33. *ODC*, no. 14: 34. The *Introduction* states, "After the singing of the Litany,

ing, covering and lighting the altar express in visible signs several aspects of the invisible work that the Lord accomplishes through the church in the celebration of the divine mysteries, especially the Eucharist.[34] The anointing of the altar makes it a sign of Christ, the anointed one, who on the altar of his own body offered the sacrifice of his life for the salvation of all.[35] The altar is to stand at the heart of the parish church to symbolize that it is from the saving events of Christ's paschal mystery that the church continues to draw its strength. The walls of the building are anointed to call the parishioners to an awareness of the fact that they are living stones in God's temple. The prayer of dedication states how the parishioners are to be assimilated into the body of Christ through the church's liturgical and sacramental life. It is Christ's blood which sanctifies the church.[36] As the church and altar are incensed and illuminated, the rites continue to point out to the assembly the importance of giving themselves over to Christ that he may transform them and they may bring him to those that they encounter. Incense is burned first on the altar to signify that there Christ's sacrifice is perpetuated in mystery and rises to the Father as a sweet offering. The people are then incensed because they too are to offer their lives through Christ to the Father.[37] The altar is then covered

---

depending on the circumstances, the relics of a Martyr are to be deposited to signify that the sacrifice of the members has drawn its origin from the Sacrifice of the Head. When the relics of a Martyr are not available, however, then the relics of another Saint may be deposited in the altar."

34. *ODC*, no. 16: 34. The *Introduction* states, "The rites of the anointing, the incensation, the covering, and the lighting of the altar express in visible signs several aspects of the invisible work which the Lord accomplishes through the Church in the celebration of the divine mysteries, especially the Eucharist."

35. *ODC*, no. 16 a: 34. The *Introduction* states, "By the anointing with Chrism the altar is made a symbol of Christ who, before all others, is and is called 'The Anointed One'; for the Father anointed him with the Holy Spirit and constituted him High Priest, who on the altar of his Body would offer the sacrifice of his life for the salvation of all."

36. *ODC*, no. 62: 56. The prayer of dedication states, "This house brings to light the mystery of the Church, which Christ made holy **by the shedding of his blood,** so that he might present her to himself as a glorious Bride, a Virgin resplendent with the integrity of faith, a Mother made fruitful by the power of the Spirit." The bold has been added for emphasis.

37. *ODC*, no. 16 b: 34. The *Introduction* states, "Incense is burned on the altar to signify that the Sacrifice of Christ, which is there perpetuated in mystery, ascends to God in an odour of sweetness; this is also a sign that the pleasing and acceptable prayers of the faithful rise up to the throne of God.

Moreover, the incensation of the main body of the church indicates that the dedication makes it a house of prayer; but the People of God are incensed first, for they are the living temple in which each faithful member is a spiritual altar."

so that all may understand that it is by feeding on the sacrifice of Christ's body and blood that they are gathered as one and sustained in the gift of salvation. The identity of Christ as the light of the world who illumines the church so that its members may bring his light to the nations is made manifest in these rites as first the altar is lit and then the church. As this occurs the bishop is to say, "Let the light of Christ shine brightly in the church, that all nations may attain the fullness of the truth."[38]

The place that is given to the celebration of the Eucharist in the rites of *ODC* gives the most powerful testimony to the place that Christ is to have in the life of the parish community. The *Introduction* declares that the Eucharist is the most important and one thing that is necessary for the dedication of a church.[39] Likewise, it is only Christ's presence in the parish's Eucharistic celebration which transforms the local gathering into a cell of his body.[40] Christ and his paschal mystery, as it is represented in the Eucharist, are the one thing that is necessary for the life of the parish. As *Sacrosanctum concilium* stated, the parish itself is established so that the Eucharist can be celebrated there and Christ's church can be made manifest throughout the world.[41] Because Christ himself is received in the Eucharist and builds the church into one, it is called the *sacramentum unitatis*.[42] For this reason, the Sunday Eucharist is to be given the great-

---

38. *ODC*, no. 70: 61. This image is taken directly from the first paragraph of *Lumen gentium*. The Constitution states, "Christ is the light of humanity; and it is, accordingly, the heart-felt desire of this sacred Council, being gathered together in the Holy Spirit, that, by proclaiming his Gospel to every creature (cf. Mark 16:15), it may bring all men [and women] that light of Christ which shines out visibly from the Church."

39. *ODC*, no. 15: 34. The *Introduction* states, "The celebration of the eucharist is the most important rite, and the only necessary one, for the dedication of a church."

40. This point is powerfully expressed in The Second Vatican Council, *Lumen gentium* when it states, "Really sharing in the body of the Lord in the breaking of the eucharistic bread, we are taken up into communion with him and with one another. 'Because the bread is one, we, though many, are one body, all of us who partake of the one bread' (1 Cor. 10:17). In this way all of us are made members of his body (cf. 1 Cor. 12:27), 'but severally members one of another' (Rom. 12:4). See *Lumen gentium*, no. 7: 354–56. This is also the theme which runs throughout the entire encyclical entitled *Ecclesia de Eucharistia*, which was released by Pope John Paul II on Holy Thursday of 2003. See John Paul II, *Ecclesia de Eucharistia*.

41. The Second Vatican Council, *Sacrosanctum concilium*, no. 42: 15. The Constitution states, "But as it is impossible for the bishop always and everywhere to preside over the whole flock in his church, he must of necessity establish groupings of the faithful; and, among these, parishes, set up locally under a pastor who takes the place of the bishop, are the most important, for in some way they represent the visible Church constituted throughout the world."

42. John Paul II, *Dies Domini*, no. 36: 735–36.

est priority in the life of the parish. At it the parishioners are built up into that people whom Christ won for himself in his death and resurrection and are made one as the Father, Son, and Holy Spirit are one.[43] Every time that the Eucharist is celebrated, the parish is to experience that its life must be founded in, nourished, and sustained in Jesus Christ alone.

The essential place that Christ is to have in the life of the parish is also expressed in the procession after communion that takes the Eucharist to the altar of reservation.[44] The Eucharist must be reserved in a parish church.[45] The procession and the reservation of the blessed sacrament in the church give witness to the reality that the parishioners must always journey with Christ and that they must keep him at the heart of their community's existence. If the parish does not exist in relationship to Christ and his mystical body, it ceases to exist as a theological entity—it ceases to exist as a part of the church.

## The Holy Spirit is the Wellspring of the Parish's life within the Body of Christ

In the rites of *ODC*, the preface, which must be used at the Mass of dedication, gives the most complete synthesis of the role that the ritual attributes to the Holy Spirit in the life of every community within the church. The portion of the prayer which is of concern here states:

> Here is foreshadowed the mystery of the true Temple,
> here is prefigured the heavenly Jerusalem.
>
> For you made the Body of your Son, born of the tender Virgin,
> the Temple consecrated to you,
> in which the fullness of the Godhead might dwell.
>
> You also established the Church as a holy city,
> built upon the foundation of the Apostles,
> with Christ Jesus himself the chief cornerstone:
> a city to be built of chosen stones,
> given life by the Spirit and bonded by charity,
> where for endless ages you will be all in all

---

43. *ODC*, no. 1: 31.
44. *ODC*, no. nn. 79–82: 386–87.
45. *Code of Canon Law*, can. 934, §1.

PART THREE

and the light of Christ will shine undimmed for ever.[46]

The preface alludes to the reality of the workings of the Holy Spirit as revealed by scripture. By the power of the Holy Spirit, Jesus Christ was conceived in the womb of the Virgin Mary and consecrated as the temple of the Father's glory.[47] After Christ's death and resurrection, the Holy Spirit descended upon the apostles so that they could continue to build up the church in the world as the dwelling place of God.[48] The preface states that the Holy Spirit continues to construct the church with chosen stones that are enlivened by the Holy Spirit and cemented together in love. It is the Spirit who binds the individual members of the parish together in Christ and unites their community as a living cell in the body of Christ. The Spirit produces the *koinonia* by which the local assembly is joined to the rest of the church. The manner in which the Holy Spirit works as the unifying power within the church is beautifully described in *Lumen gentium*:

> The one People of God is accordingly present in all the nations of the earth, since its citizens, who are taken from all nations, are of a kingdom whose nature is not earthly but heavenly. All the faithful scattered throughout the world are in communion with each other in the Holy Spirit so that "he who dwells in Rome knows those in most distant parts to be his members" (*qui Romae sedet, Indos scit membrum suum esse*).[49]

The 1977 rites of *ODC* show that the Holy Spirit accomplishes the work of building up the body of Christ through the parish principally by the celebration of the church's liturgical and sacramental rites. The building itself is dedicated so that the community may gather within it to hear God's word proclaimed, celebrate the sacraments and be fed on Christ's body and blood.[50] In the rites of *The Liturgy of the Word*, the word is

46. *Preface: The Mystery of God's Temple*, Ritual Mass for the Dedication of a Church., 1215 and *ODC*, no. 75: 64.

47. Luke 1:35.

48. Acts 2:1–15.

49. The Second Vatican Council, *Lumen gentium*, no. 13: 364–65.

50. *ODC*, no. 30: 40. In his opening admonition to the assembly, the bishop says, "Beloved brothers and sisters, we have gathered with joy to dedicate a new church by celebrating the Lord's Sacrifice. Let us take part in these sacred rites with loving devotion, listening to the Word of God with faith, so that our community, reborn from the one font of Baptism and nourished at the same table, may grow into a spiritual temple and, brought together at one altar, may advance in the love from on high."
In this regard see also The Second Vatican Council, *Lumen gentium*, no. 4: 351–52.

proclaimed so that the community may be formed by the Holy Spirit into a portion of that New Covenant people that Christ won for himself by his death and resurrection. Many of the readings that might be used at the celebration of the dedication proclaim the role which the Holy Spirit is to play in building the church into the body of Christ.[51] The rites of sprinkling conclude by asking that the grace of the Holy Spirit may cleanse the members of the assembly, for they are the temple of God's presence.[52] It is by the grace of the Holy Spirit that each individual becomes both a temple of the Holy Spirit and a member of Christ's body in the saving waters of baptism. The prayer of dedication articulates the many ways in which the Holy Spirit is to be active in the parish's sacramental life, building up the community to take its proper place in Christ's body. *ODC* shows that it is most especially through the celebration of the Eucharist that the Holy Spirit is to be active in the life of the parish, transforming those who receive Christ's body and blood into a portion of his mystical body. Just as it is the Holy Spirit who made Christ present in the Virgin Mary's womb and changes the bread and wine into his body and blood, so too it is the Spirit that makes the assembly a cell in the living body of Christ. By the grace of the Holy Spirit received in the Eucharist, the individual members are joined by love and charity to Christ, to each other, and to both the church on earth and in heaven. Living in communion with their Lord and Savior in this life, they will be brought by the grace of the Holy Spirit at the end of their earthly pilgrimages to live in perfect communion with the Trinitarian God for all eternity.

## The Parish Community, a Living Cell in the Mystical Body of Christ, Must Be Founded upon and Nourished through the Church's Liturgical and Sacramental Life

*Sacrosanctum concilium*, the Second Vatican Council's Constitution on the Liturgy, states the following in regard to the role that the liturgy plays in the church's life:

> For it is the liturgy through which, especially in the divine sacrifice of the Eucharist, "the work of our redemption is

---

51. See especially 1 Cor 3:14–17; Eph 2:19–22; and 1 Pet 2:4–9.

52. *ODC*, no. 50: 50. The prayer after the rite of sprinkling says, "May God, the Father of mercies, dwell in this house of prayer and, by the grace of the Holy Spirit, cleanse us who are the temple where he dwells."

accomplished," and it is through the liturgy, especially, that the faithful are enabled to express in their lives and manifest to others the mystery of Christ and the real nature of the true Church. The Church is essentially both human and divine, visible but endowed with invisible realities, zealous in action and dedicated to contemplation, present in the world, but as a pilgrim, so constituted that in her the human is directed toward and subordinated to the divine, the visible to the invisible, action to contemplation, and this present world to the city yet to come, the object of our quest. The liturgy daily builds up those who are in the Church, making of them a holy temple of the Lord, a dwelling-place for God in the Spirit, to mature measure of the fullness of Christ. At the same time it marvellously increases their power to preach Christ and thus show forth the Church, a sign lifted up among the nations, to those who are outside, a sign under which the scattered children of God may be gathered together until there is one fold and one shepherd.[53]

Further on, when speaking about the sacraments, the same Constitution states:

> The purpose of the sacraments is to sanctify men [and women], to build up the Body of Christ, and finally, to give worship to God. Because they are signs they also instruct. They not only presuppose faith, but by words and objects they also nourish, strengthen, and express it. That is why they are called "sacraments of faith."[54]

The rites of ODC communicate to the assembly that is having its building dedicated the role that the church's liturgical and sacramental life must have in its existence. It is very similar to that which is articulated in *Sacrosanctum concilium*. The ritual illustrates that it is through the proclamation of the word in the liturgy and the celebration of the sacred mysteries, most especially the Eucharist, that the gathered assembly becomes a living cell in the body of Christ. Through the church's liturgy, Jesus Christ, who was sent by the Father to redeem humanity, is encountered by the power of the Holy Spirit and Christians are formed

---

53. The Second Vatican Council. *Sacrosanctum concilium*, no. 2: 1–2.

54. The Second Vatican Council, *Sacrosanctum concilium*, no. 59: 20. See also *Lumen gentium*, no. 11: 361–63. This paragraph from *Lumen gentium* contains an excellent synthesis of the role played by the sacraments in the life of the church. It is very much the same as that which is attributed to them in the prayer of dedication that is found in *ODC*.

into that New Covenant people that Christ gained for himself through his death and resurrection. This study has also shown that in the normal course of events the Catholic faithful are to celebrate the church's sacraments in their proper parish.[55] In this regard, the rites of ODC properly demonstrate to the parish community that it must be founded upon, and base its entire pastoral program on, the church's liturgical and sacramental life.

One of the important implications of this fact, as it is expressed in these rites, is that the parish must be an evangelizing community. As it is Jesus Christ, the Word made flesh, who attracts men and women to the parish, it is his gospel that the faithful are to announce to all whom they meet in the events of their lives.[56] The evangelizing nature of the community will be apparent by the fact that it regularly welcomes new members through the celebration of the sacraments of initiation. As those who are already members were grafted into the body of Christ through a baptismal font is some parish, they too must seek to bring others to the saving waters so that they may also experience the freedom of God's children.[57] The profession of faith that follows the homily symbolizes that the proclamation of the gospel requires a response.[58] It is to be one that causes those who receive God's saving message to bring it to others. It should also entail a reaction that acknowledges the need to deepen constantly in the Christian life through the practice of a penance that allows Christians to grow in the awareness of their baptismal vocation.[59]

---

55. This fact was established earlier by showing that the Code of Canon states that the ordinary place for an individual to celebrate Christian initiation, marriage and the funeral liturgy is to be that persons proper parish. This can also be seen from the fact that the Code of Canon Law obliges the pastor of the parish to celebrate these sacraments for those parishioners who are properly disposed. See *Code of Canon Law*, can. 528–can. 530.

56. The evangelizing quality that God's word is to have in the community's life is emphasized by the bishop when he holds up the lectionary and says, "May the word of God resound always in this building, to open for you the mystery of Christ and to bring about your salvation within the Church." *ODC*, no. 53: 51.

57. *ODC*, no. 62: 40. The prayer of dedication states, "Here may the flood of divine grace overwhelm human offenses, so that your children, Father, being dead to sin, may be reborn to heavenly life."

58. *ODC*, no. 56: 51.

59. *ODC*, no. 48: 48–49. The bishop is to say before the sprinkling: "Dear brothers and sisters, as we solemnly dedicate this house, let us humbly call upon the Lord our God to bless this water he has created with which we are to be sprinkled as a **sign of repentance** and a memorial of Baptism and by which the new walls and altar will be purified, May the Lord support us with his grace so that, docile to the Spirit whom we

At the heart of the rites of *ODC* is the message that the parish community must be a Eucharistic community. It is through the Eucharist, celebrated by a validly appointed minister, that the members of the assembly are bound in communion with Christ the head and the entire body of his church. Eating Christ's body and blood, the parishioners are assimilated into his likeness and by the power of the Holy Spirit they receive the gift of his love and charity.[60] As Mauro Paternoster has pointed out, *ODC* has restored the Eucharist to its central place in the rites of dedication.[61] By doing this, they indicate that the Eucharist is to be at the center of the parish's life. The Sunday celebration of the Eucharist must be at the core of the entire pastoral program which animates the community's life.[62] At it the diverse members of the assembly are transformed into a living cell in the one body of Christ.[63] All of the parish's programs, events and outreach efforts are to flow from and be oriented towards the Eucharist. That Christ's presence in the Eucharist is to be the heart of the parish's existence is witnessed to in the rites of the procession and reservation of the blessed sacrament in its church.[64]

The third implication that follows from the nature of the parish's identity as a sacramental and liturgical community is that it must be conscious of its eschatological end in the new and eternal Jerusalem. The sacraments and the liturgy place the members of the earthly church in communion with the heavenly church.[65] Through the sacrament of baptism Christians are joined to Christ the head, who sits at the right hand of the Father in heaven. The relics of the saint or martyr enclosed in the altar and the singing of the Litany of the Saints testify to the reality of this communion. The prayers in *ODC* state that the word is proclaimed and the sacraments are celebrated in the building so that the faithful may be sanctified and led to their heavenly home.[66] As members of the body of

---

have received, we may remain faithful in his Church."

The bold print has been added here for emphasis. The sprinkling is to have a penitential element, calling the baptized to be faithful to their baptisms.

60. See The Second Vatican Council, *Apostolicam actuositatem*, no. 3: 768–69.

61. Paternoster, "Analisi ritual e contenuti teoloogici dell," 610.

62. See The Second Vatican Council, *Sacrosanctum concilium*, no. 42: 15, and John Paul II, *Dies Domini*, no. 36: 735–36.

63. The Second Vatican Council, *Apostolicam actuositatem*, no. 10: 777–78.

64. See *ODC*, nn. 79–82: 67–69.

65. The Second Vatican Council, *Sacrosanctum concilium*, no. 8: 5; and *Lumen gentium*, no. 50: 410–12.

66. One example of such a prayer can be seen in the prayer for the blessing of

Christ, the parishioners must have their eyes set on heaven. The parish's programs should keep this ultimate end in mind.

An Instruction from the Congregation for the Clergy, entitled *The Priest, Pastor and Leader of the Parish Community*, addressed the attention that the pastor is to give to the church's liturgical and sacramental life in the parish. To the extent that *ODC* is concerned to call the entire assembly to an awareness of the importance of the celebration of the liturgy and the sacraments, the words of this Instruction are relevant here as well. The 1977 rites of *ODC* call the parish community to base its pastoral program on the liturgy and the sacraments of the church. The life-giving nature of programs so founded is such that:

> [They do] not require the invention of new pastoral programmes, since the Christian programme, revolving around Christ, is always one of knowing, loving and imitating Him, of living the life of the Holy Trinity in Him, and of transforming history with Him by bringing it to completion: This is a programme which does not change with the shifts of times and cultures, even though it takes account of time and culture for the sake of true dialogue and effective communication.[67]

## The Parish is a Cell in the Hierarchically Structured Body of Christ

The rites of *ODC* illustrate that the parish community is a cell within the hierarchically structured body of Christ. They show that in order for it to exist in communion with the entire body of Christ, and to fruitfully celebrate the church's liturgical and sacramental life upon which it depends, the parish community must be ordered to reflect this hierarchical structure. Because, as was seen in the previous subsection of this chapter, the parish's life within the church is nurtured and sustained in and through the celebration of the liturgy and sacraments, the assembly itself requires

---

the water in the *Introductory Rites*. This prayer concludes with the following petition: "Sanctify + therefore with your blessing this water you have created, that sprinkled on us and on the walls of this church, it may be a sign of the cleansing waters of salvation, in which we have been washed in Christ and made a temple of your Spirit. Grant that, with all our brothers and sisters who will celebrate the divine mysteries in this church, we may come at last to the heavenly Jerusalem. Through Christ our Lord." See *ODC*, no. 48: 49.

67. The Congregation for the Clergy, *The Priest, Pastor and Leader of the Parish Community*, no. 27.

the services of those ordained ministries that were established by Christ for the transmission of his saving grace. Those who exercise the ordained ministries discharge a service for the good of God's people, so that the body of Christ may be built up to completion.[68] Theirs is to be a ministry to the people of God, by which Christ's word is proclaimed and his sacraments are celebrated. By the exercise of this ministry, Christ's presence and salvation are communicated to the assembly by the power of the Holy Spirit and they are transformed into members of his body. Those who offer their lives to Christ and his church, through ordination into the priesthood of Christ the high priest, do so in order that those who have been baptized into the royal priesthood might fulfill their vocations in the world and come to eternal life in the heavenly Jerusalem.[69]

The rites of *ODC* suggest that a new church is to be dedicated during a full stational Mass of the local church. At such a celebration, presided over by the local bishop, a full manifestation of the church occurs as the diverse members of the assembly participate in the liturgy according to their office within the church.[70] This type of epiphany of the church reveals the body of Christ as a hierarchically structured entity. The 1977 rites of *ODC* reveal this nature of the church as they call for the building itself to be designed in such a way that all of the members may take that place within the church which is suitable for their proper participation in the liturgy.[71] The procession to the new church is to take place in an orderly fashion, with all being located within it according to their liturgical role in the assembly.[72] Upon arriving inside the church, all are to go to their appropriate places, the bishop going to his chair ("*cathedra*") and the priests, deacons, and other ministers to the spots assigned to them in the sanctuary.[73] As mentioned earlier in this study, of note is the fact that the presider's chair at this Mass, because it is here to be occupied by the bishop, is referred to as the "*cathedra*" in the Latin *editio typica*

---

68. The Second Vatican Council, *Presbyterorum ordinis*, no. 2: 864–66.

69. At the risk of stating the obvious, those who give themselves to the ordained ministries are to do so also because it is the vocation to which God calls them to find fulfillment and joy in this life and by which they are to come to eternal life with him.

70. The Second Vatican Council, *Sacrosanctum concilium*, no. 41: 14–15.

71. *ODC*, no. 3: 31. The *Introduction* states, "Hence the general arrangement of the sacred building must be such that in some way it conveys the image of the assembled congregation and allows the appropriate ordering of all the participants, as well as facilitating each in the proper carrying out of his function."

72. *ODC*, no. 31: 40.

73. *ODC*, no. 35: 43.

of the rite. This is to indicate the fundamental role of the local bishop who makes Christ the high priest present in the diocese entrusted to his pastoral care.[74]

Dramatically evident in this ritual is the diocesan bishop's role as the principal dispenser of the mysteries of God within the local church. It is his function to direct, promote, and protect the liturgical life of the church entrusted to his care.[75] In recognition of this fact, the *Introduction* states that it is the bishop's responsibility to dedicate all churches within his diocese. Should he be unable to do this, it remains for him to delegate another bishop, or in extraordinary circumstances a priest, to do this for him.[76] His role as chief pastor of the diocese is demonstrated as members of the assembly present the building to him, indicating its connection to his sacramental ministry.[77] It is also he who asks the parish priest, who will be assigned to the community by him, to open the doors of the church for the faithful; he invites the faithful to enter the building, and he convokes the assembly from the chair ("*cathedra*"). In *The Liturgy of the Word*, the essential role of the bishop in proclaiming the gospel is illustrated as he holds the lectionary up to the assembly and then passes it on to the lector as God's word.[78] The bishop is shown as the high priest of the diocese as he presents the building to God on behalf of the community, declares in the prayers that it will be the place where God's word and sacraments will be celebrated, and offers the Eucharist there for the community. That the other ordained ministers are to cooperate with him, to assist him in his ministry, is shown by the fact that it is he who is to decide if they are needed to help with the anointing of the walls,[79] the priests concelebrate the Eucharist with him, and the ministers are to take their places in the sanctuary around him. By way of the references to the church which Christ founded upon the apostles, in both the prayers and in the readings, the rites point to the role of the bishop as the successor of the apostles in the diocese. When the walls of the church are anointed in twelve places, this gesture alludes to the role of the apostles and their

---

74. The Second Vatican Council, *Lumen gentium*, no. 21: 372–74.

75. The Second Vatican Council, *Christus Dominus*, no. 15: 571–72.

76. *ODC*, no. 6: 32

77. *ODC*, no. 33: 41.

78. *ODC*, no 53: 51. For the importance of the bishop's role as one called to proclaim the Gospel, see The Second Vatican Council, *Lumen gentium*, no. 25: 379–81; and *Dei verbum*, nn. 7–10: 753–56.

79. *ODC*, no. 64: 58.

PART THREE

successors in keeping the many living stones that make up the church united to Christ. The essential role of the bishop in binding the local to the universal church[80] is also proclaimed in this, and every other Eucharistic celebration, by the fact that it is always offered in communion with the local bishop and the pope. Throughout, the ritual shows the bishop to be the head of the local church, who, in the place of Christ the high priest, builds it up into a healthy portion in the body of Christ.

The rites of *ODC* also give witness to the identity of priests, especially parish priests, as the principle collaborators with the bishop in the ministry of Christ the high priest.[81] Sharing in his priesthood, priests make the bishop present in his absence, building the church up into the one body of Christ.[82] This is demonstrated by the fact that in extraordinary cases a priest may be delegated to dedicate a church in the bishop's place.[83] More typically, it will be for the pastor to exercise pastoral care for the parish in the place of the bishop when he departs after the celebration. This role is illustrated by the bishop's asking the priest to open the doors of the church to the faithful.[84] This symbolizes the responsibility that the priest will have in opening the mysteries of Christ to the faithful by proclaiming his word and celebrating his sacraments on their behalf. The identity which priests have as collaborators with the bishop is also made apparent by the fact that he may associate them with him in anointing the walls of the church.[85] Because the bricks in the church's walls represent the living stones that make up the church, this gesture alludes to the bishop's sending of the priests to minister to the People of God in the diocese. As the priests serve as concelebrants with the bishop at the Mass of dedication, they are also shown as those who offer the sacrifice of the Mass with the bishop on behalf of the church. After he leaves the community that is celebrating the dedication, it will fall to the priest to build the church up on the bishop's behalf and, by so doing, make Christ's body present in that specific locality.[86]

80. See The Second Vatican Council, *Lumen gentium*, no. 26: 381–82.
81. The Second Vatican Council, *Christus Dominus*, no. 30: 581–82.
82. The Second Vatican Council, *Presbyterorum ordinis*, no. 1: 863.
83. *ODC*, no. 6: 33. The *Introduction* states, "... in altogether special circumstances, to a Priest, to whom he is to give a special mandate."
84. *ODC*, no 33: 41.
85. *ODC*, nn. 63–64: 58.
86. The Second Vatican Council, *Lumen gentium*, no. 28: 384–87. *Lumen gentium* states, "In each local assembly of the faithful they represent in a certain sense

These rites speak poignantly to the role which the pastor is to have in the parish community. As *Sacrosanctum concilium* states, because the bishop may not be present everywhere in his diocese, he must divide it into smaller groupings, the most important of which is to be the parish, so that the Eucharist may be celebrated there.[87] It continues by saying that under the leadership of the pastor, who takes the bishop's place, the Eucharist is to be celebrated in the parish so that the church may be made manifest throughout the world. The 1977 dedication ritual calls attention to the significance that the pastor must give to the celebration of the Eucharist. It does so by showing that it is the Eucharist that makes the church and builds the assembly into the body of Christ. Because of its importance, the pastor must give the Sunday celebration of the Eucharist the greatest priority in his ministry. As it is the pastor who bears the fundamental responsibility for making the bishop present in the parish after the ceremony, it can also be noted that he will assume many of the functions played by the bishop during the rite. It will be for the pastor to assure that the gospel is proclaimed and to build the parish up in communion with the whole church. Others assigned to the parish are to assist him in these responsibilities. In order to fulfill his responsibilities, the pastor must exercise his pastoral ministry in a way that recognizes the parish to be a part of the diocese and the diocese as a part of the universal church. This is accomplished most fruitfully when he exercises his functions of teaching, governing, and sanctifying in communion with both the local bishop and the universal church.[88] This rite, which illustrates so beautifully the unity of the one body of Christ, warns that should the pastor fail to exercise his ministry in a way that is conscious of the parish's communion with the universal church, he jeopardizes the ability of the parish to flourish as a healthy cell within the life-giving mystical body of Christ.

There are a number of other ministries exercised in the rites of dedication. For the most part, however, they do not contribute to an understanding of the theology for a parish that the ritual yields. The function

---

the bishop, with whom they are associated in all trust and generosity; in part they take upon themselves his duties and solicitude and in their daily toils discharge them. Those who, under the authority of the bishop, sanctify and govern that portion of the Lord's flock assigned to them render the universal Church visible in their locality and contribute efficaciously towards building up the whole body of Christ (cf. Eph. 4:12)."

87. The Second Vatican Council, *Sacrosanctum concilium*, no. 42: 15.
88. The Second Vatican Council, *Christus Dominus*, no. 30: 581–82.

of the deacon points to other ways in which the ordained ministers are to be at the service of the assembly. The role of the extraordinary ministers highlight in a liturgical setting some different aspects of the baptismal vocation that belongs to the lay faithful.

The explanatory rites of *The Prayer of Dedication and the Anointings* illustrate both the great dignity and the responsibilities that belong to the baptized. As anointed stones in God's temple, they have been made consecrated members of Christ's royal priesthood.[89] By availing themselves of the church's liturgical and sacramental life, they are to be sanctified and come to eternal life at the end of their pilgrimages. The crucial mission that the rites attribute to the members of the lay faithful is discussed latter in this chapter in a separate section entitled, "The Parish is Portion of the People of God, Sharing in Christ's Priestly, Prophetic, and Kingly Mission."

This section has investigated the principle theological theme that is put forward in *ODC* for a parish community—that of the parish as a cell in the mystical body of Christ. It was seen that the parish is but a part of the one body that has Christ as its head. It exists as a result of the gratuitous gift of salvation that is offered to humanity by the Father in the person of his Son, Jesus Christ. This offer of salvation is communicated to men and women of every time and place by the Holy Spirit. The Holy Spirit brings this offer to the nations through the Christ's mystical body. Humans throughout history have this offer of salvation conveyed to them through the church's sacramental and liturgical life. By it, they are incorporated into the living body of the church and configured to Christ in such a way that they are called to bring him to others. In order that the church may be built up by the sacraments, Christ established the church as a hierarchically structured body, calling men to be configured to his high priesthood so that they may make him sacramentally present to all. Those who in cooperation with the successors of the apostles build the church up by exercising the high priesthood of Christ the head, are to do so at the service of the lay faithful. Jesus Christ established the priesthood to build up his mystical body to completion and bring its members salvation. The church establishes parishes to be those places where Christ's body is made manifest throughout the world.

Our study now turns to examining two other theological images for the parish that can be drawn from *ODC*. These complement that which

---

89. The Second Vatican Council, *Apostolicam actuositatem*, no. 3: 768–69.

was presented in this section. For this reason, the treatment of them is less elaborate.

## THE PARISH IS A PART OF THE ONE, HOLY, CATHOLIC, AND APOSTOLIC CHURCH

Describing the manner in which the church is made present when the local bishop celebrates the Eucharist, *Lumen gentium* states:

> In each altar community, under the sacred ministry of the bishop, a manifest symbol is to be seen of that charity and "unity of the mystical body, without which there can be no salvation." In these communities, though they may often be small and poor, or existing in the diaspora, Christ is present through whose power and influence the One, Holy, Catholic and Apostolic Church is constituted.[90]

In regard to those occasions when a priest presides at Mass, the same Constitution says:

> In each local assembly of the faithful they represent in a certain sense the bishop, with whom they are associated in all trust and generosity; in part they take upon themselves his duties and solicitude and in their daily toils discharge them. Those who, under the authority of the bishop, sanctify and govern that portion of the Lord's flock assigned to them render the universal Church visible in their locality and contribute efficaciously towards building up the whole body of Christ. (cf. Eph. 4:12).[91]

The rites of *ODC* call the attention of the parish to the reality that its community is a part of the One, Holy, Catholic, and Apostolic Church. While this is true in the most complete sense at a Mass celebrated by the diocesan bishop, the ritual also calls the assembly to understand that this truth about its identity is also valid when Mass is celebrated by a priest. This section will demonstrate how *RDC* draws the community's attention to each of the four marks of the church which must be part of the parish's identity.

---

90. The Second Vatican Council, *Lumen gentium*, no. 26: 381.
91. The Second Vatican Council, *Lumen gentium*, no. 28: 385–86.

PART THREE

## The Parish is a Part of the One Church

The rites of *ODC* communicate to the parish that it is a part of the one church founded by Jesus Christ. They do this by pointing out the communion that must exist between the parish and the local bishop, through whom it is united to the one church. For the procession at the Mass of dedication, when it is possible, the entire assembly is to process to the new building from another neighboring church.[92] The connection that exists between the community having its church dedicated with the entire church is powerfully illustrated by this procession. The mandate that the anniversary of the dedication of the diocesan cathedral be celebrated as a feast within all of the churches in the diocese also serves to emphasize the connection between the parish and the local church that *ODC* wishes to bring to the attention of each of these individual assemblies.[93] Through the diocese the parish is linked to the universal church.

While the communion that makes the parish a part of the church is to be maintained by ecclesial structures, the *Introduction* also makes it clear that the source of this unity is Jesus Christ and his paschal mystery. By this, Christ has gathered a holy people to himself, and made them one as the Father, Son, and Holy Spirit are one.[94] The members of this holy people are themselves made participants in Christ's paschal mystery by the celebration of the church's sacraments, most especially the Eucharist. The parishioners are incorporated into the church in the one baptismal font of the Lord and are to be nourished at his one altar.[95] No parish may have its own private set of sacraments. Communion with the Triune God, which is communicated by the Holy Spirit, depends upon the

---

92. *ODC*, no. 29: 39.

93. *ODC*, no. 26: 38.

94. *ODC*, no. 1: 31. The *Introduction* states, "Through his Death and Resurrection, Christ became the true and perfect temple of the New Covenant and gathered a people to be his own.
Moreover, this holy people, made one by the unity of the Father, Son, and Holy Spirit is the Church, that is, the temple of God built of living stones, where the Father is worshipped in Spirit and in truth."

95. *ODC*, no. 30: 40. The bishop's words here state, "Beloved brothers and sisters, we have gathered with joy to dedicate a new church by celebrating the Lord's Sacrifice. Let us take part in these sacred rites with loving devotion, listening to the Word of God with faith, so that our community, reborn from the one **font of Baptism** and **nourished at the same table**, may grow into a spiritual temple and, brought together at one altar, may advance in the love from on high." The bold print has been added here for emphasis.

church's sacramental life. When the Gospel is proclaimed in the liturgy, and authentically preached by the bishop and the ordained ministers who assist him in his ministry, it is to lead all of the faithful to profess the one faith of the church.[96]

The parish is shown to be a part of the one church in ODC not just because of the communion that it shares with the pilgrim church on earth. The relics of the saint that are deposited under the altar, when this is possible, and the singing of the Litany of the Saints, recognize the relationship that exists between the gathered liturgical assembly and the heavenly church. The two are different portions of the one church. The New Jerusalem is the destiny to which all of the members of the church are called.[97] The parish community must be aware of this.

## The Parish is Part of the Holy Church

That which identifies the parish as a part of the holy church is very similar to that which points to its identity as a cell within the body of Christ. What makes the church holy is Jesus Christ. As the prayer of dedication explains, the church is made holy (sanctified) by the blood of Christ.[98] In the *Prayer of Dedication and the Anointings,* the altar is anointed so that it may become a sign of Christ, who is to stand in the midst of his church.[99] Christ is the cornerstone around whom the entire church must rise and be defined.[100] In the parish church, the men and women of a particular

---

96. ODC, nn. 55–56: 51.

97. See *Solemn Blessing at the End of Mass,* Ritual Mass for the Dedication of a Church, 1220 and ODC, no. 84: 69–70. This is expressed in many of the prayers of the rites of dedication. One such example is the last petition of the final blessing that concludes the rite. It states, "May you be made thoroughly clean, so that God may dwell within you and may you possess with all the Saints the inheritance of eternal happiness."

98. ODC, no. 62:56–57. The prayer of dedication states, "This house brings to light the mystery of the Church, which Christ **made holy by the shedding of his blood**, so that he might present her to himself as a glorious Bride, a Virgin resplendent with the integrity of faith, a Mother made fruitful by the power of the Spirit." The bold print has been added for emphasis.

99. ODC, no. 64: 58. Before the bishop anoints the altar, he says, "May the Lord by his power sanctify this altar and this house, which by our ministry we anoint, so that as visible signs they may express the mystery of Christ and the Church."

100. See *Preface: The Mystery of God's Temple,* Ritual Mass for the Dedication of a Church. 1215 and ODC, no 75: 64. The preface for the Eucharistic prayer states, "You also established the Church as a holy city, built upon the foundation of the Apostles, with Christ Jesus himself the chief cornerstone: a city to be built of chosen stones, given

place are cleansed from their sins in baptism and joined to Christ. There, at the Sunday Mass, they receive the Eucharist and are filled with the Holy Spirit to become like Christ. The call to holiness that is addressed to all of the baptized is witnessed to by the saint's relics that are placed under the altar and the Litany of the Saints. These celebrate the victory that Christ has accomplished for those who have already reached their goal. The failure to respond to the call to holiness that is occasionally the fate of members of the pilgrim church is acknowledged in the opening rites of sprinkling. Here the bishop refers to the water that will be used as a sign of penance and a memorial of baptism.[101] By the experience that the faithful have in their parish community with the living Christ present in his word and sacraments, they are sanctified and are able to live in communion with God and his church. The goal of the parish must be the sanctification of its members—and of those who live in its vicinity—and the celestial destiny to which Christ calls all.

## The Parish is a Part of the Catholic Church

Immediately before the candles for the altar and the church are illuminated, the bishop is to declare: "Let the light of Christ shine brightly in the church that all nations may attain the fullness of truth."[102] As the candles in the church are being lit, the canticle of Tobias proclaims that all nations will come to adore God in his holy city. Throughout these rites of dedication, Christ is proclaimed as the one sent from the Father for the salvation of all peoples.[103] In him the human condition is to find

---

life by the Spirit and bonded by charity, where for endless ages you will be all in all and the light of Christ will shine undimmed forever."

101. *ODC*, no. 48: 48. The bishop is to say, "Dear brothers and sisters, as we solemnly dedicate this house, let us humbly call upon the Lord our God to bless this water he has created with which we are to be sprinkled **as a sign of repentance and a memorial of Baptism** and by which the new walls and altar will be purified. May the Lord support us by his grace, So that, docile to the Spirit whom we have received, We may remain faithful in his Church." The bold print has been added for emphasis.

102. *ODC*, no. 70: 61.

103. *Solemn Blessing at the End of Mass*, Ritual Mass for the Dedication of a Church, 1220 and *ODC*, no 84: 69–70. The second petition in the final blessing states, "May God, who has willed that all his scattered children be gathered in his Son, grant that you become his temple and the dwelling place of the Holy Spirit." This provides just one example of the prayers that seek to see all drawn to the Church so that they might experience Christ's salvation.

fulfillment and freedom from all that binds it.[104] Because it is through the many diverse parish communities that the church is to be made manifest in the world,[105] the Decree on the Church's Missionary Activity, *Ad gentes divinitus*, states that it is the responsibility of these communities to announce the salvation found in Christ to the nations.[106] The parish must serve the church's universal mission of announcing Christ's salvation by making him known to all within its locality and by integrating the many different persons it encompasses into the universality of the church.[107] It must also encourage and support the church's efforts at evangelization which extend beyond its own borders.

The success that the parish has in fulfilling its mission as a part of the Catholic Church depends upon its faithfulness to the liturgical and sacramental program that may be ascertained from *ODC*. As it is in Christ alone that mankind is to find salvation, his must be the message that illumines the parish's struggles and difficulties. It can not place its hopes in the passing political and social theories of the times. Its pastor must exercise his office of teaching by proclaiming the gospel in communion with the local bishop and the church's magisterium. The mandate that belongs to the parish as a part of the Catholic Church demands that its work will not be finished until all people have been gathered into the one flock that has Christ as its shepherd.

## The Parish is a Part of the Apostolic Church

The preface for the Eucharistic prayer that is used for the dedication of a church states, "You also established the Church as a holy city, built upon the foundation of the Apostles, with Christ Jesus himself the chief cornerstone."[108] The ritual asserts the reality that Jesus Christ founded his church to be spread throughout the world on the witness and ministry

---

104. *ODC*, no. 62: 57. The prayer of dedication says of the church: "Here may the poor find mercy, the oppressed attain true freedom, and all people be clothed with the dignity of your children, until they come exultant to the Jerusalem which is above."

105. The Second Vatican Council, *Sacrosanctum concilium* no. 42: 15.

106. The Second Vatican Council, *Ad gentes divinitus*, no. 37: 850. The Decree states, "Since the people of God live in communities especially in dioceses and parishes, by means of which, in a certain sense, they become manifest, it belongs to such communities to bear witness to Christ before the nations."

107. The Second Vatican Council, *Apostolicam actuositatem*, no. 777–78.

108. Preface: *The Mystery of God's Temple*, Ritual Mass for the Dedication of a Church, 1215 and *ODC*, no. 62: 56.

of the apostles and their successors, the bishops.[109] By their profession of faith and witness to his resurrection, Christ's saving message is passed on through the church from one generation to another. As a result of Pentecost, they transmit the Holy Spirit to the nations. The rites of *RDC* show that the parish depends upon its relationship with the bishop for its ecclesial identity. It is through him that Christ is transmitted to the community.[110] By its relationship to him, Christ the high priest continues his work of sanctifying and shepherding his people. As has been illustrated, the role of the bishop as the principle dispenser of the mysteries of God within his diocese is demonstrated in many ways throughout the ritual.[111] Without its connection to the local bishop, the parish community cannot access the church's sacraments. The bishop is the agent of *koinonia* through whom the parish is related to the rest of the church. It also depends upon him so that Christ's gospel message may be authentically transmitted to it.[112]

As has already been stated, because they refer to the priest—or pastor—to whom pastoral care of the community will be entrusted,[113] the rites of *ODC* point to the role that will be played by the pastor in making the bishop present in the parish. Since he represents the bishop and makes Christ the high priest present in its midst, without the priest, the

---

109. This theme is also articulated in the prayer for the dedication of a church, which states, "Blessed is the Church, God's dwelling-place with the human race, a holy temple built of living stones, standing upon the **foundation of the Apostles** with Christ Jesus its chief cornerstone." The bold print has been added for emphasis. See *ODC*, no. 62: 56–57. This theme is also expressed in many of the readings that might be used for the liturgy of the word, most especially Eph 2: 19–23; Rev 21: 9b-14; Matt 16: 13–19. It is also a theme that is expressed in some of the ritual gestures of the rite as when the church walls are to be anointed in twelve places.

110. See The Second Vatican Council, *Lumen gentium*, no. 21: 372–374; and *Sacrosanctum concilium*, no. 41: 14–15.

111. It was shown earlier in this study that the rites of *ODC* point to the role of the bishop as the principle dispenser of the mysteries of God in his diocese as the building is entrusted to his care; he passes the word on to the community; he dedicates the building to God on the community's behalf; and he celebrates the Eucharist for the community.

112. See the Second Vatican Council, *Dei verbum*, nn. 8–10: 754–756; and *Lumen gentium*, no. 25: 379–381.

113. *ODC*, no. 33: 41. The rubric states, "Then the Bishop calls upon the Priest to whom the pastoral office of the church has been entrusted to open the door of the church." See also *ODC*, no. 9: 33. Here the *Introduction* states, "It is fitting that the Bishop should concelebrate the Mass with the Priests who are associated with him in carrying out the rites of dedication and with those who have been given the office of directing the parish or the community for which the church has been built."

parish is not an ecclesial community in the full sense.[114] His presence allows the parish to realize its identity as a part of the apostolic church.

This section has investigated the manner in which the rites of *ODC* point to the parish as a part of the One, Holy, Catholic, and Apostolic Church. To a large degree this has involved a discussion of the ecclesiological structures that bind the parish in communion with the church. In order to complete the theology of a parish contained in the 1977 rites of *ODC* it is necessary to turn to the mission that the rites show belongs to the lay faithful. This is the work of the next section.

## THE PARISH IS A PORTION OF THE PEOPLE OF GOD, SHARING IN CHRIST'S PRIESTLY, PROPHETIC AND KINGLY MISSION

The Second Vatican Council's Decree on the Apostolate of Lay People, *Apostolicam actuositatem*, states:

> From the fact of their union with Christ the head flows the laymen's [and laywomen's] right and duty to be apostles. Inserted as they are in the Mystical Body of Christ by baptism and strengthened by the power of the Holy Spirit in confirmation, it is by the Lord himself that they are assigned to the apostolate. If they are consecrated a kingly priesthood and a holy nation (cf. 1 Pet. 2: 4–10), it is in order that they may in all their actions offer spiritual sacrifices and bear witness to Christ all over the world. Charity, which is, as it were, the soul of the whole apostolate, is given to them and nourished in them by the sacraments, the Eucharist above all.[115]

From the fact that the rites of *ODC* communicate the identity of the parish community as a cell within the mystical body of Christ, they also show it to be a portion of that Holy People consecrated through baptism and confirmation to offer spiritual sacrifices and bear witness to Christ throughout the world. To complete the theology of a parish that is presented in the 1977 rites of *ODC* it is necessary to investigate the manner

---

114. See Congregation for the Clergy, *Priest, Pastor and Leader*. This is also why the Code of Canon Law stipulates that only a priest may be named a pastor. When no priest is available to be named pastor, the Code states that one must be placed in charge of the pastoral care of the parish until such time as a priest can be named as pastor. See *Code of Canon Law*, can. 517–21.

115. The Second Vatican Council, *Apostolicam actuositatem*, no. 3: 768–69.

PART THREE

in which they articulate the mission which belongs to the lay members of the parish community. These rites provide a powerful catechesis for the laity about the mission that belongs to them as members of God's people sharing in Christ's priestly, prophetic, and kingly people. They are to be a people who are sent out from the liturgical celebrations that take place within the church to proclaim the marvellous works of Christ, wherever they might be sent in the world.

## The Parish is a Portion of the People of God, sharing in Christ's Priestly Mission

The people for whom a church is dedicated using the rites of *ODC* have a mission. The ritual places before the assembly, which is the subject of this *ordo*, the nature of this mission. The building, which is the object of these liturgical gestures, is to be made into a visible sign which reminds those who are the subject of the rite of their obligations.[116] Part of the calling that the building is to manifest to those for whom it stands as a sacred sign is that aspect of their vocation to share in Christ's priestly mission. In *The Introductory Rites* the people are sprinkled with holy water to remind them that through baptism they became members of God's holy people.[117] The anointing of the altar and the walls of the church point to the responsibility that the Christian people have to model their lives on that of Christ, who was anointed by the Spirit and offered his body as a sacrifice to the Father.[118] Following Christ's example, Christians who are also anointed by the Spirit and consecrated as members of his people, must also offer their own lives as a sacrifice to the Father, giving praise to him for the wonderful works of salvation that he has accomplished for them through his Son. This same point is proclaimed whenever the reading from 1 Pet 2: 4–9 is read in the liturgy of the word. That the sacrifices which the faithful are called to make as members of Christ's priestly people are always to be associated with those of their head is testified to by the placing of the relics of a saint or martyr under the altar.[119] The rel-

---

116. *ODC*, no. 2: 31.
117. *ODC*, no. 48: 48–49.
118. *ODC*, no. 16 a: 34. The *Introduction* states, "By the anointing with Chrism the altar is made a symbol of Christ who, before all others, is and is called "The Anointed One"; for the Father anointed him with the Holy Spirit and constituted him High Priest, who on the altar of his Body would offer the sacrifice of his life for the salvation of all."
119. *ODC*, no. 14: 34. The *Introduction* states, "After the singing of the Litany,

## A LITURGICAL THEOLOGY FOR A PARISH COMMUNITY

ics, which have already been shown to point to differing realities, in this case signify that all of those who profess Christ are to bring to completion his saving mission by offering their own lives as a spiritual sacrifice to the Father through him. The nature of this offering is expressed in the beautiful prayer that accompanies the burning of incense, as the bishop prays, "Let our prayer rise, O Lord, like incense in your sight; and as this house is filled with a pleasing fragrance, so let your Church be fragrant with the aroma of Christ."[120] The aroma of the sacrifice which Christians offer the Father is to fill the whole world with its sweetness and by so doing call others to him. The most powerful way in which the faithful are to be reminded of their vocations as members of Christ's holy people is through the sacrifice of the Eucharist. As is shown by the place that is given to it in the rites of *ODC*, the Eucharist is to be at the center of the entire Christian life. It enables the faithful to live their vocations as members of Christ's priestly people.

For the parishioners having their church dedicated, the 1977 rites of *ODC* announce the truth that they must live their priestly vocations in the world in order that Christ may become fully known to every nation and epoch.[121] It belongs to them to offer all of their work, their prayers, family and married life, relaxation and hardships as a spiritual sacrifice acceptable to God through Jesus Christ. This they do by joining all their efforts to Christ's sacrifice at the celebration of the Eucharist. In this way the laity are to consecrate the world to God.[122] The mission that belongs to the laity is absolutely crucial to the life of the church.[123] It is their role to bring Christ and the message of his church to the many corners of the world to which they go in their temporal and secular endeavors. The life of the parish must be orientated to supporting them in these efforts. In all parishes this will require that sacramental encounter with the Lord,

---

depending on the circumstances, the relics of a Martyr are to be deposited to signify that the sacrifice of the members has drawn its origin from the Sacrifice of the Head."

120. *ODC*, no. 66: 381.

121. The Second Vatican Council, *Lumen gentium*, no. 13: 364–65.

122. The Second Vatican Council, *Lumen gentium*, no. 34: 391. *Lumen gentium* states, "Hence the laity, dedicated as they are to Christ and anointed by the Holy Spirit, are marvellously called and prepared so that even richer fruits of the Spirit may be produced in them. For all their works, prayers and apostolic undertakings, family and married life, daily work, relaxation of mind and body, if they are accompanied in the Spirit—indeed even the hardships of life if patiently borne—all these become spiritual sacrifices acceptable to God through Jesus Christ (cf. Pet. 2:5). In the celebration of the Eucharist these may most fittingly be offered to the Father along with the body of the Lord."

123. The Second Vatican Council, *Apostolicam actuositatem*, no. 5: 772.

most especially the Eucharist, which the rites of *ODC* place at the heart of the entire Christian life. In different parishes, according to the time and need, it will demand the other types of social, economic and community support that make the sacrifices necessary to live the Christian life possible. All of these must flow from the Sunday Eucharist. Here all of the members of the parish community are to find the grace to identify their struggles with the sacrifice of Christ and to make him present throughout the world.

## The Parish is a Portion of the People of God, Sharing in Christ's Prophetic Mission

The rites of *The Liturgy of the Word*, the second section of *ODC*, witness to the fundamental role that the word of God has in forming the members of the community into the New Covenant people of God. The importance of God's saving word in the life of the assembly is testified to as the bishop holds up the lectionary and says, "May the word of God resound always in this building, to open for you the mystery of Christ and to bring about your salvation in the Church."[124] After he has done this, the bishop passes the lectionary on to a member of the faithful so that he or she may proclaim the word that is handed down to God's people through the bishops. By God's word, as the bishop's exhortation makes clear, the faithful are to come to know the saving mysteries of Christ. Those who hear the word are to respond to it by professing the faith of the church.[125] As a result of their consecration through baptism and confirmation the faithful are to share in Christ's prophetic office.[126] This means that having accepted God's word, they are also obliged to proclaim it to those whom they encounter in the world so that they too may come to know God's salvation and be gathered into his church.[127] They are to share Christ's word with other Christians, so that they may be invigorated by it; and with non-Christians, so that they may come to know God's salvation.[128] It is through God's word that new Christians are drawn to the church, come to baptism, are saved from the snares of evil

---

124. *ODC*, no. 53: 51.
125. *ODC*, no. 56: 51.
126. The Second Vatican Council, *Lumen gentium*, no. 12: 363–64.
127. The Second Vatican Council, *Lumen gentium,*, no. 17: 368–69.
128. The Second Vatican Council, *Lumen gentium,*, nn. 15–16: 366–68.

and sin, and that the church is built up to completion. The efficacy that God's word has in forming the Christian community is the point that is communicated by the mandatory use of the first reading from Nehemiah, which shows how the assembly is convoked by the proclamation of the word. The lighting of the candles in the church is a gesture which speaks poignantly to the responsibility that belongs to each Christian to share in Christ's prophetic mission by making his saving works known throughout the world. Here the building, which is associated with the living members of the church, is illuminated as the bishop proclaims, "Let the light of Christ shine brightly in the Church, that all nations may attain the fullness of truth."[129] By their efforts in the world, the parishioners are to make the parish a place from which the word of God is announced to all the nations.[130]

The rites of ODC invite the parish community to the awareness that it is a portion of God's people, called to share in Christ's prophetic mission. In order to fulfill their mission in the world, the parishioners must be aware of the difficulties and trials that face the men and women of their time, so that they may bring God's word to the different situations faced by their contemporaries.[131] They may at times even have to relate these difficulties to their pastors to ensure that they give them the best pastoral assistance possible, helping them to live the gospel in their daily realities.[132] While the clergy assigned to the parish are bound to give the parishioners the spiritual, liturgical, and sacramental assistance that they require to fulfill this aspect of their mission, it belongs to the faithful to spread the gospel to all areas of their temporal and secular lives.[133] To do this, each lay person must vigorously live the parish's liturgical and sacramental life, so that he may encounter Christ here in word and sacrament and be nourished to live his vocation in the world.[134] The parish itself must also be animated by programs that support the laity in the mission of evangelization and that are open to receiving those drawn to the church by the testimony that they give to God's saving action in the world. These programs, which are to flow out of God's word and the Eucharist, must be concerned to evangelize both those in the near vicinity

---

129. *ODC*, no. 70: 61.
130. The Second Vatican Council, *Ad gentes divinitus*, no. 37: 850–51.
131. The Second Vatican Council, *Gaudium et spes*, no. 62: 966–68.
132. *Code of Canon Law*, can. 212, § 2; and § 3.
133. The Second Vatican Council, *Lumen gentium*, no. 35: 391–93.
134. The Second Vatican Council, *Lumen gentium*, no. 42: 400–402.

PART THREE

of the parish and those in distant parts of the world—being conscious of the universal nature of the church's mission. The homilies, which are to assist the faithful to live the gospel, must be orientated to the difficulties and challenges faced by the men and women who make up that community. Those who respond to the community's testimony of faith must be received joyfully and properly catechized by the parish community and, where possible, led to the sacraments of initiation and the Eucharist. In this way those who are drawn to the community as a result of God's word can share in the mysteries of his salvation and likewise be sent out into the world to share in the mission that belongs to the people of God.

## The Parish Is a Portion of the People of God, Sharing in Christ's Kingly Mission

When addressing the subject of the people of God, *Lumen gentium* states:

> That messianic people has as its head Christ, "who was delivered up for our sins and rose again for our justification" (Rom. 4:25), and now, having acquired the name which is above all names, reigns gloriously in heaven. The state of this people is that of the dignity and freedom of the sons of God, in whose hearts the Holy Spirit dwells as in a temple. Its law is the new commandment to love as Christ loved us (cf. Jn. 13:34). Its destiny is the kingdom of God which has been begun by God himself on earth and which must be further extended until it is brought to perfection by him at the end of time when Christ our life (cf. Col. 3:4), will appear and "creation itself also will be delivered from its slavery to corruption into freedom of the glory of the sons [and daughters] of God" (Rom. 8: 21).[135]

From this, it can be said that when Christians model their lives on the Eucharist, by offering themselves as a sacrifice to the Father, and live their prophetic missions according to God's word, they are also participating in Christ's kingly mission. This is true because when they witness to Christ's word, pattern their lives on his paschal mystery, and manifest these values in their daily affairs, they live according to his law and subject those areas of the world where they make him present to the rule of his kingdom. For the faithful, participating in Christ's kingly mission on their earthly pilgrimages is intimately connected with them sharing in

---

135. The Second Vatican Council, *Lumen gentium*, no. 9: 359–60.

his priestly and prophetic mission in their day to day dealings. By witnessing to the gospel values in their lives, the faithful make the parish community a place in which the following petition from the prayer for the dedication of a church may become a reality: "Here may the poor find mercy, the oppressed attain true freedom, and all people be clothed with the dignity of your children, until they come exultant to the Jerusalem which is above."[136] The parish community, therefore, must be one that proclaims the dignity that belongs to the children of God, assists the poor and oppressed, and seeks justice for all persons, born and unborn. It must also be a place where people are taught about the great freedom to be encountered by those who turn away from sin, accepting Christ as their savior. However, essentially it must be a community that proclaims a fundamental confidence that true justice and mercy are to be found only in Jesus Christ at the end of time. In order to live their vocations in the world, the rites of *ODC* proclaim that God's people must have their eyes set on the ultimate end of their journeys, the New and Eternal Jerusalem.

The 1977 rites of *ODC* accomplish this by asking God to establish the building both as a sign of the church on earth and an image of the church in heaven.[137] As has been seen throughout this study, the entire ritual program is intended to remind the earthly assembly that its destiny is to join the victorious Christ in God's celestial kingdom.[138] The objective that is consistently sought for God's people in the prayers is that by sharing in Christ's word and sacrament they might be strengthened to arrive in the kingdom of heaven. In the Eucharist the faithful share in a foretaste of the eternal banquet, for which Christ's body and blood are food for the journey. For the parish that is dedicating its church building, these rites announce that its members are not citizens of this earth. They are citizens of heaven and it is only here that all of the promises which Christ has made to them will be fulfilled. Their mission on earth depends upon them not losing sight of their goal. In order for them to be true to this mission, the members of the parish community must be aware

---

136. *ODC*, no. 62: 57.

137. *ODC*, no. 2: 31. The *Introduction* states, "Because the church is a visible building, this house is a special sign of the pilgrim Church on earth and an image of the Church dwelling in heaven."

138. This is evidenced by the procession to the new church which makes use of psalms that speak of the assembly coming to Jerusalem, by the association of the assembly with the heavenly church through the relics, the litany of the saints, anointing of the walls in twelve places, numerous scripture passages which draw the analogy, and, most importantly, by the celebration of the Eucharist.

PART THREE

that they are a portion of God's people called to share in Christ's kingly mission and that their inheritance is the salvation which he has won for them by his passion, death, and resurrection.[139]

## SUMMARY

The *Introduction* of *ODC* begins by stating:

> Through his Death and Resurrection, Christ became the true and perfect temple of the New Covenant and gathered a people to be his own.

Moreover, this holy people, made one by the unity of the Father, Son, and Holy Spirit is the church, that is the temple of God built of living stones, where the Father is worshiped in Spirit and in truth.

> Rightly, therefore, from ancient times the name "church" has also been given to the building in which the Christian community is gathered to hear the Word of God, to pray together, to take part in the Sacraments, and to celebrate the Eucharist.[140]

The rites of dedication that follow ask God to accept the building that is to be dedicated to worshiping him and to make it a sacred sign, while at the same time providing for that community which will gather within the building a catechesis that expounds what it means for it to be that people which Jesus Christ has redeemed by his passion, death, and resurrection, to worship the Father in spirit and truth. The content of this catechesis is such that it elaborates for the living church, which gathers within the building, the nature of its identity as God's people according to the spiritual, ecclesial, and missionary dimensions. By doing so, the rites are intended to make of the church a sign that will call the people that worship within it to be what they are to be as God's holy people and to announce to those who encounter the edifice the offer of salvation that God extends to all persons through his living church. So effective are the

---

139. *ODC*, no. 48:48–49. The prayer for the blessing of the water states, "Sanctify + therefore with your blessing this water you have created, that, sprinkled on us and on the walls of this church, it may be a sign of the cleansing waters of salvation, in which we have been washed in Christ and made a temple of your Spirit.

Grant that, with all our brothers and sisters who will celebrate the divine mysteries in the church, **we may come at last to the heavenly Jerusalem.**" The bold print has been added for emphasis.

140. *ODC*, no. 1: 31.

rites of *ODC* in communicating the essence of what it means to be a part of the living church that, as was indicated earlier in this thesis, they have led Ignazio Calabuig to state about them:

> Si può asserire che l'Ordo dedicationis ecclesiae et altaris *occupa nel quadro dei libri liturgici restaurati un posto simile a quello della costituzione* Lumen gentium *tra i documenti conciliari: come la* Lumen gentium *è un documento-sintesi dei molteplici aspetti del "mistero dalla Chiesa," così l'*Ordo dedicationis *è un rito-sintesi dei molteplici temi cultuali delle assemblee ecclesiali.*[141]

The ritual unfolds for the community that celebrates it that spiritual reality which must define its existence, the ecclesial structures which nourish and sustain its life, and the mission that belongs to it as a result of the saving action that God has worked for it. For the community that is properly prepared for the celebration of this rite, *ODC* provides it with a liturgical formation that will lead it to an understanding of its theological and ecclesial nature.

This formation is such that it calls both the community and its members to an awareness that their entire life and purpose are to be founded upon Jesus Christ and the offer of salvation that comes through faith in him. Sent by the Father to redeem humanity, Christ is to be the reason for the community's existence. The community and its members must live in communion with their Lord and Savior if they wish to receive that gift of salvation which the Father sent his Son into the world to bestow upon his children. This communion can be received only through the Holy Spirit, who proceeds from the Father and the Son. As the rites clearly indicate, the Holy Spirit is transmitted to the men and women of every epoch and nation through the liturgy and the sacraments of the church which Christ himself established on the testimony and life of the apostles and their successors. The Christian community, therefore, must be one that is founded upon, sustained, and defined by Christ's presence

---

141. Calabuig, "Un 'rito' per una Chiesa che vive," 41. My translation of this important quote from Calabuig is as follows: It can be asserted that *Ordo dedicationis ecclesiae et altaris* [*ODC*] occupies in the sphere of restored liturgical books a place similar to that of the Constitution *Lumen gentium* among the documents of the [Second Vatican] Council: As *Lumen gentium* is a document that synthesizes the multiple aspects of the mystery of the church, so too *Ordo dedicationis* [*ODC*] is a rite that synthesizes the multiple cultic (liturgical) themes of the church assembly.

Although Calabuig is referring to the Latin *editio typica* of the rite in his comments, his remarks are equally valid when applied to *ODC* or any other approved language translation of the revised rites of dedication.

PART THREE

in his word and sacrament, most especially by that in which he is fully and completely present—the Eucharist. The spiritual formation that is conveyed in the celebration is to ground the assembly upon the truth that as a portion of the church founded by Jesus Christ, it is a cell of his mystical body. In order for it to be fruitful it must derive its entire life from the Eucharist. It is the Eucharist which makes it what it is to be.[142]

The ecclesial formation that it passes on is such that it expresses those fundamental aspects of the church's nature that are necessary for the assembly that gathers within the building to encounter Jesus Christ within her liturgy and sacraments. The community does not exist in and of itself; it is but a portion of the one church that Christ founded upon the apostles for the sanctification of all humanity. Its life is dependent upon the successors of the apostles and those who are sent by them to fulfill the mission that Christ bestows upon those who are configured to his likeness as high priest through ordination. To these, Christ entrusts the vocation of offering his sacrifice to the Father in order that the church may be built up into his likeness. To these priests is given the task of exercising Christ's work of teaching, governing, and sanctifying the community. This they are to do in obedience to the bishops they have been called to assist, in conformity to the sacramental rites they are to celebrate, and in the service of the people of God to whom they have been sent. It is their duty to build the community that they serve into a healthy portion of the One, Holy, Catholic, and Apostolic Church in which Christ is encountered.

Fundamentally, these rites are celebrated and the building is dedicated so that the people of God may recognize the great dignity and responsibilities that they are called to as members of the holy people that Christ has formed through his paschal mystery. Not only are they called to the kingdom that Christ has prepared for them through his death and resurrection; by the fact that he has sent the Holy Spirit upon them, it is their vocation to extend his kingdom here on earth. As a result of their priestly, prophetic, and kingly missions, Christians are to offer their lives in thanksgiving to the Father, proclaiming the marvels that he has worked for them through Jesus Christ (1 Pet 2: 4–9). By so doing, they are to extend his kingdom to all nations, complete his work of salvation, and come in the end to the new and eternal Jerusalem, where they will enjoy intimacy with the Father, Son, and Holy Spirit for all time. Until

---

142. See John Paul II, *Ecclesiae de Eucharistia*, no. 1.

the day comes when they achieve this eschatological destiny, Christ's faithful are to intimately encounter him here on their pilgrim journeys by receiving him in that precious gift of himself that he has given to his church—his sacred body and blood. In the Eucharist, they receive that food to sustain them on their pilgrimages as members of his church and a foretaste of the celestial banquet. As it is in the Eucharist that the faithful receive that which sustains them as members of the living church and unites them with the church in heaven, the rites of *ODC* ask God that through the celebration of the Eucharist in the rites of dedication, the building in which it is celebrated may become a sign of the pilgrim church on earth and an image of the church which is gathered with him in his celestial home. In the end, the effects of these rites is to emphasize for the community that celebrates them that its ecclesial and theological identity depends upon it being a liturgical and sacramental one—one which derives it existence primarily from Jesus Christ, as he gives himself to it and its members in the Eucharist.

The 1977 rites for the dedication of a church present a theology of what a Christian community ought to be. Realistically, this study has shown that they provide a concrete synthesis of the theology that is to animate a parish community. The Code of Canon Law shows that it is normally to their parish that the faithful are to turn for the sacramental nourishment that these rites show to be at the heart of the Christian life. It is the parish that the code requires to have the baptismal font in which the Christian life begins. Here, the faithful are to find a pastor who is charged by the church with providing for their spiritual welfare. Other priests and communities may agree to care for the spiritual needs of the faithful when, and if, they are able. The pastor of a parish must provide the spiritual care for those that he is appointed to serve. The parish community must welcome those who live within its territorial boundaries. A monastery chapel, a religious shrine, or an oratory in a religious house will always be places in which certain sacramental celebrations occur. The parish church will be the home of all the liturgical and sacramental realities that the rites of *ODC* describe as being essential for the Christian life. It will also normally be that place from which the faithful in a particular territory will be sent out into the world to fulfill that mission which belongs to them as members of God's people.

Sadly, there are parishes in the world that do not have access to the priestly ministry that the 1977 rites of *ODC* show to be essential for a full ecclesial life. However, as has been shown, the code also regards this as an anomaly to be tolerated only for as long as conditions make it necessary.[143] As soon as it becomes possible, the bishop is to appoint a priest as the pastor of the parish so that it may be nourished by the sacramental food that is essential to its life—the body and blood of Jesus Christ.

*Sacrosanctum concilium* states that because the bishop is not able to be present everywhere in his diocese, he is to set up parishes under the care of pastors so that the church may become visible throughout the world.[144] Within *ODC* is to be found the theology and ecclesiology, which if lived by the parish community, leads to the realization of that reality for which *Sacrosanctum concilium* states they are to be established. The rites of *ODC* present to the parish community a catechesis about how it is to play its part in making the church visible throughout the world and in so doing come to know the joy of the eternal salvation which Jesus Christ has won for those who share in his paschal mystery. Certain aspects of the ecclesial and theological realities that these rites describe will be found in the many different types of communities that make up the church. Within the parish community, properly established under the care of a pastor who has been duly appointed by the diocesan bishop, all of the realities described by the *ordo* will be encountered. The rites of *ODC* contain a theology for a parish community.

Before concluding this chapter, it is necessary to say a few words about a number of the factors that may contribute to how well the sign value that the rites of *ODC* ask God to bestow upon the church building may be appreciated by the members of the local community. All of these factors are referred to in some way in the *Introduction* of *ODC*. These factors may be described briefly under the categories of: 1) preparation; 2) architecture; and 3) memory.

The actual celebration of the dedication of the church must be preceded by a preparation that will allow the members of the community to understand both the significance of the rite itself and the various parts of the church.[145] As has been mentioned, this preparation ought to allow the community to understand the spiritual, ecclesial, and missiological aspects of the ritual. Such preparation will not be easy. The complexity of the rite dictates that this effort is to be given the attention that it deserves over a sufficient period of time. When it is a new building that is being

---

143. See *Code of Canon Law*, can. 517, §2. For the interpretation of this canon see Cusack and Sullivan, ix–xiv.

144. The Second Vatican Council, *Sacrosanctum concilium*, no. 42: 15.

145. *ODC*, no. 20: 36.

dedicated, this preparation should play an important part in the actual planning of the building. In this way it could help the community understand the meaning of the various parts of the church as they go about planning its construction. It can also play a vital role in helping to define the community as a healthy part within the church. When the people for whom the church is being built have only recently been established as a parish, this preparation can offer a tremendous beginning to the community's life. For one that has existed for a number of years, but is acquiring a new building or remodeling an older structure, this preparation offers a revitalizing force. When the assembly celebrating this rite has not been properly prepared and included in the celebration of the dedication ritual, a great opportunity to catechize the community about its place and mission within the church is lost. Such opportunities are few and far between.

A second significant factor which contributes to the appreciation of the sign value that is bestowed upon the church by the celebration of rite is that of architecture. The *Introduction* of *ODC* says in this regard, "A church, as its nature requires, should be suitable for sacred celebrations, dignified, evincing a noble beauty, not mere costly display, and it should truly be a sign and symbol of heavenly realities."[146] It goes on to speak of the importance of respecting those guidelines which are proposed by the church for the construction of sacred spaces. The building must in some way reflect both the ecclesial and celestial images to which it is to point. This allows for the greatest freedom of expression among the many different cultures that are to be found within the Catholic Church. However, if the structure does not represent in some way the sign value which the rite is intended to bestow upon the building, no amount of preparation will be able to lead the members of the faithful to recognize this value in the edifice. For this reason, the rite itself has a great deal to offer the community which is in the process of building or remodeling its church. It has the power to clarify for them what this structure should express and the values they should be seeking to "incarnate" within their church. So significant is this question of architecture that one almost always assumes that a beautiful church building has been dedicated and has had this sign value bestowed upon it. It is much like seeing someone dressed in a monk's habit—one merely sees a monk and does not ask if he has been solemnly professed.

---

146. *ODC*, no. 3: 31.

PART THREE

The third factor to be noted is that the question of memory impacts greatly on the ability of the faithful to appreciate the sign value which the rite asks God to bestow upon the building. In the normal course of events, a church is dedicated but once; while it is hoped that it will stand for many years after that. In order that the building may testify to the fact that it has indeed been set aside permanently for the worship of God, the *Introduction* states that an inscription is to be placed in a suitable spot so that the date of dedication may be made known to those who visit, as well as the name of the bishop who celebrated the rite and the title given to the church.[147] More importantly, the anniversary of the dedication is to be celebrated each year as a solemnity.[148] This date provides the community with an outstanding opportunity to revisit the significance which this event holds for it. Within the perspective of the rites of ODC, it provides for an occasion to reflect upon the place of the community within the universal church and to refocus its efforts upon its mission and eschatological destiny. In his article entitled "*Dedicazione senza consacrazione. Ossia: teologia liturgica in una storia rituale*," Salvatore Marsili suggests that the anniversary of the dedication of the church should be marked by the parish community with a day of retreat.[149] During the course of such a retreat, he says it would be appropriate to relight the candles from the day of dedication and for the community to be provided with a mystagogical commentary that develops the significance of the various parts of the ritual which was celebrated on the day of dedication. Such a wonderful idea would keep before the eyes of the members of the parish that excellent vision of its identity which was placed before them when their church was dedicated through the celebration of the rites of *ODC*.

Finally, to conclude this chapter, it is important to state that a dedicated church is not a necessity upon which a parish community is absolutely dependent for its existence. There are many parishes around the world for which such a building would be a great luxury. Some of these celebrate the faith in conditions of persecution and poverty. Often it is these dire conditions that help them to understand the nature of their identity as God's people far more than any building ever could. However, perhaps the church building may in some ways be compared to a crucifix. An individual does not need to own a crucifix in order to be a Christian. Many are able to identify with Christ's cross from the sufferings that they

---

147. *ODC*, no. 25: 37–38.
148. *ODC*, no. 27: 38.
149. Cfr., Marsili, "Dedicazione senza consacrazione," 599–601.

experience in their own lives. However, the crucifix is a sign. It points to that covenant which God the Father has generously entered into with a people that has not merited the death of his Son. It points to the eternal life which God's Son has won for all people by his death and resurrection. In a similar way, the church building is to point to the presence of that church which Christ purchased at the cost of his blood. The building is to proclaim that here, within this living church, is to be encountered Jesus Christ and the salvation that he came to bring to all. Here, Christ continues to live in his body and to be present through his church's liturgy and sacraments. Here is to be found all for which the human heart longs. Here is to be found eternal life. It is a sign that challenges the parish community to be that people which manifests Christ's church within their vicinity. The rites of *ODC* provide the members of the parish with a ritual by which they are catechized about what it means for them to be the living church in their locality. From this church building, and the sacramental celebrations which take place within it, Christians are to be sent out into the world to bring the good news of Christ's salvation to all who they encounter in their daily lives.

# CONCLUSION

# Conclusion

IN THE YEAR 1205 A.D., while at prayer before the cross, in the church of San Damiano, just outside the walls of Assisi, Saint Francis had a vision that would change both his life and the life of the church. From the cross of San Damiano, Jesus said to him, "Francis, don't you see my house is crumbly. Go then and restore it." Assuming that the Lord was referring to the many church buildings around Assisi that were in a state of ill repair, Francis and his followers set out to repair these church buildings. Among the churches that Saint Francis and his followers were to repair were both the church at San Damiano and that of the small church of Santa Maria degli Angel that stood at Porziuncola.

Today this beautiful little church at Porziuncola, which Saint Francis restored with his friends, stands within the heart of the much the larger and glorious Papal Basilica of Santa Maria degli Angeli. As it rests in the heart of this beautiful Papal Basilica, many pilgrims enter into the peace and tranquility of the smaller church of Porziuncola to draw near to Jesus in the blessed sacrament and remember the great saint who by his simple acts of faith changed the church. This smaller church building lies in perfect harmony at the center of the larger basilica. It is in fact protected from the many different elements in the environment and of time as it rests under the dome of the larger basilica. It is also obvious to all who visit that despite the grandeur of the large basilica, its great strength comes from this smaller church that lies in its heart.

This image of the church of the Proziuncula resting within the Basilica of Santa Maria degli Angeli is a good one with which to conclude this study. In order to begin the reform that God had called him to within the church, Saint Francis began in his own local church. From here blossomed a movement which would change the entire church and its evangelization efforts. An authentic re-evangelization of the entire world will emerge from parishes that are renewed by a liturgical and sacramental life that places Christ at the center of the parish's life and allows the Holy Spirit to nurture and mold God's people for the mission to take the good news to the entire world that they are called to through baptism and confirmation.

The liturgical theology of a parish that is found in the rites of *ODC* is one that invites Christian Catholics to discover that encounter with Christ that awaits them in their parish's celebration of the liturgy. Here they are invited to listen to Christ's word and be formed into his people as they are fed with his body and blood in the community's celebration of the Eucharist. The rites of *ODC* effectively communicate the place that the parish is to have within the mystical body of Christ, they emphasize the liturgical and sacramental life which must be at the heart of the community's life in order for it to realize its authentic ecclesial and spiritual identity, and they point to the ecclesial relationships and structures that are necessary for the parish to live the sacramental life upon which it is dependent. Most significantly, the place which these rites gives to the celebration of the Eucharist, making it essential for the dedication of a church, highlights the place that the Eucharist must have in the life of a parish and its members. In this regard, the 1977 rites for the dedication of a church must be said to offer to the parish community that is having its church dedicated, or which seeks to understand the significance of its dedicated church building, an extremely powerful ritual for pastoral and liturgical catechesis. Here is found a catechesis which speaks directly to the theological, ecclesiological, and missiological identity of the parish community. Effectively conveyed to the parishioners, it would provide them with the formation to live that mission which the documents of the Second Vatican Council so beautifully articulates as belonging to the people of God as those whom Christ sends out in to the world to share the good news.

The goal of this study has been to articulate the powerful and unique liturgical theology for a parish community and the new evangelization that is contained within the rites of *ODC*. What makes this liturgical theology so significant and of such great value is the fact that it is not the work or creation of a particular author or school of thought. It is the theology of the church for a parish community as it is contained and articulated in an important liturgical rite of the church. As has been clearly demonstrated in this study, the ordo of *ODC* is a ritual which catechizes the parish community as to how it must realize the mission set out for it in *Sacrosanctum concilium* 42—that of making the visible church manifest within its locality so that it may cooperate in making the church manifest throughout the world. It is hoped that this study will lead pastors and members of the lay faithful to a deeper understanding of the tremendous resource for their pastoral ministry that is to be discovered in this ritual. It contains theological material to assist them and the community that they serve to become all that the Lord calls them to be as workers and ministers of the new evangelization. The rite asks God to make their parish church a sign that calls them to become the body of Christ, present within their locality, bringing the good news of his salvation to all whom they are sent. It also requests that God should make of the church building a sign of the church in heaven. Here, the parishioners are to receive the Eucharist, that food which is to sustain them on their pilgrim journeys, so that they, and those to whom they are sent to bring his good news, may reach the true home that Jesus Christ has won for all by his passion, death, and resurrection.

# Bibliography

Acerbi, Antonio. *Due ecclesiologie: Ecclesiologia giuridica ed ecclesiologia di comunione nella "Lumen gentium."* Bologna, Ital.: Edizioni Dehoniane, 1975.
Addleshaw, G. W. O. *The Beginnings of the Parochial System.* 2nd ed. York, UK: St. Anthony's Press, 1959.
———. *The Development of the Parochial System from Charlemagne to Urban II.* 2nd ed. York, UK: St. Anthony's Press, 1970.
Alberigo, Giuseppe, ed. *L'ecclesiologia del Vatican II: Dinamismi e prospettive.* Bologna, Ital.: Edizioni Dehoniane, 1981.
Alberigo, Giuseppe, et al., eds. *The Reception of Vatican II.* Washington, DC: Catholic University of America, 1987.
Alberigo, Giuseppe, and Franca Magistretti. *Constitutionis dogmaticae Lumen Gentium synopsis historica.* Bologna, Ital.: Istituto per le scienze religiose, 1975.
Allemen, Jean Jaques von. "L'Église locale parmi les autres églises locales." *Irénikon* 43 (1970) 512–37.
Amato, Angelo, ed. *La chiesa locale.* Rome: Libreria Ateneo Salesiano, 1976.
Ambrose of Milan. *Epistola XXII.* PL 16, cols. 1062–69.
Andrieu, Michel, ed. *Le pontifical romain au Moyen Âge.* 4 vols. Vatican City: Biblioteca Apostolica Vaticana, 1938–41.
———, ed. *Les "Ordines romani" du haut Moyen Âge.* 5 vols. Spicilegium sacrum lovaniense 11, 23, 24, 28, 29. Louvain: Spicilegium sacrum lovaniense, 1931–61.
Arnold-Foster, F. E. *Studies in Church Dedications.* 3 vols. London: Skeffington, 1899.
Atchley, E. G. Cuthbert. *A History of the Use of Incense in Divine Worship.* London: Longmans, Green, 1909.
Augustine. *Sermo CCLXXII.* PL 39, col. 2266–68.
Baima, Thomas A., ed. *What Is a Parish? Canonical, Pastoral, and Theological Perspectives.* Chicago: Hillenbrand, 2011.
Bargellini, Emanuele. "Ecclesiologia e tempio." *Vita Monastica* 145 (1981) 6–35.
Baudot, Jules. *La Dédicace des Églises.* Paris: Libraire Bloud, 1909.
Bausch, William J. *The Parish of the Next Millennium.* Mystic, CT: Twenty-Third, 1997.
Beinert, Wolfgang. "Die Kirche Christi als Lokalkirche." *Una Sancta* 32 (1977) 114–29.
———. "Dogmenhistorische Anmerkungen zum Begriff 'Partikularkirche.'" *Theologie und Philosophie* 50 (1975) 38–69.
Bernard, Theophile. *Les cérémonies d'une consécration d'église d'après le pontifical romain.* Paris: Berche et Tralin, 1899.
Blöchlinger, Alex. *The Modern Parish Community.* New York: Kennedy, 1965.

## BIBLIOGRAPHY

Bo, Vincenzo. *Storia della parrocchia*. 4 vols. Rome: Edizioni Dehoniane, 1988–92.

Bordelon, Marvin, ed. *The Parish in a Time of Change*. Notre Dame, IN: Fides, 1967.

Borella, P. "Il Prefazio ambrosiano della Dedicazione ed un carme anonimo del terzo secolo." *Ambrosius* 39 (1963) 271–85.

———. "La riforma del Pontificale Romano e la Dedicazione del tempio." *Ambrosius* 38 (1962) 3–16.

Braga, C. "In secundam partem Pontificalis romani." *Ephemerides liturgicae* 76 (1962) 201–84.

———. "La liturgia della dedicazione." In *Il Tempio: Atti della XVIII Settimana Liturgica Nazionale a Monreale*, edited by Centro Azione Liturgica, 65–83. Monreale, Ital.: Centro Azione Liturgica, 1968.

Brennan, Patrick J. *Re-Imagining the Parish*. New York: Crossroad, 1990.

———. *The Evangelizing Parish: Theologies and Strategies for Renewal*. Allen, TX: Tabor, 1987.

Bruce, F. F. *The Epistle to the Hebrews*. 2nd ed. The New International Commentary on the New Testament. Edited by F. F. Bruce. Grand Rapids, MI: Eerdmans, 1981.

———. *The Epistles to the Colossians, to Philemon, and to the Ephesians*. 2nd ed. The New International Commentary on the New Testament. Edited by F.F. Bruce. Grand Rapids, MI: Eerdmans, 1984.

Bugnini, Annibale. *The Reform of the Liturgy (1948–1975)*. Translated by Matthew J. O'Connell. Collegeville, MN: Liturgical, 1990.

Cabié, Robert. "Christian Initiation." In *The Church at Prayer*. New ed. Vol. 3, *The Sacraments*, 11–100. Edited by A. G. Martimort. Translated by Matthew J. O'Connell. Collegeville, MN: Liturgical, 1988.

*Caeremoniale Episcoporum*. Editio typica. Vatican City: Typis Polyglottis Vaticanis, 1985.

*Ceremonial of Bishops*. Collegeville, MN: Liturgical, 1989.

Calabuig, Ignazio. "Il rito della dedicazione della chiesa." In *Scientia Liturgica*. Vol. 5, *Tempoe spazio liturgico*, 373–420. Edited by A. J. Chupungco. Casale Monferrato, Ital.: Edizioni Piemme, 1998.

———. "Il segno teologico della chiesa e dell'altare nel nuovo 'Ordo dedicationis ecclesiae.'" *Vita Monastica* 145 (1981) 36–92.

———. "'L'Ordo dedicationis eccelsiae et altaris': Appunti di una lettura." *Notitiae* 13 (1977) 391–450.

———. *The Dedication of a Church and an Altar: A Theological Commentary*. Washington, DC: United States Catholic Conference, 1980.

———. "Un 'rito' per una Chiesa che vive." *Rivista di pastorale liturgica* 16 (1978) 41–51.

Canals J. M. "La liturgia, 'epifanía' de la Iglesia. Aspectos eclesiológicos en la eucología del Misal Romano." *Phase* 27 (1987) 439–45.

Cattaneo, Enrico. "Tempio pagano, ebraico, cristiano." In *Il Tempio: Atti della XVIII Settimana Liturgica Nazionale a Monteale*, 19–37. Monreale, Ital.: Centro Azzione Liturica, 1968.

Chengalikavil, Luke. "La dedicazione della chiesa e dell'altare." In *Anàmnesis*. Vol. 7, *I Sacamenti e le Benedizioni*, 65–109. Genova, Ital.: Marietti, 1989.

———. *The Mystery of Christ and the Church in the Dedication of a Church: A Historical and Theological Study on the Rite of Dedication in the Roman Liturgy*. PhD diss., Pontificium Athenaeum Anselmianum, 1984.

Chéno, Rémi. "L'homélie, action liturgique de la communauté eucharistique." *La Maison-Dieu* 227 (2001) 9–34.

Chupungco, Anscar J., ed. *Handbook for Liturgical Studies*. 5 vols. Collegeville, MN: Liturgical, 1997–2000.
Coccopalmerio, Francesco. *La Parrocchia: Tra Concilio Vaticano II e Codice di Diritto Canonico*. Milan, Ital.: Edizioni San Paolo, 2000.
*Codex Iuris Canonici*. Benedicti Papae XV auctoritate promulgatus. Vatican City: Typis Polyglottis Vaticanis, 1926.
*Codex Iuris Canonici*. Auctoritate Ioannis Pauli II promolgatus. Vatican City: Libreria Editrice Vaticana, 1983.
"Concilium Agathense." *Corpus Christianorum*. Series Latina. Vol. 148, *Concilia Galliae a. 314- a. 506*, 189–225. Turnholti: Typographi Brepols Editores Pontificii, 1963.
"Concilium Epaonense." *Corpus Christianorum*. Series Latina. Vol. 148A, *Concilia Galliae a. 511-a. 695*, 20–35. Turnholti: Typographi Brepols Editores Pontificii, 1963.
Congar, Yves M.-J. *Il mistero del Tempio: L'economia della Presenza di Dio dalla Genesi all' Apocalisse*. Translated by Monastero Domenicano di Alba. Rome: Edizioni Borla, 1994.
———. *Le concile de Vatican II- son Église: Peuple de Dieu et Corps du Christ*. Paris: Beauchesne, 1984.
———. "L'église, ce n'est pas les murs mais les fidèles." *La Maison-Dieu* 70 (1962) 105–14.
Congregation for the Clergy. *The Priest, Pastor and Leader of the Parish Community*. Vatican City: Libreria Editrice Vaticana, 2003.
Contreras, E. "La dedicación de una iglesia. Una reflexión sobre un ritual." *Phase* 27 (1987) 469–489.
Coriden, James A. *The Parish in Catholic Tradition: History, Theology and Canon Law*. New York: Paulist, 1997.
Crichton, J. D. *The Dedication of a Church: A Commentary*. Dublin, Ire.: Veritas, 1980.
Cusack, Barbara Anne, and Therese Guerin Sullivan. *Pastoral Care in Parishes without a Pastor: Applications of Canon 517, § 2*. Washington, DC: Canon Law Society of America, 1995.
Cuva, A. "Il segno 'Tempio.' Da una rilettura del Rito della dedicazione di una chiesa." *Liturgia* 26 (1992) 282–92.
Davids, Peter H. *The First Epistle of Peter*. The New International Commentary on the New Testament. Edited by F. F. Bruce. Grand Rapids, MI: Eerdmans, 1990.
Davis, Charles. "The Parish and Theology." *Clergy Review* 49 (1964) 265–90.
De Puniet, Pierre. "Dédicace des églises." In *Dictionnaire d'Archéologie Chrétienne et de Liturgie*, vol 4, edited by Fernand Cabrol, 374–405. Paris: Librairie Letouzey et Ané, 1924.
———. *Le Pontifical romain. Histoire et commentaire*. 2 vols. Louvain-Paris: Desclée de Brouwer et Cie, 1930–31.
De Zan, Renato. "Bibbia e liturgia." In *Scientia Liturgica*. Vol. 1, *Introduzione alla liturgia*, edited by A.J. Chupungco, 48–66. Casale Monferrato, Ital.: Piemme, 1998.
Deiss, Lucien. *Célébration de la Parole*. Paris: Desclée de Brouwer, 1991.
Donghi, Antonio, ed. *I Praenotanda dei Nuovi Libri Liturgici*. 3rd ed. Milan, Ital.: Editrice Àncora Milano, 1995.
———. "La liturgia come itinerario educativo. La dedicazione della chiesa e dell'altare." *Ambrosius* 65 (1989) 443–56.
Dubosq, R. *La dédicace des églises*. Tournai, Belg.: Desclée, 1946.
Eidenschink, John Albert. "Dedication of Sacred Places in the Early Sources and in the Letters of Gregory the Great." *The Jurist* 5 (1945) 181–215, 323–58.

## BIBLIOGRAPHY

Eliade, Mircea. *The Sacred and the Profane: The Nature of Religion*. Translated by Willard R. Trask. New York: Harper & Row, 1961.
Eusebius of Caesarea. *Historia ecclesiae*. 4 vols. *Sources chrétiennes* 31, 41, 55, 73. Edited by Gustave Bardy. Paris: Les Éditions du Cerf, 1952–1960.
Évenou, Jean. "La dedicazione, festa della Chiesa." In *Assemblea santa.Manuale di Liturgia pastorale*, edited by J. Gelineau, 584–90. Bologna, Ital.: Edizioni Dehoniane, 1990.
———. "Le nouveau rituel de la dédicace." *La Maison-Dieu* 134 (1978) 85–105.
Falsini, Rinaldo. "Dalla Chiesa-comunità alla chiesa-luogo." *Rivista di pastorale liturgica* 16 (1978) 52–62.
———. "Dal tempio luogo sacra alla comunità tempio." *Vita Monastica* 145 (1981) 93–118.
Fensham, F. Charles. *The Books of Ezra and Nehemiah*. The New International Commentary on the New Testament. Edited by R. K. Harrison. Grand Rapids, MI: Eerdmans, 1982.
Ferraro, G. "Aspetti di ecclesiologia nel rito di dedicazione della chiesa e dell'altare." *Theologica & Historica. Annali della Pontificia Facoltà Teologica della Sardegna* 7 (1998) 185–217.
———. "Il mistero della Chiesa nella liturgia della dedicazione." *La civiltà cattolica* 133 (1982) 250–61.
———. "Temi di cristologia liturgica nelle letture bibliche dell' 'Ordo dedicationis ecclesiae et altaris.'" *Notitiae* 34 (1997) 147–67.
Flannery, Austin, ed. *Vatican Council II: The Conciliar and Post Conciliar Documents*. 2 vols. New rev. ed. North Port, New York: Costello, 1998.
Floristan, Casiano. *The Parish-Eucharistic Community*. Notre Dame, IN: Fides, 1964.
Francis, Pope. *The Joy of the Gospel—Evangelii Gaudium*. Washington, DC: United States Conference of Catholic Bishops, 2013.
Garijo-Guembe, Miguel M. *Communion of the Saints: Foundation, Nature, and Structure of the Church*. Translated by Patrick Madigan. Collegeville, MN: Liturgical,1994.
Gaspari, S. "La dimora del Tempio vivente." *Liturgia* 26 (1992) 539–43.
Geldenhuys, Norval. *Commentary on the Gospel of Luke*. 2nd ed. The New International Commentary on the New Testament. Edited by F. F. Bruce. Grand Rapids, MI: Eerdmans, 1983.
Giavini, Giovanni. "Per una teologia biblica del tempio." *Rivista liturgica* 66 (1979) 568–77.
Ginami, Luigi. "Nel Rito della Dedicazione i cristiani si riconoscono Chiesa." *Liturgia* 26 (1992) 455–462.
Grasso, Giocomo. "Perche le chiese?" *Rivista liturgica* 66 (1979) 553–67.
Gregory the Great. *Registrum* XI, *Epsitola* 56. CCL 150A, 961.
Gremillion, Joseph, and Jim Castelli. *The Emerging Parish: The Notre Dame Study of Catholic Life Since Vatican II*. San Francisco: Harper & Row, 1987.
Grenfield, Patrick. "The Church Local and Universal: Realization of Communion." *The Jurist* 49 (1989) 449–71.
Grosheide, F.W. *Commentary on the First Epistle to the Corinthians*. 2nd ed. The New International Commentary on the New Testament. Edited by F. F. Bruce. Grand Rapids, MI: Eerdmans, 1984.
Hani, J. *Il simbolismo del Tempio Cristiano*. Rome: Arkeios, 1996.
Heuschen, L. *Construire, consacrer et vivre une église*. Vol. 15, *Paroisse et liturgie*. Bruges, Belg.: Biblia, 1963.

Himes, J. Michael. "The Development of Ecclesiology: Modernity to the Twentieth Century." In *The Gift of the Church. A Textbook on Ecclesiology*, edited by Peter C. Phan, 45–67. Collegeville, MN: Liturgical, 2000.
Holstein, Henri. *Hiérarchie et Peuple de Dieu d'après "LumenGentium."* Paris: Beauchesne, 1970.
Ivo of Chartes. "De sacramentis dedicationis." PL 162, col. 527–35.
John Chrysostom. Homilia XX, In secundam corinthios epistolam commentarius. PG 61, col. 536–41.
John of Malalas. *Chronographie. Liber XVIII.* PG 97, col. 627–718.
John Paul II. *Dies Domini.* AAS 90 (1998) 713–66.
———. *Ecclesia de eucharistia.* Vatican City: Typis Vaticanes, 2003.
Killian, Sabbas J. *Theological Models of the Parish.* New York: Alba, 1976.
Kloppenburg, Bonaventure. *The Ecclesiology of Vatican II.* Chicago: Franciscan Herald, 1970.
Komonchak, Joseph A. "The Church Universal as the Communion of Local Churches." In *Where Does the Church Stand?*, edited by G. Alberigo and G. Gutiérrez, 30–35. Concilium 146. New York: Seabury, 1981.
———. "The Local Realization of the Church." In *The Reception of Vatican II*, edited by G. Alberigo et al., 77–90. Washington, DC: Catholic University of America Press, 1987.
Lara, Antonio. "Dedicazione della chiesa e dell'altare." In *La celebrazione nella chiesa.* Vol. 3, *Ritmi e tempi della celebrazione*, edited by Dionisio Borobio, 599–612. Torino, Ital.: Editrice elle di ci, 1994.
Lathrop, Gordon W. *Holy People: A Liturgical Ecclesiology.* Minneapolis: Fortress, 1999.
———. *Holy Things: A Liturgical Theology.* Minneapolis: Fortress, 1993.
*Lectionarium.* Editio typica. 3 vols. Vatican City: Typis Polyglottis Vaticanis, 1970–72.
*Lectionary of the Roman Missal.* 4 vols. Ottawa: Canadian Conference of Catholic Bishops, 1992–2014.
Legrand, Hervé-M. "La réalisation de l'Église en un lieu." In *Initiation á la pratique de la théologie*, vol. 3, edited by B. Laurent and F. Refoulé, 143–345. Paris: Les Éditions du Cerf, 1983.
Lengeling, E. J. "Bild der Kirche—Zeichen für Christus. Der erneuerte 'Ordo Dedicationis Ecclesiae et Altaris.'" *Gottesdienst* 11/2 (1977) 153–54.
Lodi, E. "Il luogo dell'assemblea celebrante." *Rivista di pastorale liturgica* 32/1 (1994) 3–10.
López-Illana, Francesco. *Ecclesia unum et plura: Reflessione teologico-canonica sull'autonomia della Chiesa locali.* Vatican City: Libreria Editrice Vaticana, 1991.
Lubac, Henri de. *The Motherhood of the Church, followed by Particular Churches in the Universal Church.* Translated by Sergia Englund. San Francisco: Ignatius, 1982.
Maggiani, Silvano. "Come leggere gli elementi costitutivi del libro liturgico." In *Celebrare il mistero di Cristo. Manuale di liturgia a cura dell'Associazione Professori di Liturgia.* Vol. 1, *La celebrazione: introduzione alla liturgia cristiana*, 130–41. Rome: C.L.V.—Edizioni Liturgiche, 1993.
———. "Il linguaggio liturgico." In *Scientia Liturgica.* Vol. 2, *Liturgia fondamentale*, edited by A. J. Chupuncgo, 231–63. Casale Monferrato, Ital.: Edizioni Piemme, 1998.
———. "Interpretare il libro liturgico." In *Il mistero celebrato. Per una metodologia dello studio della Liturgia. Atti della XVI Settimana di Studio dell'Associazione Professori di Liturgia*, 157–92. Rome: C.L.V. -Edizioni Liturgiche, 1989.

———. "La chiesa come luogo della comunità celebrante." *Rivista liturgica* 66 (1979) 616–29.

———. "Teologia e sacro: Per una sintattica del sacro nella liturgia." In *Teologia e sacro: Prospettive a confronto*, edited by Carmelo Dotolo, 77–119. Rome: Edizioni Dehoniane, 1995.

Magrassi, Mariano. "Il mistero della chiesa locale." *Rivista liturgica* 59 (1972) 9–28.

Mancini, F. "Lo Spirito Santo costruttore del tempio della comunità cristiana." *Vita Monastica* 145 (1981) 119–46.

Marsili, Salvatore. "Dal tempio locale al tempio spirituale." In *Il Tempio:Atti della XVIII Settimana Liturgica Nazionale a Monreale*, edited by Centro Azione Liturgica, 51–63. Monreale, Ital.: Centro Azione Liturgica, 1968.

———. "Dedicazione senza consacrazione. Ossia: teologia liturgica in una storia rituale." *Rivista liturgica* 66 (1979) 578–601.

———. "Il tempio nella storia della salvezza." In *Il Tempio: Atti della XVIII Settimana Liturgica Nazionale a Monreale*, edited by Centro Azione Liturgica, 39–49. Monreale, Ital.: Centro Azione Liturgica, 1968.

———. "La chiesa locale comunità di culto." *Rivista liturgica* 59 (1972) 29–53.

Martimort, A.G. "Le nouveau rite de la dédicace des églises." *La Maison-Dieu* 70 (1962) 6–31.

———. "Le ritual de la consécration des églises." *La Maison-Dieu* 63 (1960) 86–95.

———, ed. *The Church at Prayer*. 4 vols. New ed. Translated by Matthew J. O'Connell. Collegeville, MN: Liturgical, 1988.

Mazza, Enrico. *The Eucharistic Prayers of the Roman Rite*. Translated by Matthew J. O'Connell. New York: Pueblo, 1986.

Mazzarello, S. "Il nuovo rito della dedicazione di una chiesa." *Liturgia* 12 (1978) 674–86.

McBrien, R. "The Parish We Are Shaping." In *Parish: A Place for Worship*, edited by M. Searle, 13–28. Collegeville, MN: Liturgical, 1980.

McDonnell, Kilian. "Themes in Ecclesiology and Liturgy from Vatican II." *Worship* 41 (1967) 66–84.

McGourty, Michael. *A Theology for a Parish Community: A Reading of Ordo dedicationis ecclesiae*. Complete doctoral thesis as published for Pontifical Institute for Liturgy. Rome: Pontificium Atheneaum Anselmianum, 2004.

Merendino, Pius. "Eucharistia e chiesa locale: Reflessioni biblico-pastorali alla luce di San Paulo." *Rivista liturgica* 59 (1972) 93–107.

Michaels, J. Ramsey. *John*. Vol. 4, *New International Biblical Commentary*. Edited by W. Ward Gasque. Peabody, MA: Hendrickson, 1989.

Michiels G. "Le rituel de la dédicace." *Questions liturgiques* 76 (1995) 138–45.

*Missale Romanum*. Editio typica tertia. Vatican City: Typis Vaticanis, 2002.

Militello, Cettina. "Ecclesiologia e liturgia." In *Liturgia: itinerari di ricerca. Scienza liturgica e discipline teologiche in dialogo. Atti della XXV Settimana di Studio dell'Associazione Professori di Liturgia*, 321–41. Rome: C.L.V.— Editione Liturgiche, 1997.

———. "Teologia dello spazio liturgico." In *Scientia Liturgica*. Vol. 5, *Tempo e spazio liturgico*, edited by A. J. Chupungco, 437–54. Casale Monferrato, Ital.: Edizione Piemme 1998.

Mounce, Robert, H. *Matthew*. Vol. 1, *New International Biblical Commentary*. Peabody, MA: Hendrickson, 1991.

———. *The Book of Revelation*. The New International Commentary on the New Testament. Edited by F. F. Bruce. Grand Rapids, MI: Eerdmans, 1977.
Muncey, R. W. *A History of the Consecration of Churches and Churchyards*. Cambridge, UK: Heffer, 1930.
Murnion, P. "Parish: Covenant Community." *Church* 12/1 (1996) 5–10.
Neunheuser, Burkhard. "Pluralismo e uniformità nella liturgia della chiesa locale." *Rivista liturgica* 59 (1972) 71–92.
O'Gara, James, ed. *The Postconciliar Parish*. New York: Kennedy, 1967.
*Ordo benedicendi Oleum Cathechumenorum et Infirmorum et Conficiendi Chrisma*. Editio typica. Vatican City: Typis Polyglottis Vaticanis, 1971.
*Ordo Confirmationis*. Editio typica. Vatican City: Typis Polyglottis Vaticanis, 1973.
*Ordo Dedicationis Ecclesiae et Altaris*. Editio typica. Vatican City: Typis Polyglottis Vaticanis, 1977.
*Ordo Dedicationis Ecclesiae et Altaris deque aliis Locis et Rebus Sacrandis*. Editio typica—bozze di stampa. Vatican City: Typis Polyglottis Vaticanis, 1973.
*Ordo Initiationis Christianae Adultorum*. Editio typica. Vatican City: Typis Polyglottis Vaticanis, 1972.
*Ordo Lectionum Missae*. Editio typica altera. Vatican City: Typis Polyglottis Vaticanis, 1981.
O'Rourke, John J. "The Office of Bishop and Its Relationship to the Particular Churches and to the United States." *Studia Canonica* 5 (1971) 227–44.
Oury, G. M. "Le nouveau rituel de la dédicace des églises." *Esprit et vie* 88 (1978) 155–60, 175–76.
Paternoster, Mauro. "Analisi rituale e contenuti teologici dell' 'Ordo dedicationis ecclesiae et altaris.'" *Rivista liturgica* 66 (1979) 602–15.
Paul VI. *Ad pascendum*. AAS 64 (1972) 534–40.
———. *Ministeria quaedam*. AAS 64 (1972) 529–34.
Peters, Edward N. *The 1917 Pio-Benedictine Code of Canon Law: In English Translation with Extensive Scholarly Apparatus*. San Francisco: Ignatius, 2001.
Pilarczyk, Daniel E. *The Parish: Where God's People Live*. New York: Paulist, 1992.
Pistoia, A. "L'assemblea come soggetto della celebrazione: una verifica sui 'praenotanda' e sui modelli celebrativi dei nuovi libri liturgici." In *Ecclesiologia e liturgia. Atti della X Settimana di studio dell'Associazione Professori di Liturgia*, 90–126. Casale Monferrato, Ital.: Marietti, 1982.
Pocknee, Cyril E. *Liturgical Investure: Its Origin and Development*. London: Mowbray, 1960.
*Pontificale Romanum*. Editio princeps (1595–1596). Vol. 1, *Monumenta Liturgica Concilii Tridentini*. Study edition with notes prepared by Manlio Sodi and Achille Maria Triacca. Vatican City: Liberia Editrice Vaticana, 1997.
*Pontificale Romanum*. Editionis iuxta typicam anno 1962. Study edition with notes prepared by Anthony Ward and Cuthbert Johnson. Rome: C.L.V.—Edizioni Liturgiche, 1999.
Power, David N. *Gifts that Differ: Lay Ministries Established and Unestablished*. New York: Pueblo, 1985.
Reinhold, Hans Ansgar. *The American Parish and the Roman Liturgy*. New York: Macmillan, 1958.
Repsher, Brian Vincent. *"Locus Est Terribilis:" The Rite of Church Dedication in Medieval Christendom*. Chapel Hill, NC: The University of North Carolina, 1994.

## BIBLIOGRAPHY

———. *The Rite of Church Dedication in the Early Medieval Era*. Lewiston, NY: Edwin Mellen, 1998.

Richter, Gregor, and Albert Schönfelder, eds. *Sacramentarium Fuldense, Saeculi X: Cod. Theol. 231 der K. Universitätsbibliothek zu Göttingen*. Fulda, Germ.: Fuldaer Actiendruckerei, 1912.

*Rite of Christian Initiation of Adults*. Ottawa: Canadian Conference of Catholic Bishops, 1987.

Ryan, Desmund. *The Catholic Parish: Institutional Discipline, Tribal Identity and Religious Development in the English Church*. London: Sheed & Ward, 1996.

Sacred Congregation for the Discipline of the Sacraments. *Immensae caritatis*. AAS 65 (1973) 264–71.

Sartore, Dominico. "L'Eucaristia nella dedicazione di una chiesa e di un Altare." In *Il Messale Romano del Vaticano II: Orazionale e Lezionario*, vol. 2, 281–307. Torino, Ital.: Editrice elle di ci, 1981.

Sheerin, Daniel, J. "The Church Dedication 'Ordo' used at Fulda, 1 November 819." *Revue Bénédictine* (1982) 304–16.

Simons, Thomas G. *Holy People, Holy Place: Rites for the Church's House*. Chicago: Liturgy Training, 1997.

Sirboni, Silvano. "La dedicazione dell'altare." *Rivista di pastorale liturgica* 28 (1990) 39–48.

Sorci, P. "Per una Teologia dell' Altare." In *Gli Spazi della Celebrazione Rituale*, 63–88. Milan, Ital.: Edizioni OR, 1984.

Sullivan, Francis A. *The Church We Believe In: One, Holy, Catholic and Apostolic*. New York: Paulist, 1988.

Tangorra, G. *Dall'assemblea liturgica alla chiesa. Una prospettiva teologica e spirituale*. Bologna, Ital.: Edizioni Dehoniane, 1998.

Tanner, Norman P., ed. *Decrees of the Ecumenical Councils*. 2 vols. London: Sheed & Ward, 1990.

Tarazi, P. N. "The Parish in the New Testament." *St. Vladimir's Theological Quarterly* 36 (1992) 87–102.

Tena, P. "Ritual de dedicación de iglesias. Comentario al ritual." *Phase* 19 (1979) 183–221

*The Ordo of Baptism of Children*. Ottawa: Canadian Conference of Catholic Bishops, 2020.

*The Order of the Dedication of a Church and an Altar*, English Translation according to the Typical Edition. Ottawa: Canadian Conference of Catholic Bishops, 2018.

*The Rites of the Catholic Church as Revised by the Second Vatican Council*. 2 vols. Study ed. Collegeville, MN: A Pueblo Book, 1998.

*The Roman Missal*. Canadian (third) ed. Ottawa: CCCB Publications, 2011.

Triacca, Achille Maria. "Chiesa locale e liturgia." *Rivista liturgica* 59 (1972) 108–21.

———. "Le benedizioni 'invocative' in genere, e su 'persone.'" In *Anàmnesis*, Vol. 7, *I sacramentali e le benedizioni*, 110–152. Genova, Ital.: Casa Editrice Marietti, 1989.

———. "Le benedizioni 'invocative' su 'realtà cosmiche.'" In *Anàmnesis*. Vol. 7, *I sacramentali e le benedizioni*, 153–66. Genova, Ital.: Casa Editrice Marietti, 1989.

———. "Voi siete il tempio santo: linee teologico-liturgiche. In margine al rito della 'Dedicazione della Chiesa e dell' Altare.'" In *La dimora di Dio tra gli uomini. Tempio e assemblea. Atti della XLIII Settimana Liturgica Nazionale*, 63–94. Edited by Centro di Azione Liturgica. Rome: C.L.V.—Edizioni Liturgiche, 1993.

Trudu, Fabio. *"Haec aedes mysterium adumbrat ecclesiae." Immagini simboliche dell'Ecclesia nel linguaggio dell' Ordo dedicationis ecclesiae*. Complete doctoral thesis as submitted to Pontifical Institute for Liturgy. Rome: Pontificium Atheneaum Anselmianum, 1999.

Turner, Paul. *New Church, New Altar: A Commentary on the Order of Dedication of a Church and an Altar*. Collegeville, MN: Liturgical, 2021.

———. *Our Church, Our Altar: A People's Guide to the Dedication of a Church and Its Anniversary*. Collegeville, MN: Liturgical, 2021.

Valenziano, Crispino. "Chiesa particolare e liturgia dell' uomo." *Rivista liturgica* 59 (1972) 54–70.

———. "Il razionale sulla idea del sacro e la sua relazione al divino." In *Teologia e sacro: Prospettive a confronto*, 15–54. Edited by Carmelo Dotolo. Rome: Edizioni Dehoniane, 1995.

———. *Liturgia e antropologia*. Bologna, Ital.: Edizioni Dehoniane, 1997.

Vigilius, Pope. *Epistola ad Profuturum episcopum Bracarensem, IV*. PL 69, col. 15–19.

———. "Liturgia e simbolo." In *Scientia Liturgica*. Vol. 2, *Liturgia fondamentale*, edited by A. J. Chupungco, 46–62. Casale Monferrato, Ital.: Edizioni Piemme, 1998.

Villar, José R. *Teología de la Iglesia particular: El tema en la literatura de lengua Francesa hasta el Consilio Vaticano II*. Pamplona, Spain: Universidad de Navarra, 1989.

Vorgrimler, Herbert. *Sacramental Theology*. Collegeville, MN: Liturgical, 1992.

Wall, Robert W. *Revelation*. Vol. 18, *New International Biblical Commentary*. Edited by W. Ward Gasque. Peabody, MA: Hendrickson, 1991.

Ward, Anthony, and Cuthbert Johnson. *The Prefaces of the Roman Missal: A Source Compendium with a Concordance and Indices*. Rome: Tipografia Poliglotta Vaticana, 1989.

White, Michael, and Thomas Corcoran. *Rebuilt: The Story of a Catholic Parish: Awakening the Faithful, Reaching the Lost and Making Church Matter*. Notre Dame, IN: Ave Maria, 2013.

Wilkinson, John. "New Beginnings and Church Dedications." In *Creation and Liturgy: Studies in Honor of H. Boone Portier*, edited by Ralph N. McMichael, 251–64. Washington, DC: Pastoral, 1993.

Wood, Susan K. "Priestly Identity: Sacrament of the Ecclesial Community," *Worship* 69 (1995) 109–27.

———. *Sacramental Orders*. In the *Lex Orandi* Series. Edited by John D. Laurance. Collegeville, MN: Liturgical, 2000.

Wordsworth, John. *On the Rite of Consecration of Churches*. London: SPCK, 1899.

Zambon, G. "Ministeri locali e ministerialità della Chiesa." *Presbyteri* 30 (1996) 711–20.

Zbignievus, Joseph T. *Actualisatio ecclesiae univeralis in ecclesia locali Iuxta Concilium Vaticanum II*. Rome: Angelicum, 1970.

Ziolkowski, Thaddeus S. *The Consecration and Blessing of Churches: A Historical Synopsis and Commentary*. Washington, DC: The Catholic University of America Press, 1943.

Zizioulas, J. D. "La communauté eucharistique et la catholicité de l'Eglise." *Istina* 14 (1969) 66–88.

www.ingramcontent.com/pod-product-compliance
Lightning Source LLC
Chambersburg PA
CBHW071235230426
43668CB00011B/1447